Highlights from *Mafia Wiseguys*

"The Mafiosi are not romantic figures like you see in the movies. They are men of violence, men who let gross amounts of money rule their actions. I think there is only one way to overcome the Cosa Nostra, and that is to educate the people, to let them see what these men really are, and how dangerous they are to a civilized society. Then, and only then, will law enforcement truly win its fight against organized crime."

—TOMMASO BUSCETTA, member of the Sicilian Mafia and "Man of Honor" within La Cosa Nostra

"Next time he calls me a fat mother____, I'm going to kick his ____. Mr. O'Malley called me a fat scumbag mother____. Did you say it? You yellow mother____. He called me a fat scumbag mother____, Judge...."

—Defendant JACKIE DINORSCIO complaining to U.S. District Judge Harold A. Ackerman about a federal prosecutor

"It's my experience that trials, like true love, often do not run smoothly. Anyone who's ever been in the courtroom knows that. Things happen...."

—U.S. District Judge HAROLD A. ACKERMAN, who presided over *The United States of America* v. *Anthony Accetturo, et al.*

Mafia Wiseguys

The Mob That Took On the Feds

Robert Rudolph

A division of Shapolsky Publishers, Inc.

Mafia Wiseguys

S.P.I. BOOKS
A division of Shapolsky Publishers, Inc.

ISBN 1-56171-195-0

Previously published in hardcover as *The Boys from New Jersey* by William Morrow and Co., Inc.

For any additional information, contact:

S.P.I. BOOKS/Shapolsky Publishers, Inc.
136 West 22nd Street
New York, NY 10011
212/633-2022 / FAX 212/633-2123

Printed in Canada

1 3 5 7 9 10 8 6 4 2

To Mary Grace, Jonathon, and Alessandra—
for their patience, understanding, and most
of all, their love

"The Mafiosi are not romantic figures like you see in the movies. They are men of violence, men who let gross amounts of money rule their actions. Until the public really understands the true nature of the Cosa Nostra, its power and its violence will continue. I think there is only one way to overcome the Cosa Nostra, and that is to educate the people, to let them see what these men really are, and how dangerous they are to a civilized society. Then, and only then, will law enforcement truly win its fight against organized crime."

—Tommaso Buscetta, member of the Sicilian Mafia and "Man of Honor" within La Cosa Nostra

"Next time he calls me a fat motherfucker, I'm going to kick his fuckin' ass. Mr. O'Malley called me a fat scumbag motherfucker. Did you say it? You yellow motherfucker. He called me a fat scumbag motherfucker, Judge. . . ."

—Defendant Giacomo DiNorscio complaining to U.S. District Judge Harold A. Ackerman about a federal prosecutor

"It's my experience in trials that trials, like true love, often do not run smoothly. Anyone who's ever been in the courtroom knowns that. Things happen. . . ."

—U.S. District Judge Harold A. Ackerman, on the opening day of testimony in *The United States of America* v. *Anthony Accetturo et al.*

CONTENTS

ACKNOWLEDGMENTS

Special thanks to Tom Brazaitis and Lois Rozanski, court reporters extraordinaire, who heard every word, for their generous assistance.

To S. H. Lohman, Elisabeth Scharlatt, and Sherry Arden, who got the ball rolling.

To Michael Critchley, for his unstinting time, cooperation, and candor, without which much of the story would have remained untold. And to the rest of the defense team, especially David Ruhnke, Matthew Boylan, Robert Gigl, John P. McDonald, Alfred Gellene, John Sogliuzzo, Henry Asbill, Miles Feinstein, Dennis Mautone, John Vantuno, and the other attorneys who labored in the case, including Donald McCauley, Luanne Peterpaul, Cathy Waldor, and Brenda Cuba.

To the prosecutors, Joseph Braunreuther, V. Grady O'Malley, Thomas W. Greelish, Robert Stewart, and Samuel A. Alito, Jr., and to the law enforcement officers who are the daily combatants in the war on crime, especially Dennis Marchalonis and the agents of the FBI, the DEA, and the New Jersey State Police. Also to present and former law enforcement officials Clinton Pagano, Robert Buccino, Robert Weisert, Robert Hopkins, Charles Coe, Arthur Borinsky, Armando Fontoura, Dirk Ottens, Edwin Steir, and Mark Malone.

To U.S. District Judge Harold A. Ackerman, a fair and honorable man, which is what a judge should be.

To Donald J. Volkert, Jr., my own personal "consigliere" and good friend, a true "lawyer's lawyer."

To Ted Sherman, an outstanding writer and reporter, for his friendship and encouragement.

To Mort Pye, Andy Stasiuk, Charles Harrison, and Leonard J. Fisher, and the editors, photographers, and staff of *The Star-Ledger*, for their support, and to the journalists whose work has exposed the world of organized crime, including Guy Sterling, Dan Wakin, Gerry Campion, Anthony F. Shannon, Arthur K. Lenehan, Roger Harris, Patrick Jenkins, Bruce Bailey, Tex Novellino, Charles Garrity, Tim O'Brien, Gordon Bishop, Kenneth Woody, Peter Bridge, Stuart Marques, Judy Peet, and Maureen Castellano. And to Arnold Markowitz for his generous assistance.

To John Stone, for filling in the gaps. And to Walter Towers.

To Robert Blakey, for helping to make the law clear.

And to my editor, Susan Leon, who helped put it all together.

CAST OF CHARACTERS

THE PROSECUTION

Thomas W. Greelish	U.S. attorney for New Jersey
V. Grady O'Malley	attorney for the U.S. Justice Department Organized Crime Strike Force
Joseph Braunreuther	Assistant U.S. attorney
Barbara Miller	attorney for the U.S. Justice Department Organized Crime Strike Force
Dennis Marchalonis	FBI agent who led the investigation

The Defendants	**Their Alleged Roles**
Anthony (Tumac) Accetturo	boss of the New Jersey faction of the Lucchese crime family
Michael (Mad Dog) Taccetta	underboss of the New Jersey organization
Martin Taccetta	*consigliere* and enforcer
Thomas Ricciardi	family "soldier" and manager of gambling operations
Michael Perna	"adviser" and intermediary between "families"

Giacomo (Fat Jack) DiNorscio	cocaine acquisition and distribution
Alfonse (Tic) Cataldo	supervisor of numbers and loan-sharking
Jerome (The Vog) Voglino	deputy supervisor, numbers and loan-sharking
Robert (Spags) Spagnola	supervisor of sports bookmaking and loan-sharking, operated "the bank"
James Fede	acquisition and distribution of counterfeit credit cards
James Gammero	numbers operator
Michael Ryan	manager of video gambling operations
Walter Esposito	cocaine sales
Joseph (Scoops) Licata	loan-sharking
Robert (Bucky) Caravaggio	manager of Carmata Oil
Gerald (Jerry the Jew) Cohen	cocaine acquisition and distribution
Gerald Deluca	cocaine acquisition and distribution
Victor Cantillo	counterfeit credit cards
Manuel Monteiro	cocaine courier
John Redman	cocaine sales
Daniel Ricciardi	cocaine sales

THE DEFENSE ATTORNEYS

Michael Critchley	(for Michael Taccetta)
David A. Ruhnke	(for Martin Taccetta)
Milton Ferrell, Sr./ Stephen Skoller	(for Anthony Accetturo)
Harvey Weissbard	(for Thomas Ricciardi)
Raymond A. Brown	(for Michael Perna)
Alfred Gellene	(standby counsel for Giacomo DiNorscio)
William J. Martini	(standby counsel for Alfonse Cataldo)
John B. Sogliuzzo	(for Jerome Voglino)
Henry Asbill	(for Robert Spagnola)

Robert L. Brown	(for James Fede)
Kenneth W. Kayser	(for James Gammero)
Roy B. Greenman	(for Michael Ryan)
John P. McDonald	(for Walter Esposito)
Miles Feinstein/ John Saykanic	(for Joseph Licata)
Robert Gigl	(for Robert Caravaggio)
Thomas B. Ashley	(for Gerald Cohen)
Thomas J. Cammarata	(for Gerald DeLuca)
Peter V. Ryan	(for Victor Cantillo)
Dennis Mautone	(for Manuel Montiero)
John V. Vantuno	(for John Redman)
Maria D. Noto	(for Daniel Ricciardi)

THE JUDGE

Harold A. Ackerman	U.S. District Court Judge

THE WITNESSES

P. J. Jumonville aka Joe Sansone	undercover FBI agent
Joseph (Little Joe) Alonzo	former drug addict who turned informant after he failed in murder attempt on mob figure
Alan Amador	confessed drug dealer
Robert Fisher	confessed drug dealer
William Hawley	convicted killer
Raymond Pinto, Jr.	convicted drug dealer
Nicholas P. Mitola, Jr.	professional gambler and drug dealer

PROLOGUE

It was 11:39 A.M. on Wednesday, February 16, 1983, when Colonel Justin Dintino, executive officer of the New Jersey State Police, walked into Room SD-430 of the Dirksen Senate Office Building in Washington.

Seated at a raised semicircular dais were members of the U.S. Senate Judiciary Committee. Strom Thurmond, the garrulous septuagenarian senator from South Carolina, sat in the center position as chairman of the committee.

The room was crowded with spectators, Senate staffers, and news reporters. A court stenographer's machine clicked softly, taking down every word that was spoken.

It was the second day of hearings into the subject of organized crime in America. It had been billed as the first time since the Kefauver hearings of the 1950s that the subject would be so thoroughly and publicly addressed.

Thurmond, a confirmed teetotaler with a honey-dipped southern drawl, looked up from the dais and nodded at Dintino.

Dintino was there to testify about organized crime in New Jersey, a subject he knew well. He had been a member of the

New Jersey State Police for thirty years and served at least half that time as a supervisor of the agency's intelligence operations, organized crime, and narcotic bureaus.

New Jersey, he acknowledged, had developed a national reputation over the years as a state "infested" with organized crime. It was a reputation, he said, that the state had fought hard to overcome.

Drawing on information developed from investigations, informants, and electronic surveillance, Dintino had put together an outline of organized crime in the Garden State, listing what he called the seven key crime families and identifying the men who controlled them.

In South Jersey, there was the Bruno family from Philadelphia, which had been engaged in a long-running iternecine battle that eventually catapulted a violent Atlantic City mobster named Nicodemo (Little Nicky) Scarfo into a position of power. In Central Jersey, there was the state's only indigenous crime organization, founded and controlled by the silver-haired patriarch Simone Rizzo (Sam the Plumber) DeCavalcante.

And in the north, there were the five New York families: the Genovese, Gambino, Colombo, Bonanno, and Lucchese organizations, each named for crime bosses of the past whose inglorious deeds had propelled them into lasting infamy—Carlo (Don Carlo) Gambino, Joseph (Joe Bananas) Bonanno, Vito (Don Vitone) Genovese, Joseph Colombo, and Gaetano (Three-Finger Brown) Lucchese.

Among the most lucrative, aggressive, and well-organized of these groups was the Lucchese organization. Its influence, Dintino said, was felt from the affluent New York bedroom communities of Bergen County through the densely populated Essex, Morris, Passaic, and Union counties, which represent the heavily industrialized and commercial heart of the state, to the bucolic pasturelands of Sussex County in the northwest. And the Lucchese family's influence was expanding—its power was being felt in the south, along the state's beachfront resorts, in Ocean and Monmouth counties, as well as in Atlantic County, where sunbathers and gamblers were being drawn in equal proportions to the glistening shoreline and to the gambling palaces of the state's burgeoning casino industry.

The family's activities, Dintino said, comprised the full gamut of criminal operations: illegal gambling, loan-sharking, narcotics trafficking, takeover of legitimate businesses, fraud, cigarette smuggling, extortion, and, to a lesser extent, race fixing, arson, pornography, and stolen property.

The family was represented in New Jersey, he went on to say, by a relatively small but powerful group of individuals, chief among whom were Anthony Accetturo and Michael Taccetta.

In August of 1985, U.S. authorities in New Jersey, emboldened in part by a series of successful organized-crime prosecutions in major cities across the country, elected to undertake their own strike against the mob.

The goal: to take down the entire hierarchy of an organized-crime family—from midlevel operatives to the men at the top—in one fell swoop.

The weapon: RICO, the acronym for the awkwardly named Racketeer Influenced and Corrupt Organizations Act, a complex anticrime law rumored to have been named in tribute to the character of "Rico," played by Edward G. Robinson in the classic gangster film *Little Caesar*.

The targets: Anthony Accetturo, Michael Taccetta, and the New Jersey faction of the Lucchese crime family.

A respected *caporegime* (or "captain") in the national crime fraternity, Accetturo was the undisputed overlord of the New Jersey branch of the Lucchese crime family, and a reclusive mob "godfather" who had lived for more than a decade in self-imposed exile in Florida. A man of almost unlimited luck, Accetturo, forty-seven, had long avoided prosecution by claiming to have Alzheimer's disease, only to experience a miraculous "cure" when he slipped and fell in a prison shower after the case was closed. An earlier case against him was halted when the government's star witness had a heart attack on the witness stand.

While Accetturo, who had fled New Jersey to avoid being forced to testify before a state investigating committee, ruled his faction of the family as a sort of absentee landlord, Taccetta served as his hands-on manager in New Jersey.

Michael Taccetta, the thirty-eight-year-old philosophy-spouting underboss, had risen from street hood and local gang leader to become a ruthless mob chieftain, who prosecutors said "made grown men grovel."

The evidence in the case was to be the combined result of more than a decade of investigations by federal and state law-enforcement agencies. It would weave together information from a successful undercover foray, which exposed the inner workings of some of New Jersey's most powerful underworld apparatuses, with a wealth of new data obtained from wiretaps, surveillance operations, and a virtual army of informants.

The RICO law, which had been signed into effect in October 1970, gave sweeping new powers to government prosecutors, enabling them to hold top leaders of organized crime, who had long been insulated from the daily routine of criminal activities, responsible for the actions of their foot soldiers.

However, a U.S. Senate report noted that although the RICO law was hailed for over a decade as "the most comprehensive and powerful tool" possessed by law enforcement in the war on organized crime, it "remained the least used of weapons" in the arsenal. The sheer complexity of the law had rendered it dormant.

But by the 1980s, prosecutors had begun to recognize its value. The law had been drafted as a means to "give a thematic structure to the disparate elements" that went into creating the real world of organized crime by providing a means to tie together the gambling, the drug trafficking, and the labor corruption that made up the way of life of the Mafia. It had been designed to supplant the earlier, far more restrictive conspiracy laws and to recognize that just as society had become more complex, so had the criminal underbelly of society.

In New York, the law was used to invoke an all-out assault against the Mafia's ruling "Commission," the secret governing body that had controlled national organized crime since the era of Al Capone. It was used to cripple mob leadership in cities such as Boston, Buffalo, Chicago, Cleveland, Kansas City, Los Angeles, Philadelphia, and New Orleans.

And by August of 1985, federal authorities in New Jersey, which had become virtually synonymous with organized crime, were poised to launch their own attack on the mob.

Thomas W. Greelish, the U.S. attorney for New Jersey at the time, heralded the case against the Lucchese family as historic in scope.

"It is the first time in the history of New Jersey," Greelish said, "where virtually an entire organized-crime family has been indicted in one prosecution.

"Obviously," he went on, "everyone is going to be watching. Not only the public, but the organized-crime power structure itself."

A report issued by the FBI to the U.S. Senate Permanent Subcommittee on Investigations during the midst of the subsequent trial boasted that "the effect of this prosecution, if successful, will result in the removal of the current management structure of the Lucchese Family in New Jersey, which should prove devastating to its operation."

It was to have been the government's shining moment in the war on the mob.

PART ONE

NEW JERSEY AND YOU

1

It was a cool afternoon in late summer of 1985 when Vincent Grady O'Malley drove his car into the tree-shrouded driveway leading to the secluded Morris County home of U.S. Attorney Thomas W. Greelish.

O'Malley had followed the directions he had been given leading him onto a winding country road on the outskirts of Morristown, the historic suburban community where General George Washington set up his military command during the winter of 1779.

Tom Greelish's home was located on a cul-de-sac off a side road, just west of Jockey Hollow, a vast tract of woodlands and field where Washington's army spent that winter in log cabins and tents, while their commander in chief enjoyed the hospitality of a wealthy hostess who owned a mansion adjacent to the sprawling acreage.

Two hundred years later, the area still retained its country charm. It remains staid, comfortable, and staunchly Republican, and Greelish found the area just as much to his liking as did Washington.

The Greelish house was a two-story white clapboard colonial, with a gray brick front and black shutters situated on a two-acre plot at the end of his street.

The trees and shrubs that lined the driveway rustled gently in the easy breeze as O'Malley slammed shut the door of his car and approached the house. Summer seemed to have ended early—it was almost as if it were autumn.

It was an important day for O'Malley. He had come to see Greelish to discuss a case that had consumed his professional life for the past several years. He was carrying a final draft of an indictment that he planned to present to a federal grand jury that week. It encompassed the entire leadership of the Lucchese crime family in New Jersey. The indictment was historic in scope. It spelled out charges against more than two dozen persons accused of participating in a racketeering conspiracy that had spanned more than a decade and that involved a multitude of criminal offenses, ranging from gambling and loan-sharking to extortion, fraud, and drug dealing.

O'Malley, a former pro-basketball player with the Atlanta Hawks who had a reputation for aggressiveness, had hung up his sneakers after a single season to pursue a career in law enforcement. He had carried his aggressiveness with him.

The indictment he had prepared was to be a major debilitating blow to the mob. But O'Malley needed one thing to proceed: Greelish's stamp of approval.

On this Sunday morning, O'Malley passed the flower garden outside the rear of Greelish's home, where a collection of perennials provided a colorful backdrop for an old-fashioned sundial that served as the centerpiece of the garden. The sundial registered nearly high noon.

As U.S. attorney for New Jersey, Tom Greelish was the top federal law-enforcement officer in the state, and, as such, no indictment could be prosecuted without his signature. Although O'Malley was technically assigned to the U.S. Organized Crime Strike Force, which was at that time a separate U.S. Justice Department unit directed out of Washington, previous U.S. attorneys had exerted their political muscle and influence and had kept the New Jersey outpost of that agency under the aegis of the U.S. Attorney's Office. Thus, every indictment prepared by the strike force had to be approved and signed by the U.S. attorney.

Greelish did not know O'Malley well. The two had met at a Christmas party for federal prosecutors several years earlier, when a mutual acquaintance, spotting the two six-foot-five men towering over the crowd, took it upon himself to introduce them—apparently believing that because of their height, they would have a lot in common. As it turned out, they didn't.

In the corridors of the Federal Building in Newark, the two passed one another occasionally and would nod or exchange a brief pleasantry. But they were far from friends.

And this Sunday, Greelish was not relishing the thought of this visit. Greelish knew O'Malley to be an intense man with a short fuse and a hot temper. The summer was just cooling down—he didn't need to heat it up again.

Greelish, lanky, with a shock of straight dark hair, had the appearance of a towering farm boy. His professional demeanor was like that of a country lawyer, with an "Aw, shucks" courtroom style straight out of *Mr. Smith Goes to Washington.*

The grandson of an Italian butcher, Greelish had been raised in the bucolic Hunterdon County community of Califon and had followed a winding and sometimes bumpy road to his present position.

A college dropout, he had worked as a laborer in a local brewery before finally deciding to return to school, where he eventually settled on a career in law. While working his way through Seton Hall Law School, Greelish so impressed a federal appeals-court judge during the school's annual "moot court" competition that he was recommended for a job as the first law clerk for Frederick B. Lacey, a crime-busting federal prosecutor who had just been appointed a federal judge. Later he was placed as an assistant prosecutor under Lacey's successor, Herbert J. Stern, an equally aggressive headline-making crime fighter.

As the following anecdote attests, Greelish did not exactly fit the mold of the typical prosecutor.

One day early in his law-enforcement career, he wandered into a courtroom during the prosecution of a mob trial. A government informant, his face swathed in bandages to conceal his appearance, sat on the witness stand, testifying against a notorious New York Mafia figure.

When Greelish entered the room, the witness hesitated, then motioned to the judge. A moment later, the judge granted an adjournment. Something was clearly wrong.

The something was Greelish. Wearing a dark shirt, jacket, and tie, Greelish hardly resembled a government lawyer. The witness had taken one look at him seated in the rear of the courtroom and had immediately panicked.

The informant had to be taken aside and convinced that Greelish was actually a government prosecutor, one of the good guys, and not the mob hit man he'd been mistaken for.

When he was an aide to Stern, however, few mistook Greelish for anything but what he was—a top-drawer prosecutor. Greelish quickly found himself immersed in a host of sensational corruption cases, including the prosecution of Cornelius Gallagher, one of New Jersey's most influential members of Congress. And eventually, after a brief stint in private practice, Greelish returned to the public sector, where he was tapped in 1983 to join the U.S. Attorney's Office.

O'Malley, on the other hand, had followed a much different route.

As the second-oldest son of an old-line Irish family from Boston, O'Malley had grown up in comparative wealth in the upper-middle-class Boston suburb of Newton. His father, who had a law degree and an MBA from Harvard, was a banker, and his grandfather had been an editor of the old *Boston Herald.*

Ever since high school, O'Malley knew he wanted to be a trial lawyer. His height, however, offered an alternative. O'Malley had made his mark in college as captain of the Manhattan College basketball team and had acquired a reputation as a hustler on the court, grabbing thirty-five rebounds in his sophomore year. He had been overlooked in the college draft after having missed several games in his senior year and, as a result wound up being drafted twentieth and last, and then only on the recommendation of his coach to a longtime friend, Richie Guerin, who was then coach of the Atlanta Hawks.

It was not a good career move. After a single, lackluster season (he was on the court a total of 113 minutes and averaged 2.1 points per game), O'Malley decided that his future lay in another court—and he enrolled in Boston College Law School.

Before joining the Justice Department, he worked in the New York District Attorney's Office in the Bronx, getting his feet wet in the courtroom by prosecuting a host of major, multiple-offender street-crime cases, developing and honing his courtroom expertise, and learning about life on the seamier side of the tracks.

When he crossed the Hudson River to join the staff of the U.S. Strike Force in New Jersey in 1977, O'Malley began building a reputation as a no-nonsense prosecutor who could take even a marginal case and bulldoze his way to victory. In fact, he never lost.

"Prosecutors shouldn't lose cases," O'Malley declared during a discussion of his philosophy toward his work. "Cases, when they're indicated, are indicted because the evidence is there. . . ."

And on that summer day in 1985, that was what he had come to convince Greelish of—that the evidence against the bosses and followers of a powerful organized-crime family was there, and that he should be given the final authorization to proceed with the prosecution that would destroy them and their organization.

For O'Malley, it was the capstone to a series of investigations that had begun nearly a decade before. It was 1979, and he had been supervising an investigation involving a firm that was supposed to have fireproofed a vocational-education school in Hudson County, New Jersey. Instead, the company just threw a coat of paint over the walls and claimed the job was done.

During the investigation, agents began to encounter an individual named Michael Taccetta. He was using an office at the fireproofing company and could be seen coming and going, hosting meetings in a back room. As a result of the federal investigation, the company went bankrupt. Taccetta moved on—and the government followed.

The sons of a known bookmaker, Michael Taccetta and his brother, Martin, had been tagged by the New Jersey State Police with the nickname of the "Bowling Balls."

Both stocky (although by the time of the trial, Martin had slimmed down and looked more like a Hollywood leading man), they were known for bullying their way through areas of Essex and Morris counties, terrorizing local business owners—particularly those who had a penchant for gambling, and gambling badly. Whenever these businessmen fell into debt, authorities claimed, they found they had new friends—Taccetta and his boys.

In one instance, Taccetta was portrayed as being a sort of "unofficial host" of a prominent Morris County eatery—drinking, eating, and doing business from its tables during the day, while an aide would dip freely into the cash register for spending money, claiming the money was owed to him by the owner as interest on his gambling debts. The situation became so outlandish, authorities reported, that the restaurant owner—whose credit was drying up quickly—had friends take out loans under their own names and give the money to him to appease the Taccettas.

By May 1982, Taccetta and his associates, who by now had become familiar faces to the men watching him, had moved to another location: the Hole in the Wall, a storefront luncheonette in the Down Neck section of Newark, nestled between warehouses and factories in a seedy industrial area of the state's largest city.

After watching a collection of Cadillacs and Mercedes-Benzes parading to the luncheonette at all hours (a reporter for *The New York Times* had written that when the patrons of the luncheonette wanted to eat, they ordered out), O'Malley and the FBI were able to obtain a warrant from a federal judge authorizing the installation of wiretaps and "bugs."

Those taps and "bugs" produced hundreds of hours of recordings in which the suspects were overheard discussing everything from loan-sharking debts to concerns over their wives attending a neighborhood demonstration of frilly nightwear—a sort of Tupperware party for negligees.

The information gathered on those tapes eventually served as the basis for the charges contained in O'Malley's proposed indictment.

The strike-force prosecutor had approached Greelish in his office with the paperwork on the case. He had drafted an indictment formalizing the charges and was prepared to present it to the grand jury. It was ready, O'Malley said, for Greelish's signature.

A grand jury is a group of between sixteen to twenty-three citizens who have received a special jury-service notice—in most cases, not a particularly welcome one. Instead of sitting on a trial, they are asked to come back week after week for months. In New Jersey, the usual term of service is eighteen months, but in some instances it can be as long as three years.

Technically, the grand jury is the arbiter of "probable cause," the organ of the court that decides whether someone's name will show up in the following day's newspaper as "charged with . . ." some offense. In reality, however, many legal experts maintain, they are little more than "rubber stamps" that do what the prosecutors want.

One former top state law-enforcement official admitted that at one time during his tenure, the state of New Jersey utilized three types of grand juries. One was used for politically sensitive cases that everyone in authority would like to see just go away—and that eventually indicted no one. The second was just the opposite—it indicted anyone the prosecutors wanted it to, evidence or not. The third did just what it was supposed to do—it evaluated the evidence and decided for itself.

In federal cases in New Jersey, grand juries and prosecutors tended to see eye to eye. There have been relatively few cases where a grand jury has refused to indict if the prosecutor recommended it. Generally, this is because the cases are fairly good ones. But there is always the chance that something might slip by.

Despite O'Malley's insistence, Greelish was not prepared to act as quickly as the strike-force prosecutor might have liked. He wanted to review O'Malley's case for himself before he signed off. He wanted to be certain that this was a case that should be brought and, just as important, that it was a case that the government was going to win.

O'Malley, who had earned a reputation for brashness among his colleagues, was not a man who took lightly what he perceived to be criticism. He was combative and aggressive, even with his superiors. In arguments, he would get loud, red in the face, and bluster his way through—pointing his finger at the target of his ire. It was a combat technique he would use against virtually anyone with whom he came into verbal conflict—including the U.S. attorney, Greelish.

Greelish, on his part, wanted to avoid a direct confrontation with O'Malley. He also didn't want the meeting to turn into an all-day event.

He was cordial when O'Malley arrived, and ushered him onto the back porch.

It was clear from the outset that O'Malley was not pleased with the situation. He had spent years on this case; he knew it inside and out. It was, as far as he was concerned, a clear-cut winner.

Greelish offered O'Malley a seat at a redwood table located in the center of a screened-in porch. The house was bustling with noise and family activity, and this spot offered the best opportunity for privacy.

The two men were both dressed casually. Greelish was wearing jeans, Topsiders, and no socks; O'Malley, sneakers and a warm-up suit.

As they spoke, Greelish was candid in expressing his position: He was not going to put his signature to anything that he wasn't convinced deserved to be brought. Furthermore, what O'Malley was proposing was as historic as it was ambitious: Never before had an entire organized-crime family been indicted. This thing had to be right: Greelish wanted to make sure the case was airtight.

"And I may want to do more than just review the indictment," Greelish told O'Malley. "I may want you to sit down and delineate for me all of the proofs in this case."

O'Malley flushed.

"This is my case," he shot back. "I'm a professional. You should be able to take my word for this. . . ."

Greelish was not cowed. He spoke slowly but with increasing force and volume.

"I am the United States attorney," he said. "I'm the chief law-enforcement officer in this district. I've got a responsibility to the people of the state. I've got to be satisfied that this indictment ought to be brought."

O'Malley got to his feet and glared down at Greelish. Greelish pushed himself away from the table and got to his feet and stared eyeball-to-eyeball at O'Malley. Neither made a move until O'Malley spoke.

"I know this case," O'Malley shouted. "I know these people. . . . I've lived with it. . . . the bureau has spent years on it. . . ."

"I don't give a damn how long anybody has worked on it," Greelish shouted back. "It doesn't make a difference."

Greelish was more than aware of the responsibility he had. In the midst of the argument, he felt both frustration and worry. If he didn't sign that piece of paper, that prosecution, however historic it might be, just wasn't going to happen. And whatever O'Malley had to say, however angry or incensed he might be, and no matter how much he blustered and carried on, the ball was totally in Greelish's court. And the more that O'Malley argued, the more insistent Greelish became that he had to be satisfied that everything was in order.

O'Malley had to accept that no assistant prosecutor could unilaterally decide whether an indictment, particularly one as important as this one, should be brought. No assistant could do that. And before this, no one had ever tried.

"Look," said Greelish, lowering his voice. "We're on the same team. We share the same goals and ambitions. We want the same thing . . . we want this thing to be right."

O'Malley tried to convince Greelish to sign the document then and there. O'Malley had been given his head by the strike force and had concentrated his energies into putting the case together. Now someone was questioning his judgment.

Greelish, however, refused to waver. He wanted more time. He knew the stakes. If a case this big were to be lost, the results could be devastating. Not only would it be an embarrassment to law enforcement, but it would wind up enhancing the reputations of the men they had set out to convict.

It would make the mob even stronger than before.

Greelish stayed up late that night. He read and reread the indictment. And the next morning, he read it again.

The following week, he met with O'Malley again. The meeting lasted into the night. The two men started over, rehashing the facts of the case and the proofs that substantiated the charges. O'Malley explained and explained until, finally, Greelish was satisfied. The case appeared to be solid—the evidence was all there. Even the Justice Department—which prescreens all racketeering indictments—had agreed, and had approved it for prosecution. Greelish was the last obstacle.

Leaning over his desk, Greelish finally did what O'Malley had wanted. He took his pen and signed off.

And on August 19, 1985, a federal grand jury in Newark, New Jersey, returned the indictment, which was sealed by the federal court and placed in a vault in the federal courthouse in Newark.

Two days later, the FBI and the U.S. Attorney's Office issued dual press releases:

> The FBI in New Jersey today announced the arrest of nineteen individuals in New Jersey and Florida, based on a . . . Federal indictment returned in Newark, New Jersey . . . charging them with racketeering violations committed between 1976 and July 1985.
>
> Teams of FBI agents in New Jersey, Florida, and New York made the arrests shortly after dawn this morning. The charges against these individuals include violations of the RICO statute and their participation in an organized criminal group which reaped millions of dollars in profits from trafficking in cocaine and marijuana, loansharking, gambling, counterfeit credit cards and infiltration of legitimate business. . . .

Other arrests would soon follow. The two principal defendants were Anthony Accetturo and Michael Taccetta.

As the arrests were being carried out, Tom Greelish stood at the window of his fifth-floor command center in the Federal Office Building in Newark, a panoramic sprawl of the city spread out before him. In a few moments, he would make his announcement to the public. His staff had summoned representatives from the press and television stations in the New York–New Jersey area, and cameras and reporters were already waiting in the conference room for the press conference to begin. Greelish had been briefed on the operation by his aides. He checked his watch and slipped on his suit jacket. He was ready.

Downstairs, Greelish wove his way through the packed audience of television cameras and print reporters and stepped up to the dais. He took his place behind a podium, flanked by representatives of a host of federal and state law-enforcement agencies. O'Malley was among them. Greelish cleared his throat and made his proclamation.

The arrests carried out that morning, he said, had brought "a dramatic halt to the operation of one of the five families of organized crime here in New Jersey."

It was, Greelish declared forcefully, the most "comprehensive" set of charges ever to be brought against organized-crime figures in New Jersey.

As the cameras whirred, he described how FBI agents had meticulously gathered evidence that had been pieced together from a multitude of wiretaps and electronic "bugs" planted in the mob's own headquarters, a tiny luncheonette in Newark's heavily industrialized Down Neck section.

He spoke of mob "sit-downs," threats of victims whose "heads were going to be busted"; of "takeovers" of legitimate businesses; and of loan-sharking operations that demanded payment of interest rates in excess of 156 percent a year.

He then turned over the podium to one of the other law-enforcement officials.

Robert Wright, the assistant special agent in charge of the FBI for New Jersey at that time, told the audience that the New Jersey faction of the Lucchese crime family, headed by Accetturo and Taccetta, had risen to power during the last decade, following the "untimely deaths" of members of another crime family, the Bruno organization of Philadelphia, whose leadership was decimated as a result of a bloody battle for control of the crime empire. Those deaths, Wright sternly averred, created a vacuum that was filled by the Accetturo-Taccetta organization.

"They filled the vacuum very aggressively," Wright declared, as he paused and leaned into the microphone on the podium for dramatic effect. "And I think we can say that we have created another vacuum."

2

New Jersey has a rich and varied heritage.

The first motion picture was developed by Thomas Alva Edison in his West Orange laboratory in 1889; it was the home of the first brewery in America, which opened in Hoboken in 1642; and it was the site of the first highway "cloverleaf," the prototype of that bewildering array of ramps and roadways that has helped turn the face of America into a pretzellike maze of intersecting superhighways.

The first can of condensed soup was produced in New Jersey in 1897, the first drive-in movie theater was opened on a ten-acre field in Camden County in 1933, and the first organized baseball game was purportedly played in Hoboken in 1846.

New Jersey was where saltwater taffy, that curiously misnamed confection (there is no saltwater in the candy) was born, to the delight of dentists and orthodontists everywhere, and it was the location of the first boardwalk in America, built in Atlantic City, where fifty-one years later someone would have the notion of adding to the nation's cultural wealth by instituting the first Miss America Pageant at the same seaside resort.

But when New Jersey's patrician governor, Thomas H. Kean, took to the billboards, airwaves, and glossy advertising supplements to tell the world that "New Jersey and You" were "Perfect Together" in an effort to urge tourists to patronize the pristine beaches and pastoral mountains of the "Garden State," he might well have instead been addressing another segment of society—a segment that truly believed that they and New Jersey were "Perfect Together."

For decades, New Jersey has battled the reputation spread and perpetuated by movies, television shows, and magazine features that, among all its other attributes, it has served as a virtual breeding ground for organized crime.

Hardly a program on the mob is aired without some reference to an "Uncle Louie from Jersey," or some such black sheep of the family. In fact, when CBS premiered its much-acclaimed crime drama *Wiseguy,* the setting for the first "cycle" of episodes was . . . where else but New Jersey. The fact that the show was filmed in Canada only seemed to add to the state's reputed ambience. Obviously unfamiliar with New Jersey geography, the show's writers included references to "dumping a body into the Jersey River" (there is no such body of water) and to Newark State Prison, a fictitious institution, which, given all its other ills, the city of Newark is undoubtedly glad it does not play host to.

But while the state's professional image polishers are ever vigilant to defend New Jersey against such mob-ridden stereotypes, the state's reputation as a hotbed of organized crime is one that is not entirely undeserved. After all, how many other states can boast the distinction of having had an entire police department indicted and suspended for accepting gifts from a Mafia chieftain?

An indictment returned in the early 1970s accused a five-member police department in northern New Jersey of accepting cash Christmas gifts from Vincent (Chin) Gigante, the man who was later to become the boss of the powerful Genovese crime family. Gigante, who was acquitted in 1968 of charges stemming from an assassination attempt on Mafia boss Frank Costello, had been "living quietly" in the tiny North Jersey community when he and his wife, Olympia, allegedly attempted to show their appreciation for the fine work being performed by their local constabulary.

But in addition to all its other claims to fame, New Jersey has also played host over the years to the lives—and deaths—of a veritable rogues' gallery of underworld luminaries.

There was Albert Anastasia, the chief executioner of the infamous Murder, Inc., the organization that elevated the traditional mob rubout to the level of a boardroom directive and that became a national wholesale house for murder. And as he grew from waterfront thug to mob power broker, his desire for the trappings of wealth grew with him, eventually leading him from the docks of New York to the green, tree-shaded suburbs of Fort Lee, New Jersey, where he made his home until his death, in a hail of bullets, in the barbershop of a New York City hotel. There, high atop the New Jersey Palisades—the sheer rock cliffs that border the west bank of the Hudson River—Anastasia ruled over a Mediterranean-style palace where the crime lord insured his privacy with the aid of a pack of killer dogs, a spiked iron fence, and floodlights that pierced even the darkest shadows of the sprawling manicured grounds.

It was in this lavish mansion that Anastasia entertained the elite of the New Jersey underworld—people like Joe Adonis, a gambling czar and close associate of Lucky Luciano, who also found New Jersey the perfect climate for the health of his operations, and Willie Moretti, the New Jersey gang leader who was gunned down over dinner when the mob decided that the only way to treat his increasingly unstable mental condition (he was suffering from the ravages of syphilis) was to blow his brains out.

Anastasia, who came to America in 1917 by jumping ship in New York, had made an auspicious debut in his adopted country.

Four years after arriving, he was convicted and sentenced to the electric chair for the murder of a longshoreman in Brooklyn. Although sent to Death Row, Anastasia was granted a reprieve when an appeals court reversed the conviction and ordered a new trial.

The only problem was that Anastasia had learned his lesson the first time around, and he didn't take any chances the next time out. Before the new trial could take place, four key witnesses "disappeared," and Anastasia was acquitted.

In the ensuing decades, other witnesses demonstrated a penchant for staging similar vanishing acts. One, a crusading longshoreman who hoped to thwart Anastasia's control over the waterfront, was discovered later to have been dumped into a lime pit in Lyndhurst.

In the 1950s, a retired New Jersey contractor, who was to have been a witness at a tax-evasion prosecution against Anastasia, also disappeared, along with his wife. The home was splattered with blood and in disarray, but the bodies were never found.

Anastasia, who had ducked prosecution for one murder case by "hiding out" in the army—where no one thought to look for him—had a long run of luck in evading prosecution for his crimes.

Between 1932 and 1941, Anastasia was publicly implicated in at least four murders, including the curious demise of former Murder, Inc., triggerman-turned-informer Abe (Kid Twist) Reles, who mysteriously decided to exit a Coney Island hotel, where he was being held under heavy police guard, by jumping out of an eighth-floor window. Reles died, and with him the chance to bring Anastasia to trial for his role in Murder, Inc.

But Anastasia was far from alone in his affinity for the Garden State. Aside from Adonis and Moretti, there was Arthur Flegenheimer, the Prohibition-era beer baron, who came to be known by the much more colorful appellation of "Dutch Schultz."

Schultz, who some claim sealed his own death warrant by plotting the murder of then-crime-busting New York district attorney Thomas E. Dewey, met his demise at a Newark tavern known as the Palace Chop House in what became a legendary killing, setting the standard for gangland executions for years to come. He reportedly became so incensed over Dewey's crackdown on the rackets that he declared, "Dewey's got to be knocked off. It's got to be done. If nobody else does it, I'll do it myself."

On October 23, 1935, Schultz had retired to the mens' room when three men burst through the front door of the tavern with their guns drawn. Schultz, who had downed a prodigious amount of beer that evening, was trapped in the bathroom, where he was cut down as he tried to zip up his fly after relieving his overburdened kidneys. There were also three bodyguards, caught unawares at a table in the tavern, who were gunned down in their seats.

Supposedly, the story goes, it was Anastasia's organization, Murder, Inc., which brokered the murder contract that led to Schultz's death, the slaying reputedly sought by Schultz's own gang members. Convinced that Schultz had gone around the bend, they were fearful of the heat a hit on Dewey would bring.

But not all of New Jersey's underworld society met with such violent ends. One man, who was to become the most influential of the crime leaders who called New Jersey their home, died quietly in his sleep in 1969.

His name was Vito Genovese, the man who nearly consolidated all organized crime in America before being convicted and sentenced to prison on a narcotics-smuggling charge. He died while an inmate at the federal prison at Fort Leavenworth, Kansas. After his death, the man whom Dewey had crowned the "King of the Racketeers" was flown back to Newark Airport, where a waiting hearse took his body to a funeral home in South Jersey just a few miles from the tiny resort town of Atlantic Highlands, where he had made his home for more than forty years.

Genovese had come to the United States at the age of sixteen, and quickly discovered that America was indeed a land of opportunity. During Prohibition, the coves and inlets of the Jersey Shore provided easy access for bootleggers seeking to dart past the three-mile limit and quench the great American thirst. As a result, the area became a magnet for mobsters like himself.

Eventually settling in a modest one-story clapboard house, in the Highlands section of New Jersey, Genovese became a well-thought-of neighbor, even while orchestrating the rise to Mafia leadership that would eventually make him the most powerful of the nation's godfathers, vested with unquestioned authority that never diminished—even during his final ten years behind bars.

Praised by a local police official as "a good father," who raised his children to be "well behaved" and "religious," Genovese became something of an enigma to the local populace. He lived quietly, eschewing the gaudy glamour of some of his infamous contemporaries, and affecting such a low-key appearance that some say he would have looked more at home behind the counter of a small grocery store than seated around the conference table with the nation's most powerful crime leaders.

But the image of the modest little man with the tinted glasses and the soft-spoken personality was somewhat shattered by two separate sources.

One was the infamous Joe Valachi, the former underworld insider who first spilled the beans on the existence of the Mafia in America after being convinced that Genovese had marked him for death.

Valachi, a low-level member of Genovese's crime organization, had become a cellmate with his onetime boss when Genovese surprised him by kissing him on both cheeks. Rather than interpreting the gesture as one of affection, Valachi believed it was the traditional Mafia "kiss of death" and that his days were numbered.

Terrified, Valachi mistook another inmate for a would-be murderer and decided to get him first. Rather than face prosecution for the murder, Valachi became the most famous "rat" in mob history, providing authorities with an Arabian Nights–like tale of murder and intrigue involving the secret society of underworld criminals.

When he pointed the finger at Genovese, the modest, unassuming "Squire of the Highlands" was suddenly thrust into the national spotlight.

But Valachi's testimony was not the only source of notoriety for Genovese. Another came from a source much closer to home—his wife.

In a bitter divorce battle, his ex-wife told a court that her former husband was worth millions, reaping some thirty thousand dollars a week alone in take-home proceeds from illegal lottery operations.

And he was also, she said, a man with a violent temper. When she arrived in court in Freehold, New Jersey, to tell her story, she sported two black eyes and a face covered with bruises. Gentle Vito, she said, once broke her nose, set her hair afire, and threatened to kill her.

Genovese's only response to the accusations was shock and bewilderment.

"What she step on my heart for?" he asked in his broken English.

His most notorious bout of publicity, however, came when New York State Police and federal agents raided a private estate in Apalachin, New York, and surprised an enclave of dozens of reputed gangland figures—the most prominent of whom was Genovese, who had hoped to use the meeting to formally claim the coveted title of "Boss of Bosses" of organized crime, and to seize ultimate control over the underworld empires once dominated by such ganglords as Lucky Luciano and Frank Costello.

He would never officially wear that crown. In 1958, he walked through the doors of a federal penitentiary to begin serving a term for narcotics smuggling that he would never live out.

Despite playing host to such luminaries as Genovese, Anastasia, and others, New Jerseyites remained, for the most part, content to regard such infamous neighbors as a colorful minority, who, by chance, only happened to live within the confines of the Garden State, but whose goings-on had little impact on the lives of the average citizen.

Then the son of a U.S. Supreme Court justice gave a speech that shattered such illusions. In 1968, residents of New Jersey were shocked by a proclamation by then–assistant state attorney general William J. Brennan III charging that organized crime had infiltrated virtually every facet of life in the Garden State, with the exception of the Church.

In a speech delivered before the New Jersey chapter of Sigma Delta Chi, the society of professional journalists, Brennan, who was directing a state investigation into mob activities, called organized crime "the most serious internal problem which the state and the nation face today.

"Organized crime," Brennan told the assemblage of reporters, who took pen in hand to spread the good news to a waiting world, "has infiltrated businesses such as vending machines, trucking, motels, restaurants, bars, banks, the securities industry, construction and several others."

"It has extensively infiltrated some labor unions," Brennan asserted, a charge that would be borne out decades later when Harold A. Ackerman, the federal district judge who was to sit on the Accetturo case, issued a historic opinion, wresting control of Teamsters Local 560, one of the largest and most powerful labor unions in the state, away from its elected leaders, and appointing a trustee to oversee the union's operations because of alleged mob domination.

Indeed, while Assistant Attorney General Brennan appeared almost prescient in his comments about labor corruption in New Jersey, there were other areas he targeted in his remarks during that fateful address to reporters. "Too many local governments," he said, "are responsive more to the mob than to the electorate that put them in office."

In this direct reference to the New Jersey State Legislature, Brennan charged that even that sacrosanct body of politicians was not immune. There were, he claimed, legislators who were "entirely" too comfortable with members of organized crime."

Within the next year, scandals would rock New Jersey that would make Brennan's comments appear all too accurate.

A triumvirate of federal prosecutors, led by U.S. Attorney Frederick B. Lacey and two of his top aides, Herbert J. Stern and Jonathan L. Goldstein, launched a crackdown on crime and corruption in New Jersey that was unparalleled in the nation's history, resulting in the prosecutions of dozens of public officials ranging from current and former congressmen to high-ranking state and local officeholders.

Their techniques were so successful that prosecutors throughout the nation sought the advice of their New Jersey peers in rooting out corruption in their own states. In fact, when federal prosecutors in Maryland initiated an investigation into the finances of then–vice president Spiro T. Agnew, they consulted with New Jersey's Stern, who had succeeded Lacey as U.S. attorney, for advice on how to best build their case.

The first and most sensational of the prosecutions to grow out of the Lacey-Stern-Goldstein crackdown involved the mayor of Newark, once New Jersey's queen city, which despite decades of decline remains the largest metropolis in the state.

In 1969, Hugh J. Addonizio, a former seven-term congressman who had been touted by those in the know as a potential candidate for governor of New Jersey, was completing his second term as mayor of the state's largest city and preparing for a third run for that office. Amid the background of a heated mayoral campaign that was to mark the last hurrah for the old-line white power structure in the increasingly black-dominated city of Newark, Addonizio and fourteen other persons were indicted by a federal grand jury on extortion-conspiracy charges that tied Addonizio to reputed Mafia boss Anthony (Tony Boy) Boiardo, the son of the flamboyant Prohibition ganglord, Ruggiero (Richie the Boot) Boiardo.

The story of Addonizio's rise to power had been described in *The Star-Ledger* of Newark, the state's largest newspaper, as "an urban saga of high drama that might have been culled from the pages of American fiction."

"It was," the paper stated, "at first, a classic success story of a young man of humble beginnings who found room at the top beyond his wildest imagining. And later, it altered to an equally melodramatic tale of a powerful man's downfall."

This was true. As an all-state quarterback for St. Benedict's Prep who later went on to play football on the Fordham University team, Addonizio had spent his youth working in his father's tailor shop, dreaming of a better life.

His college career complete, Addonizio enlisted in the army, where he rose from corporal to the rank of captain and returned home a hero with a Bronze Star.

His political career began in 1948 when he became the first Democratic congressman to win election in a district that had been unshakably Republican, and from there his rise was meteoric. In 1962, he returned from Washington to Newark to run for mayor. And after a hugely successful 1966 reelection campaign, Addonizio began to dream again—this time of becoming the state's first governor of Italian heritage.

But a year after his second election victory, the dream began to fade and his image to tarnish. In July 1967, violence erupted among the city's black inner-city population in a rampage of looting, arson, and shooting, which required the National Guard to be brought in to restore order. When it was over, entire city blocks had been destroyed, twenty-six persons had been killed, and Addonizio's career was in ruins.

A blue-ribbon commission selected by then-governor Richard Hughes was appointed to probe the cause of the uprising. Their report cited a "pervasive feeling" of corruption that had left the dispirited minorities with the belief that everything in Newark government was for sale—at the right price. And then, on December 17, 1969, a federal grand jury gave reality to that supposition by indicting Addonizio.

He was subsequently convicted and sentenced to ten years in a federal prison. When he was released six years later, he retired to a home in the rural Monmouth County community of Tinton Falls, far from the scene of his turbulent public career. Two years later, Addonizio died quietly, the victim of a massive heart attack. In one of those moments of ultimate irony that only the political area can generate, his successor as mayor, Kenneth A. Gibson, ordered all the flags lowered in Addonizio's honor.

But beyond exposing the corruption of Addonizio and his cohorts, the prosecution of the former Newark mayor had served another purpose. It made something of a household name of Richie the Boot and Tony Boy, and reawakened public awareness of the role of the Mafia in New Jersey.

Richie the Boot had been one of the true celebrities of Prohibition-era New Jersey. Portrayed by authorities as the reigning patriarch of organized crime in New Jersey until his death in 1984, Boiardo had risen from immigrant stonemason to become one of the most powerful and feared member's of the state's organized-crime power structure.

His son, Tony Boy, had been indicted along with Addonizio, but was severed from the trial when he suffered a heart attack. Although he subsequently became a familiar figure at his favorite golf courses, he never recovered his health sufficiently to be able to stand trial.

On April 20, 1978, the younger Boiardo, who had adopted a more sedate and businesslike image than his once-boisterous father, and who was reputedly fronting for underworld forays into the world of legitimate business, died at Community Hospital in Montclair after lingering for weeks in critical condition since suffering a heart seizure on Good Friday.

Although he was alleged to have been the key link between the Addonizio administration and the mob, Tony Boy had remained for years in the almost legendary shadow of his father.

In his declining years, the elder Boiardo had become something of a recluse, rarely venturing from the cloistered confines of his sprawling baronial mansion, which was located just over the crest of the West Orange Mountain in suburban Livingston. Guarded by wrought-iron gates and stone pillars topped with bronze swans, the house was located at the head of a winding drive, hidden from the road by a forest of tall trees and shrubbery. The main house was constructed of imported Italian stone, resembling the dark, brooding fortress of a feudal lord.

There, behind the walls of his private sanctuary, the once-robust Boiardo had passed his time puttering in a vegetable spread that, in a final glimmer of his once-characteristic humor, he had marked with the sign GODFATHER'S GARDEN.

Boiardo outlived his son and heir presumptive by more than six years, passing away at age ninety-three, a frail, stooped, white-haired shadow of his former image as a brawling, gun-toting hood who had survived an assassin's bullet in the early 1930s.

But in his prime, Boiardo was something else—a Prohibition-era bruiser who modeled himself after Al Capone and who sported a five-thousand-dollar diamond belt buckle that earned him the nickname "Diamond Richie."

A familiar figure in Newark politics, who as local ward leader mingled freely both with the prominent and the notorious, Boiardo had slipped from public view when the Addonizio case propelled him and his son back into the limelight.

The public attention was heightened when the press began publicizing stories about Boiardo's fortresslike home and the goings-on that were rumored to have taken place there. The estate was featured in a double-page spread in *Life* magazine, which described the home, aptly enough, as designed in "Transylvanian traditional." For along the dark drive leading up to the main house was a bizarre collection of statuary: likenesses of the entire Boiardo family, their busts and nameplates arrayed on pilasters surrounding the *padrone* of the dynasty, a youthful Richie the Boot, outfitted in formal riding wear, sitting astride a prancing white stallion.

A less familial, but grisly feature of the estate was a private crematorium. It was here, underworld rumor had it, that Boiardo disposed of his enemies, burning them on a huge iron grate after they had been murdered.

"Oh he just did it to show everybody what a great guy he

is, that he got guts," one mobster explained. "He'd tell them he'll take anybody's headaches, they give him the bodies. . . ."

Perhaps the greatest single wealth of information to be developed about the mob in New Jersey was revealed almost by accident.

In 1969, a defense attorney for Simone Rizzo (Sam the Plumber) DeCavalcante, so named because of his ostensible profession as a plumbing contractor, filed a motion in federal court in Newark seeking disclosure of any information obtained against his client through electronic surveillance. In response, then–U.S. attorney David M. Satz gladly obliged. He filed thirteen volumes of transcripts documenting the results of the surveillance with the court.

The resulting furor produced a steady stream of newspaper accounts of the conversations, not only depicting meetings between DeCavalcante and his buddies, but also dropping the names of embarrassed public officials whose prominence made them grist for gangland gossip.

DeCavalcante's attorney, Chris Franzblau, had not anticipated that his motion to gain access to the material would wind up being released to the press as well: "I expected I would have gotten the information before it was made public," Franzblau declared at the time.

DeCavalcante, the son of an alleged bootlegger who emigrated to the United States from Sicily, could have been the model for Marlon Brando's portrayal of *The Godfather*. With crisp, wiry silver-black hair and a neat graying mustache, DeCavalcante spoke in a hoarse, asthmatic whisper while gesturing expressively with his hands.

Called some years later to a meeting with state investigators, DeCavalcante had been polite, noncommittal, and even gracious in offering a state official a pack of cigarettes. It was only after DeCavalcante had gone that the official looked down and noticed something unusual about the package. It lacked a federal tax stamp.

The tape transcripts proved great reading. They not only recounted the foibles, the squabbles, and even the romantic interludes of many of the ranking crime figures in the state (also peppered by mentions of political figures), they were also remarkable for the grisly details they provided about a way of life that had only been whispered about before by the general public.

In one recording, a man identified as "Tony" reminisced proudly about a murder he had once committed. Describing the situation to DeCavalcante, Tony told how he and two other men put a soon-to-be victim on a truck and tied him up. They drove him to a park, but the location proved unsatisfactory, so they loaded him back into a car and drove him to a farm, where they concealed the car in a garage.

Tony and his friends turned on the car radio to drown out his screams. Then one of the men put a gun to the victim's head, while another cut his throat. They buried the body near the farm, and then later, for a reason that was never made clear, they decided to dig up the corpse and move it.

At this point, Tony said, "I saw a sight that I never had seen before. I was scared.

"We dug him up after he died, and his hair was still growing. The dead man was hairy. I never saw this before."

Possibly the most important and lasting impact from those tapes, however, was the fact that they documented once and for all the existence of the Mafia's high Commission, the governing council of organized crime, which was established to end the gangland wars of the Roaring Twenties and to bring a modicum of peace to an otherwise unruly profession. It was designed as a nine-member board of directors, comprised of the leaders of the nation's most powerful organized-crime families. And "to defy the Commission," as one mobster proclaimed, "is to defy the world."

Finally, a year later, a similar set of transcripts, recounting conversations involving Gyp DeCarlo, was also released. Although branded by then–U.S. attorney Herbert J. Stern as a "brutal, sadistic" man who "would violate any laws," he was granted, inexplicably, a pardon by President Nixon from his twelve-year extortion–loan-sharking conviction shortly before his death in 1973.

Stern made one final effort to have DeCarlo jailed for failing to pay an outstanding twenty-thousand-dollar fine.

As grandchildren watched from the upstairs window of DeCarlo's lavish colonial-style home, U.S. marshals first threatened to break down the door of the house, and were then allowed to enter peacefully, help DeCarlo into a bathrobe, and place him on a stretcher to be delivered to court. His young wife shouted protests at the treatment.

He was released several hours later when he began spitting up blood in a courtroom. He died within weeks of the episode.

His legacy, however, lingers. The tapes of his conversations, recorded at a secluded retreat known as "the Barn," sketched a graphic portrait of graft and corruption throughout New Jersey.

It was the second of a double-barreled blast leveled at the heart of the Mafia in New Jersey.

The disclosures, combined with the spotlight trained on the mob by the release of the DeCavalcante tapes a year earlier, took the underworld of crime out of the shadows, and into the glare of the daily press.

The secret society was no longer secret.

PART TWO

THE INVESTIGATION

3

It was like love at first sight.

For Placide "P. J." Jumonville, an undercover FBI agent posing as a streetwise "high roller," Jackie DiNorscio was the man who held the key to the magic kingdom—the great wizard of the underworld, whose words would provide the "open sesame" he so desperately needed to fulfill his mission. DiNorscio was the man who could provide him with instant access to the inner circle of the Mafia.

For Jackie, a great blob of a man whose appetite for money was exceeded only by his appetite for food, Jumonville fit the bill on both accounts. Secretly bankrolled by the government, Jumonville made no secret of his seeming wealth, nor his readiness to expend large portions of it with the ease that can be mustered only by a man who deep down inside knows that it's really somebody else's cash.

In sum, to Jackie, Jumonville was "raw meat"—and Jackie was more than ready to chew him up. They were made for each other.

It was September 1976, and for the Federal Bureau of Investigation, it was a time of transition. Gone were the days of the square-jawed college boys with crew cuts who filled the ranks of J. Edgar Hoover's dreams. The agency was moving into a new era. After decades of denial, it had finally admitted that organized crime existed. And now the federal law-enforcement tacticians were trying what was for them a new technique to combat it: undercover work.

Jumonville was breaking new ground when he met Jackie DiNorscio. He was one of several federal agents from the Newark field office who had been handpicked to participate in an operation known as "Project Alpha," which was being coordinated jointly with the New Jersey State Police.

It was a prototype operation, a precursor of the celebrated "Abscam" project, which in years to come would net the Bureau a bevy of politicians (including the senior U.S. senator from New Jersey, Harrison A. Williams, Jr.) and make virtually every mobster and politician in America think twice about who it was they were talking to.

But in 1976, America was a gentler, more trusting place to live. A mobster was a mobster—or so the mobsters thought.

A native of Louisiana, Jumonville had come to the assignment with a background not in criminal administration, but in zoology and chemistry. In terms of upbringing, Jumonville had about as much in common with the streets of New Jersey as Jackie DiNorscio would have had were he turned loose in the bayous. But he had the dark, intense good looks of his French-Cajun heritage, and somewhere along the line someone realized that he wouldn't make a half-bad imitation Italian.

So Joe Sansone was born. The name was picked out of a telephone book. And on September 8, "Joe Sansone" made the acquaintance of Jackie DiNorscio for the first time.

DiNorscio came into this world on July 23, 1940, as Giacomo DiNorscio, the son of Dominick DiNorscio, a ranking member of the Bruno organized-crime family who was known to his associates as "Tommy Adams."

A proven "earner" for the organization, the elder DiNorscio was eventually elevated to the post of *caporegime.* Although based in Philadelphia, the "family," named for its founder, Angelo Bruno, maintained a branch office in the Down Neck section of Newark, the heavily industrial section of the city that was also known as "the Ironbound" because of its location between the major rail lines that serviced the city.

Jackie's lineage was a lucky break for him, because without the respect afforded his father, it is questionable how long Jackie would have survived on his own. Jackie, his friends openly admit, had a problem. He was nuts.

"He's been crazy all his life," one Mafia figure confided. "He's not just, you know, a little funny. He's really nuts."

To prove that the description was not given lightly, an acquaintance of Jackie's related a story, possibly apocryphal, perhaps not:

"Ten years ago, Jackie didn't know anything about drugs. He grew up in the city, and as far as he knew, drugs were for losers. But then, after a prison stint, he went to Florida. There, it was a different story. He looked around, and he saw these people making millions. And he wanted to make some too.

"So he decided to do what he knew how to do best. He decided to pull a scam. He got in touch with some Colombians, not to buy drugs, but pretending to be selling them. He set up a meeting.

"Jackie told me when they came to pick him up, they were driving this fancy car. It was the first time he ever knew what a 'Marcedes' Benz was. He couldn't even pronounce the name.

"Anyway, he didn't give a fuck who he was dealing with. These guys put him in the car, blindfolded him, and took his gun. Then they drove him to some place and brought him into a room where there were these five Colombians waiting.

"One of these guys opens up a suitcase and shows the money. I don't know how much it was, but it was a lot.

"Suddenly, Jackie pulls out a gun from the small of his back that he had hidden when they searched him and says, 'Guys, this is a stickup.'

"They're just staring at him, and he motions with the gun, which is this little thing, and tells them that even though he doesn't have enough bullets to kill them all, 'I'll shoot four, and the fifth I'll beat to death.'

"He took the money, and he drove away with the 'Marcedes' Benz. He really liked the car.

"He would go up against anybody."

The assessment proved true even during the trial.

Already convicted and sentenced to thirty years for cocaine trafficking while in Florida, Jackie was in custody throughout the entire two-year span of the Accetturo trial. But during that time, he would call the lead federal prosecutor a "yellow motherfucker," tell the trial judge the court was "full of shit," and challenge a government attorney to a wrestling match.

It was no wonder that when FBI agents later wiretapped telephone conversations of the "boys," they immediately knew who was being talked about when somebody said, "I went to see the maniac yesterday, he's coming home Tuesday . . . fucking nut."

But in 1976, when "Joe Sansone" first walked into DiNorscio's life, Jackie was an inmate at Rahway State Prison, a brooding, fortresslike structure that, despite its name, is not in Rahway at all, but in the neighboring community of Woodbridge Township. Years later, responding to the sensitivities of residents of the town of Rahway, New Jersey officials rechristened the institution the East Jersey State Prison. But despite the official name-change, it still is known best simply as "Rahway."

The prison, its walls topped by great castlelike turrets, sits incongruously like the center of a feudal city on a great expanse of flat earth in the middle of a lightly industrialized area of Union County.

An ugly silver-colored dome hovers over a Grecian-style entrance of brick and cement. Yellow, peeling paint obscures the natural red of the brick, and blends in a sickly pastel with the painted cement walls, which form the starlike extensions that radiate out from the dome in all directions.

These are the "wings," housing rows of cramped closetlike cells, illuminated by the flat and inadequate glow of institutional-fluorescent lighting. Built in 1901 to serve as a low-security reformatory, the building has been expanded over the years into a decaying mélange of architectural styles denoting a bewildering array of minimum-, medium-, and maximum-security sections.

Unlike many prisons, purposely placed in remote areas where they remain largely unseen by the public, the entrance to Rahway is separated from Rahway Avenue, a two-lane thoroughfare slicing though the northernmost corner of Woodbridge Township, by a small parking area used by the guards and other workers at the prison. A wrought-iron fence and gates topped with coils of barbed wire divide the parking area from the actual prison entrance.

Outside, a stagnant pond attracts the children of visitors, who cluster around to toss stones at the unwary ducks seeking refuge in the brackish water. The pond, a breeding ground for mosquitoes to torment the prisoners during the warmer months, serves as the only break in the landscape leading to the visitors' parking area, where motorists are first directed by signs into what looks like an immense auto junkyard—complete with rutted rows of dented and decaying vehicles—and then warned by crudely painted signs to PARK AT YOUR OWN RISK.

In the winter, the dome, whose illuminated arc makes the prison an easily recognizable landmark by night, seems more like a sieve than a roof, with streams of water pouring into the prison during inclement weather. In the summer, despite the thick walls, the lack of ventilation and the simmering crush of humanity turns the prison into an oven that bakes the prisoners in their cells.

The visitors' room at Rahway State Prison is probably no better and no worse than hundreds like it across the country: grimy, institutional green walls; scratched and fogged Plexiglas dividers; and scarred and rickety metal and wood furniture coated with an overlay of sweat, grease, and other residue of bodily contact, left as unintentional souvenirs by the thousands of prisoners, family members, girlfriends, boyfriends, and, in Jackie's case, business associates like Sansone who came to the room each year.

While in prison, Jackie had heard through the grapevine that there was a new boy on the block who was throwing money around and seemed to have some connections. Jackie had sent word that he wanted to meet him.

Jumonville described how he was set up in his character:

"They provided me with a flashy apartment in New York City, East Side, Manhattan. Automobile, money, furnished apartment, that sort of thing. And ultimately, a business enterprise . . .

"I was given a driver's license, credit cards, things of this nature, under an assumed name, to utilize in carrying out this identification of myself as a high-roller type of individual. . . ."

He explained that he was also given money to host dinner parties for the underworld associates with whom he was trying to connect.

"I established myself in the neighborhood where I was living, around some of the restaurants, some of the bars. I would go in and, you know, see to it that I left substantial tips with people that worked in these places so that they knew who I was. They would remember me if I came back again. That was important to me because I had to create a background for myself. I didn't have a criminal background. I wasn't involved in mob activities, so I had no one in back that would vouch for me as being credible in the world of organized crime."

Jumonville acknowledged that "I paid for these entertainment expenses, if you want to call it that, for many different members of organized crime."

And it was on the basis of this background that Jackie DiNorscio had decided he wanted to meet "Joe Sansone."

The two looked at each other for the first time through a full-length screenlike divider off the main visitors' area.

"This is Joe," a mutual acquaintance who had accompanied Jumonville to the prison told DiNorscio, "the guy I was talking to you about."

When Jackie met Joe Sansone, DiNorscio was already serving an eight-year sentence on a bookmaking conviction. "He's been inside for four years," their mutual acquaintance had told Jumonville as they were waiting on a bench outside the visiting area. "The parole board turned down his appeal because of his organized-crime reputation."

In fact, one friend once quipped that Jackie "never had a three-year run" when he was not in jail for something. It wasn't far from the truth.

"What's your last name?" Jackie inquired of his newfound friend.

"Sansone," Jumonville replied easily.

Jackie appeared thoughtful. "I used to have a good friend named Sansone," he muttered, and then appeared to drop the issue when Jumonville didn't react.

Jackie had looked upon his meeting with Sansone as a potential bonanza. Ultimately, it was going to wind up costing him even more time.

But incarceration never proved much of a deterrent to Jackie. If nothing else, the prison provided him with a rent-free office for him to conduct his own business.

State police detective Robert Delaney, who worked with Jumonville on "Project Alpha," described in testimony before a U.S. Senate subcommittee his dealings with Jackie and his associates.

As related by Delaney, Jackie had made himself right at home in the prison. Not satisfied with the limited access inmates are given to telephones, Jackie had taken matters into his own hands.

"Somehow," Delaney said, "he had arranged to have his own telephone actually connected to his cell.

"What he had done was figure out where the telephone lines were in the prison. He discovered one near his cell and plugged an unauthorized extension into it."

To cover his tracks, Jackie arranged to have the calls billed to an outside party, so the charges wouldn't show up on the prison phone bill and make the prison officials suspicious. Only Jackie didn't want to pay for those calls either. So he had them billed to a trucking company that was being used by the state police and the FBI as a front for their undercover operation, and which Jackie was bent on muscling into.

Before prison officials finally found out what was going on and pulled the plug on Jackie's personal phone, DiNorscio had run up several thousand dollars in phone bills, all of which were picked up by the government.

But the phone line wasn't the only thing DiNorscio forced the government to pay for. While he was in prison, he arranged to have his wife placed on welfare. Even though he was still earning substantial income from his criminal operations, she was able to qualify because, ostensibly, he wasn't working. He also demanded to have his girlfriend collect unemployment insurance—again sticking the tab on the FBI–state police front company.

"He told me to arrange for her to receive unemployment insurance," Delaney recalled. "That would have been easy enough to do, except she never had been an employee of ours. She had not even been a no-show employee. We had no record of her ever having worked for us.

"That didn't trouble DiNorscio. He just assumed I could fix it for him."

Not content with providing an income for both his wife and his girlfriend, DiNorscio even demanded that the company provide the girlfriend with a car. And again, the government would have to pick up the tab.

"As you will note," Delaney said in relating the incident during an appearance before a U.S. Senate subcommittee inquiry on organized crime, "when someone talks to you like this, it is difficult to say no."

A government tape recording presented to the subcommittee recounts one such conversation between Delaney and DiNorscio:

DELANEY: Hello?

DINORSCIO: Bobby? This is, you know who this is, right?

DELANEY: Oh yeah, how ya doing?

DINORSCIO: Ah, did you tell me we could go get that yesterday?

DELANEY: I told ya I'd do what I could. I'm having a problem getting the money.

DINORSCIO: You having a problem? Did I tell you to lay it out personally?

DELANEY: I'm having a problem personally.

DINORSCIO: Hey, Bobby, what are youse trying to do, make a fuckin' jerkoff out of somebody?

DELANEY: Hey, there's nothing like that being done.

DINORSCIO: Nothin' like that? I mean, what the fuck you think, I'm a fuckin' beggar or something?

DELANEY: Nobody's saying that.

DINORSCIO: Well, I asked ya for fucking one motherfuckin' favor, and youse are gonna tell me that youse are gonna have a problem with fifty? I mean, you wanna see me blow my fuckin' top down here?

DELANEY: No, I don't want to see that. I don't want to have a problem with anybody.

DINORSCIO: A problem? I mean, what the fuck, youse are trying to make a fuckin' fool out of somebody then. [Look], I never begged a motherfucker in my life and I'm not gonna start now, especially with my fuckin' moves. You tell me you got a problem with that little cocksucker [another undercover agent who

> is posing as Delaney's business partner]. I'm gonna show him. I'm puttin' a fuckin' man down there, and I want to see the fuckin' thing the way it's being run, if I can't get it [the money for the car].

There was a method to Jackie's madness. He confided to Jumonville why it was so important that his girlfriend have a car. According to an FBI report, she came every Saturday to give Jackie a "blow-job" in the visiting area, and she had to have a car to get there.

But according to Delaney, Jackie was not merely content with having the government foot the bill for his extramarital relationships. He expected the same courtesy to be extended to his own family. Reported Delaney, "Jackie DiNorscio, still in Rahway prison, sent word to me that he wanted his wife, Marlene, and two children and his mother to have a vacation at Disney World in Orlando, Florida."

Jackie, it seemed, wanted them to be the "guests" of the trucking company.

"I sent word back to him that the answer was no," Delaney said.

But that wasn't the last of it.

"William (Woody) Brown was DiNorscio's enforcer," Delaney explained. "He was a big man, physically. He came to me with Jackie's latest message, the point of which was that I should change my mind and have Alamo Transportation (the government company) pay for the family's vacation."

The result was, Delaney recalled, that Alamo did pay for most of the DiNorscio family's vacation. And the government picked up the tab for Jackie one more time.

Jumonville was well aware of Jackie's propensity to ooze himself like some giant protoplasm over any person or business that came his way, and engulf it for himself.

"Jackie DiNorscio was like many of the other fellows I met in organized crime," Jumonville later recalled during the trial. "They want somebody else to pay the bill."

And "Joe" was Jackie's kind of man.

Jackie began by attempting to woo Jumonville to his "family."

"He was talking about his father's affiliation with the mob," Jumonville testified later. "And that he had a standing reputation, that they were a very strong group, and they could open a lot of doors to the Mafia. If we wanted to go along, or if I wanted to go along, you know, working with him in the business."

"You know where he [the elder DiNorscio] is and the weight he carries," Jackie had told Jumonville on their very first meeting.

Jackie, in fact, had big things in mind for the undercover agent.

Within weeks of his meeting with "Joe," Jackie and his associates had: asked "Joe" for fifteen thousand dollars in loans to finance a "big" deal in Nigeria; sold him stolen cars; tried to sell him stolen bearer bonds; asked him to use his "influence" to help arrange for Jackie to "relocate" to more pleasant surroundings in a minimum-security prison; wanted to know if he could locate a buyer for a bronze sculpture; offered to sell him a Stradivarius violin; asked him to arrange to have a car crushed so Jackie's brother could collect on the insurance; and asked him for fifty dollars.

Within a month, in fact, Jackie began asking if Sansone would be "willing to give up a piece" of the undercover trucking company that the FBI and state police were using as a front. He was moving right into Jumonville's web—and, like a happy spider, Jumonville was welcoming him.

But Jackie wasn't the only DiNorscio to fall into the agent's web. His brother, Ralph, was just as eager to take advantage of the agent's generosity. Ralph was right in there pitching too, repeatedly asking for loans of twenty-five dollars, thirty-five dollars, or even a few hundred dollars.

But it wasn't only money that he was seeking when Ralph put the touch on Sansone. Sometimes, he wanted favors. Like the time he decided he wanted to see his father—and asked Sansone to go along. The trouble was Ralph's father was then living in Pennsylvania, having taken up official residence at Lewisburg Federal Penitentiary, located in a historic but drab little community near the banks of the Susquehanna River.

By this time, Jumonville, in his undercover guise, had been called upon to do a lot of things he would never have done ordinarily. He had picked up the dinner tabs for some of the most notorious mob figures in the state, he had even "warned" them of an impending bust in order to show he had valuable "contacts" of his own, and he had been forced to "sample" marijuana and cocaine in order to keep from drawing suspicion to himself.

All of these incidents would come back to haunt him when he was called back to the witness stand a decade later during the trial.

But one of the biggest tests of his undercover abilities came not while attempting to walk an emotional tightrope negotiating deals with suspected mob dons, but when he was asked to accompany Ralph DiNorscio on his Pennsylvania adventure.

Ralph, as was his wont, had been out on a drinking binge the night before and was still woozy when he met Sansone early that morning in the parking lot of a bowling alley on Route 22 in Union, New Jersey. When Sansone pulled into the lot in his late-model Thunderbird and spotted the underworld figure, it was obvious Ralph was not in good shape.

Sansone followed as DiNorscio drove to his own home in a nearby residential area of the township, dropped off his own car, and went into the house while the agent waited.

DiNorscio emerged a few moments later carrying a newspaper, a brown manila folder, and a brown paper bag.

"What's in the bag?" Sansone asked as Ralph climbed into the Thunderbird.

Proudly, DiNorscio displayed his "gifts": a raw steak and a five-ounce bottle of Cepacol mouthwash, which he had filled with scotch at a tavern around the corner from his house.

"I'm going to sneak them in," DiNorscio declared.

The ride to Lewisburg was a long one. And for Ralph, it was a thirsty one as well. Slouching back in the seat, he reached into the paper bag and quietly unscrewed the cap on the mouthwash bottle. He would just take a sip, he assured Sansone, just enough to make the trip go a little more smoothly. . . .

In a display of what one attorney later dubbed a heart-tugging example of filial devotion, Ralph DiNorscio drank all the scotch intended for his father.

When DiNorscio and the undercover agent stopped for lunch at a restaurant in Blakeslee, Pennsylvania, Ralph refilled the mouthwash bottle, then treated himself to another belt or two. He became visibly intoxicated.

Now he had a problem. As DiNorscio and Sansone continued on their way, nature began to take its course: Ralph had to take a leak; in fact, to be more accurate, several of them.

"Pull over," he told Sansone repeatedly. Sansone obliged, and swerved the Thunderbird over to the roadside. DiNorscio staggered out of the car. Bleary-eyed and wobbly, he unfastened his trousers . . . and missed.

Now he had several problems. He was drunk. And his pants were soaking wet.

It was two o'clock by the time Sansone and DiNorscio arrived at the prison. As they passed through the entrance gates, DiNorscio told Jumonville, "The bottle and the steak are in my socks."

Once inside the main auditorium, DiNorscio headed for the bathroom. Out of sight, he pulled down his socks and took out the steak and the bottle and transferred them to his pockets. Back in the public area, however, a guard spotted the bottle bulging out of DiNorscio's back pocket.

Ralph reacted quickly.

"C'mere," he told Jumonville, calling him over to the soda machine and simultaneously tossing the steak onto the floor. "The guards are on to me. Put it in your pocket."

Jumonville stooped down, quickly retrieved the steak, and sat down on a nearby bench while DiNorscio tried to explain to the guards about the bottle. Somehow, Jumonville managed to slip the steak into his pocket, while Ralph DiNorscio began engaging the guards in a less than cordial conversation.

Jumonville was sitting quietly when he was approached by a guard.

"You with him?" the guard asked, indicating DiNorscio, who by now was hurling abuses at the other prison guards who had been questioning him. "You can't bring liquor into this prison. We're going to toss the two of you out of here."

Jumonville attempted to intervene in order to aid DiNorscio, when one of the guards turned to him.

"We've called the head of security," the guard said. "He's on his way down here now. We're probably going to lock both of you guys up."

DiNorscio was swearing heatedly. The guards escorted

Jumonville and DiNorscio to a side room near the main entrance. When DiNorscio became enraged, the guards pulled Jumonville into an adjoining office.

"What's your connection with this guy?" a prison official asked.

"Just a friend of the family," Jumonville replied with a straight face.

"Did you know he was bringing liquor into this prison?" the official demanded.

Jumonville tried to calm the situation.

"The guy's an alcoholic," he told the guard. "I hope this isn't going to cause a problem for his father."

The guard said, "Your friend has violated a federal law that could subject him to ten years in prison."

But the guards relented on the arrest. "Since he's drunk, I'm going to let you get him out of here. But only if he goes quietly."

Moments later, Jumonville and DiNorscio were escorted out of the main entrance of the prison. They never did get to see Dominick DiNorscio, and were lucky to get out of the prison without being arrested.

But the story did not end there. DiNorscio said he would leave town only on one condition—that Jumonville get him more to drink. After all, the guards had confiscated his last purchase, and the ride home was going to be a thirsty one.

So the agent gave in, drove DiNorscio to a state liquor store, and bought him a pint of vodka.

Back in the Thunderbird, DiNorscio settled happily back in his seat as the undercover agent drove them home to New Jersey.

The story of that eventful jaunt would later emerge as one of the more bizarre elements of what was to become one of the most bizarre cases in the war on organized crime.

4

Project Alpha remains one of the most successful incursions ever undertaken by law enforcement into the world of organized crime, and would provide a springboard for even more ambitious offensives against the mob bosses. The wheels that were put into motion by Alpha would eventually turn full circle a decade later as the government sought to crush the Lucchese crime family in New Jersey.

In addition to aiding authorities in amassing dozens of arrests, the Alpha probe provided investigators with an unparalleled insight into the inner workings of the mob. And although the actual Alpha investigation ended in 1977, the fallout of that three-year operation would continue to blight the mob for years to come.

In many ways, the intelligence information obtained from Alpha served as a sort of Rosetta Stone for decoding the theretofore incomprehensible machinations of the secret underworld societies operating in New Jersey; it was a playbook listing who's who, and how they fit into the hierarchy.

The information garnered by the probe was not based solely on information from informants, but from firsthand experience by the men who risked their lives to penetrate those secret societies, FBI agents like Jumonville and a group of dedicated state police detectives who donned the false identities that would bring them face-to-face with some of the top criminal figures in the Garden State. In a very practical sense then, Alpha would lay the groundwork for the FBI probe that would eventually lead to the indictment of Accetturo and the entire New Jersey branch of the Lucchese crime family.

Operating out of a top-secret command post located in a penthouse suite in a Newark office building on Broad Street, a team of handpicked state and federal law-enforcement officers manipulated the strings controlling the investigation. The cover for their headquarters was an engineering firm located on Broad Street in Newark.

Among the key targets of the operation were John DiGilio, a former professional prizefighter who ruled the Hudson County waterfront with an iron fist; Tino Fiumara, the handsome and deadly young mob boss who was being groomed by the organized-crime hierarchy to assume a place among the highest echelons of underworld power, only to have his future snatched away at the hands of a government informant; and Jackie DiNorscio, who had alliances with at least three mob families and who played the role of mob "godfather" as though he were born to the position.

Project Alpha was put together in part by Colonel Clinton Pagano, who was later to become superintendent of the New Jersey State Police. It was a federally funded project that was carried out with all the secrecy of a CIA covert action.

Pagano recalled that the operation was known only to a select few—the U.S. attorney and even many prosecutors were kept in the dark as to what was actually in the works. Because there were lives on the line, there could be no room for innocent leaks. The undercover operatives were targeting the key players in the mob—and those players played for keeps.

As a law-enforcement success story, Project Alpha has few parallels. According to Pagano, it "opened up a whole new view of the organized-crime hierarchy in New Jersey" including the burgeoning Lucchese empire and spawned a series of cases that extended for years beyond the termination of the undercover phase of the operation.

When Project Alpha became public in late September

1977, it coincided with the arrests of some thirty persons, who were apprehended by FBI and state police agents in a series of predawn raids. The suspects were herded into a holding pen set up at the National Guard Armory in West Orange.

The charges ranged from loan-sharking and interstate transportation of stolen property to unlawful sale of handguns to a variety of other state and federal offenses.

But the charges didn't stop there. Subsequent indictments, both federal and state, were eventually returned against the three top targets of the probe—DiGilio, Fiumara, and DiNorscio, all of whom were eventually convicted. DiNorscio, in fact, was already in prison on an earlier charge. Only DiGilio never went to prison. Although he stalled his prosecution for more than a decade by feigning "organic brain damage," he was eventually tried and found guilty. Before a sentence could be imposed, however, he disappeared, and his body was found floating near a north Jersey marina several weeks later.

The first step in setting up Project Alpha was to place the undercover operatives in the known haunts of the mobsters and to allow them to become familiar figures to the men they would be investigating. Initially, they went to the Bayonne area, which was DiGilio's base of operations, obtained apartments, and found work in the port area, either at trucking terminals or on the docks. By day, they established their names and faces in the area. By night, they frequented the locations of the known mob hangouts.

Working with a source, Pat Kelly—a corrupt businessman who was favored by the mob because of his ability to engineer financially profitable scams—a handpicked team of state-police operatives, Robert Delaney, Robert Weisert, and Ralph Buono, worked hand in hand with selected FBI agents, including P. J. Jumonville.

For three years, these troopers and the agent lived in a shadow world of criminal activities, living and socializing with the very people whom they were actively investigating. It was an alien environment. These were police officers. Now they were cast into new roles—emulating the very men they were assigned to get.

It was more than a full-time job. Weisert recalled working from seven in the morning until one the next morning, and then starting the routine over again. They were always on the job, and their nerves were raw. Weisert would get up in the morning and throw up from the tension. "And it got worse from there on."

As part of the cover, Weisert was given a penthouse apartment just south of Fort Lee. There, he and Kelly would host parties for their organized-crime targets. But the good times were for the bad guys. For the good guys, it was a nerve-racking nightmare. They had tape recorders and microphones hidden in planters and wine buckets. "We were always under the constant fear that someone would pick up a wine bucket and the tape would fall out, or it would malfunction and start beeping," he recalled.

To facilitate the operation, Delaney and the others were directed to establish a trucking business, Alamo Transportation Company, a firm that eventually grew—with the help of mob friends—into such a large operation that it had some thirty-five tractor trailers on the road, delivering produce such as seafood, vegetables, and meat throughout the United States. The company employed twenty-five workers and fielded its own company baseball team. It was this firm that Jackie had sought to treat as his private-slush fund.

The letterhead of the company, which was headquartered at 231 Communipaw Avenue in Jersey City, even bore a slogan: WHEN TRUCKING, REMEMBER THE ALAMO.

Alamo was outfitted with transmitters and microwave equipment. Video surveillance cameras were mounted behind grills, recording all that went on in the offices. The signals were bounced back to a dish antenna, located on the Newark office building where the command center was based.

"We had the most sophisticated equipment. . . ," Weisert recalled. "A push-button phone would activate a room."

Delaney posed as the owner and president, Buono was his confidant and best friend, and Weisert served as the business manager and as a "buffer" between Delaney and the main targets.

Initially, Jumonville worked with Delaney, but later, Delaney pretended to "buy out" Jumonville. This allowed the FBI agent—who was described as a bit of a lone wolf—to spin off on a series of independent investigations, including those that brought him into contact with DiNorscio's cousin Joseph

Alonzo, the man who would eventually become the key to the government case against DiNorscio, Accetturo, and Taccetta.

But the success of Alamo brought with it its own headaches. Even an undercover operation has to pay Social Security and other benefits, and the paperwork was as cumbersome as any private company must endure.

"We were getting too big," one state-police officer recalled.

The problems were growing, and even the dangers were increasing. In one instance, targets threatened to "come down and torch the business" and murder one of the operatives.

They also had their hands full fielding overtures from organized-crime groups of all types who wanted to take advantage of the benefits the undercover company had to offer.

Dirk Ottens, a former state-police detective who served as an administrator for Project Alpha, recalled that not all of the bad guys were particularly skillful at what they did. In some cases, it was a wonder they hadn't been locked up years before.

Ottens related one incident in which he had received an emergency telephone call from one of the undercover operatives in the early hours of the morning.

"You're not going to believe it, but we've got a hijacked load of refrigerators," the operative explained. "We don't know what to do with it. There's only two of us here, and we've got to unload it."

A crew of independent hijackers had made off with a truckload of refrigerators from a port area trucking firm, and had decided to fence the goods with the state operatives.

Ottens considered the situation. "Tell them they're not getting paid until they get that trailer out of there."

It was a stall for time. He had to arrange to rendezvous with the men to slip them some cash. He got in his car and turned on the radio. That was when he went pale. The radio was broadcasting an alert. The hijacking had been reported, and police were looking for the truck.

Holy shit, he thought to himself. That truck is right there . . . at our dock. It could blow our whole undercover operation.

Using a code name, Ottens called in to the office. "Tell them to get it out of there right away. We can't afford to be set up like this. . . . Tell them they don't get any money until that truck's out of there. You don't want anything hot laying around."

It was a miracle it had ever got that far in the first place. Apparently, the hijacking began with two ne'er-do-wells walking into a truck depot "looking around for a trailer" to steal. No high-tech scheme carried out with precision timing and inside information this. They just decided to steal a truck. They spotted the trailer loaded with refrigerators and realized they could be worth something.

So they hooked a truck tractor up to the trailer. Only they weren't mechanical marvels either. They inadvertently crossed the connection lines, and wound up locking the trailer brakes in the On position. The truck wouldn't move.

At this point, one of the men from the depot noticed the activity, and wandered over to the truck.

"What's going on?"

The hijackers were brazen. "Well, we got to take this truck out, but it won't go."

The depot employee took a look and realized what was wrong.

"You jerkoff, you got the lines crossed."

He reached down and fixed the error, and the two men climbed into the truck cab and started it up.

A moment later, it dawned on someone else at the truck yard that there was no authorization for that truck to be going anywhere. He started yelling from the office, "Hey . . ."

The hijackers revved up the truck and barreled ahead. They steamrollered their way out of the lot, taking down a cyclone fence and a telephone pole along the way.

"They were definitely not truck drivers," Ottens said. "When they got to our place, they took off half of the dock roof with the trailer. We almost had to forfeit our lease because the owner of the property was all upset, we were ruining his building. Needless to say, we didn't worry too much about getting another case together on them."

The coordinators of Project Alpha had gone into the operation with a strategic perspective: There were cases they wanted, there were people they wanted to get, and there was information they needed. They knew whom they were going after, and after three years, they knew they had got what they needed.

Unlike the situation that developed in the Accetturo case a decade later—which, in hindsight, some critics contend was permitted to grow too large to handle—the people who ran Project Alpha realized that from a prosecutorial standpoint, enough was enough. Some of the Alpha cases would take years to develop and bring to trial. At some point, there would be just too much to handle. So the decision was made to wrap it up.

There was also another reason: The operation had become so successful, according to state-police lieutenant John Liddy, that it was beginning to attract the attention of other law-enforcement agencies, who were oblivious to the true nature of Alamo Transportation. Local and county law-enforcement agencies had begun taking their own look at Alamo, and they were beginning to conduct surveillance operations of their own. The watchers, in short, were now being watched themselves.

The main undercover operative, Delaney, used the undercover name Bob Covert—his last name being an ironic play on his real role. Delaney-Covert played the part of a rich kid whose parents had been killed in an auto accident, and who had become wealthy as a result of the settlement and was putting the money into the trucking business.

"In a typical undercover operation," Ottens said, "the first thing a cop does is grow a beard, put jeans on, and wear brogans and a field jacket."

But this technique, he said, is limiting. It gets you in the door, but only to the level of the street hoods. But the mob bosses are known to be greedy; so the thought was, present them with a guy with bucks, and they're not going to want to share him with their underlings—they'll skip right to him themselves. With this in mind, they disguised Delaney in a four-hundred-dollar suit.

The mob bought the ruse completely. It had the two essential components that suck the mob in—money and an easy mark.

"The thing to keep in mind with these so-called wiseguys," declared state-police sergeant Bob Hopkins of the state-police intelligence bureau, "is that they're really nothing more than street-level con men. Their whole thing is to make a buck, and they're not as sophisticated as the media, and even law enforcement, tends to make them. It gets down to simple human behavior. They find a kid that's gullible, they find an individual who is vulnerable, and then they ask the question—does the guy have money? . . . and then they move in."

When it came to Alamo Transportation, they didn't ask for large amounts. They picked away small pieces. They'd go to restaurants and charge three-hundred-dollar meals.

That technique, Weisert said, was particularly popular with DiNorscio. "When the phone rang and it was Jackie calling from prison saying I need three hundred dollars right now for my girlfriend or whatever . . . we had to give it to him. And if we didn't, there'd be yelling and screaming on the phone and there'd be threats."

But the demands didn't stay small. In addition to the piecemeal bilking like Jackie's telephone scam at Rahway State Prison—Alamo eventually found itself paying out nearly 25 percent of its profits in payoffs of one sort or another to mob figures.

Pat Kelly, the informant, was the link between the undercover operatives and many of the mob figures—including Jackie DiNorscio. Every Wednesday night, he would come in and go over the books, and settle the accounts. DiNorscio would get one third, DiGilio would get one third, and Fiumara would get the other third. But the factions weren't happy with the setup. They each wanted it all.

Initially, it had been DiNorscio's baby. Pat Kelly was his man, and Alamo trucking was his mark. He was the one who had found Jumonville. He was the one who introduced Kelly to Fiumara. And he was the one who vouched for Kelly to DiGilio.

Kelly was described by Delaney in Senate testimony as "an extraordinary man." A very successful businessman, whose interests in real estate, construction, and other ventures had made him quite comfortable financially, Kelly had cut some corners, made some questionable financial transactions, and had come to the attention of law enforcement.

"Kelly found organized crime fascinating. He was the kind of smooth-talking, cordial, and imaginative person, who can be extremely helpful to law enforcement."

Kelly (who Delaney noted would probably have become a "made man" in organized crime if he had been Italian rather than Irish) had been given a choice: face prosecution for his own crimes, or cooperate. He, of course, chose the path of least resistance: cooperation.

Pat Kelly was held in high regard by the mob. He was an earner, but a special kind of earner. He not only brought in money, he was also an innovative thinker. He showed them new ways to move.

He was in sharp contrast to the man who served as his greatest booster, Jackie DiNorscio.

Jackie, Hopkins revealed, "wasn't real bright to begin with. He has the distinction of being one of the very few, if not the only guy, that ever did eight years for bookmaking. He had a lot of good opportunities, and he had great opportunities with Pat Kelly." But his primary interest at the time was how to get a quick five hundred dollars.

"He [Jackie] was always trying to bleed us," Ottens recalled. "For a while, we were like his blood bank for money."

He also was "mixing it up" with some pretty major players, including DiGilio and Fiumara. Some thought it was out of disregard for their positions. Others thought he was just used to bullying and blustering his way through situations. Whatever, he didn't display great acumen.

"One of the things that used to irritate the hell out of me," Hopkins declared, "was that the picture is always painted with these guys that rather than being a 'little deviant' toward society, they would be the Lee Iacoccas [of the underworld]; that they're really sharp guys who could cut through all the red tape. Well, that is not the case. We used to wait literally months for a simple load to get boosted, with all the dickering back and forth about can they put it together, and all the infighting about who's going to do what."

Even simple things became difficult—like stealing cars. One plan called for mob figures to steal Lincolns and Cadillacs. Now, there were Lincolns and Cadillacs all over the streets, but it took forever for them to decide which ones they were going to take.

"These meatballs," Hopkins said "used to say that before they could pull a heist, they had 'to get our balls up.'" Which meant "they had to go get lit up in a gin mill and drink their bravery. But these lushes would end up so blitzed, they couldn't do the job."

One acquaintance of Jack DiNorscio once quipped that if law enforcement really wanted to put an end to organized crime in New Jersey, all it had to do was leave DiNorscio out on the street. He had a particular talent for bringing down the heat on otherwise successful operations.

"He was stupid," a state-police investigator explained. "He was in jail, and he wasn't sensitive to what was happening out on the street. He had this cavalier and self-centered idea of what his role was."

And until authorities were able to "ingratiate themselves" with Fiumara and DiGilio, Ottens said, "DiNorscio was our ticket to undercover success."

As a result, the three separate factions all attempted to lay claim to the Alamo operation. And they all wanted to help nurture Alamo into the bonanza they dreamed it could become—they were competing for the prize.

"With us," Hopkins said, "they knew they had something good. And they wanted to milk it nice and slow."

As one mob figure told Weisert, "Bobby, this is just a little infant, a little baby. You don't want to hurt it now, it's gotta grow."

And grow it did.

Delaney compared the relationship between Alamo and the mob to lovers during courtship. The company reaped the benefits of having supporters in organized crime, which Delaney said was the "romancing stage."

"It is comparable to courtship and marriage. The suitor may treat the maiden much better during courtship than he treats her during the marriage. At this point, Alamo was in the courtship stage."

Jackie, Delaney noted, was, of the three, the least effective suitor. "He was greedy and always tried to intimidate people."

This became evident in a tape recording of a conversation between Kelly, a DiNorscio associate, Woody Brown, and Delaney about the issue of Alamo's sending his family on a vacation to Disney World.

•

KELLY: Now, what's the situation on these ah, tickets with Jackie?

BROWN: We got, we need the money for the travel agency. . . .
KELLY: The tickets are $1,325.29.
BROWN: Right.
KELLY: That's for Marlene [Jackie's wife].
BROWN: That's for Marlene and the kids.
KELLY: The two kids and the mother-in-law, right.
BROWN: The mother.
KELLY: The mother, I mean.

Delaney, however, was adamant. He wasn't going to pay. Or so he thought.

DELANEY: That would be it, I mean. I'm not gonna. You know, after that's over, there's something else.

Then Brown made DiNorscio's message crystal-clear.

BROWN: Well, Jackie said, this is his wife all right, and if we can't do this here for him, he said that he'll call Tino and Johnny and he'll shut everything down. There won't be nothing moving out of here.

Eventually, Alamo sprang for the vacation.

As Alamo grew, Weisert managed to do what nobody else had done before—get close to DiNorscio and the other mob figures they were after. State-police and FBI units had been trying to get to them for years; no one had even come close.

Except for DiNorscio, even in their dealings with Alamo, the others used buffers. DiGilio and Fiumara used Kelly as an intermediary. The direct contact the authorities were seeking was still missing.

But Weisert had a breakthrough. He had been working on DiGilio with the idea of getting loan-shark money to set up his own operation, under DiGilio's tutelage. He had been trying for months to get a personal sit-down with the elusive mob figure. DiGilio was as cagey as he was wary, but eventually, he couldn't resist.

Arrangements were made for a meeting in a car.

Weisert was understandably nervous.

It was a green Lincoln Continental. DiGilio was in the passenger seat. A driver was behind the wheel. Weisert was picked up for a little ride.

The plan was for two other troopers to tail the meeting by installing a beeper under the bumper. Weisert was, of course, wired.

"Keep an eye out back," DiGilio told his driver. And they set off through the streets of Bayonne, as the conversation began.

The last thing the backup crew saw was Weisert driving away—then they realized that the beeper wasn't working. DiGilio kept looking out the back window. The follow-up car had to hang back to avoid being noticed. It hung back so far, they lost sight of the Lincoln.

When Weisert got in, his heart was in his mouth; but after about five minutes, he settled down. After all, his support team was right behind him—or so he thought.

To top off the situation, DiGilio suddenly shouted, "I think we're being followed. Better start making some turns."

Weisert was confident. After all, even if they lost visual contact, there was always the beeper, which he, of course, had no idea wasn't working.

"That damn car," DiGilio muttered, looking out the rear window. "It's still behind us." To his driver, he barked the order, "Go into the park."

Now, Weisert was beginning to worry. They were going to become suspicious. They were going to spot the tail, and they were going to find the recorder. And he wasn't carrying a gun.

I'm dead, Weisert thought to himself.

DiGilio checked the rear window again. "That yellow car is still behind us," he muttered.

Suddenly, Weisert perked up. "Yellow car?" He turned around. It was a little sports car. Whoever it was, it wasn't the state police. The state-police car was no where to be seen.

That's when Weisert almost went into cardiac arrest for real.

Fortunately, the car was innocent—it wasn't tailing anybody, and Weisert went on to play out the next act. DiGilio eventually promised to make Alamo "one of the biggest in the country."

No one, however, was ever able to get quite so close to Fiumara.

Tino was alleged to have once strangled a rival with piano wire, shot several men in cold blood, and had acquired a reputation for ruthless bloodletting.

Fiumara had a beautiful home in suburban Bergen County. As a favor, Alamo allowed Fiumara to send the company a bill for a soil test on his lawn. Alamo also sent truck drivers up with sandblasting equipment to resurface his swimming pool.

Apparently, the workers weren't doing the job the way he thought they should have been doing it. And Fiumara—who was rumored to have tried to chop out someone's heart with an ice pick during a dispute—lost his temper.

The workers came back in a state of shock.

"He went crazy," one worker told the undercover troopers who had sent him to the house. "He grabbed a ten-pound sledgehammer, walked over to his brick barbecue, and, starting at the top, he kept hitting it until he leveled the entire thing right to the ground."

Much of his reputation for violence may have been exaggerated, but no one wanted to take the chance of finding out. He had cold, piercing eyes and a penchant for leveling a "death stare" on those with whom he was not enamored. Most chose to stay out of his way, and many of his subordinates were reluctant even to speak his name aloud.

He was so brazen, one police official said, that he was reported to have secured the door to the old FBI office after the agency relocated its Newark headquarters from the federal courthouse to the more spacious facilities at the Gateway office complex. (This was not such a farfetched story. After all, DiGilio was prosecuted for engineering the theft of his own FBI dossier from the same FBI office. He arranged to have the documents smuggled out in the panties of a female clerical worker.)

When Fiumara was eventually brought to trial, it was testimony from the informant Kelly that finally brought him down.

Along the way, the Alpha investigation revealed some interesting tidbits about organized crime, and many of them involved Tino, who in many ways was a prototype for the traditional "godfather": People seeking his favors would come to him and kiss his ring. And he would bestow his blessings.

Delaney noted that a lot of younger mob figures used the movie *The Godfather* as a sort of preparatory course in mob etiquette—they used it as a way of learning how to behave.

"They had a lot of things taught to them through the movie. They try to live up to it. The movie was telling them how."

On one occasion, Delaney noted, Joseph Doto, the son of the legendary old-time mobster Joe Adonis, handed a waiter a handful of quarters and had him play the theme to *The Godfather* all through dinner.

Even the kisses of respect, which would later become an accepted part of mob protocol, received a boost from the motion picture—although not everyone was familiar with the meaning.

On one occasion, Delaney recalled, Fiumara and several members of his crew had come into a bar, and started exchanging kisses of greeting. The bartender was new. He didn't know who these people were and made a comment: "What is this, a fag bar?"

The remark, Delaney said, made Tino "very upset." He took his underboss, Michael Coppola, aside and told him to have a little talk with the bartender. Coppola did as he was instructed; he grabbed the bartender, and told him firmly that his remark was not appreciated.

"And when the bartender came back," Delaney said, "he was obviously upset and was having a hard time even figuring out how to pour a drink."

As a result of Alpha, federal prosecutions would be mounted against Fiumara, DiGilio, and DiNorscio.

DiGilio would fight on for years, feigning insanity off and on until his death while the Lucchese trial was still in progress. Fiumara would go to jail on a twenty-year jail term, to be followed by a subsequent twenty-five-year conviction in federal court in New York.

DiNorscio . . . well, DiNorscio did what he did best. He stayed in jail, until eventually he would be released and relocate to Florida. There, his path would cross that of exiled mob boss Anthony Accetturo.

It was a meeting that would prove potentially disasterous for both men—and critical to government efforts to build its case against the Lucchese family in New Jersey.

Even in the Sunshine State, it turned out, the "boys from New Jersey" never forgot their roots. And when those roots were uncovered, the new leaders of the Lucchese organization, men like Michael Taccetta and his brother Martin, would be exposed.

5

The last thing Michael Taccetta looked like on the day of his arrest was a Mafia boss.

The man who was regarded by many as the "philosopher king" of organized crime and who quoted as freely from the "Great Books" as from homespun Sicilian folktales, was something less than a vision of sartorial splendor.

Wearing beach sandals, Hawaiian print shorts, and a sweatshirt covering a stomach that could best be described as expansive, he resembled nothing so much as a vacationing pizza-pie maker. But according to authorities, Taccetta was one of the most powerful leaders of the Lucchese crime family in New Jersey.

Although relatively small by comparison with the larger Genovese and Gambino families which continue to dominate the New York area underworld, the Lucchese organization had grown steadily in power and influence since its founding by Gaetano "Three Fingers Brown" Lucchese in the 1930s.

One of the so-called original "five families" of the Mafia in America, the organization was represented on the mob's high Commission, the board of directors of organized crime headquartered in New York. And like each of those five families, the Lucchese organization maintained a presence in New Jersey. By the mid-1980s, that presence had grown into a force to be reckoned with.

Accetturo, authorities reported, had evolved from a brazen street hood, who is reputed to have once set fire to a police surveillance van while the police were inside, forcing the officers to flee or roast, to become the grand old man of Lucchese operations in the Garden State.

And when he fled to Florida to avoid the heat law enforcement subsequently brought to bear on him, Accetturo allegedly turned the day-to-day operations over to Michael Taccetta.

According to authorities, the family controlled lucrative gambling and loan-sharking operations in large areas of northern New Jersey. Authorities also reported that the family successfully infiltrated legitimate businesses in the region, including the construction, solid waste, garment, and trucking industries.

In addition, authorities contend that the family also became enmeshed in the financing of narcotics trafficking, and formed alliances with South American drug organizations—allegations, however, that have been adamantly disavowed by the Taccettas.

On August 21, 1985, Michael Taccetta was led into the federal courthouse in Newark in the company of FBI agent Dennis Marchalonis, the man who had made the capture of Taccetta and his companions his life's work.

Marchalonis, in contrast to Taccetta's casual attire, looked like Mr. Rogers. Impeccably neat, his close-cropped hair parted precisely to the side and combed in layered symmetry over a high brow, Marchalonis was the picture of fastidiousness. Thin, sharp-featured, and bristling with energy, the FBI agent had ushered the handcuffed mob boss out of the FBI car and into the rear entrance of the pillared courthouse, the entrance reserved for those unfortunate enough to be placed under arrest or shipped off to prison after their convictions.

In many ways, Marchalonis looked like what he was, a former high school teacher. He had grown up in the coal-mining region of eastern Pennsylvania, and had taught an array of courses ranging from world history to economics, anthropology, and criminal justice. He held a bachelor's degree in social studies from East Stroudsburg State College and a master's in political science from the same school.

Nearly a decade had elapsed since he left the world of academia to join the button-down world of the FBI. And the pursuit of Michael Taccetta had occupied a good percentage of his time since then.

Early that morning, Marchalonis and a team of agents had entered a motel room on the Jersey Shore where Taccetta was spending the night. The air-conditioning was running full blast, and Taccetta was attempting to escape the problems of a chronic asthma condition that had plagued him most of his adult life. He was in bed when the agents walked in.

Taccetta had expected something. Rumors had been circulating that the government was getting ready to make a move. It was common knowledge that the Taccetta-Accetturo operations had been under investigation for several years, ever since FBI agents swept through northern New Jersey with a parcel of search warrants, seizing paperwork and evidence related to what was believed to be an abundant array of illicit activities. The evidence included notebooks with names and numbers, merchandise that had been acquired under suspect circumstances, and a smattering of other potentially incriminating materials.

The agents gave Taccetta time to dress before leading him down to their waiting car.

As they got in the vehicle, Marchalonis handed Taccetta a copy of the indictment in the case. Taccetta thumbed through it. It contained the usual—gambling and loan-sharking-type charges. But there was something else—it accused Taccetta of being part of a drug-distribution ring, headquartered in Florida, which was shipping large quantities of cocaine into New Jersey.

Taccetta looked at Marchalonis intently. "What's this?" he asked, jabbing a handcuffed hand at the indictment.

"You'll see," Marchalonis said, and settled back in the seat for the long drive back to Newark. . . .

Marchalonis and Taccetta already knew each other at the time of the arrest. The two had met months before during a four-hour search at the Berkeley Heights, New Jersey, home of Victor Cantillo, a suspected associate of the mob chieftain.

As the agents rummaged through the house looking for evidence, Taccetta and Marchalonis had settled down in the kitchen for a quiet talk. It was a moment that the agent recalled vividly.

He had been assigned to the Taccetta investigation in June of 1982. From that date until June of 1985, he had immersed himself in the operations of Taccetta's illegitimate and legitimate businesses. He had conducted surveillance of Taccetta, he had listened to his voice on wiretap and "bugs," and he knew virtually everything there was to know about him. But he had never actually met the man face-to-face before this moment.

And now the man who had been the target of his work for the past three years; the man he was building a case against and hoped to put behind bars; the man who was considered by law-enforcement authorities to be one of the most powerful mob figures in New Jersey—was seated across a kitchen table from him asking his name. And both the agent and the suspect well knew that the time was coming when they would face each other again, in a courtroom.

"Marchalonis," the agent said, introducing himself, "Dennis Marchalonis." He repeated it twice. Taccetta seemed not to have heard it before.

And as the other agents went about searching the house, Taccetta and Marchalonis embarked on a rambling conversation that touched on subjects as diverse as patriotism, family, and crime, as well as the "code" of the streets.

Taccetta also revealed himself to be a man who was equally comfortable discussing Socrates and Machiavelli as he was talking of "snitches, stool pigeons, and informants."

It was this conversation, ironically, that would several months later become the subject of cross-examination by Taccetta's attorney, and be turned from a virtual admission of guilt by the key figure in a mob empire to a challenge to the credibility of the man who was sworn to bring him to justice.

Yet on that particular afternoon, it was as though two old friends had come to talk.

Marchalonis and another agent went into the Cantillo house through the garage. The door led directly into the kitchen.

Michael Taccetta and Victor Cantillo were seated at the table along with two women and two children.

Taccetta gestured at the women and children.

"You mind if they leave?" he asked.

Marchalonis smiled. "I have no problem at all," he replied, and the youngsters were led out of the room by the women.

Agents, meanwhile, were roaming around the house, looking for possible evidence to use in the case against the Taccetta organization. Several were looking through the drawers and cabinets in the kitchen.

Marchalonis pulled up a vacant chair and sat at the table.

"You want a soda or something?" Taccetta asked.

Marchalonis settled back in the chair. "Yes, please," he said. Cantillo went to the refrigerator and returned with a can and a glass. Marchalonis thanked him, poured the beverage, and took a drink. He set down the glass and looked across at Taccetta.

Taccetta lit up a cigarette as he studied the agent in the neat tie and jacket seated across from him. He drew deeply on the smoke, and his eyes narrowed. Taccetta's asthma was chronic; he had suffered repeated attacks. The cigarettes were killing him. But so was the weight. Whenever he became nervous, he ate and smoked. He could polish off a half-gallon container of T&W ice cream in a single sitting. He didn't know how many packs of cigarettes he went through.

His voice was a low, raspy rumble.

"You know, they keep putting my name in the paper along with these guys when they get arrested," he said. "That just ain't right."

Taking a drag on his cigarette, Taccetta asked the agent a direct question.

"What's your opinion of the kind of guy that would come forward or tell or snitch or be a stool pigeon regarding other individuals?"

Marchalonis looked at Taccetta and replied thoughtfully. "As an FBI agent," he said, "I'm not in a position to judge. But to someone in my position, their information could prove very helpful."

Taccetta then asked the agent: "There was an FBI agent in Los Angeles the other week. He was arrested for espionage, for giving secrets to the Russians. How do you feel about that kind of guy?"

"As far as I'm concerned," the agent said, "he is a traitor to his profession."

Taccetta smiled knowingly, sitting back in his chair. "I feel the same way about a guy who would tell on others in my profession."

Taccetta never specified what "profession" he was talking about, but the meaning was clear.

"Socrates," Taccetta went on to say, "had a code to live by. No matter what, you kept your mouth shut.

"They gave Socrates a choice when he got into trouble with his government," Taccetta explained. "He could either leave Greece and no longer come back—and go against everything he had been taught—or he could drink the hemlock poison.

"Socrates chose to drink the hemlock," he said. "He chose to live, or in this case to die, for what he believed in."

The agent carefully considered what the man across the table was telling him.

"People in my profession," Taccetta said in a hushed voice, "have a code to follow. . . . You have to take the good with the bad. . . ."

As the conversation progressed, the two men turned to other topics—children, families, and even the economics of crime.

"You got any kids?" Taccetta asked the agent.

"Yeah," Marchalonis replied. "Two."

Taccetta laughed. "Me," he said, "I got four."

Taccetta, who had been arrested years earlier on a gambling charge, waxed nostalgic about the changes in the business since those days.

"You know," Taccetta told the agent, "a lot of people exaggerate the amount of money to be made in the numbers business. They think you can make, like, seventeen percent profit." He shook his head and laughed. "Only the banks with the credit cards do that good.

"In the numbers business," he said, "it's more like ten percent."

Taccetta drummed on the table as if gathering his thoughts. "Ten, fifteen years ago, maybe you could pay a runner seventy-five or a hundred twenty-five dollars a week to run around collecting numbers.

"Today," he laughed, "you got to pay them three, four hundred dollars for the same work—and this eats up the profits."

As they spoke, the smoke in the room grew thicker.

Taccetta drifted once again into philosophical musings. "Are you familiar with Machiavelli?" he asked the agent.

Marchalonis, who had once taught Machiavelli's political theory, indicated he was. The sixteenth-century Florentine stateman's work *The Prince* was regarded as the classic treatment of power and government.

Taccetta applied Machiavelli's teachings to the role of leadership, how to rule and how to command.

"Me," Taccetta said, "I grew up in the streets. I didn't have the benefit of making a lot of mistakes."

Taccetta squinted through the smoke of his cigarette. "You," he told the agent, "you could probably make two million mistakes and you wouldn't have any problem."

He hooked his thumb back at his own chest.

"Me," he said, "I make one mistake—it could be my last."

6

The call notifying attorney Michael Critchley of the indictment came to his house early in the morning. Alerting him to the arrest was a friend of Taccetta's.

His first response was to moan, "Oh, shit." He knew it was inevitable, but deep down he had hoped it would never happen.

He rolled out of bed, made a cup of coffee, and began making calls. He found out some of the names of the others arrested, and he found out where the arraignments were to take place.

The first hearings were before U.S. Magistrate G. Donald Haneke. Haneke's courtroom was a tiny, paneled room tucked away at the rear of a fourth-floor corridor of the federal courthouse in Newark. The room was crowded, packed with lawyers and defendants. A window air conditioner was whirring. News reporters filled the first three rows of seats.

The door opened, and Grady O'Malley, the man who had brought the case to indictment, walked into the room. His mere physical presence was electrifying. His jaw was set, and he moved with the assurance of a natural athlete. He exuded confidence.

The government wanted Taccetta held as a "danger" to the community. Haneke demanded to know on what evidence the request was based. There were tape recordings, prosecutors said, referring to someone named "Rocky" who would be put "in blackness"—although nobody was quite sure who "Rocky" was, or for that matter, what had happened to him.

There was evidence that a suspect in a related investigation had been murdered, authorities said, but Haneke ruled that the evidence was inadmissible. Nobody in this case had been charged with the crime.

Critchley asked questions of the FBI agent who supervised the investigation, Dennis Marchalonis. The agent acknowledged that he had never seen Taccetta with a gun; never saw him strike anyone; never saw him engage in any violent act.

When the hearings were over, Haneke ordered Taccetta released on bail. The government, the magistrate ruled, had "not met its burden" to keep him from setting bail. Critchley had won the first round.

As the prosecutors walked out of the courtroom, O'Malley looked angry. Critchley put out his hand. He had won, but he knew it was just as easy to lose. And the next round might go to O'Malley. You win some, you lose some. O'Malley had lost this one, but there would be another time.

O'Malley ignored the hand and walked past the defense lawyer. Critchley looked at him walk away with Marchalonis at his side.

"Okay, Grady," he muttered to himself. "I'll remember that."

Michael Critchley was born in Newark, in an area not far from the same neighborhood, predominantly Italian, and predominantly poor, in which Taccetta and his friends were raised.

The youngest of six brothers, he was raised in a cold-water flat—he was twelve years old before he found out what steam heat was. His father was a roofer, and his mother picked up what money she could at odd jobs.

His father died when he was thirteen, and his mother died four years later. It was Holy Thursday night when Critchley came home and found her body, cold and stiff.

No one in his family had ever gone to college. In fact, he could not recall anyone from his neighborhood even considering such a venture. When a child turned sixteen, the normal routine was simply to quit school and get working papers.

Critchley recalled an older boy from the neighborhood once asking him to go for a ride with him. The boy was headed for a factory to apply for a job, but he couldn't fill out the application. He couldn't read or write.

It wasn't uncommon for friends to be locked up. When they needed nine men to play a game of sandlot baseball, they often had to go looking to other neighborhoods to fill up the team, because their own players were in jail.

The biggest success stories were those who got civil-service jobs—the pay was decent, the benefits good, and, best of all, you were protected. College never entered into the picture, because even if a child had the grades, there was no money to pay the tuition.

After graduating from high school, Critchley found work as a roofer. He had in fact worked his way through a good portion of high school hammering nails on the off-hours when class was not in session, often falling asleep in class.

After his mother's death, Critchley moved in with an older brother.

"I didn't know what I wanted to do, I didn't know where I wanted to go." But he did know he wanted out. He was a bright kid, and he knew there was something better out there somewhere.

A number of his brothers were police officers who supplemented their incomes with roofing. It was in the blood. It was something Critchley knew, so he did it too.

At Port Newark, that first winter after high school, it was so cold that after he drove in three nails, his fingers would freeze up, and when he hit them accidentally, they were so numb, they would swell up and begin to bleed. The others in his family had put up with it, but he was sick of it—the cold in winter and the blazing heat in summer. He made up his mind to find something else.

He signed up for a few courses at Bloomfield College, structuring his schedule so that he could take courses both during the day and at night, leaving time in between to roof two or three days a week and earn enough money to carry himself through school.

In his third year, as an education major, he had signed up for the junior practicum course, which takes the students into an actual classroom setting. There, he struck up a friendship with a teacher he was assigned to work with. One day, he noticed his friend was in a hurry to leave school early.

"What's the rush?" Critchley asked.

"I have to get to my other job," the man explained.

"Other job? What's your other job?"

"I sell hot dogs," the man said.

As Critchley watched him leave, he found himself with a hollow feeling in his stomach.

"Mike," he said to himself, "you're not doing all this to get a part-time job selling hot dogs."

So Critchley took a shot. He changed his major to political science and decided to try for something he had only dreamed about: law school.

By the time he finished college, he had married and already had one child; and to support himself and his family, he was still roofing.

But law school was different from college. The amount of reading was overwhelming. By the time he got to class, he was exhausted. He felt he'd never make it through.

His family had developed political contacts in the area. Some were policemen, some were firemen. So he put their contacts to use, and wound up with a job as a sheriff's officer in Essex County. It was a good job, and he worked for a while in the detective bureau, learning the basics of criminal investigation. Soon, he wanted to be closer to the courts; he wanted to see how the law really worked. Through a contact of his brother, Critchley became court attendant to state superior-court judge Brendan T. Byrne. It was 1970.

The two men got on well together. Byrne did not have an official court clerk, and in his nearly three years there Critchley found himself, for all practical purposes, cast in that role. The law student drafted many of Byrne's written opinions, participated in settlement conferences, worked on motions, and, all the while, was in charge of administering the courtroom operations. He talked to defense lawyers, as well as to prosecutors. Alone in the courtroom, he would practice opening addresses to an imaginary jury. He was learning the judicial system from the inside out.

On occasion, Byrne would shock attorneys by interrupting discussions and turning to his uniformed court attendant, who was standing in the court with his holstered gun and badge.

"Mr. Critchley," he would ask "what do you think about this?"

The attorneys were generally surprised when the uniformed attendant presented a perceptive analysis of the issues.

When Critchley graduated, Byrne called him in to see him. Byrne was moving on—he had been named assignment judge for Morris County.

"Mike," Byrne asked him, "what are you going to do? It would be silly to come with me. You don't need to work as a law clerk—you've essentially done that. Whatever you want, I'd like to recommend you. Whatever it is, whatever law firm, whatever position . . ."

Critchley didn't have to think twice about his answer.

"I'd like to be an assistant prosecutor," he said.

Sometime later, Byrne pulled Critchley aside. "I've talked to Joe Lordi," Byrne said. "Take your résumé and go down and see him."

Lordi was then the prosecutor for Essex County. When Critchley met him, the prosecutor took one look at the uniform and made the same mistake many of the attorneys in Byrne's court had made.

"Judge Byrne sent me," Critchley said, handing his papers to Lordi. Lordi looked at him and asked, "What do you want, to be an investigator?"

Critchley was used to it by now. "No." He smiled. "I went to law school. I want to be a prosecutor."

Critchley was sworn in as a prosecutor two weeks after he was notified that he had passed the state bar exam. He had gone from uniformed court attendant guarding the courtroom on one day to a full-fledged assistant prosecutor the next day. The irony was, his pay dropped—from $14,000 a year to $12,000.

Despite the drop in pay, Critchley decided to give up roofing for good.

He worked there for a year, gathering trial experience—handling every sort of case thrown at him. By then, Byrne had become governor of the state, and remembering his old attendant-turned-lawyer, invited Critchley to join his staff at the state capitol. He accepted and was named assistant counsel to the governor.

A year later, Critchley opened up shop for himself and soon began trying cases. He went into criminal law because it was the easiest way into a courtroom; there simply weren't that many civil cases to be had, and by now Critchley was not only supporting a growing family, but carrying a mortgage in addition to his school loans.

His first big case arrived when an officer in the Prosecutor's Office came to him with a request. His brother was in trouble—he was a police officer accused of protecting an alleged narcotics dealer known locally as "Popjaws."

Critchley was young and relatively inexperienced. He had only been in practice for two years at that time, and was surprised that he was being asked to take on the case.

"He gave me his brother's life," Critchley said. "I told him I would take care of it."

He kept his promise, and it was the beginning of a reputation that began to grow.

Critchley had known of Michael Taccetta as a teenager, and the two had seen each other at dances. Critchley even participated in the drum corps sponsored by St. Rocco's, the church that was located near Taccetta's home. They weren't friends, but they knew of each other's ways.

Critchley belonged to his own gang and had had his share of fights, some involving clubs, some even involving guns. There were turf wars over neighborhoods, someone saying something unpleasant about a friend's girlfriend or mother, someone calling someone a punk at a movie or messing with his girl at a dance. He still bears a slight scar near his right eye where he was whacked in the face with a board during a gang rumble.

Critchley had been picked up a few times for petty juvenile offenses, but because his brothers were police officers, he was able to get out of a number of close scrapes with the law without a record. They weren't serious offenses; breaking into a car for a joyride, stealing a car battery, fighting.

"I think from the time I was ten until the time I was nineteen, when you realize it's not that important, I was fighting every month. There was always some fight, somewhere, involving someone or something.

"I've been fighting all my life," Critchley said. "If I had a theme song, it would probably be called 'Keep Punching.'"

He was an Irish kid in an Italian neighborhood. An outsider. Sometimes it helped. Sometimes it hurt. But one thing it did was help him to understand the background from which the defendants in the Accetturo trial had come, as well as the defendants themselves.

"Some people think we all start from the same line and can't understand why everybody can't keep pace with the pack. But the fact is, we don't all start from the same line. Some of us start from ten yards behind, some of us start from forty yards behind . . . and it takes time to play catch-up. Sometimes you never catch up. You can't catch up from an education you haven't received. You can't catch up from an environment where education is not stressed as being important. You can't catch up when you don't have strong family support making certain you go a certain way.

"And sometimes you can't catch up when the peer pressure and surroundings are such that you don't know any alternative. . . ."

They filtered into the restaurant one by one, gathering first in the bar area.

There were lawyers, dressed like lawyers, and there were "wiseguys," dressed in their usual attire—pullover shirts and casual slacks. It was only in the movies, or among those who liked to imitate the images they saw in the movies, that mob figures wore the expensive clothes. In fact, this was generally how you told the lawyers and their clients apart.

It was around 7:00 P.M. on this warm early September night in 1985 when Michael Critchley arrived, fashionably late. Most of the others were already there, at the bar, chatting and drinking.

Critchley was clearly the man in charge. He darted about like a host at a singles' mixer. He knew most of the guests personally, but a lot of them did not know each other.

This was to be the first formal meeting of the defense team, and he wanted to establish some glue, some consistency, to ensure that they would be a team that played together. He was the manager of the ball club, and he was determined that they would have a winning season.

But Critchley was nervous. Although he had been

through this sort of thing before, this was the big game—it was like playing in the World Series. For 162 days a year, a guy plays baseball: It's the same game, with the same white lines, the same umpire, and the same pitchers. But when it comes to the World Series, there are some players who just can't hit. In the room that night were people who were clearly capable of hitting home runs, but Critchley wanted to make sure that everyone was at least capable of getting a base hit.

His first goal was to engender a spirit of camaraderie. To this end, Critchley had made arrangements to reserve a private room above a popular Italian restaurant on Bloomfield Avenue, the heart of what once had been a thriving Italian-American enclave, but that had gradually given way to newer immigrant groups.

Critchley wanted a place that afforded some privacy, was convenient, and where some fifty lawyers and defendants could feel comfortable. There were simply too many people to meet in a normal conference room, and they needed the space that a restaurant or catering hall could provide.

Almost all the defendants and their attorneys, with the notable exception of Anthony Accetturo—the man who was alleged to be the leader of the Lucchese organization—showed up. Critchley threaded his way through the dining area toward the bar where the others were waiting.

That was when he spotted a familiar face.

Seated at one of the tables was Irwin Kimmelman, the attorney general for New Jersey. With him was another state official. Critchley and Kimmelman were not close, but they knew each other by sight.

Critchley nodded. "Hello, General," he said, recovering from his surprise at seeing the top legal officer for the state seated just yards away from a gathering of some of the most notorious crime figures in New Jersey. It was apparent from his greeting that Kimmelman did not know who the others were. But it was an awkward moment, and in fact, the situation was to become even more awkward as the evening progressed.

It was about an hour later, when the defendants and their lawyers were in the midst of their private meeting, that the owner of the restaurant approached Critchley, clearly concerned over how to handle the situation.

"Mike, Mike, I got to talk to you," she appealed, interrupting him.

"What's the matter?" he asked.

She hesitated, and then stammered out the problem. "The attorney general wants to come up," she declared. "He saw all the attorneys coming in," she said, "and he thinks it's a bar association meeting. I don't know what to tell him."

Critchley laughed. She apparently didn't want to tell the attorney general who really was meeting in her restaurant. He took the woman by the arm. "Just tell him," he suggested, "that it's a private meeting. Tell him it really wouldn't be appropriate for him to attend."

It was a masterpiece of an understatement.

The defense attorneys were getting on well. Some of the defendants barely knew their own lawyers, so the evening served as a get-acquainted time for them as well.

All of the lawyers and defendants involved in the case—even the one female attorney—were a group of practiced "ball-busters." If somebody did or said something foolish, he was going to have to eat it. The aim, however, was to keep it on that level, to avert any backbiting or criticism that could spark dissent down the road.

They stayed at the bar long enough for another round of drinks. Critchley wanted to make certain key attorneys were present before the official meeting was called to order. It was crucial in his mind that men like Harvey Weissbard and Tom Ashley be present, because he needed their input.

As the group reached its full complement, Critchley adjourned the gathering and led the crowd up the stairs to the reserved meeting room. Inside, banquet tables had been arranged in a large U-shape configuration, with Critchley seated at the head. The table was set as though for a feast.

As the lawyers and defendants were led to their seats, waitresses began bringing in family-style platters of pasta, veal, and wine, which were consumed with much relish.

As their appetites and thirsts were quenched, conversation quieted. Critchley pushed back his chair, dabbing his mouth with a napkin. Somebody clinked a glass for silence.

"This is our first meeting," Critchley declared. "I know it's unusual to do it this way"—he swept his hand over the plates of food—"but I could think of no other way."

"In many ways," he said, "this is like a legislative body. There are probably some states which don't have as many legislators as we have attorneys and defendants. . . ."

One by one, Critchley had the attorneys and lawyers stand and introduce themselves.

Critchley had already worked out a preliminary battle plan. He knew it was going to be a large case with a lot of defendants, and he knew that if he was to work with other lawyers, he wanted people he could count on—he knew whom he wanted on the case. In fact, he had personally recommended the lawyers to some of the clients, and the clients to the lawyers.

The defendants knew Critchley's reputation. He was not a guy who pleaded clients out. He fought for them. They knew his recommendations were solid. They knew these weren't just his friends he was suggesting. They were people who had specialized skills, people who could be counted on. He wanted the best he could get—even if some were relatively young and unknown.

He needed technicians, people who were knowledgeable on the law. He needed people who were experts on the rules of evidence. He needed people who were experts on the rules of federal procedure. And he needed another sort of lawyer, what he once termed "trial terrorists," attorneys who were prepared to go into battle in the courtroom, yet also work within the rules.

He needed people who were skillful trial attorneys, and he needed "crazies," the kind of lawyers who could be counted on to hold up their end of a fight.

When it came time for Critchley to begin assembling his defense team, he had reached out for a well-rounded group of lawyers to form the nucleus of his twenty-six-man team. He had known the case was coming, so he had had time to give the matter some consideration. He also knew that the defendants would be likely to accept his recommendations.

Accetturo, who had been living in Florida away from the day-to-day operations, was the sticking point. The lead defendant in the case, as the titular head of the Lucchese mob, Accetturo was not satisfied with the way the defense was being handled in New Jersey. He kept recommending a lawyer from

Philadelphia and telling Critchley and the others how they weren't doing it right and were "shooting each other in the foot."

Accetturo brought in Milton Ferrell, Jr., a prominent defense attorney from Florida. He also wanted to retain former U.S. attorney general Ramsey Clark to handle motions challenging the government wiretaps in the case.

"Why?" Critchley had asked Accetturo. "Tell us what areas we are deficient in. Don't just say we need to file more motions; we've filed motions. Tell me if somebody reviewed them and felt there was a point they could cover better."

Ferrell and Critchley did not mesh, and eventually, Ferrell was replaced by his father, Milton Ferrell, Sr. It was to be the last case the senior Ferrell would ever try—he was dying, but no one knew it.

Nor did Critchley get on well with Accetturo. But in a way that did not matter. Critchley was representing the man who was ultimately the key figure in the trial. Although Accetturo was alleged to be the leader of the organization, it was Taccetta who authorities claimed was the day-to-day manager. It was around Taccetta that everything else revolved.

And it was around his lawyer that the defense was going to revolve.

Critchley wanted to make certain that his rear and his flanks were covered. And as far as he was concerned, Michael Taccetta's brother, Marty, represented an area of potential vulnerability for his client. Authorities claimed that Marty was the *consigliere* of the organization—the man who represented Michael in overseeing the family's interests. So he wanted to make sure that Marty Taccetta had one of the best lawyers in the case.

Critchley recommended Marty to David Ruhnke. Ruhnke, a former federal public defender, had been quietly building a practice along with his wife, who is also an attorney.

Critchley regarded Ruhnke as one of the brightest lawyers in the state. Conservative, understated, but extremely persuasive in legal matters, Ruhnke has a unique professorial style. A vegetarian who would often use the luncheon recess as an opportunity to jog, he would serve as a perfect counterpoint to Critchley's rough-and-tumble, street-fighter courtroom style.

For Thomas Ricciardi, regarded by the government as one of the Taccetta organization's inner circle, he recommended Harvey Weissbard. "He is skillful, tactful, and in a group of attorneys with a great deal of ego, he is going to be a balancing factor," Critchley had said. "He is a levelheaded guy, respected by the courts, with a tremendous amount of experience."

Weissbard had been involved in challenging the federal government's landmark effort to take over control of New Jersey's mob-dominated Teamsters Local 560, one of the most powerful union locals in the nation. He knew RICO law, and as Critchley saw the team putting together its case, he came to regard Weissbard as giving the defense "legitimacy."

For Michael Perna, another alleged member of the Taccetta inner circle, he recommended Raymond M. Brown, the son of one of New Jersey's most highly regarded defense attorneys, Raymond A. Brown. The younger Brown had developed his own reputation as a skillful defense lawyer, but as it turned out, he became embroiled in another trial involving former U.S. secretary of labor Raymond Donovan, and his father stepped in to fill his shoes.

The elder Brown is something of a legend in legal circles. A tall, elegant black attorney who had been an outspoken proponent of civil rights, he had "knocked around" the South and had become involved in battling the Klu Klux Klan before returning to practice in New Jersey. He integrated the New Jersey National Guard and retired as a full colonel. He had made his reputation in the celebrated trial of "Dr. X," a New Jersey physician accused of the deaths of numerous patients. He won an acquittal in that case, and made his name as one of the most skillful courtroom advocates in the metropolitan area. He was also instrumental in winning a gaming license for Resorts International, the giant casino conglomerate that became the first firm to pioneer legalized gambling in Atlantic City.

Henry Asbill of Washington, D.C., was brought in as one of the only two out-of-state attorneys in the case, and he and his firm proved to be a major asset. Asbill represented Robert Spagnola, an ex-cop who was accused of running the sports-betting operations for the organization.

With Asbill, who was regarded as a key strategist, the defense also received the benefits of his partner, Samuel

Buffone, who Critchley said "represented the state of the art in regard to RICO law," even lecturing around the country on it.

There were others, Thomas Ashley and Robert Brown, both black attorneys, whose abilities and skin color gave Critchley a double dose of what he was after. Both were sharp and talented, and would also serve as a counterpoint to the impression that this was simply an Italian organized-crime case.

Robert Brown brought with him an added bonus. During the course of the trial, Brown was to become the first black mayor of Orange, the suburban Essex County community where Accetturo had been born. And the man who presided over the swearing-in ceremony was none other than the Honorable Harold A. Ackerman, U.S. district-court judge—the trial judge in the Accetturo case.

The jury was precluded from reading press accounts of the trial, but there was no prohibition from reading newspaper accounts and photos about Brown's election and swearing-in by the very judge who was trying his client.

To complete the picture, other defense attorneys around the table included: Peter Ryan, Miles Feinstein, John McDonald, Thomas Cammarata, John Vantuno, John Saykanic, John Sogliuzzo, Roy Greenman, Dennis Mautone, Robert Gigl, Ken Kayser, and, the only woman in the case, Maria Noto.

When the introductions were over, Critchley took center stage.

"Guys," he began, "I've been living with this case for a long time, since 1983. I think I know what they have, and I think I know what they don't have. I *know* what they don't have."

In his view, the heart of the case was gambling. He had monitored the investigation from its inception and knew that investigators had seized records purporting to link the defendants to gambling operations.

"We have to fight this with our motions, throw some body punches, soften them up, get as many hearings as we possibly can, and develop a trial strategy."

It was more like a pep rally than a legal discussion, and when it was over, Critchley asked everyone to sign a joint defense agreement, which would make whatever was said in their joint defense meetings privileged information.

"We are in this together," he told the gathering. "It's us against them. And the 'us' are in this room. We've got to stand tight, stand strong, and nobody, hopefully, will break rank."

"We definitely can win this case. Don't believe what you see in the paper.

"We may have some problems on the gambling counts, we may fall, but we can beat the big picture. They can never put a RICO together."

The words were prophetic.

8

At the turn of the nineteenth century, Newark was listed among the "Great Cities of the World," right up there with London, Paris, and Rome.

In 1890, it was home to a population of 182,000 residents, and was described as boasting a confluence of "broad and beautiful streets, many of them elm-shaded and lined with handsome buildings and private residences." Teeming with business, industry, and pride, it was the queen of New Jersey cities, and home to numerous notables from Stephen Crane and Washington Irving to the Ritz brothers and former New York mayor Edward I. Koch.

Today, despite boosterism, Newark suffers from the ravages of most old inner-city metropolises. Its population is largely minority, poor, and ill educated. Its schools are troubled; its municipal resources are overburdened; and its reputation is one of a hotbed for crime. It is a reputation that, at least in part, has been honestly—or dishonestly—earned.

The police force is undermanned, and workers who commute to the city by day flee to the suburbs by night. FBI agents have been mugged on the streets, their guns and identifications stolen. Assistant U.S. attorneys have been held up at gunpoint after leaving their offices. One prosecutor's car was stolen by joyriders who were involved in the shooting of two police officers and who then totaled the vehicle in a violent attempt to run a police roadblock.

Newark, in short, has seen better days.

However, in recent years the city has been attempting to make a comeback. New office complexes have been created; school campuses expanded; and plans have been announced for development of a waterfront area and a cultural center.

Unquestionably, Newark has a future, although it remains to be seen where that future will lead.

One industry that has remained constant, from the days of Dutch Schultz and the beer barons through the demise of Newark Mayor Hugh Addonizio and Richie the Boot Boiardo, has been organized crime. Sociologists would probably conclude that it was a natural outgrowth of the struggles of the largely Italian immigrant populations that swept into the city during the early part of the century.

And it was there, in the depths of the inner city, where the "boys from Jersey" were bred and where they forged the alliances that would decades later propel them into prominence as the bosses and underbosses of powerful criminal groups, capable of commanding at once both fear and loyalty among the local populace.

Alfonse Cataldo—known as "Tic" to his friends—was one of the original "boys," and Newark was his home. Michael and Martin Taccetta were his cousins and would later become fellow defendants. Tic operated a candy store in the old neighborhood, located near Fourteenth Avenue and Bruce Streets in the heart of the old Central Ward.

It was in that neighborhood that the race riots that eventually tore apart the city during the 1960s erupted. But at that time, it was a self-contained neighborhood of tenements of two- and three-family homes, where "aunts lived upstairs from aunts, cousins lived down the street, brothers and sisters married other brothers and sisters and moved down the hall from each other." It was not an area where money flowed freely, and although there was hot water in the apartments, it was not unknown for five families to have to share a single bathtub.

It was also a neighborhood where some lessons were learned early.

According to Cataldo, there was a game the boys played in that neighborhood called *"pasta fagioli,"* a reference to the bean-and-noodle soup that was a staple of some Italian peasant diets.

"And the type of game it was," Cataldo said, "the little guys, maybe the guys that were ten, eleven years old, if you wanted to go to the candy store on top of the hill, you had to run up the hill, and you had the guys that were maybe thirteen, fourteen, fifteen years old. They'd take their belts out. If you wanted to get into the candy store, you had to run past them, and they hit you with the belt. So you tried to get into that store as fast as you could."

During the Accetturo trial, Cataldo told that story to the jury.

"I'm still mad at Vic Cantillo for some shots he hit me with when I was a kid," he said, referring to one of his co-defendants in the case. "By the same token, I bet you Michael Taccetta is still mad at me with some of the shots that I hit him with when I became one of the older guys.

"But I think," he concluded, "that game was developed to roughen us up, to teach you to take your licks. . . . I have taken my licks."

The neighborhood was teeming, with bars, candy stores, social clubs, barbershops, and drugstores. It was a city within a city. Most of the residents were second-generation Italian, and the culture reflected the ethnic makeup. Some families came from the same towns in Italy. Others developed their bonds within the neighborhood.

When families fell on hard times, others would come to their aid. When one mother died leaving a family of small children, another's parents took them in, fed them, and clothed them.

It was also the type of area where gambling was a regular and accepted pastime. Friday night gambling was a ritual. One of the "boys" recalled being hoisted on his father's shoulders and brought to the local social club when he was five years old. He would stretch out on the sofa while the television blared the fight. His father would sit down to play cards, generally pinochle.

"I never once saw a round of the fights," he said. "I would fall right asleep. The next thing I would know, it would be Saturday morning, and I would wake up in my bed."

There might have been seven or eight of those clubs in a three-block area. On corners, older men would sit on the stoop, playing cards for a penny a point. No one looked on it as if it was wrong.

Many of the older men were professional club fighters who earned extra money sparring for money. Ironically, they had to obscure their own ethnic heritage, fighting under made-up Anglo-Saxon names.

In summers, people would sleep on fire escapes to stay cooler. But it wasn't all sweetness and nostalgia—it was a tough area. There were street gangs and fights, and if you weren't from the neighborhood, you risked a beating to venture onto forbidden turf.

And as the "boys" grew older, the criminal behavior became less benign.

According to the government, Michael Taccetta and Jackie DiNorscio, for a time, committed break-ins at stores and businesses on an almost daily basis. And they "registered" their activities with Anthony Accetturo, who by then had already become a major figure in the local crime hierarchy.

It was important to "register" with Accetturo, and to have his blessing. Those who didn't felt his wrath.

A government informant described how another of the "boys" from the neighborhood, who was a bookmaker with his own "club," wound up turning his club over to Accetturo after one particularly violent incident.

"Michael Perna and his father, Joe Perna, were out drinking. They went to a tavern, where eventually a fight erupted," the informant said. "Michael and his father were stabbed. I was in a club up at the next corner with Giacomo DiNorscio, shooting crap in the back room. I heard a commotion out in the front. I went out, and there was an individual named Buddy holding a knife in his hand full of blood. People were running around him. He left in a car, just took off. Joe Perna came running up the street. He looked like somebody had thrown a bucket of black paint over him. He was full of blood. He chased them up the street. Michael Perna was following, coming up the street toward us. Giacomo DiNorscio and I were standing on the corner. Michael came walking up slow and lifted up his sweater. He said: 'They got me, *Cugino*.' As soon as he said that, as soon as he lifted the sweater up, a spurt of blood shot out. His father looked in much worse shape than he did."

Michael was in worse shape than his father, who had only superficial cuts. But both survived. After that, Perna worked for Accetturo. And everybody lived happily ever after.

But the relationships between the people who grew up in the neighborhood endured. Many were cousins; others just friends. And they hung together despite the changes. For some, it would be unusual for more than a few days to pass without them talking. Daily meetings were the routine.

Change in the old neighborhood would come as the ethnic mix shifted, as the Italian-Americans moved out toward the outer wards, toward Vailsburg and North Newark, and as more and more blacks gravitated toward the inner city the Italians left behind.

9

While Michael Critchley was busy assembling his defense team and trying to figure out the best way of countering the government case, U.S. authorities were busily assembling their own team.

Tom Greelish had some hard decisions to make. The case had originally been developed by the U.S. Organized Crime Strike Force, a now-defunct Justice Department unit that had been established during the Kennedy years as an elite band of professional prosecutors who could operate free from local political interference. That was the concept.

In New Jersey, the reality was that the strike force was essentially an arm of the U.S. Attorney's Office, which operated more or less as an adjunct to that agency. The strike force was eventually abolished, with its attorneys absorbed into the U.S. Attorney's Office.

At the time of the Accetturo indictment, the strike force was in a state of flux. There had been some problem cases, and there had been some personnel changes.

The situation was exacerbated when Robert Stewart, the strike force chief for New Jersey and a veteran prosecutor who is uniformly praised for his dogged pursuit of a case and his meticulous attention to detail, was assigned to work on the Pizza Connection case in New York.

For Greelish, the options were few. He had met with Justice Department officials in Washington to discuss the situation. They had considered assigning a member of Greelish's own staff to take over the helm of the strike force in Stewart's absence, but then rejected the move as a bad personnel decision, as the move would undoubtedly be resented by the strike-force staff. Besides, there just were not that many people to go around. At the time Greelish took over the U.S. Attorney's Office, 70 to 80 percent of the senior people were doing drug cases.

The solution settled on by the Justice Department called for the assignment of a temporary replacement for Stewart, and Greelish adopted a policy that had proved successful in some past cases. He assigned a senior member of his own staff to work in tandem with strike-force lawyers on their major cases.

Greelish had long realized that a lot of the success of a prosecution involves personality, and where more than one prosecutor is working on a case, he recognized a need to have people who respect each other and who can get along on a personal level.

Volatile, opinionated, and stubborn, Grady O'Malley was a bulldog in the courtroom. But the same traits that made him a tenacious prosecutor created in him a less-than-easygoing personality. But this was his case, his baby, and Greelish had to find the right people to match up with him.

The first of these was Barbara Miller, who had already been assigned by the strike force as a junior assistant. A bookish young woman whose manner of dress—severely tailored suits and what used to be known as "sensible" shoes—made her appear ten years older than she really was, and who frequently kept her long hair tied back in granny knots, Miller looked in many ways more like a prototypical librarian than a prosecutor. In sharp contrast to her looks, it shocked some to find she maintained what one acquaintance termed a "wicked" sense of humor.

During the trial, she became the object of some of the cruder comments muttered by some defendants. Even in the courtroom, there was an undercurrent of kissing noises, which have become the national "love call" of certain ethnic groups. Miller, however, never lost her composure.

With some defendants, she was less than popular because she was the member of the prosecution team primarily assigned to making certain that medical complaints that kept them out of court were real and not feigned. They often accused her of insensitivity. Others noted that her behavior denoted justifiable cynicism.

In any case, Miller, like O'Malley, projected a sense of mission. This was serious business—and she was as serious as they came. During one of the first trial sessions, attorney Dennis Mautone had been brought in to meet his client, Manuel Montiero, who had already been convicted of serving as a drug courier and was charged in the Accetturo case with serving the same role.

Mautone was approached by Miller, who inquired, "Who are you?"

Mautone, a gregarious sort with a quick smile, responded in a sprightly manner, "I'm Dennis Mautone."

He turned to his client, whom he had just met, and clapped his arm around the client's shoulder. "I represent Manuel Montiero," he beamed, "a fine fellow in his own right."

Miller only scowled in response. "That's your opinion," she snapped, and quickly turned away.

Mautone soon realized that there was no love match in the offing.

A former federal prosecutor, who was representing a client in another mob-related prosecution, recalled a similar encounter with Miller in the Federal Building cafeteria. As he related it, Miller was nothing if not blunt: "How can you defend that scum?" she asked.

For most defense attorneys, it was easy. It was a job, and it paid the rent.

Like Dennis Marchalonis, the FBI agent who put together the basic case, Miller had been raised in rural Pennsylvania. She had been an anthropology graduate from Bryn Mawr college and, following her graduation from Georgetown University Law School, had served as a law clerk with the U.S. Labor

Department and later with the Justice Department before joining the Justice Department's Organized Crime Section. She had transferred to New Jersey in 1984.

For the final member of the prosecution team, Greelish was determined to find someone from his own staff. The man he finally chose was thirty-one-year-old Joseph Braunreuther. He was probably the best choice Greelish could have made.

Bright and capable, Braunreuther had the dark good looks of his Irish-German heritage that gave him a sort of rakish charm—something that Grady O'Malley sorely lacked. People liked "Joe B."—and they respected him.

And although intellectually adroit—he had been editor of the Law Review at St. John's Law School—he was far from a bookworm. A solidly built six footer, with a dark mustache and thick black hair, Braunreuther was a match for O'Malley as an athlete. A former captain of the New York Rugby Club, who enjoyed the continuous action of that demanding sport, Braunreuther also had developed into an expert skier.

Born in a lower-middle-class neighborhood in Queens, New York, not far from the location where mob boss John Gotti would later make his headquarters, he was the son of a sanitation worker who eventually became a court clerk, and then worked his way through law school to become an attorney. His father had encouraged him to do the same.

Braunreuther took a circuitous route to accomplish his goal.

One of four children, he was never in want of food or shelter, but his family could not provide the money he needed for school. So he joined the merchant marine, enrolling in the U.S. Merchant Marine Academy at Kings Point, Long Island. It was a good school, and the education was free. But there was a catch. Once he graduated, he was obligated to several years of service.

From the streets of Queens, Braunreuther found himself on a series of round-the-world adventures: shepherding supertankers around South Africa to Kuwait and Iran and wrestling giant container ships to Singapore and Hong Kong. He weathered the experience, from storms at sea where he watched giant, truck-sized containers swept into the ocean by the fury of the storms, to picking his way through a barroom brawl with a brawny Norwegian in a Malaysian nightclub.

On one occasion, he had learned the folly of playing peacemaker. After trying to intervene in a budding fight, he had jokingly told one foreign seaman, "You're a real pisser."

It was supposed to have been a comradely salute, but the seaman took it as an insult. "You call me a pisser . . ." he shouted in his accented voice. He stopped talking and started swinging. Braunreuther was fortunate to make it back to the ship intact.

The experience that Braunreuther gained at sea gave him an air of confidence that served him well in the trial. Whatever the "boys from Jersey" had to throw at him, the boy from New York City was well equipped to handle it.

In late October 1986, Thomas W. Greelish had made a decision: The U.S. attorney for New Jersey wanted out.

The lanky prosecutor walked into a small anteroom on the second floor of the Federal Office Building in Newark. The room was filled with rows of chairs. Greelish threaded his way through a crowd of reporters and cameramen and took his position at a podium at the end of the narrow room.

It had all the trappings of a full-blown press conference, similar in many ways to a scaled-down version of the one he had convened when he announced the return of the Accetturo indictment just one year before.

For Greelish, however, that was all behind him. There would be no more indictments. He had reached a decision. After ten years of public service, Greelish was relinquishing the spotlight and returning to private practice.

"I'm very proud to have been United States attorney," he declared somberly, and then added, "I look forward to the future. . . ."

The announcement came just days before the scheduled start of jury selection in the Accetturo-Taccetta trial. It was a coincidence that, to this day, Greelish feels may have played a role in the outcome of the trial.

Greelish's initial months in office had been turbulent. His son, who was later to succumb to a lifelong battle with muscular dystrophy, had been in critical condition and hospitalized in Pennsylvania. As a result, Greelish spent most of the first months of his term virtually phoning in his duties. The hospital had given him a desk and a telephone line in the intensive-care unit, and between caring for his son, he attempted to juggle the responsibilities of his office, spending the bulk of the day on the telephone conferring with his subordinates.

After his initial head-to-head with O'Malley regarding the Accetturo indictment, Greelish had put the case on a back burner as far as his own priorities went. There were other cases that were more pressing, and eventually, there was his own decision to leave office to be dealt with.

Greelish had hoped to be able to stay on until a replacement was sworn in—but that was not to be.

Bureaucratic delays in Washington held up the appointment of a new U.S. attorney, and after repeated warnings to the Justice Department, Greelish made good his promise and left the office.

Meanwhile, the chief of the strike force, Robert Stewart, was immersed in his own concerns over the development of the Pizza Connection case in New York.

For a critical period, the ship was essentially without a captain.

10

In the late summer of 1985, Harold A. Ackerman, a U.S. district judge assigned to the federal court in Newark, New Jersey, was luxuriating on a lounge chair on the poolside patio of a resort in Positano, Italy.

The resort, located southwest of Naples, was built on a plateau on the side of a sheer cliff that plummeted down into the clear waters of the Mediterranean. It had been voted among the world's great vacation retreats by no less a standard-setter than *Lifestyles of the Rich and Famous.*

That morning, basking in the warm glow of the sun, Ackerman stirred from his reverie to note to a traveling companion that the natural beauty of the setting had been augmented by the arrival of two young Frenchwomen, who had sauntered onto the patio, clad only in their bikinis and tans.

A discrete and worldly man, not wanting to appear to be overly awed by the imported Gallic scenery, Ackerman picked up a copy of the *International Herald Tribune* and made as though to concentrate on the news of the world.

Within moments, however, the vistas that had attracted him seemed to disappear. His concentration on the paper was no longer feigned. He was focusing on an article that reported some two dozen members of a crime family in New Jersey had been arrested as the result of an indictment that had been returned in Newark, New Jersey.

As he read the article, which gave a brief sketch of what had occurred, Ackerman experienced a moment of queasiness and a fleeting sensation that, somehow, the tranquillity and peace of his European sojurn were to dissipate—and soon.

Just ten days later, when he arrived home, he telephoned his secretary. In addition to the usual pleasantries, she had news.

"You know," she told the judge, almost as an afterthought, "you have a big case."

In New Jersey federal courts, cases are assigned by a random "wheel," which spins off each new case to the next judge in line. This time, Ackerman's number had come up. In fact, his secretary didn't even have to tell him what case she was speaking of. Somehow, he knew.

Harold A. Ackerman is a man who loves life. He can be loud, he can be funny, and he can be irritating.

He is a man who appears larger than he really is, who has been fighting a long battle with his waistline, and who is almost constantly on a diet. He is a brilliant man with an effusive personality, who frequently masks his intellectual abilities behind a facade of self-deprecating humor. In a world where judges are frequently held in an exalted position only to find their egos inflating like weather balloons, Ackerman treads the earth with the mortals. A born raconteur, he genuinely enjoys people, and is ready at the drop of a gavel to chatter away with anyone within earshot about the latest developments in world politics, motion pictures, and culinary discoveries. An avid reader and enthusiastic traveler, he is a man of insatiable curiosity. He frequently pops into the pressroom at the federal courthouse in Newark on his way to and from court to exchange pleasantries and gossip with reporters on the latest developments in the world. He can be compassionate and warm, but he can be a harsh judge of those who have violated the strictures of society, as many who have stood before him for sentencing might attest.

Harold Ackerman was born and bred in New Jersey. He

grew up in Irvington, a community that is part of the vast urban sprawl that spread westward from Newark, in a lower-middle-class neighborhood not unlike those that spawned Taccetta and the rest of the "boys."

He was the son of a furniture salesman. Although close to his mother, he was never close with his father and remained estranged from him most of his life. He was forced to go to work at age fourteen at which time he worked thirty-three hours for three dollars—a munificent salary of eleven cents an hour.

He enlisted in the army as soon as possible after he turned eighteen. He took to the army, was promoted quickly, and was eventually assigned to a security post with the super-secret Manhattan Project.

When his enlistment was over, he went to school, aided by the G.I. Bill. Initially, he had wanted to be a journalist, but thought better of it and changed to the law. He passed the New Jersey bar in 1951.

As an attorney, he became increasingly drawn to the struggles of the labor movement and became a lobbyist for the CIO in Trenton. He practiced labor law for a time, but soon found that it was not to his liking. Although he enjoyed people and loved the law, he found he hated clients—not a good trait for someone whose livelihood depends upon their good graces.

In 1955, he started working for the state of New Jersey under Governor Robert Meyner and was instrumental in helping the new administration to clean out what *Time* magazine described as a "scandal ridden Department of Labor."

Within a very short period of time, Ackerman was named a judge in the Workman's Compensation Court, and then, later, made a supervising judge. Ackerman was gathering what, for a man then in his late twenties, was an unparalleled variety of experience that would serve him well in his later appointments.

On June 10, 1965, he took his oath of office for the Union County District Court and became the presiding judge of that court, which was essentially a small-claims court. Four years later, he was nominated to the Union County court, where he obtained his first taste of criminal cases, but where he became stalled due to political pressure from a local state senator, who was attempting to use the appointment as a lever for his own ambitions. In 1970, Governor William T. Cahill pushed through the appointment, and in 1973, he was advanced to superior-court judge for Union County, one of the most populous counties in the state.

In late 1978, he was one of sixty-one persons within New Jersey who were being screened by a special committee set up by President Jimmy Carter as potential appointees to the federal judiciary. He was one of thirteen recommended, and one of the four ultimately selected, taking his oath of office as a U.S. district-court judge in early January of 1980.

In many ways, Harold Ackerman may have been the perfect choice to sit as judge in the Lucchese mob trial; in other ways, he may have been the worst. He was a human being, and humanity was the last thing the prosecution needed to win its case.

Critics have since suggested that Ackerman should have seen the trouble coming, that he should have recognized the case as virtually unmanageable, and split the charges into several smaller trials. But the federal government was adamant in wanting the case tried intact, and he gave the government what it wanted.

Later, Ackerman would remember that the first emotion he felt as he assumed the bench for the beginning of the trial was a basic and honest one—fear. It was a unique case. He had read the articles in the press indicating that a record number of potential jurors had been summoned to the courthouse for the start of the selection for the jury panel.

The government was predicting that the trial would last six months. Ackerman had a sense that that might not be as accurate a prediction as the prosecution team might have hoped. It was a massive indictment, involving massive charges. And as he sat at the bench for the first time in that case, looking out over the sea of faces before him—lawyers, defendants, a standing-room-only crowd of spectators—there was a sense that this case was going to be different from all the others he had ever tried.

Normally, most judges feel a sense of excitement and pleasure at the start of a significant case. It is what they have prepared all their professional lives to do, preside over a case of major and lasting importance. But Ackerman did not take pleasure in assuming the bench that first day. He realized, as he looked at those faces, that this was going to be a very awesome challenge—and an ordeal—perhaps the greatest he, or any judge, would ever face.

Indeed, Harold Ackerman's role in the trial was destined to be more than just that of a judge. He would learn to become a ringmaster, presiding over a three-ring circus complete with its own clowns.

There would be days when the sheer scope of the case would tax both his stamina and his intellect.

The image would be forever engraved in his memory of twenty lawyers, leaping to their feet in seeming unison, shouting repeated "objections" to the prosecution, and then falling into a virtual firing line of legal sharpshooters, each taking their turn and peppering the court with their most inventive arguments. And for every objection registered by the defense, the prosecution would have to respond. The sheer weight of numbers could wear down the prosecutors and, at the same time, exhaust the judge.

It was all part of the grand defense strategy developed by Critchley: Keep punching, hit the prosecution every chance they had, like a prizefighter firing body blow after body blow to try to weaken the opponent and knock him off balance.

And in addition to the oral arguments—the spontaneous debates that could erupt at a moment's notice—there was the avalanche of paperwork being ground out by the munchkins ensconced in the back rooms of the law offices.

Defense attorneys later acknowledged that part of their strategy was to distract the prosecution, to keep the prosecutors busy. Every paper filed by the defense had to be met by a written response from the prosecution. And every issue had to be reviewed and decided by the judge.

They called out Ackerman's name; they waved their hands, they refused to take "no" for an answer. It was a hydra-headed monster of legal demons. When he would lop off one head with a definitive ruling, three more would pop out of their seats, baring their legal fangs, ready to strike at any vulnerable area of either the court or the prosecution.

Ackerman struggled valiantly, at times like a man on the verge of drowning. He had to listen to the legal arguments and evaluate them on the spot: a major misstep could scuttle the trial or create grounds for reversal by an appeals court. He had to filter out the substance from the meaningless babble. He had to strain to maintain order against a tide of disruptions. And, amid it all, he would have to deal with Jackie DiNorscio—the man who threatened to turn the proceedings into a virtual one-man side show.

And so on that first day, as Ackerman looked into the faces of the attorneys, the defendants, and the prosecution, he was dead-on right in his abiding sense that this would be a fight to the finish.

PART THREE

THE TRIAL

11

Jury selection seemed to go on forever.

They came by the hundreds, day after day, ordinary people who had the good, or bad (depending on how they looked at it) fortune to be summoned for jury duty.

One thousand notices had been sent out, and this number eventually climbed to more than fifteen hundred before the final panel was seated. It was the largest single jury call ever conducted in New Jersey. The candidates had been culled from a computerized master file, compiled largely from voter-registration and driver's-license lists. They came from eight counties all over North and Central Jersey; Morris, Sussex, Union, Bergen, Essex, Hudson, Passaic, and Middlesex.

Judge Harold Ackerman was determined that the jury he picked would be able to sustain what even then was projected to be a trial of record-setting length. He told the jurors it could last at least six months. He could just as easily have said it would last at least a week—either would have been accurate. No one knew exactly how long it would really be.

The courthouse in Newark, which is located on the upper floors of the central post office building, was in turmoil. It appeared in a virtual "state of siege."

Shotgun-toting marshals surrounded the building and blue lights from patrol cars flashed in the streets, while inside the building, more marshals and security guards manned metal detectors and X-ray machines as the jurors, defendants, and visitors filed toward their eventual rendezvous in the courtroom.

It was November 19, 1986, and the air was cool and clear. The cold of winter had not yet swept in, and a sense of autumn lingered in the air. Michael Taccetta, wearing a canvas windbreaker, walked into the entrance past a phalanx of photographers and television cameramen. Michael Critchley, businesslike in a black overcoat, walked at his side.

"This is a farce," Taccetta grumbled, and then added, "but I guess it's the only show in town."

The line to enter the courtroom was long as everyone entering waited to pass through the metal detector, designed to screen against possible weapons. Keys, pocket calculators, and coins, however, were enough to set it off, and each time, visitors had to empty their pockets before they would be allowed to pass through.

In the corridor, it was reminiscent of the wedding scene from *The Godfather*—only without the band and the food.

The band never did play, but in the months that followed, the food did arrive. Luncheon recesses were marked by a banquet of Italian-style hot dogs, laden with fried potatoes, onions, peppers, and a heart-stopping quotient of grease. The marble benches were covered with bakery boxes containing pastries. A local specialty store offering every variety of nuts did an unprecedented business, as defendants brought in bag after bag of fresh-roasted peanuts, cashews, and Brazil nuts.

Anthony Accetturo, who prided himself on his own cooking, brought in his own sandwiches. He gained forty pounds during the trial. Taccetta, known to law-enforcement officials as "the Fat Kid," tried to diet. His wife, a petite and pretty brunette, would bring him bags of fresh vegetables. It didn't help—somehow he absorbed calories anyway.

The seats in the front of the courtroom were reserved for the defendants and their lawyers. The furniture had been rearranged to accommodate them all, and seats had been assigned by lottery, with Ackerman picking the names out of a brown paper bag. The idea was not to give any of the defendants undue prominence by virtue of his position in the courtroom. Ironically, however, the man charged as the boss, Anthony Accetturo, drew one of the first seats. He was right where he belonged. Taccetta drew a seat in the approximate center of the room. His brother, Martin, pulled a number just one seat away.

It was afternoon, before all the preparations were complete, that the first group of potential jurors was called into the room. The room became quiet as the judge, in his flowing black robes, took the bench.

"My name is Judge Ackerman," he said softly and distinctly into the microphone, "and we're about to pick a jury in a criminal matter. . . ."

It was a process that was to last four months.

By March 16, Ackerman thought he finally had a jury. He was wrong. When he assembled the panel, he realized he had problems. One of the jurors didn't show up, another announced she was pregnant, and another's boss took the enlightened position that he thought the only people who should serve on juries should be welfare recipients and retirees.

"Murphy's Law must be operating today," Ackerman muttered. He had just received a call from a minister on behalf of one of the jurors. She had complained of being sick and had been sent home for rest. When the juror arrived home, however, she found her house had burned down—and her dog was dead.

"Yeah," one of the defendants quipped bitterly in the corridor. "They found it in the back of a late-model Cadillac with a bullet hole behind its ear. . . . The FBI thinks it was a hit."

Even through the jury selection, Critchley still had some hope of working something out. The potential penalties under a RICO conviction are staggering. For most people, it would mean virtual life sentences if the judge imposed the maximum—and Ackerman was not a lenient judge. Several years before, a former mayor of Atlantic City had pleaded guilty in connection with a mob-linked corruption scandal. He was shocked when Ackerman sentenced him to fifteen years in prison. The defendants knew that if they took a plea, without some guarantees, they would get as much as Ackerman could give them. And for most of them, that was too much.

It was around six o'clock in the evening on the last day of the marathon jury selection process. Critchley and Assistant U.S. Attorney Joseph Braunreuther walked out of the courtroom and down the marble corridor of the courthouse to Judge Ackerman's chambers. The buzzer controlling the electronic lock sounded, and they opened the door and walked in.

Ackerman's chambers were the poshest in the courthouse. Rich, deep-set wood paneling, ceiling-high bookcases, a sitting area, and a separate study alcove gave the inner room the spacious grandeur of the library of a private club.

Ackerman sat at his polished barrister desk, a massive and ornate piece of furniture that is suited perfectly to the classic decor of the room.

After some friendly chatter, Ackerman sat back in his high-back leather chair and rocked comfortably as the two attorneys faced each other. They were there to discuss the possibility of a plea.

According to Critchley, the government had taken a hard-line position on negotiation. As far as they were concerned, he said, there were no negotiations. There was nothing even to negotiate. They had the case locked up solid. And it was either plead to the whole package, or else go to trial.

Critchley had his own theory about the case. The government had sold it to the press as the biggest organized-crime prosecution in New Jersey history, but Critchley viewed it far differently. To him it was nothing more than big, sexy, sophisticated, and overblown. At heart, he viewed it as essentially a gambling case.

Critchley still had hope at this point—guilt or innocence was irrelevant. The goal was to cut losses so that a defendant could one day hope to see daylight, rather than a lifetime of endless shadows from inside a prison cell.

"This case, Joe, is not what you think it is," Critchley told the prosecutor. The government attorney, however, was not convinced.

"You're looking to put my guy inside for a decade and a half," Critchley told Braunreuther, calculating how much time would actually have to be served on a twenty- or twenty-five-year jail term. "And he don't have that many decades and a half left to go." Taccetta was already in his forties.

The arguments went back and forth. Tempers began to grow heated.

"Joe," he said, "I think you think I'm bullshitting. We are going. I'm going to pound the shit out of you. And if you beat me, it's not going to be because I gave it to you. It'll be because you took it."

Critchley looked at his opponent. "Let me tell you something, Joe. There's no fucking way," he shouted, "that I'm pleading my guy to twenty-five years.

"You think you got a good fuckin' case? Well, I think I got a good fuckin' defense. Now let's go get it on. . . ."

12

Opening day of the trial in March 1987 was like opening day at a Broadway show, complete with crowds, cameras, and limousines.

The defendants, dressed in their Sunday best, three-piece suits and sports jackets, smiled with capped teeth and coiffed hair at television news crews as they filed into the courthouse.

It was the first time they had dressed up, and it was to be the last. Within days, the de rigueur dress was polyester and pullovers. One defendant was eventually reprimanded when he attended court in a T-shirt and Bermuda shorts.

Michael Taccetta, dressed in a gray jacket and black slacks, walked up the ramp leading to the front of the courthouse. He was accompanied by his attorney, who flashed a quick smile at the cameras. Taccetta, a chain-smoker despite a severe case of asthma, took one last greedy drag at a cigarette before tossing it aside into the shrubbery as he entered the building.

For the prosecutor, V. Grady O'Malley, walking into the courthouse was like running a gauntlet. As the defendants clustered in groups in the corridor, there were muffled invectives, "Ah, fucking O'Malley . . . scumbag."

There was also a muted chorus of greeting, "Yo, Vinnie . . ."

The pressure was on.

O'Malley recognized the significance of the trial. From his perspective, it was the biggest case anybody in that courtroom would ever try. And he didn't believe in losing. "You win a case, you're a hero," he said. "If you lose it, you're a bum."

He had turned down the plea-bargain offers from the defense. They had wanted too much. "I'd rather lose the case," he said, "than just give the case away."

Stern-faced and intense, O'Malley stood and faced the jury. He was dressed in a light brown suit. He scowled and put his hand in his pocket as he began.

In a stark, no-nonsense address, reminiscent of Robert Stack's portrayal of Eliot Ness in *The Untouchables,* O'Malley grimly described the inner workings of a "tightly knit organization" whose members "breathed a life of crime" and reaped vast sums of illicit profits while adhering to a strict code of "respect, loyalty, and silence."

"We own New Jersey. We can make any move we want there."

These were the boasts that Grady O'Malley attributed to members of what he portrayed as the secret underworld "fraternity" that comprised the New Jersey faction of the Lucchese organized-crime family.

In a stark, staccato, almost angry delivery, O'Malley catalogued the litany of crimes attributed to the defendants, portraying their organization as controlling activities ranging from gambling to loan-sharking and credit-card fraud.

"Ladies and gentlemen," O'Malley said as he addressed the jurors, his hair close-cropped above a ruddy Irish-American face, "the term 'conspiracy' in Latin means to breathe together. And for nine years, these defendants breathed the life of crime. . . ."

He swept his hand about the courtroom to take in the massed assemblage of twenty defendants, who together with their lawyers filled the well of the courtroom. They were crowded together at long, benchlike conference tables set up in a series of concentric semicircles radiating out from the massive raised oak bench, behind which the judge sat ensconced in his ceremonial splendor, flanked by marble pillars and velvet curtains.

"These defendants commit criminal acts as a means of putting money in their pockets, putting food on the table, and obtaining the other luxuries of life."

The prosecutor told the jurors that the crime organization had a headquarters, a luncheonette in a section of Newark, New Jersey, known as Down Neck. The name of that luncheonette, he said, was the Hole in the Wall.

Later in his summation, he claimed that the luncheonette derived its name from *Butch Cassidy and the Sundance Kid* and the infamous "Hole in the Wall Gang."

On that point, he was wrong. The name, some of the "boys" freely acknowledged, was merely a nostalgic reference to a famous restaurant that had once stood in the heart of the neighborhood where many of the defendants were raised. It was the sort of mistake the son of an old-line Irish family from Boston, who grew up far away from the poverty of an Italian Newark ghetto, was expected to make. But it was symptomatic of a far greater gap of understanding. The defendants never really understood the prosecutors, or what they were doing or why they were doing it to them. And as became apparent in the months that followed, the government team never really understood the defendants, and why they did what they did.

"And I call it a luncheonette, ladies and gentlemen," O'Malley told the jurors, "but I submit to you it was a clubhouse for these defendants. They fixed it up a little bit," he said. "They put pictures on the walls of their legendary heroes, Rocky Marciano, Babe Ruth," and in the same breath he added, "Al Capone, Meyer Lansky, Lucky Luciano."

During the trial, these photos were to be introduced as evidence along with others seized from the walls of the alleged mob "clubhouse." One of those photos, ironically, was an old picture of Edward G. Robinson, whose famous portrayal of a gangster in the film *Little Caesar* provided defense attorney Michael Critchley the opportunity to emote before the jury, clutching his chest and dropping to the floor as he cried out the memorable final line of the movie: "Mother of Mercy, can this be the end of Rico?"

The jury and audience laughed at the performance. The government did not. In the aftermath of the trial, while the FBI, the Justice Department, and other law-enforcement agencies attempted to regroup their forces, the line seemed applicable to the very law under which the case was prosecuted: RICO. And the words seemed eerily prophetic.

As O'Malley continued his opening narrative, he told the jurors of mob "sit-downs" to settle differences with rival crime groups.

"This enterprise," O'Malley stressed, "is not a hobby, not a recreation or a sidelight to these defendants, but, in fact, is their livelihood."

"You don't find this organization or enterprise in the Yellow Pages," he said flatly. "It doesn't advertise. You can't apply for a job there. And you only leave this organization by growing old or going bad."

O'Malley said the defendants embellished their life-styles with the aid of counterfeit credit cards, which they used to obtain hundreds of thousands of dollars in everything from clothes to theater tickets to big-screen television sets, and charged that they "pawn" the cost off on the financial institutions that must make good on the charges.

And when it came to dealing with legitimate businesses, O'Malley said, the goal of the organization was to move in on them, "insinuate" themselves into the operation, get their "foot in the door."

The prosecutor quoted one alleged member of the organization's inner circle, Michael Perna, a reputed mob soldier, as explaining the organization's philosophy in a conversation with his boss, Michael Taccetta, that was secretly recorded by an FBI "bug" hidden at the Hole in the Wall.

"He says," O'Malley related, "'Mike, we don't push our way into joints to tell people what to do. We want them to know us'"—he paused for dramatic effect—"'and to want us.'"

O'Malley described the leader of the organization as Anthony Accetturo. The white-haired mob figure, who authorities believed was next in line to assume control of the national crime family, had fled New Jersey in the early 1970s to avoid a subpoena to testify before the New Jersey State Commission of Investigation, and had lived in self-imposed exile in a modest home in Hollywood, Florida.

But, authorities have long maintained, Accetturo continued to wield control over mob operations in New Jersey, acting as a sort of absentee landlord—overseeing business, but at a distance.

"He's not a flashy guy," O'Malley told the jury, pointing to Accetturo, who sat at the front of the courtroom in a simple sport shirt, baggy pants, and a blue sweater. "But when important decisions need to be made, he makes the decisions. Maybe it's settling a confrontation between his own people or with others. Or maybe it's protecting his territory against invasion by other organized-crime people. But in the final analysis, he has the last word, and as a result of that elevated position, he gets a piece of the action, some of the proceeds."

Michael Taccetta, the thirty-nine-year-old former Boys Town resident whose wife once won the New Jersey State Lottery and described her husband as an "oil company consultant," was identified by O'Malley as Accetturo's number-one man in New Jersey, the person who allegedly supervised the day-to-day activities of the organization.

"He [Accetturo] has delegated his representative here in New Jersey to run this organization as Michael Taccetta," O'Malley said, turning to point at the heavyset man seated in the approximate center of the courtroom.

"Mr. Taccetta," O'Malley continued, "is the chosen one. He's the corporate executive who makes the decisions that impact the daily routine of the members of this organization. And for taking on this job, he gets a piece of the action."

O'Malley described an incident in which a reputed underworld figure "messed up and cost the organization some money" and was subsequently called on the carpet by Taccetta.

O'Malley quoted the man as telling Michael, "I'd never do anything to hurt you or your money," and concluded their conversation by declaring his fealty: "Michael, I'd love to shine in your eyes."

"Who is this man, Michael Taccetta?" O'Malley asked, raising his hands in a stage gesture. "Grown men grovel, adult men vie for his attention, close associates are at his beck and call. He will be shown," O'Malley said, "to be the boss of the organization here in New Jersey for Anthony Accetturo."

It was a strong, forceful opening. And it appeared to fulfill the promise former U.S. attorney Thomas Greelish had made at his press conference. It was a major prosecution. And the government was poised to deliver the goods.

Joseph Braunreuther was impressed. The speech has been factual and businesslike. And O'Malley projected a strong presence in the courtroom. But when Michael Critchley rose to his feet, it became evident that the prosecutor had engaged a worthy opponent.

Physically, they couldn't have been more different. O'Malley, towering and powerfully built. Critchley, average height, balding, and with the physique of a wiry Irish bartender.

But Critchley had, in his heart at least, kissed the Blarney Stone. It was something that O'Malley apparently had failed to do.

The defense lawyer, dressed stylishly but conservatively in a gray suit, began by pointing to a Latin motto inscribed on the front of the wooden platform behind which U.S. district judge Harold A. Ackerman sat overseeing the proceedings.

"Now I don't know if the good brothers who taught me Latin would be happy with my pronunciation," Critchley began, "but hopefully they would be a little happy with the understanding that although my pronunciation has not improved over the years, my ability to read Latin and to understand the sacred creed has not diminished with time.

"Right in front of you, ladies and gentlemen," he said, walking over to the front of the bench and underscoring each of the words with his index finger, "it reads: Let justice be done though the heavens should fall."

The defense attorney next outlined his position. The charges, Critchley maintained, were nothing more than a hodgepodge of "absurdities," prejudice, and perjury, pieced together from paid government informants to create a "*Godfather*like" atmosphere in the courtroom.

With a dramatic flourish, he sketched the theme that was to run through the case. He attacked the government witnesses as paid liars, and he accused prosecutors of making a "compact with evil" in a desperate attempt to bolster their case.

"They have given everything away but the courthouse for one objective: not justice, but victory," he charged.

He pointed accusingly at the prosecutors. "Careers are going to be made or neutralized based on the outcome of this case. People are going to get promoted or demoted. . . ."

He contrasted the lives of the career criminals the government was preparing to call as witnesses with the men on trial.

"You'll come to hear my client is married, to Carol Taccetta." He paused and looked across the room. "Somewhere in this courtroom, I don't have my glasses." He turned back to the jury. "Seventeen years, four children. That's life-style. Goes to Holy Family Church, Florham Park. His wife teaches CCD. That's life-style." He swept his hand over the prosecution table. "They would have you apply something sinister to that. Every time there are newspaper articles about him, his kids suffer. Rumor, innuendo, and speculation. They want to convict my client on speculation. On prejudice. On guesswork . . ."

Many of the defendants, he said, were related. They were part of a "family," but not the kind the government meant.

"The family," he said, "is Martin Taccetta and Michael Taccetta. They didn't get together to join a criminal conspiracy. They got together because Mr. and Mrs. Taccetta got together. And it's called biology."

There were amused smiles on the faces of several jurors.

There were others: Michael Perna, a cousin; brothers, Daniel and Thomas Ricciardi; neighborhood friends who played together in Little League, like Robert Spagnola.

"It's called biology," Critchley said softly. "It's called love. It's called family. . . ."

He pointed again at the prosecutors.

"They would twist it, they would make it evil. . . ."

He concluded by walking back beside the motto inscribed on the front of the judicial bench.

"All we're asking, ladies and gentlemen," he told the jurors quietly, "is that justice be done though the heavens should fall."

There was silence in the courtroom as Michael Critchley walked back to his seat.

And when the trial was over, for the prosecution—which spent years of work and millions of dollars putting the case together for presentation to the jury—his words were to come back to haunt them. Their worst fears were borne out. The sky did open. And the heavens did fall.

And as the trial progressed, the rains, which began when Critchley outlined the defense, turned into a monsoon when DiNorscio took center stage.

Giacomo DiNorscio stood up to make his opening statement.

Waddling to his feet, DiNorscio pushed aside the chairs that were in his way and approached the podium set up in the center of the courtroom. On his way, he turned to the defendants and their lawyers. "Anybody got a hat?" he asked in a stage whisper as Judge Ackerman announced solemnly, "Ladies and gentlemen, Mr. Giacomo DiNorscio is representing himself, and he will present his opening statement to you."

"Your Honor," DiNorscio muttered, pointing to one of the defense lawyers, "I need this hat." Without waiting for a response, DiNorscio reached out as the hat was handed forward. "I need this hat for one minute. Now this is just serious, just for a minute."

DiNorscio turned to the jury. He was a little unsteady on his feet. He appeared a little nervous, confused. "Took four-and-a-half months to get this jury, took a lot of patience of everybody in this courtroom. I want you to know I'm satisfied with everybody on this jury."

He reached up and clamped the hat down on top of his head, and pointed up at it. "The reason I'm wearing this hat is to make me look like a gangster." He pointed down at the prosecution table, where O'Malley sat beside the rest of the prosecution team, Assistant U.S. Attorney Joseph Braunreuther, U.S. Justice Department prosecutor Barbara Miller, and FBI agent Dennis Marchalonis. "That's what they want, this table wants me to be."

There was a murmur in the courtroom. No one seemed quite certain what was happening. Some of the jurors seemed to realize that DiNorscio was making a joke. They laughed. DiNorscio paused, then pointed to his head and whipped the hat off again. "It's not even my hat."

He shambled to the podium as he passed the hat back to its owner, attorney Robert Brown.

"Thank you, Mr. Brown," DiNorscio said.

Composing himself, the defendant again turned to the jury. "My name is Jack DiNorscio, and I'm representing myself in this matter."

"After hearing all the attorneys and the lawyers for the past couple of days," DiNorscio said, "I'm what you call a relief." He paused to catch his breath. "I want to thank Mr. Critchley for telling me what the sign means under the judge's desk. I thought it meant 'No Smoking.'"

At that point, the tension, which had been building in the courtroom, broke loose. The jury, the spectators, the attorneys, and the defendants, erupted in laughter.

DiNorscio didn't miss a beat. "To get serious for a moment," he said, and then began recounting the sums of money that lawyers tabulated had been paid to one of the informants. "Eighty-four thousand dollars for '86. It's now '87. That's well over one hundred and fifty thousand."

He paused and faced prosecutor Joseph Braunreuther.

"Mr. Braunreuther," he asked in mock seriousness, "you need another guy?"

As the laughter subsided, DiNorscio went on. "Ladies and gentlemen, I thank you for your presence here today and throughout the trial and ask you for your patience. As you can see, I'm no lawyer. I only have a ninth-grade education. I'm not sophisticated in the laws like the other persons that have addressed you in this courtroom. . . .

"But I have learned," he said, "as a layman. I read the law—RICO. I can tell you that it would be more appropriate for the men involved in the Iran scandal deal for selling arms to the Contras. They should be indicted, not me."

He paused, then raised his hand to his mouth in a conspiratorial whisper and moved closer to the jury. "By the way," he told them, "Forty million is still missing."

The jurors snickered. And DiNorscio went on to another topic. "Casinos last year in this state, in New Jersey, made New Jersey six hundred million dollars. And God knows how much they make on the lottery. Guy hits lottery for two million dollars," he said, referring to the payout schedule used by the New Jersey State Lottery Commission, "they give you half for twenty years. Why don't they give me the whole thing, and I'll give them twenty?"

Before anyone could figure out what his comments meant or that the figures didn't add up, DiNorscio turned serious again. "I've chosen to represent myself in this matter because I feel strongly about this case. My defense will not be complex, because it's going to come from my heart. Let me say to you without hesitation and reluctance: I'm innocent of these charges."

A moment later, he was back into his comedy routine. It

was beginning to get difficult to tell where the serious moments left off and the jokes began. The only problem was, not all of the jokes made sense.

"Talk about being extravagant," DiNorscio began with all the bravado of a veteran stand-up comic. "Money. My wife asked me for twenty dollars and I took her in the kitchen where I have a mirror. I showed her the twenty dollars, and I told her—this is the truth—I told her, this twenty dollars is yours in the mirror. This is mine." He waved a bill in front of the jury to illustrate his story. "She went to the butcher the next day and came home." He said he asked her where the roast was.

"'You won't believe me'," he quoted her as saying. "I'm sorry," he said, "I can ask a question." With that, he said, his wife took him back into the kitchen and stood in front of the mirror, "lifted her dress, said to me, 'That's yours, in the mirror'" and then made a gesture as though she were pointing to her crotch. 'This belongs to the butcher.'"

As the jury convulsed, DiNorscio leaned on the podium, heaving with laughter. Sweat was pouring off his face, and he was mopping it with a handkerchief. "I don't mean to embarrass nobody on this jury," he said, "but I'm just showing you I'm not a gangster. I'm a comedian. . . ."

There was stunned silence.

O'Malley looked angry and disgusted. Braunreuther was both amused and disturbed. The prosecutors knew that Critchley's eloquence was one thing—but Jackie was dangerous. Braunreuther knew it would be difficult for any jury to convict someone who appeared to be just joking around.

At the same time, Ackerman was faced with an immediate dilemma. Jackie was a clown. And how does the court deal with a clown? As a judge, he had an obligation to keep control in the courtroom. But how could he stop people from laughing?

13

Jackie DiNorscio didn't start out representing himself. When the trial began, he had an attorney. The problem was, he and his attorney didn't get along.

The problem spilled out into the open one day in mid-February, while the court was in the midst of its long ordeal to select a jury panel for the trial.

Jackie had been sleeping. It was a situation that had generated a great deal of discussion and frustration in the courtroom.

Jackie claimed to suffer from an obscure ailment known as "sleep apnea." In layman's terms, the condition supposedly resulted from a constriction of Jackie's throat during the night, which impaired his breathing and caused him to awaken repeatedly, leaving him tired and exhausted in the morning. The situation, it was claimed, was aggravated by his weight.

And as a result, Jackie would nod off in the courtroom.

The problem reached the boil-over point when, on February 19, 1987, John Sogliuzzo, a young, dark-haired attorney representing Jerome Voglino—an alleged loan shark known as "Jerry the Vog"—made a formal motion relating to DiNorscio's sleeping problems.

"It's now about twenty to twelve," Sogliuzzo said, standing and looking at the clock at the rear of the courtroom, "and I know from others' records, Mr. DiNorscio has been sleeping for at least approximately twenty minutes now, and I know that jurors—particularly I've been watching number two—have been drawn to the attention of Mr. DiNorscio, [who] has had his head down."

Nodding over toward the bench where DiNorscio was slumped, Sogliuzzo paused and pointed out the inert hulk. "I think that as we stand here now," he ventured, raising his eyebrows for emphasis, "he is sleeping."

Ackerman turned to Kirk Munroe, a Florida attorney who was representing the sleeping defendant. Munroe was a tall, slender, sandy-haired attorney with a finely etched beard and a soft-spoken manner, whose firm had represented DiNorscio in a prior narcotics case but who now appeared distinctly uncomfortable seated alongside his bulky client.

Ackerman's instructions to Munroe were direct: "Wake him up."

Munroe, however, wanted to speak. He raised his hand.

"Does the court wish me to be candid with the court?" he asked, his voice colored by traces of a faint southern drawl.

Ackerman grimaced and shook his head.

"I don't put a muzzle on you, Mr. Munroe."

There was a pause, and then, as if lifting a great burden from his shoulders, Munroe explained his plight.

"It is in my personal interest as Kirk Munroe," the attorney began, "that he"—he nodded down at his client—"remain sleeping . . ." Munroe cleared his throat and added, "because he affords me no threat when he is sleeping."

There was a buzz and a few muffled snorts of laughter among the defense camp. Munroe went on, declaring to the judge, "I'm just telling you that I do not want to wake him up."

Monroe later confided to the court that he and Jackie had been at odds for some time. According to the attorney, DiNorscio had stiffed him on his fees. DiNorscio apparently had given the law firm a valuable ring as security, and when he was unable to pay, the firm tried to sell the ring to a jeweler. But Jackie, Munroe complained, sent his own representative to the jeweler, and took the ring back.

"I found out Tuesday of last week," Munroe told the court, "that my client stole from my law firm.

"It was not his stone to pick up," Munroe explained, "it was my law firm's stone. So as a victim of what I can only characterize as a criminal act on behalf of my client toward my law firm—there is no way I can continue representing him."

Munroe caught his breath and continued.

"I am very proud to be a lawyer, and I'm proud to represent people accused of crime. I do so with all my heart. I do so with all my vigor. I frankly have never had the case that I couldn't handle. And I've been practicing law for thirteen years, as criminal defense attorney for eight years or so. So I've represented a lot of people who society considers to be not very nice people. And I've never had any problem with that."

He hesitated, looking at DiNorscio. "I have never had a client steal from me. Never . . ."

Turning to the judge, Munroe went on and summed it up as succinctly as possible. "I don't want to be here."

DiNorscio, who was awake at this time, was not about to sit by silently. He waved his hand, seeking to speak.

"I didn't steal nothing, Judge," he declared angrily. DiNorscio contended that he had put up the ring as payment for an earlier appeal, and maintained that Munroe's firm had not filed the necessary papers.

"And if he don't want to handle my appeal, he don't get my ring," DiNorscio asserted. "It's as simple as that. As far as anybody getting robbed here," he blustered, "I think it's me."

Moments later, Ackerman had had enough of the bickering. He thundered like a schoolmaster, pointing his finger at DiNorscio.

"Just listen to me very carefully, Mr. DiNorscio, because I don't play games, and I assure you of that. I may smile from time to time, but I don't play games. And I just want you to understand that."

DiNorscio appeared cowed by the outburst. There was a momentary hesitation, and he then responded with a meek protest, as if bewildered by all the furor.

"I don't know what you're getting mad about, Judge."

The matter appeared settled. But only until the next morning.

Ackerman had just taken the bench when Jackie, sitting over to his far right, raised his hand like a schoolboy signaling to the teacher.

"Your Honor," he said, "I hate to disturb you this early in the morning." Then he dropped his bombshell.

"I went over everything I thought about, and I have to make a motion. . . ."

DiNorscio, like a sleeping giant awakened by a call to battle, lumbered to his feet. "I think I'm better off by myself, Judge."

He had made a decision. He wanted to be his own lawyer.

Ackerman appeared concerned. This was not a matter to be taken lightly. The judge stroked his chin and rested his head on his hands in contemplation, as he peered down from the bench at Jackie.

"Have you ever had any legal training?" he asked solemnly.

Jackie thought only for a moment, and then responded, "I've been in jail all my life."

Ackerman was clearly worried. The courts have decreed that a person has a right to represent himself. But Jackie's lack of knowledge of the law could prove a handicap for him and a positive liability for everyone else in the case.

"Let me try to put it plainly," Ackerman said patiently. "There's an old saying that a person who represents himself has a fool for a client. Have you ever heard that before?"

DiNorscio shook his head.

"No, Judge."

Ackerman was annoyed. "You never heard it before?" he snapped. "Well, you're hearing it now for the first time. Does that make any sense to you?"

DiNorscio hunched his shoulders and raised his hands as if weighing the merits of the statement.

"Is it true?" he asked.

Ackerman nodded, looking DiNorscio in the eye in an almost fatherly manner. "Sometimes it is, yes."

DiNorscio looked straight at Ackerman and announced his decision.

"And sometimes it ain't, Judge. . . ."

It was to become a turning point in the trial. Until then, Jackie had been one of the crowd, larger than most, admittedly; but seated as far away from the jury as possible, he had blended into the throng of defendants and attorneys, his only distinguishing feature being his bulk.

He was now carving out a new role for himself, one that would guarantee that he would be placed in the limelight. It was not a situation that was met with enthusiasm by the other attorneys.

For much of the jury selection, DiNorscio had dressed casually, in a jogging suit and sunglasses. The problem was, a number of the other attorneys objected to his appearance. That, and his sleeping and snoring. And now his decision to represent himself ensured that whatever discomfort they had felt over Jackie's mere presence in the case was going to a minor itch compared to the pains they anticipated.

But as Jackie was later to phrase it, "I feel like I'm best qualified to represent myself because I have a strategy that I am going to perform while I'm in this court."

It was much later that the court and the prosecution discovered what that strategy was. And by then it was too late.

Jackie got his wish. Munroe was relieved as counsel. Another attorney, Carl Herman, was initially appointed to serve as standby counsel, to assist Jackie in coping with the finer points of the law. But that solution was not a permanent one either. Within days of his appointment, Herman suffered a burst appendix and was rushed to the hospital.

The man who was called to replace him was Alfred Gellene, thirty-six, an idealistic attorney with sandy hair and a bushy mustache who was conducting a general practice in Morristown. Gellene had handled a smattering of criminal cases in his career, but nothing had prepared him for the experience he was about to face.

The day he walked into the Newark courtroom was a day he will never forget.

"There was an air of unreality about the whole thing," he said, as he looked back on the day.

"I sat there next to Jackie, and the judge said, 'Mr. DiNorscio, this is Mr. Gellene."

Jackie's response was less than enthusiastic.

He looked at Gellene, whose baby face, chubby build, and boyish mannerisms made him appear far younger than his thirty-six years. His response was less than diplomatic.

"I don't know him; I don't want him," Jackie told the court.

Then he turned and whispered in Gellene's ear.

"Kid," he asked, "you ever done a RICO [racketeering] case before?"

Gellene shook his head.

Jackie looked at him appraisingly for a moment, before responding.

"No offense, kid, but I want to get out of jail sometime."

Jackie turned to the court and made a grand gesture of pushing his chair all the way back against the wall, as far away from Gellene as he could get. "I'm not going to sit next to him," Jackie asserted.

Ackerman, however, was prepared for just such a response. He wanted no more quibbling. He was cold as he laid out the law to DiNorscio.

"Mr. DiNorscio, I don't want to tangle with you, I really do not." Then he issued his final decree, as he pointed to the chair at DiNorscio's side. "I'm going to have him sit there."

DiNorscio just shrugged. He had pushed it as far as he could. The fight was over, and the court had won.

He looked at Gellene. "He can sit anyplace he wants."

Later that day, Jackie introduced himself and Gellene to the jury. It was not the usual introduction.

"I'm a defendant in this case," Jackie began. "My name is Jack DiNorscio. I'm going to defend myself. No partners. I practice law. However, the judge appointed me a counsel—to wake me up when I fall asleep."

The jurors only stared in amazement.

And as the jury selection proceeded, Jackie dozed.

The entire situation provoked repeated protests from the other lawyers in the case. It reflected badly on the other defendants, the attorneys said, and they made motion after motion to have DiNorscio removed from the case.

"Your Honor," Critchley said early one day, summing up the frustrations the other attorneys felt, "it seems a day doesn't go by that we don't have a problem with Mr. DiNorscio. Whether it be snoring or sleeping. Every day we talk about his diet, his lunch, his food, whether he should be poked, whether he should be pinched. I think there's a point in time when enough is enough. . . . I just think that one person seems to be dominating the proceedings in this courtroom, and that's Mr. DiNorscio. Judge, maybe we could be severed from him."

The judge himself expressed his frustration.

"The record, to say the least," Ackerman commented at one point, "has been made more than complete on this score. I'm swimming in snoring or allegations of snoring in this case."

After it was over, Gellene admitted that the situation never improved. "I'd say he had to sleep through about thirty, forty percent of the trial. Some days were better than others. If he had a big lunch, he'd fall asleep right away."

14

Jackie DiNorscio's criminal career spanned four decades and is regarded by some law-enforcement officials as a sort of monument to misfortune, or at the very least, bad judgment.

Although his first public appearance was positive—a sixteen-year-old DiNorscio and a dog named Chubby were hailed as heroes in the newspaper for alerting sleeping neighbors to a two-alarm fire that severely damaged a home in his old neighborhood—his subsequent press notices were less than glowing.

Edwin Steir, a former director of the New Jersey Division of Criminal Justice and former assistant U.S. attorney for New Jersey, had kept tabs on DiNorscio during his own career in law enforcement.

"Every year or so, I'd stumble across Jackie DiNorscio," Steir recalled. "He was always getting caught. He was a very incompetent criminal. My impression is that he spent more time behind bars than he did out on the street."

Indeed, when Jackie, who had moved to Florida after serving his time as a result of the Project Alpha conviction, walked into Ackerman's courtroom, he had just been sentenced to jail yet again by U.S. District Judge Maryanne Trump Barry—the sister of flamboyant New York developer Donald Trump—to thirty years' imprisonment on federal narcotics charges. Coincidentally, DiNorscio had been tried in a courtroom located directly across the pillared marble hall from the court where the Lucchese extravaganza would play itself out.

"DiNorscio," his own lawyer had acknowledged to Barry during the narcotics case, "is a criminal. He's been a criminal for a long time."

When it came time for his summation, the lawyer told the court, "Jackie DiNorscio is not very brilliant. Another thing is, physically pretty, he's not. Socially pretty, he's not. . . ."

In fact, the lawyer admitted, "The social life of Jackie DiNorscio to many people might be disgusting.

"Some people would say," the attorney told the court, "well, you know, look at him. What a scumbag."

"He was one of the most hard-luck guys going," said Robert Buccino, deputy chief of the New Jersey Statewide Organized Crime Task Force. "I think he even got arrested twice while he was in jail."

Jackie's plight was graphically illustrated by an encounter he had with Buccino.

It was after the death of a lesser-known mob figure who was slain in the driveway of his home in suburban Essex County. Such deaths often provide a wealth of intelligence information for law-enforcement authorities. Investigators are often assigned to stake out the funeral homes to see who comes and goes, who talks to whom. It provides a candid look at the status of relationships and alliances within the underworld.

In this instance, the victim was a close friend of DiNorscio.

"So we go to cover the wake," Buccino said. "Now, I never like to sit behind a tree or something like that. If I'm going to cover it, I'm going to go stand right there, let 'em see, I don't care."

Which is exactly what Buccino did. He positioned himself in an obvious spot right in front of the funeral home and waited.

"And who comes pulling up," he said, "but Jackie DiNorscio, his wife, and a couple of other people."

Jackie wasn't shy. He recognized Buccino and walked over to him, his wife in tow.

He extended his hand to the state investigator and introduced his wife. Then the two began talking.

"While we're talking," Buccino said, "a guy walks over. I still don't know who he is. The guy walks over and he says to Jackie, 'Jackie, I gotta talk to you.'"

Jackie looked at the man and nodded.

"All right, in a little while. Can't you see I'm talking? In a little while, just a little while."

He turned back to Buccino.

But the man wasn't to be dissuaded. He tugged on Jackie's arm.

"But, Jackie," he insisted, "the load is in."

Jackie's eyes widened, and he glared at the man.

"Excuse me a minute," he said to Buccino and turned to the man. "This is Detective Buccino of the state police," Jackie said emphatically, jerking his head at the plainclothes investigator.

The man turned to the investigator and stuck out his hand, smiling. "Oh," he said, "pleased to meet you."

He turned back to Jackie. "Jackie, what should I do? Should I bring the load over to the warehouse or should I take the load . . . ?"

Jackie's face grew livid, but he tried to control his anger as he cut the man short.

"Did you just hear what I said?"—raising his voice for emphasis. "This is Detective Buccino—a *POLICE OFFICER*!"

The man nodded again, almost indignant at Jackie for shouting at him.

"Yeah, I heard. So what?"

Jackie shook his head and turned back to Buccino. He shrugged his shoulders in resignation.

"Now you know why I get pinched?" he asked.

And get pinched he did. If there was one thing Jackie DiNorscio proved himself good at in life, it was getting arrested.

Jackie's record begins at age fifteen, when he was charged

with juvenile delinquency as the result of a teenage brawl. Several more juvenile-delinquency charges followed in close succession during the next several years, culminating with his being sentenced to the state reformatory at Annandale when he was seventeen.

His adult record began just two years later. Newark police spotted Jackie and two other men loading clothes into a car. When a police officer attempted to question the young men, they fled. They were captured after a short chase and taken back to a nearby store. Police found the rear door forced open.

The incident won Jackie a trip to another reformatory, and he wasn't out long before he was in trouble again.

This time, he was charged with assault and battery on a police officer. He claimed self-defense. It seemed that police were trying to arrest his father, and being a dutiful son, he elected to intervene.

At age twenty-three, he was charged with fracturing the jaw of an acquaintance with a baseball bat. He claimed self-defense then too, and that charge was dropped.

Jackie was lucky for several years. Although his record reflects arrests for a variety of offenses during the late 1960s, most of those cases resulted in dismissals or acquittals.

His run of luck ended, however, with a case that did little to endear him to law enforcement. It was related by Charles Coe, a former New Jersey State Police officer assigned to the agency's Intelligence Bureau, who specialized in organized-crime investigations. Coe knew DiNorscio, and he remembered the incident well.

It was the summer of 1969. The scene was a popular coffee shop near the Jersey Shore. It was the early morning hours, but there was still a line of patrons waiting to be seated. In that line was Jackie DiNorscio, along with several of his friends.

Jackie, however, wasn't content to wait. It wasn't something he did well.

"These guys apparently tried to muscle in, to get ahead," Coe recalled. But one of the men on line put up a stink and held his ground. When the next booth became available, he was shown to a seat.

This, apparently, did not sit well with DiNorscio. When

the man was seated, DiNorscio and the others walked up to him, and after a few words were exchanged, he "beat the hell out of him." When it was over, the victim had a broken jaw and a crushed cheekbone.

The real problem for DiNorscio, Coe said, was that the victim was an off-duty New Jersey state trooper. And police have long memories.

Jackie's first trial ended in a mistrial, and the second time around he was acquitted. He later attributed the acquittal to a beating he allegedly received in retaliation.

But law-enforcement officials never forgot the incident. DiNorscio himself used to cringe every time he saw a trooper and wondered aloud how long it would take to live down the repercussions of the incident.

He never really did. "He made an error in judgment that night," a law-enforcement source noted, and it haunted him for the rest of his career.

If nothing else, the beating of the trooper focused law-enforcement attention on Jackie DiNorscio, and when they ran across his name in the future, they were well aware of who he was.

In a way, Jackie DiNorscio was born into crime the way Prince Charles was born to the throne. His father, Dominick (Tommy Adams) DiNorscio, a "soldier" in the Philadelphia-based Bruno crime family, had a criminal record dating back to the 1930s, and was only released from prison in 1986 at age seventy-five. For a time, he served as the acting *caporegime* of that family in northern New Jersey, but was demoted in 1980 because the family leaders felt he was not generating enough revenue.

Although Jackie has told authorities that he was harassed because of his father's criminal record, law-enforcement officials regard his father's career as the key to Jackie's "success": "The only reason he had any status at all in organized crime was because of his father," Steir said.

Jackie, meanwhile, Steir recalled, "was always getting himself in trouble. I remember periodically hearing, Oh, we locked up Jackie DiNorscio again."

But for Steir, the image of Jackie was not that of the Falstaffian figure that emerged from the Accetturo trial. It was a far more sinister image that stayed in his mind.

"It's easy to view Jackie DiNorscio as sort of a clown," Steir said, "but the fact is that he had very, very deep organized-crime connections."

During the Accetturo trial, Jackie had turned to the judge in a moment of candor. He nodded toward Accetturo, the man who grew from poverty and obscurity to become revered as one of the most powerful crime figures in the state.

As Accetturo sat, unaware of the conversation, Jackie pointed his thumb at the "boss."

"If I hadn't gotten busted," Jackie told the judge with a burst of pride, "I'd be sitting in that chair today."

15

When Joseph Benjamin Alonzo took the witness stand on April 8, 1987, it was with all the fanfare and excitement of the main event at a major prizefight.

For weeks, rumors had been circulating about Alonzo. He was to be the star prosecution witness. He knew the defendants personally and had grown up with many of them. In fact, he was to be the perfect "inside" witness for the government.

There was only one problem, the defense said. He was crazy. Before Alonzo even walked into the courtroom, the stories about him had begun to spread.

According to Critchley, Alonzo not only had undergone shock therapy, he had been diagnosed as schizophrenic. And in the summer of 1986, before jury selection in the case had even begun, Critchley launched an assault on Alonzo's reputation.

In what was viewed as one of the most outrageous legal motions to be brought in the case—and which was strongly condemned by the judge as a possible attempt to inflame the jurors—Critchley not only questioned Alonzo's mental stability, but raised the specter that he was a potential carrier of the AIDS virus, someone whose aberrational behavior could threaten the health of everyone in the courtroom.

The defense documents outlined a scenario worthy of the most sensationalistic tabloid: A crazed witness, infected with a dreaded and fatal disease, goes berserk in the courtroom in a mad attempt to infect all around him.

In an affidavit filed with the court, Critchley said the AIDS issue had developed as a result of investigations that showed that Alonzo's onetime roommate was an intravenous drug user who had recently died of AIDS. The affidavit further suggested that Alonzo, also a known drug user, could have contracted the disease from a shared hypodermic needle and demanded that the government have Alonzo tested for the disease before being brought to court.

Alonzo, it was also claimed, had a long history of erratic behavior. In addition to numerous violent episodes, the attorneys said, the witness had been under psychiatric treatment for years, and had a long history of arrests while under the influence of alcohol and drugs. In one instance, they reported, he was hospitalized after drinking a mixture of orange juice and rubbing alcohol.

Defense attorneys also cited another incident in which Alonzo broke into a house by throwing a log through a window, exposed himself to the terrified occupant, and then fled, screaming and naked, into the street.

A witness such as this, the defense declared, returning its dubious medical position, "must be controlled and others protected from a disease of epidemic proportions and fatal consequences," and then cited medical studies that claimed that the AIDS antibody—the best keys to detecting persons infected with the disease—had been found in the tears and saliva of persons infected with the virus.

"Because this disease is a baffling mystery of recent genesis and the detection of its presence in the tears and saliva occurred a short three months ago," Critchley wrote in June of 1986, "there is disagreement in the scientific community whether HTLV-III is transmitted by saliva, tears, or casual contact.

"Conclusive knowledge regarding its transmission and contagiousness," Critchley asserted in the papers, "remains a mystery. At any time while testifying, [the informant] may dribble, spit or sneeze. He may cut himself on a document, a paper clip, etc."

The attorney then demanded, "What safety measures will be taken?"

The affidavit further warned that the judge, the stenographers, the lawyers, and even the jurors risked becoming infected as a result of potential exposure to the witness in the courtroom.

"We are dealing with an incurable disease whose transmission is poorly understood," Critchley wrote, concluding his warning with the strident declaration. "The only thing certain about the disease AIDS is, if you get it, you die."

The defense lawyers presented their case with all the fervor of television ministers, but despite the days of hoopla surrounding the AIDS motions, Judge Ackerman dealt with the matter summarily: Drop the subject or the attorneys would face disciplinary proceedings.

But if nothing else, the controversy had served at least one purpose. It had kept the prosecution busy dealing with what ultimately was determined to be an entirely irrelevant issue.

It also helped to set the stage for an attack on Alonzo's credibility that made the image of a drug-crazed "Typhoid Mary," biting and spitting at everyone around him, almost pale by comparison.

When Alonzo finally arrived to face the packed courtroom of defendants—many of whom were old friends and distant relatives—he was ushered to the premier seat in the house.

Because of the logistical problems generated by the massive number of defendants and attorneys, the witnesses did not testify from the security of the witness stand, which normally is located in a raised box to the left side of the judge's bench. In an effort to permit all of the defendants and lawyers to actually see and "confront" their accusers, Ackerman had arranged for the witnesses to testify from a raised desk normally used by his court clerk, located directly in front of his bench.

The seat served its purpose—it provided the defendants with an unobstructed view of the men whose testimony was intended to put them in prison. To the witnesses, however, the scene was not unlike being placed in the center arena of the Roman Colosseum, filled with an audience hungry for blood.

"Who is Joe Alonzo?" Grady O'Malley had asked during his opening statement to the jury. "What does he know? How does he know it, and what does he have to say?"

"Well," O'Malley said in answer to his own questions, "we know he's a cousin of defendant Jack DiNorscio. Alonzo grew up in the Newark area with many of the defendants here, knows many of them, has known them for twenty years.

"Mr. Alonzo," O'Malley went on, "will give you insight into this organization. He'll describe to you Mr. Accetturo's rise from numbers runner here in Newark to the position that the government alleges that he is in now. Mr. Alonzo will explain to you what the protocol is of this enterprise, which is . . . respect, loyalty, and silence—rules that he will break when he testifies. . . ."

In return for his cooperation, Alonzo had been admitted into the hallowed ranks of the Federal Witness Protection Program. The program, administered by the U.S. Marshals Service, is designed to help law-enforcement authorities afford security and protection to would-be informants who fear they might otherwise become part of the foundation of the next mob-financed construction project.

Under the program, a witness is given a new identity and a subsidy to permit him to establish a new life in another part of the country. Without this program, many law-enforcement officials feel, the fight against organized crime could not be successful.

The old adage for mob informants—"You can run, but you cannot hide"—has been in large measure disproven as a result of the Witness Protection Program. Through it, they can run, and they *can* hide.

As far as the defense team was concerned, Alonzo was their prime target. He was the key to the government case, and he had to be discredited if the defense was to succeed.

Critchley spent a good portion of his opening remarks attempting to do just that.

"You'll hear about Mr. Alonzo," he said, his face grimacing as he spoke the name. "You'll hear that Mr. Alonzo basically has led a life of crime.

"You could," he said, "consider the fact that he's been so deeply involved in the criminal commission of crimes over his life that he has become acutely aware of how to manipulate the system. He has honed it to a science. He has sharpened it like a sharp knife. He can cut right through it, and he can get what he wants.

"When he committed his first crime as a juvenile," Critchley declared, "Dwight David Eisenhower was president. And Ronald Reagan, our president, was selling Borax soap.

"Although much has changed over the last thirty years," Critchley declared, "with Mr. Alonzo nothing has changed."

The first day on the stand, Alonzo looked like a 1960s rock musician gone to seed. Dressed in a black sports jacket and open-neck black shirt, his salt-and-pepper hair less-than-stylishly long, Alonzo appeared to be a physical and emotional wreck.

He was jittery. He was hard to understand; he looked as if he needed a drink.

DiNorscio made some noise as he stood near the far wall and changed seats with Gellene in order to get a better look at the witness. Alonzo kept his face averted as Braunreuther handed him a glass of water, which he gulped thirstily.

The buzz of anticipation, which had risen in intensity, subsided. The nervous laughter and conversation, which had spread among the defense tables, dissipated. All eyes were on Alonzo.

As the jury filed in, DiNorscio raised his hand and called out in a stage whisper to the judge.

"I'd like to talk to him, Judge. Can I talk to him?"

The question went unanswered as the jurors were ushered to their seats.

Ackerman leaned over the bench and spoke to Alonzo, instructing him to sit closer to the microphone and to pull his chair close to the desk.

Then Braunreuther began his questioning.

According to Alonzo, he contacted the FBI in February of 1985 with an offer that they found difficult to refuse. He wanted to cooperate.

"Why did you reach out for the FBI in February of 1985?" Braunreuther asked.

Alonzo's response was hushed, barely audible. "I feared for my life."

"Why?" Braunreuther asked.

Again, Alonzo kept his face down, his words muted. "I shot one of the defendants."

"Which defendant was that?" Braunreuther inquired, stepping back from the witness and glancing around the courtroom.

Alonzo did not look up. "Giacomo DiNorscio."

There was a brief murmur in the courtroom, and Braunreuther continued. "What is your relationship to Mr. Giacomo DiNorscio?"

Alonzo responded with a single-word answer: "Cousin."

"How long have you known Mr. DiNorscio?" Braunreuther asked.

"All my life," Alonzo said.

Moments later, Braunreuther turned again to the shooting of DiNorscio and Alonzo's fear that his own life was in danger.

"What was it about the shooting of Mr. DiNorscio that now leads you to fear for your own life?"

Neither the spectators nor the jurors could suppress a laugh when Alonzo responded.

"Well," he said, "I missed."

Braunreuther waited until the laughter subsided. "What do you mean by that?"

Alonzo looked up for the first time, with an expression of impatience. He had already told his story to the prosecutors. Why were they being so obtuse?

"I didn't kill him," Alonzo said in a louder, agitated voice. "And I knew the repercussions."

Braunreuther tossed back a lock of hair that had fallen over his forehead and leaned on a stack of books on the prosecution table. "What were the repercussions as you understood them?"

Alonzo glared back defiantly. "I violated a rule . . . a rule of the life that I was living for the last thirty years."

DiNorscio, he said, had been his "boss." And if he escaped retribution from him, Alonzo said, he would have had to face DiNorscio's father and others.

The situation became clear to him, he said, when DiNorscio signed a statement declaring that Alonzo was not the one who had shot him. At that point, Alonzo said, he felt he had no choice. There was only one route to go. Toward the government and the Federal Witness Protection Program.

According to Alonzo, DiNorscio was the boss of a Florida-based cocaine-distribution ring, and he had dealt with his cousin in the operation on an almost daily basis.

"I dealt cocaine," he said. "I helped package it. I weighed it."

As the questioning proceeded, DiNorscio blurted out an objection.

"Your Honor," he shouted, waving his arm for attention. "I object to Mr. Marchalonis signaling the witness." Pointing at the FBI agent assigned to supervise Alonzo seated at the prosecution table. "He signaled the witness. I want someone to keep their eye on them, Judge. Did you see him signal the witness?"

Ackerman raised an eyebrow. "Are you asking the court?"

"I'm asking my cocounsel, Judge," DiNorscio said.

Braunreuther appeared exasperated. DiNorscio was making an issue of the relationship between the agent and the witness, and he felt he had to deal with it.

"Mr. Alonzo," he asked, "was Mr. Marchalonis signaling you?"

Alonzo was resolute in his response. "No, he's not."

Some of the jurors merely smiled knowingly at the answer.

Alonzo was still nervous on his second day of testimony. The strain on him was evident, and at least some of the defense lawyers expected him to explode. He had never been an entirely stable person, and the stress of testifying against his former associates could prove too much—or so some members of the defense team hoped.

Alonzo was almost mechanical as he talked about his "schooling" in organized crime, learning the ropes, the way of the streets. His teachers, he said, included his cousin, DiNorscio, and DiNorscio's father.

"Are you familiar with Anthony Accetturo?" Braunreuther asked, as he approached the lectern positioned in the middle of the courtroom.

Alonzo darted a quick glance at the white-haired defendant seated several feet to his right.

"Yes, I am," he said in a hoarse voice.

"You recognize him here today in the courtroom?"

Alonzo nodded. "Yes, I do."

Braunreuther placed his hands on both sides of the lectern. "Would you please point him out?"

Alonzo swiveled in his seat and pointed his finger in a short jab. "Anthony," he said, and turned away swiftly.

He was almost mumbling as he told how he had become involved in illegal numbers operations, "edging" off some of the bets to Accetturo. His voice was so low that several times Critchley had to ask to have answers repeated.

"Because the witness is looking in the other direction," Critchley charged, "we really can't hear very well at all."

Alonzo had no intention of turning around. He wanted to look at the government attorneys. Not at Accetturo, Taccetta, or DiNorscio.

"Keep your voice up," Ackerman told him.

He had known Accetturo since the mid-1950s, Alonzo said, seeing him on the street corners of his neighborhood, watching his organization grow to more than fifty persons. It was important, he said, to be aligned with such a group.

"What are the benefits, Mr. Alonzo?" Braunreuther asked.

Alonzo's reply was short but informative. "Protection."

"What do you mean by protection?" he was asked.

Alonzo gathered his thoughts for a moment and then explained. "Protection from the law. Protection from other individuals robbing you. If you're not 'around' someone," he said, "people are going to try to take what you have." It was like the law of the jungle, the biggest and the strongest survive. That was the way of the streets.

Alonzo worked directly with DiNorscio, he continued, but at the time, even though DiNorscio's operations were small, they told people they were aligned with Accetturo. This way, he said, they didn't have to pay any "ice" to the law to keep from getting busted. Anthony was taking care of that for them.

How did he know that? For Alonzo the answer was simple, and practical. "Well," he told the court, "they didn't bother us."

Ackerman could only sigh. This was not proof. This was only a guess—and it was inadmissible as evidence. "The jury," he said, "will be instructed to strike the last two answers."

As Ackerman turned back and nodded to Braunreuther to continue his interrogation, there was movement to his far right. It was DiNorscio, again waving for attention.

The fat man rose to his feet.

"Judge," he shouted, "you know what the problem is here. I can't hear and watch Mr. Marchalonis doing this." DiNorscio made some exaggerated hand signals to illustrate his complaint that the FBI agent was silently coaching the witness on his answers. "Somebody keep their eye on him, please?"

Ackerman was annoyed. "Mr. DiNorscio," he said firmly, "will you kindly be seated."

The request was not firm enough. DiNorscio only became louder and more insistent. "It's true, Judge. I want somebody to keep their eye on this man," he blustered, gesturing with his hands and winking broadly in what he claimed was an imitation of the FBI man. "It's this and that and this." He turned to the judge and raised his hands plaintively. "Just watch him for me, please?"

Ackerman didn't even respond. The trial was young, and already the weight of controlling these characters was beginning to take its toll.

"Mr. Braunreuther," he said wearily, "you may proceed, sir."

Braunreuther ran his hand through his thick hair and shook his head as he looked down at his notes on the lectern.

"I'm having a difficult time remembering where I was as well, Judge. . . ."

It was late in the morning on April 8, 1987, when Braunreuther mentioned the second key name in the case.

He leaned over the lectern and asked quietly, "Are you familiar with an individual by the name of Michael Taccetta?"

Alonzo nodded. "Yes, I am."

"How long have you known Michael Taccetta?" Braunreuther asked.

"Twenty-five years," Alonzo said almost wistfully, repeating the answer a second time. "Twenty-five years."

He pointed to Taccetta, who was seated in the center of the courtroom wearing a blue suit with a gray shirt. It was one of the few times the defendants appeared sartorially proper during the proceeding. Within days, the style of dress degenerated to sport shirts, polo shirts, and, on one occasion, Bermuda shorts. The jurors for the most part were equally casual, sporting jeans, denim skirts, and sweaters. As the trial progressed, only the attorneys maintained the normal courtroom decorum. And, of course, the black-robed figure of the judge.

Taccetta, Alonzo said, was a familiar figure in the old neighborhood. He would see him at the corner hangouts, in the nightclubs, in the bars. He'd be in the local candy store, on the phone.

His feelings toward Taccetta in those days were to be echoed by others on tape recordings made by the FBI decades later.

"You know," he said, with a trace of seeming nostalgia, "I liked Michael a lot."

He was asked how Taccetta supported himself during the late 1960s.

"Gambling," Alonzo said, pausing to think and then adding, "some burglary."

"Was he affiliated with anybody at that time?" Braunreuther asked.

"Yes," Alonzo replied, dropping his voice so low it was almost impossible to hear his answer. "He was affiliated with Anthony."

Taccetta, he said, "always looked up to Anthony. He respected him."

One of the problems with mob informants, authorities concede, is that they usually bring with them their own set of baggage. In opening statements to the jurors, prosecutors are fond of disavowing any affection for the individuals they will call to testify. They are often liars, cheats, reprobates of the worst kind, authorities admit—but then add that it takes people like these to provide an inside look at criminal activities.

The difficulty is, sometimes the baggage that these witnesses carry is far more inflammatory than the information they have to provide. And unless the prosecution takes the first step to expose it, disclosure of this information can prove devastating to the government's case.

So when it came time to expose Alonzo's dirty linen, Braunreuther tried to get in the first licks. The only problem was, Alonzo's linen proved especially dirty. And despite Braunreuther's own clean-cut image, the dirt didn't all come out in the wash.

"When was the first time you were incarcerated?" Braunreuther asked.

Alonzo rubbed his face and pondered the answer. "I believe it was 1958."

The first time was for breaking and entering and burglary. The next time was for possession of a single tablet of Valium. For that he received six months.

But then came the heavy stuff: two years for cocaine distribution and two-and-a-half years for conspiracy to sell stolen securities. Then there were the crimes for which he was never caught.

When he was only eighteen, he was sentenced to a state reformatory. He was already a heroin user by then, and when he was released, he became an alcoholic. In the late 1960s, he began using heroin again. Then cocaine. And more drinking.

"I finally came out of jail in 1976," Alonzo recalled, and told how the cycle repeated itself. "I became heavily involved with the use of cocaine and other drugs, as well as alcohol, went to jail, and used narcotics and drugs and alcohol while in prison. Got out of prison in January 1981, where I continued to use cocaine and alcohol, marijuana, and Quaaludes."

But then came the bombshell.

Alonzo admitted that he had not only undergone psychiatric and electroshock treatments, but, after he began cooperating with federal authorities in mid-1985, he had also used hundreds of dollars a week in FBI money to keep himself supplied with heroin, cocaine, and alcohol. Alonzo testified that his weekly FBI allowance went for just that.

The witness explained that although Marchalonis drove him to a drug clinic for daily doses of methadone, a synthetic narcotic, he secretly supplemented his consumption with regular doses of drugs and liquor. Additionally, Alonzo revealed that he had been under the influence of drugs when he was called to testify before the federal grand jury investigating this very case.

"I was on a hundred milligrams a day of methadone. I was using cocaine on almost a daily basis. I was smoking marijuana on a daily basis and usually drinking on a daily basis."

The disclosure drew an explosion of protests from the defense.

As the jury was led out of the courtroom for the lunch break, Critchley leaped to his feet, demanding a mistrial. The defense, he said, had never been informed of this situation.

"Here we have a guy that's shooting heroin paid for by the FBI and he's testifying before the grand jury and he's, in effect, a zombie," Critchley exclaimed. "This is critical. This goes to prosecutorial misconduct."

Braunreuther leaped to the defense of the government.

"The FBI did nothing improper," he declared. "They had a witness who had a drug habit, and he went out on his own and bought cocaine. He got up on the stand in court and admitted it happened."

The furor was beginning. And the defense motions for mistrial came in rapid-fire sequence.

They were all eventually denied by the judge, but the disclosure of Alonzo's ability to acquire drugs under the very noses of the agents who were supposed to be monitoring him was to become a major factor in the case, changing the very focus of the trial. And by the time the case was over, there were those who might have concluded that it wasn't the defendants who were placed on trial, but the government itself.

16

For the next several days, Alonzo went on to detail his knowledge of the criminal activities of the various defendants.

He recounted how Michael and Martin Taccetta moved down to Florida during the early 1970s to be with Accetturo and to open a lounge at a hotel in North Miami. The business, however, was not a success, and on New Year's Eve, someone detonated a stink bomb in the club. Shortly after that, the Taccettas moved back to New Jersey.

By the late seventies, however, life had improved for the Taccettas. Michael was now in charge of his own gambling operation in New Jersey and was acting as Accetturo's anointed representative in the Garden State.

For Alonzo, however, life wasn't working out so well. His problems began with his cousin Jackie, who was then serving a sentence in Rahway State Prison, contacted him and sent him to see a man. That man was P. J. Jumonville, the undercover FBI agent.

"I had some marijuana at the time," Alonzo recalled. "He said, 'Go to this guy, Joe . . . and see what he can do with it.'"

"How do you know him?" Alonzo said he'd asked Jackie during a visit at the prison.

Jackie just waved away Alonzo's concerns, he said. "Don't worry about it," Jackie assured him, "I had him checked out. Came back A1A."

In court, Alonzo shook his head as he recalled the incident.

The trustworthy individual whom Jackie had vouched for, Alonzo said, "was an FBI guy"—P.J. Jumonville, the undercover agent.

Although the defense attempted to object to the testimony, questioning whether Alonzo had "personal knowledge" of the matter, the witness just shot back, "I was sent to jail for it. I did time for it. Yeah, I have personal knowledge."

Alonzo explained that he had tried to sell Jumonville a batch of stolen securities. For his efforts, he wound up being indicted and imprisoned.

When he was released in 1981, he was sent to a federal halfway house in Fort Lauderdale, Florida, a fortuitous placement for Alonzo as it turned out. Jackie was living not too far away, in Pompano Beach. Before long, Alonzo was back in the groove with his cousin.

"I got high with him. I smoked 'base' for the first time in my life. And talked a lot about old times. You know, I hadn't seen him in a while."

But for Alonzo and his cousin, the reunion didn't last long. Jackie, who had been released from Rahway, was not it turned out an entirely free man. He was a fugitive from a prior conviction in New Jersey. Rather than face the time, he had simply packed his bags and moved to Florida.

For several months, Alonzo said, he spent nearly every day with Jackie. He would leave the halfway house around six in the morning, drive to Jackie's home, and go back to sleep until later in the day.

Meanwhile, Alonzo said, Jackie was supporting himself by dealing drugs. And although he was technically a fugitive, he didn't live like one. According to Alonzo, DiNorscio's life-style was "extravagant and sick," blowing large sums of money on cocaine, booze, and rents. The costs would have been prohibitive, Alonzo said, except, as always, Jackie had an edge. He didn't pay for his drugs.

"He found out," Alonzo said, "you can make more money if you don't have to pay for it and sell it."

What did he do?

Alonzo's answer said it all. "Take it."

In court, Braunreuther quizzed Alonzo about the deals.

"How do you know that?" he asked.

"He bragged to me about it," Alonzo said. Describing the "rip-offs," Alonzo related how DiNorscio would enter into a deal, and then how "he would take the money or the drugs, either one."

But the idyll was not to last long. By May of 1981, the law caught up to Jackie.

He had brought his Corvette in for repairs at an auto dealership in Delray Beach. When he and Alonzo went to pick it up, Jackie was taken into custody. "The FBI was waiting there for us, and when we went in, they came down on us."

But for Jackie, Alonzo said, it was only a short hiatus in his career. Acting on his cousin's instructions, Alonzo said he withdrew some ninety-five thousand dollars from a safe-deposit box. He explained how he gave forty thousand dollars of that money to a friend of Jackie's from the old neighborhood who had followed his buddy down to Florida. The friend, Alonzo said, invested the money in cocaine. The investment paid off.

By the time Jackie got out of jail in 1983, the friend had turned the forty thousand dollars into the basis for a lucrative drug-smuggling enterprise. Jackie stayed around New Jersey for a few weeks, and then took a vacation in Acapulco. When he eventually returned to Florida, Jackie was ready to step into the driver's seat of the operation.

Alonzo, meanwhile, had got a job, he said, in a "diamond place."

Alonzo was about to embark on the story of what he later described as the best business deal he had ever become involved in—and how he claimed Jackie butted in and tried to take it all away from him.

It was this episode that eventually embittered Alonzo against his cousin and led to the breakup of their life-long friendship. And it was the motivating force behind Alonzo's decision to try to murder DiNorscio in an abortive shooting that left Alonzo with nowhere to turn except to the government for protection.

But before he could begin, Gerald DeLuca, alleged to be one of Jackie's minions, rose from his seat and walked toward an anteroom in the rear of the courtroom. He looked pale, and his eyes were glassy. He stumbled, and he fell.

DiNorscio and Cohen grabbed him and helped him to his feet. DeLuca shook his head dizzily. A pair of deputy U.S. marshals placed his arms around their shoulders and tried to help him walk out the rear of the courtroom, but DeLuca staggered and fell a second time.

As he was brought upstairs to the U.S. marshals' offices, DeLuca broke into a cold sweat and began babbling incoherently. Then he collapsed to the floor again. He was rushed by ambulance to a local hospital emergency room, where he was diagnosed as suffering from hypoglycemia, treated, and released.

DeLuca was judged well enough to return to court, but the interruption called a halt to the testimony for five days.

It did provide DiNorscio, however, with another opportunity to ask to get out of the trial. Too many people, he said, were becoming ill.

"You lost three or four people in this courtroom," he told the judge, refering to defendants and jurors who had fallen sick. "And I don't want to be the fifth."

Ackerman did his best to ignore him."

But Jackie DiNorscio was not an easy person to ignore. Before Alonzo could take the stand again the following week, he was ready with a fresh batch of objections—and complaints.

It seemed he didn't like what Alonzo had been saying.

"Judge," DiNorscio said, rising to his feet and running his hand through his hair, "I sit here and hear him talking, and I hear you listening to him. And I know you have the power in this courtroom to impeach this witness, because everything at this point is a lie. Joe is a drunk. Joe was a junkie. Joe was never coherent, and you're sitting here and allowing all this stuff to take place?" DiNorscio scratched his head again and shifted his weight. "I can't see this, Judge. I'm sitting here getting sick listening to this guy testify."

Ackerman only nodded. "Thank you, Mr. DiNorscio," he said, and then turned to other business.

But in a matter of moments Jackie was back on his feet, waving his hand like an insistent child.

"You didn't see my hand before," DiNorscio called out.

Ackerman grimaced and rolled his eyes. "Mr. DiNorscio, I haven't been ignoring you. I have given you an opportunity. I will give you another opportunity. As a matter of fact, you want to speak first?"

DiNorscio laughed. "You're a little ahead of me, Judge, and I forget."

Ackerman frowned. "I don't want to promote amnesia. Go ahead."

DiNorscio grumbled a bit and then picked up where he had left off. "Do you remember when we were picking this jury, Judge, and I said to you that everything you're doing is fair?" DiNorscio said, making a smacking sound with his lips. "I don't think so anymore, Judge.

"I know you're an intelligent fellow, Judge," DiNorscio continued, in an attempt to be conciliatory, but added, "You're sitting up there and allowing this guy to make testimony that it is impossible to be true. So where are we going with this trial, Judge?"

Ackerman rubbed his chin and then said softly, "Forward."

DiNorscio looked momentarily confused. "Forward?" he asked. It was a question that would turn out to be unusually perceptive.

Alonzo spent the rest of the day detailing his involvement in what the government had euphemistically referred to as the "gem business."

According to Alonzo, it was all a scam.

The business, known as Aron and Aron, opened in May 1983. As outlined by the witness, the business was known in the trade as a "boiler room" operation. Salesmen would sit in an office and make telephone calls to prospective customers and try to interest them in their product.

There are essentially three steps to the operation:

First, a "qualifier" calls potential investors and tells them he is sending out investment information to businessmen in their area. The information, he says, will be free, and then asks if the individual will take time to look it over. In addition, the "qualifier" asks if the individual is liquid—if he has money to invest. If the answer is affirmative, the individual is pegged as a qualified lead.

In the next step, the literature is sent out to the potential customer. In about two weeks, long enough for the person to have received the material, the salesman calls and attempts to make a sale. If he is successful, the scheme moves into its next phase: A person known as a "loader" calls with good news. The investor has already made money! He is then told that the company expects a 50 to 80 percent growth over the next year and that this would be a good time for further investments.

The pitch is convincing. The customer has already made money—or so he thinks—so why not?

As part of the sales pitch, the customer is actually sent a sample of the product—in the case of Aron and Aron, some form of gemstone—and told that if he does not like it, he can return it within ten days for a full refund.

But why would a customer want to return it? Along with the stone, he is sent certification from a "government approved" laboratory—whatever that may be.

The only problem is, the deal is like an old joke. In that joke, a man buys an over-the-counter stock. It's a great deal, his broker tells him. It keeps going up in value. Finally, the investor decides enough is enough. He wants to cash in on his investment. "Sell," he tells the broker. The broker responds, "To whom?"

According to Alonzo, this is much the way his telephone gem business worked. Once the company had a client, it would continue to sell and sell, until the customer reached the point of exhaustion.

The problem for the customer was, Alonzo said, the gems are almost never worth what they are sold for. Even if they were good stones, a person would have a hard time cashing in on them since there is no fixed value on "colored gems."

It was in just such an operation that Alonzo found a niche. In return for providing salesmen and leads, Alonzo was given a piece of the business, right up there with the two principal owners. Indeed, for the first time in his life he had a real job. Not a great one, admittedly, but a job nonetheless.

"It's on the verge of being legal," Alonzo protested under a grilling by Critchley. "Compared to the things I've been into in my life, it was legal."

But Alonzo's success was not to last. The company had problems—not the least of which, he said, was DiNorscio.

It started with a dispute over the ownership.

Alonzo received a telephone call from a man who claimed he had loaned Alonzo's partner money to start up the business. The caller, Alonzo knew, was a relative of "Corky" Vastola—a ranking member of the New Jersey–based DeCavalcante crime family. That caller, Alonzo said, told him he now had a "piece" of the company.

Alonzo had only one place to turn—his cousin. He asked Jackie to intervene.

At a subsequent meeting, Jackie laid down the law. Vastola's relative may have loaned the money, but it was never put into the business. As Alonzo noted, his wayward boss was spending up to a thousand dollars a week on "escort" agencies, and Alonzo speculated that was where the money had gone.

Vastola's relative was not satisfied. He told Vastola, and as far as Vastola was concerned, the money had been loaned to the company, so this was their company. DiNorscio didn't care. He told Vastola, in no uncertain terms, to get lost. He had assumed a proprietary interest in the company. It was now his baby.

Diplomacy was never Jackie's strong suit. Vastola was insulted and decided to take the matter up with the "family."

At this point, Jackie was still something of an independent. Because of his father's position in the Bruno family, he had been allowed to operate almost as though he himself were a member of the family.

Now, Vastola went to the Bruno family with a complaint. As a result, the elder DiNorscio was sent down to Florida to straighten things out—only that wasn't what happened.

Dominick DiNorscio by then a seventy-year-old man, looked like a smaller version of his son: short, fat, with a bulldog face and arms that looked as if they would have been right at home wrapped around someone's neck. And the senior DiNorscio was no more diplomatic than his son. A meeting between him and Vastola ended with the elder DiNorscio storming out of the room ready to explode, grabbing his son by the arm and heading for the door.

"Let's get the fuck out of here," he muttered to Jackie and Alonzo. "Fuck these guys."

Jackie picked up the cue. On the way out, Jackie made his position clear. The dispute had only served to strengthen his resolve. "We're not giving a piece of this business to anybody," he shouted. The problem was, Corky Vastola was a man of influence. And Jackie was not.

So Jackie did what he had done in the past. He called Michael Taccetta for help. Jackie and Michael had been close for years. Even when he was in prison, it was Michael that pulled strings to help out Jackie. Now, Alonzo said, Michael was the only one whom Jackie could count on to go to bat for him.

His call for help was answered. Within days, the "boys from New Jersey" arrived in Florida.

The meeting took place at the Diplomat Hotel in Hallandale Beach, Florida. Attending the session, Alonzo said, would be Taccetta and Tommy Ricciardi, an associate from New Jersey who knew Corky well. The others at the meeting would be Jackie DiNorscio and Anthony Accetturo and his majordomo, Frank (Goo Goo) Suppa.

It was early in the morning when Alonzo and Jackie arrived in the company of one of Alonzo's business partners, Mitchell Aron. Alonzo waited in the coffee shop while Jackie used the telephone and called up to Michael's room. A half hour later, Michael and Tommy came down.

Alonzo hugged them. It had been a long time since he had seen them. Jackie did the same.

While they were waiting, Suppa also arrived. Meanwhile, Anthony entered the building through a dining room at the rear of the coffee shop. The men exchanged embraces. It had been a long time since they had seen each other.

But this was a business meeting, not a social occasion, and they had things to talk about.

There was a brief discussion, and Jackie turned to Alonzo. "Take Mitch and go back to work. I'll talk to you later."

Alonzo left. And the four men who remained discussed the future of Aron and Aron.

The meeting lasted several hours. When it was over, Accetturo was hot. He didn't like the way Vastola was behaving. Vastola had clout, but Anthony was supposed to be the big cheese in this area of the world—and Vastola wasn't recognizing that. He was trying to place a lock on all the "phone room" operations—he was trying to make the rules himself.

"Nobody," Accetturo snarled in response, "nobody puts a fence around my fence."

But Accetturo didn't do anything for nothing. He had decided to intervene on behalf of DiNorscio, but in return he wanted something. What he wanted was DiNorscio himself.

"He wanted Jackie to be with him," Alonzo said. "Jackie had to agree to be with him and to be made into his crew and to do some work for him."

DiNorscio was more than agreeable to the deal.

Goo Goo Suppa made the arrangements. He went to New York to set up a "meet" with the bosses of the respective families, and approximately one month later, Suppa and DiNorscio flew back to Manhattan for the final sit-down.

Jackie was nervous. He was out of favor with his own family, the Bruno organization, and now he was supposed to be shifting alliances to the Lucchese group so that he could block a takeover of the gem business by the DeCavalcante family. Needless to say, it was not a confidence-building situation.

Jackie was afraid to go. Although it was too late to back out, he was half-afraid that the entire trip might be a setup, and that the bosses were leading him into a trap.

Before he left, he turned to Suppa.

"If you're bringing me to a bad spot," he grumbled, "I'll be waiting in hell for you with a bat."

But the meeting went as planned. When it was over, the beef had been resolved in Jackie's favor. Nonetheless, the decision was a close one and Suppa had to throw his weight around as a representative of Accetturo. In return, Accetturo wanted something else. In addition to having Jackie become one of his own, he wanted a piece of the business. A big piece—50 percent.

Alonzo sounded almost sad when he recounted the results

of the sit-down in court. The decision may have been in his favor, he said, but the outcome was far from ideal. He knew what Jackie's plans were for the business.

"I knew the business didn't have long to go," he said, and he was right.

For a while, things went on as usual, the only difference being that profits from Aron and Aron were split with Accetturo and Jackie.

One day, Alonzo recalled, Aron was squeezed out.

Jackie called Alonzo aside.

"Your friend Mitchell," he said, "he's got to go."

Alonzo knew what was coming, but he asked the question anyway.

"Why?"

DiNorscio expressed indignation. "He's been robbing you. We caught him stealing."

Alonzo looked askance. "Whaddya mean? How do you know?"

"Listen," Jackie said, "I asked him for a couple of diamonds."

"Yeah?" Alonzo responded, waiting for the second shoe to drop.

"You know what he did?"

"What?"

There was outrage in Jackie's voice. "He gave them to me. He gave me two diamonds out of inventory. Three grand worth."

Alonzo waited for Jackie to make his point.

"If he did that for me so easily," Jackie said, with what was to him impeccable logic, "how many times has he done it before? If he'll rob you here, he'll rob you down the line."

Alonzo could only wonder in admiration at the reasoning.

Things did not go well for the company after that. Bit by bit, pieces of the company were eaten away. New people were put on the payroll, and some even got cars to drive. One such person was an individual known as Tony Chocolate.

"Did he do any work for the business?" Alonzo was asked by a government prosecutor.

"Yeah," Alonzo replied tartly. "He showed up."

"What did he do?" the prosecutor demanded.

Alonzo looked at the government lawyer. "He showed up," he repeated.

Jackie, he said, still wasn't content.

He began robbing the business himself. It started when Jackie secretly opened a competing company and started siphoning off salesmen and customers. As a result, Accetturo was being cheated out of his cut of the proceeds.

As Alonzo recounted this story in court, Accetturo turned to look at Jackie. This was news to him. Accetturo only stared silently, his eyes hooded in thought, and then turned his gaze back to the witness.

"He was robbing from everybody," Alonzo continued.

By late 1984, it had all ended. The state of Florida began investigating the business and subpoenaed the records. The license to operate was taken away. But before the records could be seized, Alonzo said, Jackie came up with a solution to halt the investigation—or at least leave authorities with nowhere to go with it.

It was a simple solution, but effective. They arranged a robbery and stole the company records.

For Alonzo, it was the end of more than just a business. It was the end of his only chance to make it on his own.

He began using drugs and drinking more heavily than ever—wallowing in his resentment toward the man he blamed for it all: Jackie.

"I felt that I had been robbed," he said. "I wanted to sell the diamonds. I seen them just trying to hold me down. It was a resentment that I held. It ate away at me like a cancer for a year.

"And on February tenth, I shot Giacomo DiNorscio. . . ."

The words "I shot Giacomo DiNorscio" had all the impact of a boulder being tossed into a lily pond. The ripples spread outward, washing over everyone in the courtroom.

This was the incident that had begun it all. This was the incident that had turned Alonzo from a swaggering, street-smart "wiseguy" into a frightened government informant, from a cocky punk who shot courage into his arm with a hypodermic needle to a quivering mass of raw nerves who was turning against all those he had known and trusted in a desperate attempt to buy his own salvation; he was turning to the men who, for an entire lifetime, had represented the enemy.

But now it was too late. He could never go back. He had

broken the code of silence and had become forever an outsider to the underworld he had known and inhabited for over forty years.

On the witness stand, he had told his story. In exquisite detail, he had implicated the bosses of organized crime in an array of criminal acts. It was something that could never be taken back or forgotten. He had told secrets that were never meant to be told. He could never go up to these men afterward and beg their indulgence. He had committed sins for which there could be no forgiveness. And wherever the government agents put him, in whatever life he would lead, under whatever name he would be given, Joseph Alonzo would have to live with this knowledge.

But his immediate ordeal was not over yet. Testimony as a government witness is only the first part of an informant's obligation. The second part is even harder. He must face up to interrogation by the lawyers for the very men he is attempting to help convict.

It most cases, the prospect of facing a grueling cross-examination at the hands of a skilled defense attorney can be forbidding enough. But in this case, there were twenty-one persons waiting to take on Joseph Alonzo and place his words and his life under a microscope and expose his innermost secrets to the world.

And as Alonzo looked out into the sea of faces that stared back at him from the courtroom, he could only wonder what was coming next.

It was probably better that he did not know.

17

As outlined by the witnesses in the trial, life was good for Jackie DiNorscio in the autumn of 1985.

His cocaine business was booming. He had a Rolls-Royce and two Mercedes Benzes (although he only registered one and kept switching the plates on the other to save on the registration fees and taxes), and he had drained Alonzo's gem business dry.

He was hitting the nightspots with beautiful girls on his arms, sometimes two at a time, and he was taking them home to bed, sometimes two at a time.

On one occasion, before he swallowed Aron and Aron whole, he had swaggered into the offices of the company and called a staff meeting. It was his idea of a motivational pep rally.

"I'm already a millionaire from my other businesses," he declared, adding in a half-audible mutter, "whatever they may be." The array of salespeople and clerks, who were trying to eke out livings selling gemstones by phone, could only stare with wonderment at this figure. They thought he was the boss, although no one was quite sure why. But they had their suspicions. And now, Jackie was confirming them. "But I want everyone else here to make money"—he paused for effect—"I'd like to see a couple of other millionaires. . . ."

The gem business, he told them, was a legitimate business. But then he added the zinger.

"Anybody that doesn't want to do this and wants to be a wiseguy—if they have the courage, they can come with me."

Jackie was invincible; no one could touch him. Or so he thought.

On February 10, 1985, Jackie was sleeping off the effects of one of his wild nights of debauchery. He had been out at a local discotheque with a couple of friends and their girlfriends and had brought the party back to his house. It was late, but for Jackie, time meant little. He was doing cocaine. He had two girls with him. Jackie insisted on playing backgammon, making his plays between toots of cocaine.

When the sun came up, Jackie was still seated at the backgammon table with one of the girls, still coked to the gills. The second had fallen asleep.

There was the usual ritual of moaning and groaning as the various guests tried to pull themselves together to face the day. The second girl asked for a ride home.

Joey Alonzo had not been at the party. He arrived early the next morning in the company of Jackie's friend, Alan Amador.

Joey and Jackie were cousins, their mothers were sisters. But Joey and Jackie had been more than just relatives; they had been friends. In many ways, they were like brothers. For thirty years, they had played together, hung together, partied together, fought together, and got busted together.

On February 10, 1985, Jackie DiNorscio was probably the closest person in the world to Joey Alonzo. But in Joey's state of mind, that didn't count for much.

When Joey showed up at the house, he was in less than tip-top condition. He was coming down from a high, and the aftereffects were not pleasant.

Al was talking to Jackie from his car phone and mentioned that he had picked up Joey.

"No, no," Jackie stammered, "don't bring him over here."

Al knew Jackie had a girl with him and didn't need Joey as a chaperon.

"I'm on my way to my house," Al responded. "I can't take him there. You know why."

The "why" was drugs. Al was holding Jackie's stash of cocaine, and they couldn't afford to let Joey anywhere near it.

Al decided to stall to give Jackie time. He turned the car around and headed back to his own apartment complex and parked it in the driveway. He left Joey sitting in the car while he went up to his place. After picking up some coke, he phoned Jackie and said he had no choice. He couldn't bring Joey up to the apartment, and he couldn't stay in the car all day. Like it or not, he was bringing Joey over.

There was a reason why Joey wanted to see Jackie that morning. He was broke and needed money.

When the pair arrived at the apartment, Jackie's shot at romance was over. The second girl wanted to go home. Jackie thanked her, slipped her two hundred dollars and sent her on her way.

Joey looked at the money. This was his chance.

"I'm a little short," he told his cousin. "How about ten bucks to see me over."

Jackie was out of it. The effects of the coke were just beginning to wear off. "No," he told Joey.

Joey began to fume.

As the hours passed, Jackie collapsed in a heap in his bedroom. Exhaustion had swept over him like a wave. The artificial energy from the drug had kept him going through the night. Now all he wanted was sleep.

Joey sat in the living room. The television was on, and Jackie's daughter, Rosalie, was home. After a bit, she got up and went to her room to take a nap.

The television continued to blare. There wasn't much on, but the noise was distracting. Joey just sat. And the bitterness he had harbored for the past year began to eat at him.

He had had something. It wasn't much, but it was his. And Jackie, great, boisterous, greedy Jackie, Fat Jack the glutton, had taken it away. Now he had nothing.

Except a gun.

It was a small gun, a .22 caliber, the kind favored by the mob. They don't make much noise, and the bullet flattens out when it hits bone and ricochets around in the body, tearing up organs. It doesn't have much stopping power, but it will kill quite efficiently. And this was also a professional weapon—it had a silencer.

Joey sat on the sofa as the television droned on and absently screwed the silencer onto the barrel.

Jackie had handed two hundred dollars to a girl he had probably never seen before and probably would never see again, but he wouldn't give his own cousin ten bucks. Joey was angry enough to kill—and that was what he tried to do.

Carefully, Alonzo got up from the sofa and crept to his cousin's bedroom door. He pushed it open slowly and peered in. Jackie was lying on his bed, faceup, his mouth open and snoring loudly.

Joey walked up beside his cousin. There was only hatred and anger in his mind as he leveled the pistol at Jackie's head. He wanted to blow out his cousin's brains. He squeezed the trigger.

There was a soft *pfft* that was loud in the silence of the room.

The bullet slapped into Jackie's face just below the jaw and lodged in his throat.

The great hulk on the bed thrashed and rolled over, still breathing.

Joey leveled the gun a second time at the swell of Jackie's back. He squeezed the trigger again.

The great body shuddered a second time. Now, Jackie was fully awake. He lumbered to his feet.

He looked at Joey in wide-eyed amazement. He had often thought about death, but never at the hands of his cousin. He held out his hands to his assailant. "Joey," he cried, his voice hoarse and thick with blood from the wound in his throat. "What are you doing? I love you."

Joey just pulled the trigger again. And again . . .

In the courtroom, Joey Alonzo related the details of the shooting to Michael Critchley.

"You wanted to blow out his brains. Is that not a fact?"

"Yes."

"You did not even give him a chance, did you?" Critchley asked, with audible contempt in his voice.

"No," Alonzo said quietly, almost in resignation. His hand was near his mouth, and he was keeping his face down, his eyes averted.

"This was the person who was the closest person in life to you, correct?" Critchley sneered.

"That's correct," Alonzo said, in a half-sob.

"This was your brother, almost?"

"That's correct."

"You shot him, but you missed. You didn't get his brains. You got him in the jaw. Is that correct?"

"Yeah."

"And you know the bullet was lodged in his throat?"

"That's what I was told, yes. . . . I haven't seen the scar, but I imagine there is one there."

Critchley walked over to where Jackie was seated against the far wall.

In a loud, derisive voice, he called out to Alonzo as he gripped DiNorscio's shoulders.

"Do you want to take a look at it?" He continued, "You shot him four or five times, and you left him to die. Correct?"

Alonzo had no choice but to answer. His responses were being recited almost by rote.

"That's correct."

"You did not even give him a chance. You shot him in his sleep, correct?"

"Yes, that's correct."

Critchley waved his arm at the witness in a broad, sweeping gesture of dismissal. "I thought you were a tough guy for thirty years."

"I never said that," Alonzo muttered.

"A wiseguy?" Critchley corrected.

"Yes," Alonzo admitted, he had claimed that.

"Would you say on February 10, 1985, you showed your true character by committing a great act of cowardice?"

Alonzo took the hand away from his mouth and looked directly at Critchley.

"I think," he began, "on February 10, 1985, after over a year of resentment and hate for him for robbing me and holding me down"—he paused—"I had reached a point where I decided to take Mr. DiNorscio's life."

Critchley walked toward the witness, his voice loud and

commanding. "Isn't what you just gave me a justification in your own mind for committing an act of cowardice?"

Alonzo lowered his gaze. "Yes."

Critchley turned away, his back to the witness, the attorney looking into the eyes of the jurors as he spat out his comment.

"Even a hunter gives an animal a chance. You didn't even give him a chance. . . ."

Joey was out of his mind with desperation. He had just gunned down his cousin, and he had to get out. He raced out of the house.

He ducked into the parking lot of an apartment complex next door. He still had the gun in his hand and realized he had to get rid of it. He spotted a cluster of ferns near a black olive tree and tossed the automatic down near the base of the tree. Then he ran across the parking lot.

A man and woman were standing near the next building, washing their car.

Alonzo was out of breath, his voice raspy. And there were wet stains on his pants, dark and sticky. It was blood.

He was almost incoherent as he approached the couple. They looked at each other. Clearly, he was in need.

"Will you call a cab?" Alonzo asked the couple. It sounded as though he had come from cheering at a football game; his voice was hoarse, and he was gasping for breath.

The man walked Alonzo to his apartment and left him at the door. He walked to the phone and made the call. Alonzo thanked the man and walked back outside. He was breathing easier now.

"Can I have a cigarette?" he asked. Again, the man obliged, and Alonzo walked over near the corner of the building to wait.

When the cab arrived, police and rescue vehicles were already at DiNorscio's house.

DiNorscio was lying on the living-room floor in a pool of blood, and a trail led back to the bedroom. The silencer was lying beside the bed on the floor.

A police alert was issued almost immediately. White male, forty to forty-five years old; five foot eight inches tall; curly dark hair, barefoot, and wearing a light blue jogging suit. Armed with .22-caliber handgun.

Alonzo was aware of the sirens next door, when the cab pulled up in front of the apartment complex where he was waiting. Shaking, he pulled open the cab door and jumped into the rear seat. He stammered out an address of a friend in North Miami Beach.

He had wanted to grab some cash before he left DiNorscio's house, but there wasn't enough time. He could only hope that his friend could loan him something when he got there.

Alonzo was perspiring heavily. He was nervous. So was the cabdriver, who had seen the police cars and guessed that his fare had something to do with the commotion. As they pulled up to a light, the driver suggested that Alonzo might be more comfortable up front. He actually planned to let Alonzo out and then floor the accelerator and take off, stranding him there. It didn't happen. Instead of getting out, Alonzo climbed over the front seat.

When the driver looked over, he could see the bloodstains.

The radio barked out a message. The driver picked it up.

"I'm on my way to Miami," he said into the microphone. Alonzo looked agitated. The driver was worried.

The dispatcher was aware something was up. The message wasn't right.

"When you get clear," he said, "give me a call. We have a personal message for you."

The car sped down Route 95. Traffic was heavy, and the driver and passenger sat in silence.

"Get off here," Alonzo suddenly declared as they neared an exit. "Then I can get your money faster."

The driver eyed him warily.

"Don't worry," Alonzo said, irritably. "I'll get your money."

After a number of turns, they found the address. Alonzo got out. "I'll be back with the money," he said, and slammed the door shut.

The driver watched him go up to the house and pound on the door. Eventually, someone opened it. Alonzo took the cigarette he had in his mouth and tossed it into the grass and entered.

A few moments later, he walked out of the house and back to the cab. He had twenty-four dollars in his hand.

"This is all he's got in the house," Alonzo told the driver.

The driver was pissed. It was just as he thought—not nearly enough to cover the fare. "I'm tired of taking a bath for everybody else's problems."

Alonzo was calm now, and he just looked the driver in the eye. There was something menacing in his voice. "I'll mail you the difference . . . but why don't you just take this. . . ."

The driver took the money. As he drove away, the supervisor was on the radio. They wanted the address. So did the police. . . .

Alan Amador was at home around 6:00 P.M. that night when the door to his apartment burst open. It was two friends of Jackie's, Manny and Patty. They were looking for Joey.

"Are you hiding him?" they demanded.

"I don't know what the hell you're talking about," Al shouted back.

Patty rummaged through the apartment, while Manny kept Al by the door.

"What's going on?" Al demanded. The two men had guns, and he was beginning to get worried.

"We're lookin' for Joey," Manny said. "He shot Jackie." He paused to catch his breath. "If we catch him, we're going to kill him. . . ."

But they didn't catch Joey. The police did.

Jackie recovered quickly, picking up the partying where he'd left off—at least for a time. Jackie didn't want to be alone.

From his hospital room, he issued orders: Bring me women; they were brought. He wanted cocaine. It was brought.

He also never stopped his business. Even from intensive care, he called his contacts. He had a hole in his throat from a tracheotomy, and he gurgled when he talked. But the phone was always in use. And before long, Jackie was back. . . .

Joey was in Dade County Jail when he saw Jackie again. He was swathed in bandages on his hand and around his neck.

Jackie pointed to the wounds.

He wasn't going to prosecute, he told Joey. He had signed

a statement that Alonzo was not the man who had shot him. He gave Joey a hundred dollars and said, "I don't think we're going to see each other again."

Joey watched the fat man leave. He had made a mistake. He had left him alive. And now, he knew in his heart, he had been sentenced to death.

That was when he told the police to call the FBI.

The next time Joey Alonzo saw Jackie DiNorscio was in 1987, in federal court in Newark. It was not a pleasant reunion, but Jackie must have felt some sense of satisfaction on the morning of April 29. He was finally getting his turn to confront his chief accuser, the man who had once tried to kill him.

Lumbering to his feet, Jackie waddled across the courtroom to the podium and began rustling through a sheaf of papers in a manila folder.

On his way over, he turned to whisper to several of the defendants. He had a wide grin on his face. The spotlight was on him, and he was loving it.

Alonzo was already in the witness box when the jury filed in. They were almost as eager as Jackie. Also, word had spread, and the audience was packed. Reporters lined the front rows of benches, their pens and pads on their laps. This was going to be a show. And Jackie was to be the star.

Ackerman was formal and proper as he introduced the defendant to the jury. But he could only wonder at what Jackie had in store.

"Ladies and gentlemen of the jury," Ackerman said, "Mr. DiNorscio will now cross-examine Mr. Alonzo." He paused for a moment and then added by way of explanation, "Mr. DiNorscio is representing himself."

He gestured to the defendant. "Mr. DiNorscio."

"Your Honor," Jackie replied, "could you inform the jury I'm not a real attorney?" There was a murmur of laughter from the jury and spectators. No one could have mistaken Jackie for a professional lawyer.

"Judge," he started in again, "before we get started, I'd just like a little advice on something. Like, in other words, I know there's no cursing in the courtroom, right, Judge?"

Ackerman looked concerned.

"There's what?"

"There's no cursing in the courtroom, right?"

Ackerman passed his hand over his face. This was not starting well at all. "Hopefully," he said.

Jackie was undeterred. "The reason I was saying that," he explained, "I was going to give an example—like Mr. Alonzo's letting the government do to me what the butcher did to my wife. . . ."

Jackie's opening remarks about the butcher and his wife were still fresh in the jury's minds; there was no stifling their laughter.

"There's a couple of things I want to get straight," Jackie began.

"You're here to ask questions," Ackerman admonished, raising a finger at the defendant. "You may proceed, sir."

"Your Honor," DiNorscio said, fumbling for words, "if I don't explain this just a little bit—like, in other words, if I say butcher, you know what I mean—and I don't want to be butchered any more than I've been."

Jurors were rolling their eyes and putting their hands over their mouths to stifle outright laughter.

The prosecution was fuming, and Ackerman was becoming irritated.

"Just ask questions, Mr. DiNorscio," the judge warned.

"Okay," Jackie promised. Then he turned to the jury. "Ladies and gentlemen, I request your indulgence just for a minute."

Assistant U.S. Attorney Joseph Braunreuther got to his feet. He brushed his hair back from his brow. "Excuse me, Your Honor," he said. "Judge, if possible, this is a very serious matter, a very solemn matter . . . I ask the court—"

DiNorscio cut him off. "I'm just letting the jury know," he protested.

Ackerman waved DiNorscio to silence. "I'm listening to Mr. Braunreuther, please."

"Excuse me, Your Honor," the prosecutor continued. "I would just ask Mr. DiNorscio to limit himself to the proper scope of cross-examination—which is to ask questions of the witness."

"I told him that twice," Ackerman assured him. "That's all we want—to ask questions."

"What is he saying?" DiNorscio asked belligerently.

"He's saying what I said to you," Ackerman thundered, "ask questions, that's it."

And that is exactly what DiNorscio did.

"Joey," he said, turning to face the witness, "isn't it a fact that you blame me for everything except the Chicago fire?"

The jury laughed again.

Jackie looked around for something. He spotted a water pitcher and asked if he could have a cup. The judge directed his clerk to hand a glass of water to the defendant, and Jackie continued.

"Joe," Jackie asked, "how come you've been calling me Giacomo instead of Jackie? For forty-five years, you've been calling me Jackie. They tell you to say it?"

Alonzo fumbled for a response. He sat sideways in his seat, avoiding looking directly at the defendant. "Your name is Giacomo," he muttered.

Jackie shuffled through his papers again, dropping some to the floor. It was an effort for him to bend down to pick them up. One of the attorneys seated behind him did it for him and handed him the documents.

"Joe," Jackie said, obviously reading from notes, "is it true that you're sorry that you're testifying and lying against me here today?"

Alonzo rubbed his chin. His voice was raspy and dry. "Ah, I'm sorry that I'm here testifying, and I'm not lying here today. You know that."

"And I'm sorry I asked you that question," Jackie muttered in an undertone.

Looking up at the witness, he began again. "Joe, all of our lives when we lied to each other, we never looked each other in the face. That's when we knew we were lying. You haven't looked at me once during this whole trial. You know that?"

There was a moment of silence, and then Alonzo spoke up. This time he looked Jackie in the face. "I feel real bad for having shot you. I know I was wrong, and there's no way I'll ever be able to make that amends—and it does bother me to look at you, Jack."

Jackie rambled on a bit about the shooting, told him about his wounds, the tracheotomy (he called it a "triganomamy") and how he gagged "agh, agh, agh" when he tried to speak. "I hurted, Joe," he said.

He looked at the witness, leaning on the podium for support.

"Did you say I was the closest person in the world to you at one point?"

"On a number of occasions," Alonzo said, his voice low, his head down. "I said that a lot."

"You could have fooled me," DiNorscio muttered.

Jackie made some comments about "signals" passing between the prosecution and the witness.

"You're paranoid, Jack," Alonzo said.

"You're the one that's paranoid, Joe. I'm just a little nervous; this is my first cross-examination." He grinned slyly and turned to the jury. "I know you can't tell, though. . . ."

As he progressed with his questioning, Jackie went back again to the day of the shooting.

"You remember when you came in my house, I was sleeping, and I was sleeping on my stomach—you shot me once, went for my head, but you got me in the jaw and once in the back, and I got up." He looked piercingly at Alonzo. "What did I say?"

Alonzo kept his face averted. His voice was barely audible. "Ah, 'I love you, Cuz.'"

"Then you shot me three more times."

Jackie picked up the folder of papers in front of him and pushed them aside.

"Joey," he asked quietly, "in spite of everything, you believe I still love you?"

Alonzo stared at DiNorscio for what seemed forever. The courtroom was still.

The witness shook his head and averted his eyes once more. "No," he said.

Jackie pointed to the notes.

"You know," he said, "forget these papers." He pulled himself upright behind the podium and stepped away from it in clear view of the witness. "Hey, Joe," he called, his voice sounding as if he was back on the streets instead of in the courtroom, "you came into my house and you shot me, and my daughter was in the next room; right, Joe? Was she?" Without waiting for an answer, he rushed ahead. "When you shot me the third time, I held you the last two times for you to shoot me, didn't I, Joe? Didn't I, Joe?"

Alonzo appeared to retreat. "I don't understand your—"

"When I was holding you back," DiNorscio shouted, stepping closer to the witness, "I let you put those other three shots in me, didn't I? Because my daughter was in this next room. Didn't I yell, 'Get out of the house!'?"

Alonzo remained silent.

"Joe," DiNorscio said, "if you got me, you would have killed her too?"

Alonzo kept his head down. He was playing with a pencil on the table in front in him. "I don't remember—"

DiNorscio stepped closer.

"Was she in the house, Joe?"

"You were the only one I had anything against."

Jackie raised his eyebrows in a broad gesture.

"Just you and I? Joe, was my daughter in that house?"

"Yes," Alonzo said in a small voice.

"Would you have killed her too, if you got me, Joe?"

"No."

No?" Jackie asked incredulously. "What was you going to do, leave her around? You know my mistake? Trying to come in here and act like a lawyer and a comedian." He swept his hand, gesturing to the full courtroom. "These other lawyers got you, Joe."

He paused and was silent for a moment. Then he lowered his voice. "I ask you for your own sake and mine and everybody in this courtroom, tell the truth here, Joe, tell the truth, Joe."

Ackerman cut in—this was not exactly proper cross-examination. "Is there a question before the witness?"

DiNorscio ignored him.

"Just tell the truth, Joe."

Ackerman was becoming agitated. He didn't want a scene, but this was out of line. "Just ask questions," he shouted. "Please, Mr. DiNorscio, just ask questions."

DiNorscio was oblivious to the court's warnings.

"Is it you're trying to save yourself? Is that what counts here, Joey?"

Alonzo could barely be heard. "I told you the reason what I'm here for is that I feared for my life."

Jackie pointed to the prosecution table, his finger shaking with emotion.

"You really think these people are going to stick with you for the rest of your life?"

Alonzo stammered, "I don't . . . I haven't thought about that, Jack." He looked up at his cousin. "I know I thought you'd stick with me for the rest of my life, and you sold me out and robbed me. . . ."

"You know in your heart there's only one reason why I'm here today. . . ." he said, his voice almost tearful.

DiNorscio just looked at him with undisguised contempt.

"You're here because you're a washout, Joe. . . ."

Ackerman was becoming livid. "Just ask questions," he boomed. "Just ask questions."

DiNorscio turned away.

"Do you know who paid for your mother's funeral, Joe?"

Alonzo muttered, "Insurance."

DiNorscio swiveled back to look at his cousin, who appeared to be trying to draw himself up behind the protection of the desk. "Are you aware that I'm the one that paid for your mother's funeral?"

"I don't believe that," Alonzo shot back.

Jackie pointed toward the spectators. "Ask your sister. She's right there in the audience."

Alonzo kept his head down. "If you did," he muttered, "thank you."

"Did you come to the funeral that time? If we had it arranged for you to come, would you come?"

The listeners had to strain to hear the reply.

"No," was all Alonzo said.

DiNorscio abruptly picked up his folder of notes from the podium. There was anger in his voice. "Your Honor," he said, "I'm sorry for what I did here today." He walked away from the podium slowly, heading toward his seat by the window. "I can't get next to this guy . . . I don't care to cross-examine anymore."

18

Alonzo was more nervous than he had been since he began his testimonial odyssey. His hands were shaking, his eyes darted nervously around the room, and he fidgeted in his chair. He wanted to keep his eyes on the prosecutors, as he had throughout the direct testimony, doing his best to ignore everyone else. The prosecutors were his friends. But today they would be of little help.

Today was the day the lead defense attorney was going to try to make him into a liar.

The jury filed into the courtroom, and amid a low murmur of conversation from the defense tables, they took their seats. They sensed the drama was about to begin for real.

"Good morning," Ackerman said, nodding pleasantly to the panelists. The jurors scanned the courtroom, looking to see what was coming next. Some looked at the judge and smiled.

"As I indicated to you yesterday when I sent you home," the judge said, "the next item on the agenda is cross-examination by defense counsel." The judge swept his hand in the direction of the attorney who was standing at the podium.

"Mr. Michael Critchley, who represents Mr. Michael Taccetta, will cross-examine Mr. Alonzo."

The judge nodded to the attorney. "You may proceed, Mr. Critchley."

The lawyer straightened his notes and looked at the judge. "Thank you," he said solemnly. Then he turned to the witness.

"Good morning, Mr. Alonzo," he said with a mischievous smile on his face.

"Good morning, Mr. Critchley," the witness said.

It was the last pleasantry that passed between them.

This was the day Critchley had been waiting for. He had laid his foundations and done his homework during the pretrial arguments. He had conducted his investigations and sorted through the documents provided by the government relating to the witness. He knew Alonzo better than Alonzo knew himself—and he was ready to strip the witness bare.

"Mr. Alonzo," he asked, "how long have you been either in the Witness Protection Program or in the custody of the FBI?"

Alonzo pursed his lips in thought, and then leaned close to the microphone.

"I went into the custody of the Witness Protection Program in May of 1985. I'm not quite sure of the date that I got out of the Dade County Jail where I went with the FBI."

According to Alonzo, he was being held in the Dade County lockup on a charge of "attempt to commit a capital offense." In English, that translated to attempted murder. He was charged with attempting to kill Jackie DiNorscio, even though Jackie did not press charges.

After his arrest, Alonzo said, he had asked to speak to the FBI. As far as he was concerned, they were the only ones who could help him.

But Critchley knew differently. He knew it wasn't help he wanted from the FBI, or at least not the sort of help Alonzo had suggested.

The lawyer brought up the name of a local police officer, a Detective Gooding. Alonzo recognized the name.

Hadn't Alonzo first asked something of him? "You asked for drugs, as a matter of fact, did you not?"

Alonzo hesitated. "My recollection is I asked for methadone."

But Gooding couldn't get that for him.

"Did he tell you that he could not get them?"

"Yes, he did."

"And after he told you he could not get them . . . that's when you asked to see the FBI, isn't that a fact?"

Alonzo balked at the suggestion. But Critchley led him through the events that followed his arrest on the shooting charge. He was sick; he was beginning to go through withdrawal.

Withdrawal from what? What had he been taking?

"Cocaine," Alonzo muttered.

"What else?" Critchley demanded.

"Maybe some Valium."

"What else?" Critchley asked again.

"Cocaine and methadone. Maybe some Valium"—he paused, then threw in another—"pot . . ."

Alonzo was becoming wary. Critchley seemed to know a lot about his drug use.

He admitted that he was taking one hundred milligrams a day of methadone. He had gone to a local clinic for a prescription. Although methadone, a synthetic narcotic, is widely used by drug-abuse clinics to help wean addicts off other substances, Alonzo didn't want to get weaned off anything. He had a more practical reason for going into the program.

"I went on methadone-maintenance program when the money ran out. . . ."

It was only the opening chapter of Alonzo's drug story.

Critchley took Alonzo back through the years, to 1956, when he began using heroin, on through his life in and out of prison.

"You said you went to jail and used narcotics, drugs, and alcohol. What did you mean by that?"

Alonzo was becoming testy.

"We all know there is drugs in jail."

Critchley looked at him quizzically.

"When you say 'we,' are you including me?"

Alonzo appeared almost surly. "Yeah," he spat out. "I'm sure you know."

"Okay," Critchley said, "what drugs did you use in jail?"

"Marijuana, cocaine, Quaaludes, and I think heroin once or twice."

"Drugs are available in prison," Alonzo explained. "I became a drug addict. I used drugs. I was an addict. I used drugs. Drugs were available in prison."

Alonzo said he had spent time in four federal facilities: Lexington, Kentucky, in 1978; Danbury, Connecticut, in 1978; Eglin Air Force Base in Florida in 1975, and Allenwood, Pennsylvania, around 1976.

"Of those four institutions," Critchley asked, "did you use drugs in all of them?"

"Yes, I did," Alonzo declared.

Critchley rubbed his hand over his hair and paused. He looked over at an easel that had been set up near the jury box. He weaved his way over to the easel and walked it out into the center of the courtroom so that he could display it to the jury. There was a large white sheet of paper on the easel, and Critchley picked up a black marker and began to make a list.

"You talked about heroin, right? And heroin is '56. You talked about cocaine. You've talked about methadone. You also testified as to Quaaludes. Is that correct?"

"That's correct."

Critchley scratched the names of the drugs on the easel.

"You testified as to Dilaudid?"

"That's correct. . . ."

"You've also taken Demerol. Is that a fact?"

The questioning was beginning to take on an almost automatic quality—Critchley asked, and Alonzo agreed.

"You have taken on occasion Doriden?"

"That's a fact."

"You've taken cough medicine for purposes other than a cough. Is that correct?"

Alonzo was beginning to become amused.

"Of course."

"And you've taken Darvocet?"

"Yes."

The list was beginning to look like an index from a *Physicians' Desk Reference.*

"How about Seconal? You've taken Seconal, right?"

"Have I ever taken Seconal? Yes."

"And you have taken Darvocet?"

"Yes."

"Percodan?"

"Yes."

"Percocet?"

"Yes."

"You've already referred to Valium?"

"Yes."

"You've taken Preludin, have you not?"

The repetition was broken. Alonzo was thinking.

"Ah, I'm not sure," he confessed.

"Well," Critchley asked, "do you know what Preludin is?"

That question, Alonzo could answer.

"Ah, if it's a diet pill, I never took one. I had a prescription for one. . . ."

Critchley picked up with his list.

"And you've also taken Desoxyn?"

"Yes."

"You've taken LSD?"

"Yes, once or twice."

By now the jurors were beginning to snicker. The list had already run over the page on the easel, and Critchley was still going. Considering all the drugs he had ingested, Alonzo seemed more like a laboratory test animal than a witness.

"How about Tuinal?"

"Yes."

"Speed?"

"Well, yeah . . ."

"You have O.D.'d on Mellaril. Is that a fact?"

Alonzo laughed.

"I O.D.'d on a few things. I don't remember Mellaril. . . ."

"As a matter of fact," Critchley suggested, "were you hospitalized September 25, 1971, for an overdose of Mellaril?"

"I was probably hospitalized a few times for overdoses," Alonzo laughed.

"I'll get into those," Critchley said. "I'm talking about Mellaril."

Alonzo shook his head.

"I don't know about Mellaril."

Critchley nodded. He looked at Alonzo and scrawled the name of the drug on his list. "I'll put that down. Just accept my representation. . . ."

"How about Dalmane? Do you remember O.D.ing and being brought to the Martland Medical Center on October 9, 1971?"

"Hard to O.D. on Dalmane," Alonzo quipped.

"Have you taken Dalmane?"

"I could have. A lot of drugs I was on were being prescribed in the seventies by a doctor. I don't know what they were."

Critchley did, however, and he ticked them off.

"Cogentin, Haldol. You also O.D.'d on Librium?"

"That was probably in my system. . . ."

"The question is, you O.D.'d on Librium, is that a fact?"

"Not a fact."

Critchley looked at the witness questioningly. "Do you recall June 27, 1972, your mother taking you to Clara Maas [Hospital]? That is when you O.D.'d on Librium and you ingested rubbing alcohol?"

Now Alonzo showed a flash of recollection. "Librium and alcohol together. Yes. You asked me Librium. Probably other pills I had in me too."

Critchley turned back to his list.

"Librium, I'll put over here."

Alonzo agreed.

"I'll put Librium. I'll put rubbing alcohol." He turned back to the witness. "How often did you take rubbing alcohol?

"I was a sick guy," Alonzo protested. "That was the first time I did it."

Critchley stepped back from his list. The paper was filled with names of drugs.

"I don't have any more room," he said. "Could we just put 'others'?"

Alonzo nodded as the jury tittered.

"Sure . . ." Alonzo said.

Critchley turned to face the witness.

"How often have you lied in your life?" he demanded.

"I could never put a number on it."

"About how many times?"

"Hundreds of thousands."

"Hundreds of thousands?"

"As I said," Alonzo responded, with a masterwork of understatement, "I was no saint."

"Lying comes easy to you, does it not?"

"At one time, it was part of my life. Then it came real, real easy."

Critchley's voice dripped with sarcasm.

"Then, after you came under the eyes of the government, you acquired characteristics of truth and honesty and integrity. Is that a fact? Is that what you're telling us?"

Critchley grinned at the jury, while Alonzo fumbled for an answer.

"Do you know the date that you acquired all these characteristics?" Critchley asked.

Some of the jurors laughed openly.

As the afternoon wore on, Critchley turned back to his list of drugs Alonzo had consumed. And he added a few more, painkillers, barbiturates, and sleeping pills.

"Did you ever have hallucinations from taking drugs?" Critchley asked, in a matter-of-fact tone.

Alonzo's answer was just as matter-of-fact. "Yes, I did."

One of the jurors rolled his eyes. Another rubbed his hand over his face. A third sat quietly with a bemused smirk.

"Can you describe for us the type of hallucination that you experienced," Critchley prodded.

Alonzo scratched his chin as if in thought. "Someone coming to my house that I owed money to—with a gun. I think I hallucinated that. I'm not even sure of that today."

Some of the defendants began to snicker.

"All I know is" Alonzo persisted, "I went to the hospital after that, and they said I hallucinated."

"How about another time?" Critchley asked.

"To be honest with you," Alonzo said, "I thought I heard a voice. . . ."

"What did the voice tell you?" Critchley asked mildly.

"It was Jackie's brother talking to me. . . . He wasn't there."

Critchley cast a look at the jury. They were enjoying this.

"What was Jackie's brother telling you?"

"That—we were just talking. . . ."

But the third example of a hallucination Alonzo gave was not really a hallucination. He just couldn't remember what really happened the day of November 9, 1983.

The other people involved, however, were unlikely ever to forget.

Mary Koptak was upstairs in her Pomparo Beach home

taking a shower, when she heard the noise. Banging, glass crashing downstairs. Grabbing a towel, dripping wet, she rushed out of the shower to the head of the spiral staircase. She took a tentative step down.

"What is going on?" she shouted to the housekeeper, Felice Diaz.

The housekeeper's voice was frantic. "There's a madman trying to break into the door."

The madman was Alonzo. His hair was wild, his eyes were glazed, and he was naked except for a robe, which hung open.

He knocked at the door.

"What do you want?" Diaz called out.

Alonzo just muttered incoherently, his voice rising in pitch.

"Get away from there," the housekeeper shouted.

Alonzo kept banging. The housekeeper was becoming frightened. She called out to her employer, but she didn't answer.

Mrs. Koptak stood on the staircase just staring.

Alonzo was on the steps, holding a log he had picked up from the flower garden near the house, smashing at the leaded-glass insets in the front door.

The glass smashed to the floor, and Alonzo's hand snaked inside to the latch and undid it.

Mrs. Koptak ran upstairs and into a bedroom to call the police. Her housekeeper was already on the phone, dialing frantically. She couldn't get through.

Alonzo walked in the front door.

A small baby was in a playpen on the floor, but it was as if the child didn't exist. Alonzo walked past, and the child began to scream hysterically.

The intruder dropped onto the couch.

The housekeeper dropped the phone and rushed to the baby, picked him up in her arms, and ran back to the baby's room.

Mrs. Koptak crept out of her bedroom to the balcony and peeped down to the first floor.

Alonzo just sat on the couch.

Mrs. Koptak kept frantically dialing the emergency number for the police. Eventually, she got through.

When the police arrived, Alonzo was gone.

Outside, Alonzo ran wildly down the street. A neighbor was cleaning a pool. His robe flying open, Alonzo ran to the man.

"Call an ambulance!" he screamed. "Call the police. I'm dying."

As one of the backup cars responding to Mrs. Koptak's call for help rounded the corner, the neighbor flagged down the patrol car.

"He needs help," the neighbor called out, pointing to Alonzo. "There may have been an accident. . . ."

Alonzo was approached. He was frantic. He shouted; he babbled. "Can't breathe," he muttered.

Felice Diaz was just beginning to calm down when a police officer knocked at the shattered door of the Koptak home.

They had someone in custody, the officer said, and would she come outside to see if it was the same man.

On the street, Alonzo was being loaded into an ambulance, strapped to a stretcher. Felice Diaz walked over to him beside one of the officers.

"Is this him?" the officer asked.

One of the ambulance crew propped Alonzo up so she could see his face. Alonzo looked into Felice's eyes. He was quiet now. He looked at her and just smiled. . . .

In the courtroom, Critchley was asking Alonzo about the incident.

"Do you normally go into homes by throwing a log through the door, or do you ring the bell?" Critchley asked sarcastically.

The jury laughed.

"I was in a panic, Mr. Critchley," Alonzo insisted. "I already testified that I thought I was dying. You would have thrown the log through there too."

"But is it safe to say that somebody inside that house that doesn't know you might be startled if someone comes through their door after a log, rather than either a knock or a bell?"

Alonzo was serious. "Of course. And I feel real bad about that. I mean that."

Alonzo's life was one long "trip," and a bad one at that. Jail, on the other hand, was a kind of refuge, and he described his incarceration at the federal prison facility in Lexington, Kentucky, as "probably the best jail I was ever in, in my life."

Small wonder. There were drugs, even heroin if you wanted it. Alcohol was also available.

Even sex was available—and not the usual jailhouse kind where Big Bubba decides to cornhole some unfortunate ninety-pound object of his affections.

Alonzo had the good, old-fashioned heterosexual stuff. He had a girlfriend.

"While I was in Lexington, I did have sex in jail, yes," Alonzo recalled before Critchley with a trace of wistfulness. And it wasn't just sex—it was love.

"And you had a romance?"

"I went with the same girl for about two years, yes. . . ."

Critchley shook his head, looking at the expressions on the jurors' faces. Some of them were clearly eating this up. It was better than an afternoon soap opera.

"I'll bet you didn't even want to leave Lexington."

Alonzo pursed his lips and nodded in agreement.

"To be honest with you," he said, "there are times when Lexington was a pretty good place."

While at Lexington, Alonzo also took courses: Keys to Selling—he received a certificate for that; and Transactional Analysis, for which he received a diploma. Some of the courses for which he received certificates, he never even attended. He knew the guy who gave out the documents.

One of the courses he did attend, and for which he received a certificate, was Rational Behavior Training. That was while he was passing the time with drugs and sex.

"What did you learn at the Rational Behavior Training seminar?" Critchley asked.

Alonzo grinned. "Judging by my actions after the course, not too much."

As the days progressed, Alonzo became increasingly frazzled.

He was grilled by Critchley about his medical history. He was confronted by psychiatric records showing that he had once been diagnosed as "schizophrenic" and had been given electroshock treatments on at least six occasions. And he was forced to admit that he lied to the psychologist who examined him for the government.

"I probably told him a lot of things . . . a lot of things that were untrue," he said.

"Are you saying you lied to this psychologist?" Critchley asked indignantly.

"I probably did." Alonzo shouted angrily at Critchley. Gesturing at the defendants who lined the courtroom, he shot back, "Remember, if I wasn't a liar and a thief, I wouldn't have known any of these guys."

It was Accetturo, he said, who gave him his first shot of heroin in the back of a candy store. It was Accetturo, he said, who handed him a batch of stolen checks and told him to go cash them. And it was Jackie who took his business away.

Alonzo acknowledged that after turning informant, he was taken good care of by the government. He and his girlfriend, he said, were provided with more than thirteen thousand dollars in hotel accommodations, including room service. He admitted receiving more than eighty-four thousand dollars in government funds and services, in addition to a hundred-dollar-a-day fee for appearing as a witness.

Each morning, he said, Dennis Marchalonis, the FBI agent assigned to his case, would take him to a methadone clinic. The problem was, that only whetted his appetite. When the FBI agent left, Alonzo went on to find something more substantial. He bought other drugs—and he used the FBI's money to do it.

By bus or train, he said, he would leave the hotel where he was staying, and travel to New York City to make a connection, usually in Harlem. There, he would buy cocaine and heroin in what he called ten-dollar "balloons." He would usually buy ten or fifteen of them at a shot.

"I was a heroin addict," he said. "A heroin addict will find a dealer in Harlem if he wants to. . . ."

As the interrogation proceeded, Alonzo became harder and harder to hear. And more nervous. He was beginning to bristle at the incessant questioning, and his answers were becoming more surly and argumentative.

"I told you," he burst out at Critchley, "you know, look—I bought heroin. I used heroin on a daily basis. I don't know how many times. Did you hear my answer?"

Some members of the defense team were speculating how long it would be before he was back on the bottle. Critchley kept up the pressure.

In a mock stage gesture, he cupped his ear and asked that Alonzo speak up. "Is there a reason, Mr. Alonzo," Critchley asked, "you don't want to be heard?"

Alonzo flushed. He was clearly uncomfortable. "I'm nervous. I have to apologize, and I want to be heard and get this over with."

"Would you turn around. . . ?" Critchley suggested.

Alonzo squirmed in his seat. "I'd like to sit the way I am," he said, as he angled himself away from the defendants and in the direction of the prosecution table.

"You don't want to face. . . ?" Critchley asked.

"I want to sit the way I am," Alonzo shot back. "You got me sitting in their laps anyway, what do you care?"

Critchley's cross-examination of Alonzo was taking on all the trappings of a freak attraction at a carnival sideshow.

"Why are you maligning me?" Alonzo pleaded.

"Because you are a liar," Critchley answered.

On the final day of interrogation, anyone passing the courtroom might have assumed someone was trying out a comedy routine.

The jurors, the spectators, and even the judge were roaring with laughter. Even Alonzo couldn't help himself—he began to break up too.

He sat at his desk, rolling his eyes, scratching his ears, banging his fist on the table and staring at the ceiling. Some of the attorneys wondered aloud if he were back on drugs.

Critchley expressed wonder at how much money the government had paid to rehabilitate Alonzo to get him ready for the trial. From rental cars to sixty-five dollar-a-day room-service bills, Critchley ticked off the benefits Alonzo had received.

Holding up one of the government lists itemizing the expenses, Critchley pointed to a medical bill for $3,916.

"I think that was for dental expenses," Alonzo offered.

"That was for what?" Critchley asked in amazement.

"Dental," Alonzo repeated.

Critchley scratched his head and looked at the jury.

"We paid for your teeth?"

Alonzo showed no embarrassment. "Yeah," he said.

But it wasn't only the witness who was beginning to bridle

U.S. Strike Force attorney V. Grady O'Malley prepares to enter the U.S. Courthouse in New Jersey. O'Malley, who spent years preparing the indictment against the New Jersey branch of the Lucchese crime family, had never lost a case.

Assistant U.S. Attorney Joseph Braunreuther was one of the last to join the prosecution team but came to shoulder much of the courtroom work with O'Malley.

U.S. Attorney Thomas W. Greelish outlines the charges against the twenty defendants during a 1985 press conference. *The Star-Ledger*

U.S. District Judge Harold A. Ackerman reflects on the trial during a quiet moment in his judicial chambers. Ackerman was determined to be fair, but the case would become the ultimate challenge for any judge.

Lead defense attorney Michael Critchley (*left*) walks toward court with his client, reputed Lucchese crime family boss Michael Taccetta. *The Star-Ledger*

Defense attorney David Ruhnke (*left*) with his client, Martin Taccetta, Michael's brother, called the consigliere for the Lucchese organization in New Jersey *The Star-Ledger*

Self-exiled reputed crime boss Anthony Accetturo (*left*) with his attorney, Milton Ferrell, Sr. Ferrell's subsequent death would throw the proceedings into disarray as Accetturo fought unsuccessfully to be dropped from the trial. *The Star-Ledger*

The old neighborhood

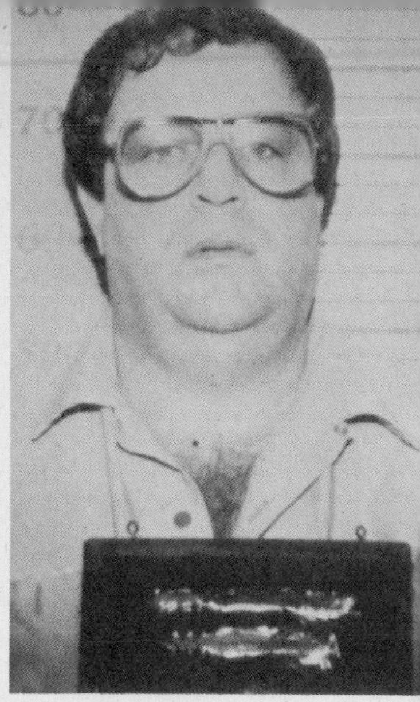

Giacomo (Fat Jack) DiNorscio as a young man and at the time of the trial

Reputed Lucchese family soldier Michael Perna, who authorities claimed acted as an adviser for the organization

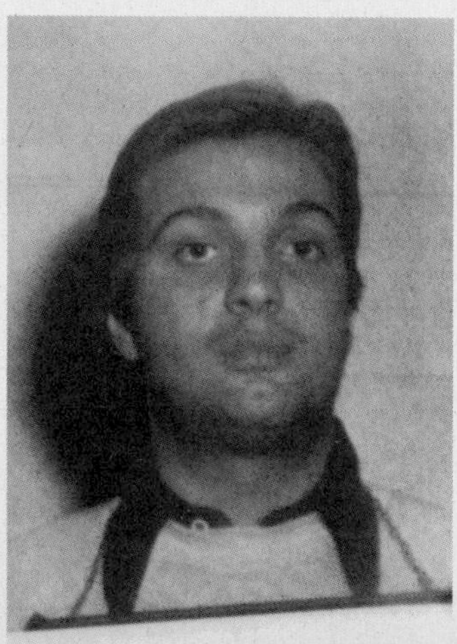

Thomas Ricciardi was alleged to manage the crime family's gambling operations.

Robert (Spags) Spagnola, who prosecutors claimed supervised "the bank" for the Lucchese's sports gambling activities

Authorities alleged that Alfonse (Tic) Cataldo ran the numbers and loan-sharking operations. Like Jackie DiNorscio, Cataldo chose to represent himself at trial but eschewed the jokes for a serious legal defense.

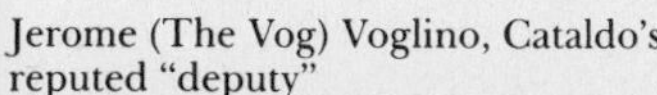

Jerome (The Vog) Voglino, Cataldo's reputed "deputy"

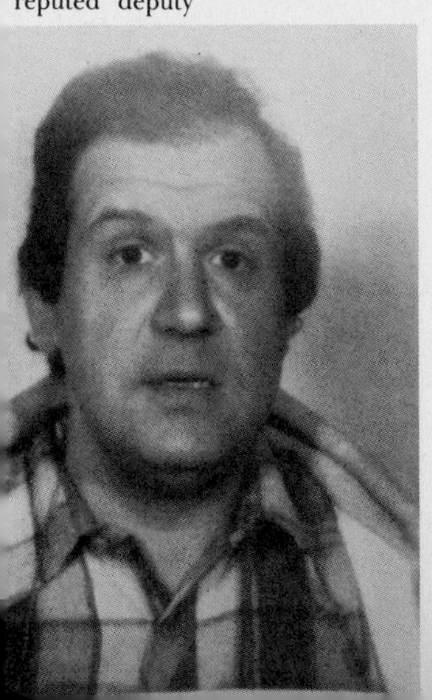

A grim-looking Michael Taccetta is led into federal court in handcuffs by FBI agent Dennis Marchalonis, who supervised the investigation leading to the arrest of the Lucchese family leaders. *The Star-Ledger*

Martin Taccetta is escorted into the courthouse by FBI agents. *The Star-Ledger*

Thomas Ricciardi is brought to court by FBI agents. *The Star-Ledger*

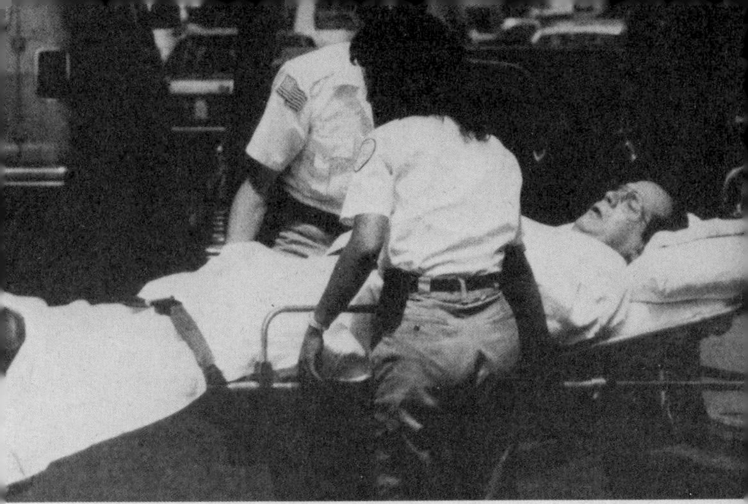

Rescue-squad workers bring ailing defendant Jerome Voglino to court on a stretcher. After Voglino claimed he was too ill to attend the trial, Judge Ackerman ordered a bed be set up in the courtroom to accommodate him. *The Star-Ledger*

The defense team *Maria Noto*

Martin and Michael Taccetta wave jubilantly to a crowd of onlookers following their acquittal on federal racketeering charges. *The Star-Ledger*

Anthony Accetturo plants a kiss of gratitude on the cheek of defense attorney Michael Critchley following the dramatic conclusion to the trial. *The Star-Ledger*

at the questioning. The government was becoming irritated over Critchley's emphasis on the care and feeding it had provided to its prize witness.

There was the matter of a rental car. Authorities had provided Alonzo with a Buick Skylark. The question was, how much did it cost?

"We've heard Mr. Braunreuther in his remarks say about three different things as to what he's representing the facts to be," Critchley said, his voice rising in pitch. "It went from thirty dollars a day to fourteen dollars a day. . . ."

Dennis Marchalonis shoved back his chair and pushed himself away from the prosecution table. He got to his feet and started out of the courtroom.

"Can Mr. Marchalonis wait until we finish?" Critchley demanded.

Prosecutor Joseph Braunreuther was on his feet. "Judge," he said in exasperation, "the man is going to make a phone call for Mr. Critchley, so we can get it right now."

"Calm down," Critchley said to Braunreuther, who was becoming increasingly heated over the dispute.

"Is Mr. Critchley going to direct the court?" Braunreuther demanded.

Ackerman rubbed his face and rolled his eyes. "Right now," he muttered, "I'm suffering from a delusion that I am administering this trial. And I would appreciate it very much if you gentlemen would just stop bickering. Just stop the bickering. . . ."

And as Alonzo's testimony wore on, even DiNorscio managed to get his two cents into the fray during one of the breaks.

"Judge," the fat man said, lumbering to his feet and waving his hand. He pointed at Braunreuther, who was standing by the prosecution table. "He's been interrupting Mr. Critchley's cross-examination all day. I thought this would be an opportune time."

He paused and smiled slyly. "Is it possible I could arrest Mr. Alonzo on a civil matter? Make a citizen's arrest?"

The courtroom began to convulse in laughter as he concluded his request. "See, he violated my civil rights."

When it was over, Critchley had accomplished what he set out to do. The government's star witness had been reduced to a habitual drug user, who had systematically worked his way through a pharmacopia of strange and curious substances and who had used government money to keep on a high even after he agreed to cooperate with authorities. He was a man who had had hallucinations, had heard voices, and who had been a criminal his entire life. It had been Critchley's goal not only to demonstrate that Alonzo's word was worthless, but that far from being a member of "organized crime," his career was one of haphazard, irresponsible acts unconnected with anyone. If he could shoot Jackie DiNorscio, the man who had been "like a brother to him," he could do anything.

Even lie to the jury.

19

Ten years had passed between the time FBI agent Placide Jumonville, alias Joe Sansone, had worked as an undercover agent in Project Alpha and the time he walked into court as a witness in the *U.S.* v. *Anthony Accetturo et al.*

A lot had changed in those years. In the 1970s, Michael and Martin Taccetta were still "the kids," young up-and-comers who were hanging out in an Orange social club and running their fledgling gambling and loan-sharking operations under the tutelage of Anthony Accetturo. But now the Taccettas had grown up. And so had their operation.

This was not the first time Jumonville was testifying about his dealings with the "boys." Years before, he had been a witness against DiNorscio in a case that had helped keep Jackie behind bars. But nothing Jumonville had been through before could have prepared him for what was to confront him when he took the witness stand in the Accetturo trial.

His testimony began innocuously enough. He had been sitting in the audience section of the courtroom when Grady O'Malley announced to the jury, "The government at this times calls Placide J. Jumonville to the stand."

Jumonville rose to his feet and deliberately threaded his way through the throng to the witness chair. He did not look at either the jury or the defendants. When he took his seat, he adjusted the microphone and looked to O'Malley for instructions on how to begin.

Under questioning by the government prosecutor, Jumonville told a story that was straightforward. It was an account of his involvement with DiNorscio, his meeting with Alonzo, and his dealings with the Taccetta brothers.

His job had been to penetrate the Mafia, he told the jury, and specifically to determine the extent of organized-crime control along the New Jersey ports.

It was a twenty-four-hours-a-day job. Weeks would go by without him seeing his family. For the most part, he worked alone, out of touch of any surveillance team, his only contact with his own superiors through telephone and infrequent face-to-face meetings. For two years, he played the role, meeting dozens of people in and associated with organized crime.

At one point, he raised his hand and indicated DiNorscio. "This is Jackie DiNorscio, right over here to my right."

He related the progression of their relationship, from conversations about stolen cars to stolen bonds. And he related his introduction to the Taccettas.

He pointed out Marty Taccetta, who was sitting in court in a blue suit. Marty merely smiled implacably and stared back. Jumonville went on to narrate how he later met with Michael in the Orange social club, where some twenty guys were hanging around playing pool and just hanging out.

"Michael told me he had just gotten off the telephone with Jackie DiNorscio at the prison. And Michael realized why we were there," he told the jury. "He knew it was in connection with the bootleg cigarette business that I had talked to Jackie and his brother about."

"Incidentally," O'Malley asked, "do you see Mr. Michael Taccetta in the courtroom today?"

"Yes," Jumonville answered solemnly, "I do." He pointed out Taccetta, who was hunched over the conference table, taking notes on the testimony.

DiNorscio had touted the Taccettas as "very close" with "Tumac," the name Accetturo was known by on the street. And he had done one other important thing: He had arranged for him to meet with Joey Alonzo.

Essentially, Jumonville was there to corroborate what Alonzo had already told the jury. It was like hearing the other side of the story, and for the most part, the two accounts meshed.

The testimony was relatively brief. It was factual, and it did what it was designed to do—it backed up the government's star witness. What it also wound up doing, however, was providing even more grist for the defense counterattack.

Jumonville had been breaking new ground in his undercover activities. It was something new for the FBI to send an agent deep undercover, and Jumonville had to play it pretty much by ear. His life was on the line, and he couldn't afford to make mistakes.

Now the proverbial chickens were coming home to roost. And armed with stacks of detailed reports prepared by Jumonville during his undercover life, the defense was prepared to pick apart his every move. And whatever eggs he had laid, the defense lawyers planned to hatch right in front of the jury.

One of the first to start warming those eggs was David Ruhnke, the number-two attorney in the defense lineup, the "intellectual" member of Critchley's first-string team.

Smiling, soft-spoken, and immensely reasonable, Ruhnke was a Dartmouth graduate whose tightly curled silver hair contrasted sharply with the devilish glint of his blue eyes. He was able to convey an impression that, if nothing else, the testimony from the government witness had been amusing.

When Ruhnke confronted Jumonville on cross-examination, he began by inquiring a little more closely into some of the "deals" that the agent claimed Jackie had proposed.

"If I'm correct," Ruhnke began, "Mr. DiNorscio, in the first conversation you had with him, said he had exactly one-hundred-and-two deals that he could get you involved in. Is that correct?"

Jumonville nodded. "He made that statement, yes."

Ruhnke looked at him quizzically. "One hundred-and-two deals?"

Jumonville remained firm. "Yes."

Ruhnke shook his head in amazement.

"Not one-hundred-and-one dalmatians; not one-hundred-and-three anything. One-hundred-and-two-exactly deals. Is that correct?"

Jumonville looked resigned. "That's what he said."

Ruhnke then turned to one of the more spectacular "deals" discussed by DiNorscio, a "Nigerian deal" that was some sort of mob swindle related to construction projects in Africa. The details were never made quite clear.

To refresh Jumonville's recollection, Ruhnke quoted from the court transcript of an earlier trial in which that same deal had been mentioned. On this point, even the judge in that proceeding appeared incredulous.

> THE COURT: Now at one point in your testimony, you referred to the Nigerian deal as a three-million-dollar deal, is that correct?"
>
> JUMONVILLE: If I'm not mistaken, I believe it was a three-hundred-*billion*-dollar deal. It was an extraordinary figure.
>
> THE COURT: You are saying three hundred *billion. . .* ?"
>
> JUMONVILLE: Yes.
>
> THE COURT: Not three hundred million?
>
> JUMONVILLE: Three hundred *billion.* I recall it being exceptionally extraordinary in terms of the size of money involved, supposedly involved.

"Yes, sir," Jumonville acknowledged after Ruhnke read the exchange, "that's my testimony."

At that point, Critchley jumped in.

"Do you know how much three hundred *billion* in 1977 would be worth today?" He rubbed his eyes as if to clear away the dream and repeated his question, his voice rising in pitch for emphasis. "You know how much three hundred *billion* would be worth today?"

Jumonville didn't appear fazed. He remained calm as he replied, "I have no idea, sir. I didn't go along with the Nigerian proposal. I really didn't have much of an interest in it. Frankly, I think Mr. DiNorscio's role in that Nigerian deal was like a sponge . . . he was just looking to absorb some of the money."

Then Critchley brought up a potentially telling point.

"Well, as a matter of fact, didn't Mr. DiNorscio ask you on one of your visits to him in state prison to loan him ten thousand dollars for the Nigeria deal?"

"That matter was brought up," Jumonville admitted. "It sure was."

Critchley's point was obvious. As the interrogation continued, he didn't mince words when he gave his own impression of Jumonville's dealings with Jackie. Jumonville, he suggested, had become more than just a "mark" for DiNorscio.

"You were maintaining the image of a mark, is that correct?" he asked with a dramatic flourish. "You know what a mark is?" He paused for effect. "I don't mean a Mark Four or a Mark Five." As several of the jurors looked at Critchley and chuckled, the attorney looked at Jumonville with a wry smile. "You know what a chump is?" he asked. Had the FBI agent been more of a mark than he realized?

There were other areas that Critchley also targeted. He questioned the propriety of an incident in which Jumonville sold pieces of Indian jewelry to an informant, which Jumonville defended by explaining that his dealings in jewelry amounted to a personal hobby—one that probably cost him money in the long run.

But the main focus of Critchley's questioning was yet to come. Jumonville had spent a great deal of time with Alonzo, who, as everyone knew by now, was a drug addict. According to FBI reports on those encounters, Jumonville had been faced with a major dilemma—what to do when Alonzo offered to share his drugs.

According to his own reports, he had been forced at times to accept what was being offered.

"This wasn't a group of Boy Scouts I was dealing with," Jumonville explained. "I was out there working alone with these people. There was no one there to back me up. It was strictly a solo operation."

"Now," Critchley asked offhandedly, "just so I understand it, you used marijuana and cocaine on numerous occasions, isn't that a fact?"

Jumonville acknowledged there were occasions when he was "exposed."

Critchley plowed ahead. Within a week of meeting Alonzo, the attorney charged, "he has you, an FBI agent, using drugs?"

Jumonville admitted he "did take a drag and blew smoke out." But he angrily defended his actions. "At this point in time, I'm an FBI agent acting in an undercover capacity, dealing with an organized-crime member. I have to establish personal credibility and personal security. . . ."

"As a matter of fact," Critchley went on, "there were two marijuana reefers . . . Alonzo has one. He hands one to you. He's saying that it's high-quality smoke. Then he tells you that he likes a man that can appreciate a good smoke." Critchley glared at the witness. "Did he tell you that?"

"Yes, sir," Jumonville said, "I believe he did."

It was Jumonville's first encounter with marijuana, but there were other occasions as well. Critchley demanded to hear about each of them in detail. Jumonville's demeanor appeared to grow increasingly incensed at the questioning, especially when Critchley turned to an incident involving cocaine.

Alonzo had been boasting about his contacts for high-grade cocaine from "people in Florida," and he brought out some of his wares during a visit with Jumonville in the agent's Upper East Side apartment in New York.

It was, the agent said, "the first time I saw cocaine. I had no idea what it was. He [Alonzo] said it was cocaine. I was kind of apprehensive, but he sampled some of it first. I felt it couldn't be poison. I sampled some."

There was a hush in the room. People were beginning to see exactly where Critchley was heading.

"I went in the kitchen and blew my nose," Jumonville continued. "I felt that I had probably inhaled a granular amount. I blew my nose out, and I got a drink."

"Are you saying," Critchley asked, almost winking at the jury as he did so, "that you stored it in your nose?"

Jumonville was firm. "I stored it in my nose." This, Critchley knew, was a physical impossibility. It would be absorbed on contact.

"How, physically, did you get it in your nose?" Critchley asked broadly, playing to the jury.

"I believe that Mr. Alonzo had a dollar bill that he rolled up."

"This was high-quality cocaine?"

"Mr. Alonzo said it was high quality. Ninety-five, ninety-three percent pure."

It may have been Jumonville's first encounter with cocaine, but Critchley noted that it wasn't his last. There was another occasion, this time at Alonzo's apartment. Alonzo was discussing a Florida drug deal and went to his refrigerator and took a plastic bag of white powder out. He poured it into a saucer and began dividing it into thin lines with a razor blade. Then he produced a red plastic straw, inhaled some of the drug, and passed the saucer to the undercover agent.

"And you inhaled the cocaine? Correct?"

"I did inhale the cocaine and—"

But Critchley cut him off. The agent put some on his tongue? Yes, Jumonville admitted, he had tasted it.

Now Critchley began moving quickly—too quickly for the government to react. He stood and approached the witness. "I have a saucer here," he said, raising each item aloft to show the jury, "and I have approximately six ounces of a white powder, and I have a straw and I have a razor blade. Could you just, please, come down, and just show us how the lines were placed into the saucer?"

By now, O'Malley was on his feet. His face was scarlet, and his voice was booming. "Judge," he cried, "I'm going to object to his. . . . There's no need for playacting. . . ."

"Unbelievable!," O'Malley shouted. "I'd like a sidebar. . . ."

He got it. And as the lawyers retired to a spare room at the side of the court to confer with the judge, the argument became heated—at least for some. Critchley had a bag of baking soda, and he wanted the witness to demonstrate exactly how he managed his feat of "faking" cocaine use.

In the middle of the dispute, however, Ackerman suddenly looked up. DiNorscio was lounging against the window, smoking a cigarette.

Ackerman waved everyone to silence. "Wait a second, please," he said. "Mr. DiNorscio, were you smoking just now?"

DiNorscio was candid. "Yes."

"Please," Ackerman said, "this is not a rest room."

Then the argument resumed, and despite O'Malley's protests, Ackerman leaned in Critchley's favor. "Demonstrations are not foreign to a courtroom," he said. "People are asked in homicide cases: How did you hold the gun? Show us how you held the knife or gun."

He overruled O'Malley's objections. "Let's see what he does," Ackerman said. "I'm keeping my options open."

As the trial resumed, Critchley called the witness down to a position in front of the jury. He handed him the saucer and asked him to reenact what had taken place that night. He handed the agent the plastic bag of baking soda.

"Mr. Jumonville," he asked, "can you do it? Can you show a reproduction?"

The agent showed his resolve. "I'm going to do it to the best of my knowledge."

The witness stood just a few feet away from the jury box. He was intent as he emptied the contests of the bag onto the saucer.

"You indicated he used a razor blade to make lines?" Critchley asked.

Jumonville tried to show how it was done. Then Critchley handed him a straw.

"You put that to your nose?" he asked.

"Yes."

"And you ingested?"

"I inhaled some in my nose. I didn't ingest it."

As Jumonville walked back and forth in front of the jury carrying out his demonstration, there were audible snickers from the defense camp. And there were smiles from some of the jurors.

The agent was trying to maintain his dignity but it was a difficult task under the circumstances. But if the jurors thought Critchley had put on a show, they had yet to see the main act, because Jackie was just warming up on the sidelines.

A decade had come and gone since the September day when Jackie had first met Jumonville in a cage in Rahway State Prison. Now, on the day after Critchley's "demonstration," Judge Ackerman gave DiNorscio the nod to stand. "Mr. DiNorscio," he said politely, "you may cross-examine the witness."

Jackie, who was normally seated in a far corner of the defense section, stood with a grin on his round, puffy face, and waddled, more than walked, toward the lectern in the center of the courtroom. Because of Jackie's bulk, some of the other defendants and attorneys had to move to the rear of the courtroom in order to view the proceedings.

Jackie took a moment to settle himself at the lectern, tapping the microphone to be sure it was working.

He smiled at the agent. "Little Joe," he said. "Don't mind me calling you 'Little Joe.' That is how I know you."

Jumonville was not troubled by the name, or if he was, he didn't let it show. "That's correct, Jackie. You used the name before, so I don't see any reason why you can't use it anymore."

Jackie shrugged. "I'm not too smart, so why don't you ask me questions?"

Jumonville was quick with the retort, "You hold your own pretty well."

Jackie was silent for a moment, then walked around the lectern and came a few steps closer to the witness.

"Do you carry your gun with you all the time?"

"On occasions I do, yes."

"Do you have it on you right now?" Jackie wanted to know.

Jumonville looked amused.

"I sure do. . . ."

Jackie looked at the jury and feigned alarm, holding up his arms in a sign of surrender.

"I'm having problems. If I ask you something you don't like, you won't shoot me?"

Several of the jurors began to laugh out loud. Others held their hands to their faces to muffle their amusement.

"I can assure you, Jackie," Jumonville said deadpan, "the thought of shooting you never crossed my mind."

Jackie raised his eyebrows questioningly, as if asking the jurors what he should do. Then he addressed Jumonville again. "Just keep your hands on the desk, okay?"

This time there was no muffling the laughter from the jurors and the other defendants.

Jackie asked Jumonville a few routine questions and then suddenly interjected. "When you first met me, I had a wife, two kids, a nice house and a little dog, right?"

Jumonville appeared confused. The question had come out of left field. "I never visited your residence. My contacts with you were at the penitentiary. I'm not sure. Your family . . ."

Jackie persisted, a bit impatient, "Would it be your information I had what I said? Wife, two kids, nice house?"

Jumonville shrugged. "If that's what you're telling me, sir.

I don't know what your house was like. I know you told me you had two children and a wife. I recall that. But I can't recall . . ."

DiNorscio grimaced. "Well, are you finished?"

"Yes, I am."

Then Jumonville found out what DiNorscio was leading up to—another joke.

"Do you know since then, I'm divorced, wife got the house, kids don't talk to me?"

The prosecutor, Grady O'Malley, suddenly saw what was happening. Angrily, he stood to object. "Judge . . ."

But he wasn't fast enough. Jackie went on, "And the dog bit me."

With that, there was no controlling the courtroom. The spectators, the jurors, and the rest of the defendants were literally rocking in their seats with laughter.

One of the few who wasn't laughing was O'Malley.

"A serious trial, Judge," he protested. "Mr. DiNorscio has succeeded in doing this every time he stands up. I ask the court to admonish him and ask his questions be directed to the witness and stop the comedy routine now."

DiNorscio turned to face O'Malley, who was now flushed with anger. "This whole trial is a joke," DiNorscio said with contempt. "You made it a joke, Mr. O'Malley. . . ."

It was later in the day, on recross-examination when Jackie took the opportunity to question Jumonville again. Only now, the mood had changed. It was as if a cloud had passed over Jackie's mind—a dark cloud. He looked troubled when he stepped to the lectern to begin a new line of questioning. Turning serious now, Jackie accused the agent of taking advantage of Ralph DiNorscio's drinking problem and brought up the abortive and drunken trip to Lewisburg Penitentiary in May of 1977.

"Just one thing, about my brother, Joe," Jackie began. "He wasn't a bad guy, was he?"

Jumonville nodded. "I didn't hold any personal ill will against your brother. . . ."

But as far as Jackie was concerned, the trip to Lewisburg was just one example of how Ralph had been taken advantage of, an accusation Jumonville vehemently denied. The agent was resolute as he defended his actions.

"I'd no intentions of abusing a problem your brother had," he declared. "And I don't feel that I did, sir."

"Joe," Jackie continued as the jury riveted their eyes on him, "I told you many times, leave my brother out of this, didn't I? Many times I told you, leave my brother out."

Jumonville was calm and polite as he responded.

"Mr. DiNorscio, that's not true, because you and your brother had conversations concerning stolen property, automobiles, and other things, wherein you encouraged me and him to both engage in these activities on the outside."

Jackie shook his head.

"Joe, you took my brother to see my father. You knew he was drunk when you left, and you bought him more liquor, and you were bringing some in to my father. And you're an FBI agent, and you're going to a federal corrections institution—"

"I did pick up your brother to visit your father at Lewisburg Penitentiary," Jumonville replied. "I didn't think we should go, because he looked like he was out all night. He was the one that insisted we should go. After I got up there, I talked to him . . . he became belligerent. You know the rest of the story."

"Did you ever get to meet my father?" DiNorscio asked.

"No, sir," Jumonville stated, "I did not meet your father at the Lewisburg Penitentiary." He paused, then added in a loud voice, "But I did meet him in 1980 in New Brunswick—when he threatened me in the corridors of the courthouse."

Jumonville suddenly pointed out to the right rear row of benches in the courtroom. "I see him in court today. I met him once in my life, but I remember his face. He's sitting right in the back."

Jackie turned to peer into the audience and spoke to his father, motioning with his hands.

"Get up for a moment." He turned back to Jumonville, his voice lowered. "My father is seventy-six years old."

The elder DiNorscio, his face stony, his voice hoarse, called out a response to the agent's comment about the threat, as jurors swiveled to see the speaker.

"He's a liar, so what can I tell you?"

Judge Ackerman cut off the exchange. "We don't need any remarks from the audience."

DiNorscio then approached Jumonville, his voice cold and without a trace of humor. "Did you know my father lives in a four-room apartment with my mother, four blocks from the cemetery where my brother is buried? You helped kill him too, Joe."

Jumonville shook his head and stared unblinkingly back at Jackie. There was a stir in the courtroom as he spoke.

"I don't believe I had a hand in your brother's demise," Jumonville said, solemnly. "I think maybe you should look at yourself. . . ."

20

If the testimony of Joseph Alonzo and P. J. Jumonville had provided a kind of historical backdrop for the people and events who made up the framework of the Lucchese trial, the next series of witnesses would attempt to bring that history to life through the stories of their own personal dramas.

The first of these witnesses was Robert Fisher, who had been living with his sister in Waterville Valley, New Hampshire, when he received a telephone call from Jackie DiNorscio. Jackie was in the intensive-care unit at a Florida hospital. He had been given a tracheotomy, and he sounded as though he were underwater when he spoke.

"Bobby," DiNorscio gurgled, "I been shot and almost passed out. . . ."

DiNorscio was difficult to understand. He was burbling more than talking. Gerald Cohen, another of the defendants and a close associate of Jackie, was in the room and took the phone.

"Cousin Joey shot Jackie five times."

Fisher closed his eyes and waited for the other shoe to drop.

Manny Montiero, another associate of DiNorscio, also got on the phone. He was the one to break the news, "Cousin Joey's with the feds. . . ." he confirmed. "He gave them the whole operation. Cousin Joey could put me and everybody else away."

Fisher, by his own account, had been one of Jackie's best customers in the cocaine trade.

A short, fat, balding former butcher with a compulsion toward braggadocio, Fisher was the kind of guy who seemed to know a little about everything. If you wanted to talk sports, he could talk sports for hours. If you wanted to talk guns, he could talk about weapons. And if you wanted to talk about drugs, well, he knew them too.

He had first met DiNorscio when Jackie was traveling through Rhode Island on his way to an evening out in Newport. For Fisher, it was a night to remember.

Jackie had been with a friend of Fisher's, and they had stopped by the house. He recalled that Jackie had been dressed in a yellow suit and was wearing a chain with a twenty-dollar gold piece surrounded by diamonds around his neck. On his wrist was a gold bracelet with his name, "Jackie," spelled in script. He was wearing a diamond pinkie ring.

"It isn't the type of thing that you see in Rhode Island," Fisher later recalled. "It is the type of thing you see on television."

It was on a Friday, June 13, 1986, when FBI and DEA agents from Rhode Island arrived at Fisher's house shortly after 5:00 A.M. Fisher was asleep, loaded from a bout of drinking the night before. The agents rapped on a sliding glass door, and Fisher staggered out of bed to let them in. A DEA agent reached into his pocket, pulled out a small card, and read it to Fisher. It was the Miranda warning: "You have the right to remain silent . . ."

He was ushered into the rear seat of a waiting car. The agent started the engine and headed back toward his office in Providence. After a brief flurry of conversation, Fisher fell silent. He seemed to be thinking.

"Can I cut a deal?" he asked out of the blue. "I don't want to go to jail."

The charges against Fisher accused him of serving as a distribution arm for a narcotics operation controlled by Di-

Norscio. Fisher's way out of the situation was simple. He agreed to talk. He was cooperating, he said, because he realized after his arrest by the FBI "there was no way out of it."

It was shortly after noon on May 20, 1987, when Fisher came to court to tell his story to the trial jury. The first thing he did was to identify DiNorscio. He pointed to Jackie, who was wearing a blue shirt, open at the neck, and then went on to tell of his dealings with Jackie and his friends.

As he related it, it had been a stormy relationship. At one point, he and Jackie had a bit of a disagreement over money. Jackie claimed he owed him. Fisher said he didn't. Jackie responded by warning him that "he was going to put me and my fucking wife in the trunk of the car."

For the most part, Fisher testified, he served as a "mule," ferrying drugs packed into the rear compartments of various cars to New England. Sometimes he drove from New Jersey. On other occasions, he went directly to Florida.

His only efforts to avoid detection were to hide the drugs, and to keep his hair trimmed and his car washed. It worked—he was never stopped.

But there was always the unexpected.

On a trip to Florida, Fisher had already picked up a load of cocaine and was driving along the intracoastal waterway, when he spotted a long-haired girl on a sailboat. There was a car coming in the opposite direction, and that driver spotted her too. She was topless.

Both drivers turned their heads to stare. They were so busy looking at the girl, they didn't see each other until it was too late. "He was checking out this girl," Fisher said, "and I was checking out this girl. We both drove into each other."

Fisher sweated out the situation and, eventually, drove away without the drugs being detected. It was only then that he realized the full irony of the incident. The "girl" on the sailboat, he said, "turned out to be a guy."

Fisher was a natural storyteller. He was clear, colorful, and had a sense of humor that was evident even in what should have been a desperate situation for him. He peppered his testimony with anecdotes. He talked about Jackie's cars, including his Corvette with the "teenybopper" paint job of blue and red flames down the side, and his Cadillacs and two Mercedes Benzes, a black four-door sedan and a red-and-black convertible.

He noted that Jackie had the same New Jersey plates on both Mercedes and asked him why he had identical tags for both cars.

Jackie's reply: "I don't like to pay taxes."

He told how Jackie insisted on sending him out to buy clothes, because he didn't dress well enough for the places Jackie liked to frequent. Jackie wanted to be sure Fisher "wouldn't look like a jerk."

Going out with Jackie was itself an experience. "It was like a movie. Jackie sat there, we all ate, thanked him, had a good time, had wine and had a good time. It was a very good time.

"He knew the maître d', knew everybody, was tipping everybody like he knew them."

They snorted cocaine, and then ordered a feast. A whole new world was opening up for Fisher: "I had some kind of crab they have in Florida where you eat one part of it, like one leg or something, some kind of crab, little necks, steaks with spaghetti sauce on it, all kinds of, like, just Italian things, like cheeses and stuff."

His beverage of choice, however, was vodka. "I don't like Italian wine, can't drink that," Fisher said.

Fisher's stories were compelling and dramatic. The jury was attentive. But it was what he had to say on the following day that was perhaps the most significant of all.

Joe Braunreuther asked Fisher what he had been told by Montiero when the two men met after the Alonzo shooting incident.

"He said that he was concerned that Joey had talked to the feds, and that he was trying to find a way to make what he said to the feds sound stupid. And that he was going to make it look like Joey was a drug addict and that he was a crazy man and he had shock treatments."

Montiero's words seemed almost prescient, for that was what the defense HAD tried to do.

The cross-examination of Bobby Fisher was—by the standards set by the rest of the trial—relatively brief. In a case where some interrogations went on for months, Fisher's cross-examination was positively Spartan—it lasted only six days.

He said he had decided to cooperate as a witness in the case after being interviewed by U.S. authorities in New Jersey.

He denied that a statement, which authorities stressed they did not consider a "threat," that they would consider indicting his wife along with him had anything to do with his alliance with the government.

"When I got to New Jersey," Fisher said, "my lawyer said to me, he says, 'Bobby, do you realize you are involved with racketeering people, gangsters?' And that is when I agreed to cooperate, because I am not a racketeer or a gangster. I was a cocaine dealer."

The testimony was beginning to accumulate, as bit by bit, the government was assembling its case. Alonzo had told his story; Jumonville came in to corroborate it, and then there was Fisher to fill in the gaps that Alonzo's testimony had left.

Outside the presence of the jury, Jackie was the first one to protest.

"Judge," he began, "can I speak in layman's terms?" He touched his head with his finger. "Something confused me here."

He gestured with both hands. "Joey comes in and testifies for the government. And we beat Joey up on the stand.

"Now you have the government bring in an FBI witness . . . and he gets beat up.

"Now," he complained, "we got Fisher coming in to clear up the problems with the government case. . . .

"The thing that concerns me, Judge, is when do you take this case over and see what they are doing? When do you see what these people are doing here?"

Ackerman looked irritated. "What do you mean, 'When do I see what they're doing?'"

"You see it, Judge," DiNorscio declared. "You're the most intelligent man in this courtroom."

Ackerman shook his head. "You said that once. It was patently untrue then. I have an equal opinion about it now."

But DiNorscio was not dissuaded. "Judge, you understand my position here? They have people coming in lying through their teeth to save their own ass. Put an FBI agent on the stand . . . to clean up what Joe did wrong. When do we get some relief in this court, Judge, with what they're trying to do? . . . When are you going to take over this courtroom and stop them from what they're doing?"

Ackerman drew himself up. "I stop any party from doing what they're doing when I think it is legally inappropriate or unfair or highly prejudicial."

"Judge," DiNorscio persisted, "I could see it, and I'm the dummy in the courtroom. How can't you see it?"

Ackerman shrugged. "Well, I guess by your standards, I'm dumber then."

Jackie waved his hand. "If you were out on the street, Judge, that would be true. But . . ."

He never finished his thought. And for his own sake, it was probably just as well.

(Note to readers: The next page will be p.229 due to the movement of the photo section for the paperback edition.)

21

June had begun and spring was fast turning toward summer when the next witness was led into the courtroom. There was an air of anticipation in the room. From the government's perspective, the testimony he would give would lend even more credence to the story sketched by Alonzo.

To the defense, however, he represented yet another lamb being led to the slaughter, to be ripped apart on cross-examination. Already, they were sharpening their verbal knives.

Alan Amador had been in jail in Cincinnati, Ohio, when he was visited by FBI agent Dennis Marchalonis.

Amador, who had begun his career as an auto-body repairman from New Jersey, was alleged to have been an associate of Jackie DiNorscio—one of Jackie's entourage—who assisted him in his cocaine-distribution business in Florida.

As a drug dealer, however, Amador had proved a total bust. The first time he had set out on his own to negotiate a sale, his customers turned out to be federal narcotics agents, who recorded the entire transaction on videotape.

"You're on video," they told him as they identified themselves and made the arrest. "You're a star."

He wound up facing forty years in jail. But Amador had a trait in common with Fisher and the other informants. Once caught, he was more than eager to talk.

Life in Florida with Jackie was nothing if not interesting, according to Amador.

He described Jackie decked out in jewelry, freely snorting cocaine in front of anybody who stopped to notice.

He also told of one of the more memorable dinners with Jackie and two of Jackie's girlfriends. Jackie arranged for one to be seated at one table and the other to be seated at another, and he kept hopping back and forth between the two. While he was with one, he would order his associates to be attentive to the second. Eventually, Amador recalled, "one took a fit because the other one was there."

He described Jackie at home, talking on two phones simultaneously, while half a dozen different people walked in and out of the rooms. Jackie bellowing orders, telling whom to go where. Jackie at a diet center, bedecked in twenty thousand dollars' worth of jewelry and diamonds, yelling and screaming at the help for better accommodations. Jackie taking a table and chairs and setting them in the middle of a hotel lobby and holding court.

"You got to understand, with Jackie, Jackie makes a game and a joke and takes over everything wherever he's at. He became the center of attraction. . . . If anybody would walk in, they would think he was the owner of the place. . . ."

Amador went on to recount the story of Jackie recuperating from his wounds in the hospital after being shot by Alonzo—demanding cocaine and women be brought to his hospital room. From there, he moved on to the subject of Jackie's array of high-tech equipment, including lie detectors and James Bond–style booby-trapped briefcases. The equipment, Amador said, included devices designed to screen for "bugs" and wiretaps, as well as telephone "scrambler" devices similar to those used by government intelligence agencies. The most elaborate, however, was a specially equipped briefcase that was used to transport drug money. According to Amador, it was wired so that if taken away from the owner, it would send out a jolt of electricity powerful enough to stun the person who had taken it.

But what Amador had to say about Jackie was, in the long run, of little significance. He was merely adding to the mountain of evidence that had already been presented.

It was what he had to say when he was shown a photo that caused a stir in the courtroom. He had identified a photo of Anthony Accetturo. There was a moment of silence as he said it. Accetturo, he declared, was "the boss, the head of everything."

It was the most significant testimony linking Accetturo to the case that had yet been presented. It was a direct corroboration of what Alonzo had said.

The witness said he had been introduced to Accetturo at a hotel where the three-hundred-pound DiNorscio was attending a diet program.

He said he was also present on another occasion when Accetturo handed three $100 bills to DiNorscio's daughter as a birthday gift.

DiNorscio, Amador said, held Accetturo in such high regard that he showed "total respect [to] even just the name. . . ."

Whenever mob figures were in a "squeeze" for money, Amador said, they would go to "Tumac," and it was apparent that he "was the boss.

"It was like him being their ace in the hole," Amador said.

Accetturo, slouched in his chair in a pullover shirt, listened to the testimony. He merely smiled and shook his head.

Amador didn't look at him.

When Jackie approached Amador to cross-examine him, he tried to defuse the testimony. Turning to the court, he asked, "Can I make a citizen's arrest now?"

The defendants laughed; some of the jurors chuckled; but the judge was not amused.

At one point, Jackie turned to Amador and recalled his testimony about bringing cocaine to him in the hospital. "I never denied doing any coke," Jackie said. He looked quizzically at Amador. "As a matter of fact," he asked the witness, "did you bring any?"

There was more laughter.

"I don't deny doing coke," Jackie said later. "I love it. . . ."

Jackie's antics might have been amusing the jury. But they were clearly not amusing the judge. At a break in the proceedings, Ackerman turned to face DiNorscio.

"Mr. DiNorscio," he began, "I have been extremely patient in the face of jokes about cats, about butchers, about your wife . . . or former wife."

DiNorscio stood and raised his hand.

"Judge—"

Ackerman refused to acknowledge him.

"Let me finish," the judge declared.

DiNorscio was heedless of the brewing storm.

"I want to tell you—"

This time Ackerman was thundering, "You let me finish."

Jackie tried to get in another word. "I know—"

"Just let me finish," Ackerman said through clenched teeth.

This time DiNorscio shouted back, "If you stop hollering—"

"I'll stop hollering when you let me finish," Ackerman stormed. "I have been extremely patient with you. You want to play a clown, that's your problem."

DiNorscio looked hurt, "Well—"

Ackerman cut him off, but only for a moment. "But when you—"

Now Jackie was shouting too. "That's my way of defending myself. . . . You're allowing that asshole to testify here. Who are you kidding? . . . I don't want to even listen . . . no more if you're going to talk to me in that tone. . . ."

"I treated you in a professional manner," Ackerman retorted.

DiNorscio laughed scornfully. "You're supposed to."

"What's that?" Ackerman snapped.

"You're supposed to," DiNorscio said in a loud voice.

"Mr. DiNorscio," Ackerman sighed, "you can say I'm wrong all day long."

Jackie merely laughed. "You can say it too, Judge."

22

Michael Taccetta, his glasses perched precariously on his nose, glanced at his notes and whispered in Critchley's ear.

Accetturo, meanwhile, sat silent, preferring to banter with the judge during breaks then to talk to the men who reputedly served as his own "soldiers."

Jackie would occasionally chat with the judge too, sometimes about his health.

"Judge," he told Ackerman in total sincerity one day, "I haven't had a bowel movement in two days."

The testimony was droning on, and although the tales of the life and times of Jackie DiNorscio had been presented in all their lurid glory, Taccetta and Accetturo thus far had been relegated to cameo appearances in the grand drama.

Jurors could only wonder what thoughts were filtering through the minds of these two men, the reputed bosses of a powerful crime family, who by an odd turn of fate had come now to share a crowded courtroom together with them for months. In some ways they were all prisoners there.

Although the defendants had laughed when it seemed appropriate, or glowered as they expressed outrage over some prosecution moves, for the most part, their faces were impassive, they betrayed nothing.

But there were stories the jurors never heard, like the one related in an FBI report about Michael Taccetta. . . .

The black car cruised slowly along the streets of Newark. It was night, and the sidewalks were in shadow. The city was almost deserted when the vehicle glided past the door of the bar.

There were two of them in the car, watching the door of the tavern, and waiting.

A lone man emerged, a black man, silhouetted against the glare of light from the interior. Briefly, the sound of music and voices drifted out to the pavement and faded as the door closed behind him. He waited, his eyes adjusting to the gloom, and then spotted the car by the curb. He started toward it.

There was a man at the wheel and another in the rear seat. He knew them both. The man in back was his boss, Michael Taccetta. As Accetturo had before him, Taccetta had retained control of numbers operations in the inner city, despite the racial changes. The color of the money hadn't changed.

The man leaned in the window and flashed a smile.

Normally, Taccetta or his representative would have got out to meet with the man. Tonight was different.

"My leg," Taccetta said. "I fell on it. It hurts to walk. Why don't you get in, and we'll talk."

The black man was nervous. There was sweat trickling under his arms, but the smile remained on his face. He placed his hand on the handle and opened the door. The man at the wheel stared straight ahead as he slid into the front seat.

Taccetta nodded, and the driver started the engine.

"We'll just ride around a little," Taccetta told the black man.

The fear began to grow. There was no reason for this change in routine. He could have handled the business curbside, even if Taccetta was injured.

Maybe they knew.

The black man was supposed to be handling the numbers in that portion of the city. It was a trusted position. But the proceeds had been down; the profits were off. And he knew why. He began to sweat more profusely. Apparently, they knew why too.

There was no conversation. The car just drove through the nearly empty streets.

And in the rear seat, Michael Taccetta reached into his pocket, pulled out a small silver .22-caliber revolver, and pointed it directly at the black man's head. He pulled the trigger.

The crack of the pistol was deafening inside the car; the smoke acrid. And the look of fear on the man's face changed instantly to shock. His eyes went wide.

So did Taccetta's. The man was leaning forward and turning his head around. And he was staring directly at the man who had shot him.

It took Taccetta a moment to realize what had happened. It was almost funny. The bullet had not done a thing. It had bounced off his head.

Now the man was whooping and in a panic. The shot might not have killed him, but it did hurt. And he might not be so lucky the next time.

Taccetta recovered from his own surprise, raised the gun a second time, and pointed it at the man's face.

The driver shouted, "Not now, there's a car coming." In the darkness, it could well have been a police car. He couldn't afford to take the chance.

"Wait till it passes before you hit him again," the driver shouted.

The black man saw his opportunity. He grabbed the handle of the door and pushed as hard as he could. The door swung open, and in the same instant he dived out onto the street. He was little more than a blur in the night as he ran off.

Two days later, Taccetta received a call from South Carolina. It was the black man.

"I'm sorry," he pleaded in a tight, high-pitched voice. "Let's forget the whole thing. I don't want no problem. . . ."

Michael Taccetta was something of an anomaly in the world of organized crime. He was not only feared and respected by his underlings, as mob bosses generally are, but he was genuinely liked. In some cases, the emotions ran even stronger—they loved him.

An FBI "bug" hidden at the Newark luncheonette used

as a sort of private club for Taccetta's organization recorded a conversation between two reputed bosses of Taccetta's gambling operations, Alfonse (Tic) Cataldo, who had grown up with Taccetta, and Jerome (Jerry the Vog) Voglino. According to authorities, Cataldo and Voglino supervised the lucrative numbers and loan-sharking operations for the mob family.

During their conversation, which took place in a back room festooned with pictures of underworld luminaries such as Al Capone, Lucky Luciano, and Meyer Lansky, the two delivered what amounted to an impromptu testimonial to the leader of the gang.

"Oh, Michael, what a guy," Cataldo declared in an almost reverential tone.

"He listens to ya," Voglino offered in his distinctive hoarse bark.

"Oh, he does," Cataldo continued. "He's the best guy in the fucking world. There ain't nobody like him."

Cataldo reiterated to his companion, "There ain't nobody like him."

One afternoon, shortly after Christmas of 1982, Taccetta paid a personal visit to the Hole in the Wall. He greeted his friends with waves, smiles, and hugs, and headed for the back room. Waiting there for him there was Frank Pisano, a member of his organization who had requested a meeting.

Pisano had been identified by authorities as a member of Taccetta's sports-betting operation. It was his job to help in tabulating the results. Only this time, there was a problem. A discrepancy had been found in his figures. Pisano was worried.

The two men acknowledged each other, and Taccetta took a seat across a table from Pisano. He listened.

Pisano explained. The problem had to do with the betting on a New York Jets game. The operation looked as if it had been hurt—and it might have been his fault.

"The only way he [his boss in the sports-betting operation] believes anything could have been wrong," Pisano declared, "is if I was involved."

Taccetta was cold when he spoke. "He said that's what happened."

"No—" Pisano said quickly, his voice rising a pitch.

Taccetta cut him off. "Right, okay."

Pisano drew a breath. "Okay, all right, I gotta tell you how I feel . . . I'm being honest with you here . . . I felt like Henry Fonda."

Taccetta registered confusion. What did Henry Fonda have to do with all this?

"Who's that?" he asked.

"*Wrong Man,* no, *The Wrong Man,*" Pisano explained, referring to the title of the classic movie in which Fonda played a man wrongly accused of murder. He was only afraid of being accused of cheating, but he knew the consequences could be the same.

"I told Michael Perna [a close associate of Taccetta] last night, if you were Idi Amin, I would be dead."

Pisano had known there was a problem for several days. But the night before, Taccetta had come to his house on routine business. And Pisano had become alarmed.

"Mike," he said, almost pleading, "I been around, six, seven years. It's the first time you've been in my house . . . I'm being honest with you, you came to my house to take a 'reading.' . . ."

He knew Taccetta had called his boss. That also had alarmed him.

"You know how I took it, that you were asking him was I short with the money. I'm saying *marone,* they must think I would misuse their money."

Pisano lowered his voice. "I'm, I'm in disfavor with you."

"No," Taccetta said, shifting in his seat. "Because I know you. I knew your fuckin' mind was gonna go. I knew that call [for the meeting] was gonna come before you knew it was gonna come. I knew it."

Pisanso breathed deeply. Taccetta sounded satisfied, but he wanted to be sure. He wanted to know that there were no doubts. Pisano admitted to Taccetta that he had a gambling problem. But everything was under control.

"I would feel this way even if I didn't gamble," he told Taccetta." I don't ever want there to be a question of my integrity. I would never take your money."

"I know you gamble," Taccetta said.

Pisano spoke almost as though to a priest, confessing his shortcomings.

"But I would never take your money," he said. He muttered a few other words and then looked at Taccetta, his eyes almost moist. "I would love to shine in your eyes . . . I would love to shine in your eyes."

He looked into Taccetta's face, his hands reaching across the simple table. "No matter what situation, what other pressures I might have, or whatever incidents, positions, I put myself in, is there any doubt in your mind that I would ever do anything to hurt you?" Pisano asked.

Taccetta's response was terse. "No," he said.

"None at all?" Pisano demanded.

"None at all," Taccetta assured him.

Pisano at last seemed relieved. He paused and then sighed, "That's all I need."

Taccetta had been born on September 16, 1947, the son of a Newark bookmaker, Angelo Taccetta, a self-employed building-materials supplier, who authorities claim doubled as a trusted "soldier" in the Lucchese crime organization.

He was a tough kid growing up in a tough neighborhood. His early record reflects an arrest at age twelve for assault and battery, a charge that led to him being sent to Boys Town, a Catholic youth facility for wayward youngsters.

While there, Taccetta attended the local high school, returning to the youth facility at the end of the school day. But he stood out among his peers. He had an entourage, and he was looked up to. There were even rumors that he was the illegitimate son of some famous gangster. When he walked down the hall, the other students stepped aside.

One classmate made the mistake of passing a comment about Taccetta's mother. It was the usual sort of teenage rankout, but Taccetta's response was to wait until the other classmate was alone in the locker room, and belt him in the stomach.

The students soon learned not to pass comments about Taccetta's family.

When he was fifteen he was arrested for "idling and loafing," a charge that many employers would like to bring against their workers from time to time. For that capital offense, he was released with an understanding that his parents would "discipline" him properly.

There were other arrests. He was picked up and released during an investigation into a car theft. He pleaded guilty to a disorderly persons' offense for a fight.

He graduated from Newark Preparatory School at age nineteen and went away for one semester to Providence, Rhode Island, where he attended the Johnson and Wales Junior College of Business. At the end of the semester, he was back in New Jersey, a student at the Essex College of Business. But he was not destined for glory in the world of academia—his grade averages hovered around the "C"–"D" mark.

Back on the streets, he worked variously as a laborer and in partnership with his brother and father in the supply of Belgium blocks and other construction materials.

He was twenty-three when he was sent to Trenton State Prison following his conviction on a gambling-conspiracy charge. It was his first big-time offense.

The Essex County Prosecutor's Office had put the case together with the aid of an informer and evidence gathered from wiretaps. Shortly after New Year of 1981, fifty-eight persons were taken into custody as county authorities raided thirty-one locations, seizing some $10,000 in cash and $137,000 in lottery slips. At the location where Taccetta was arrested, a bundle of partially burned lottery slips were found in the backyard.

Taccetta was sentenced to one to two years in Trenton State Prison.

He came out tougher than when he went in.

He once told a federal investigator who asked what he had done for a living, "Bookmaking. That's what I pled guilty to."

There were subsequent arrests for larceny, extortion, and gambling. None of the charges stuck, and Taccetta's reputation began to grow.

He was in his early twenties when he married his childhood sweetheart, Carol Ann Nozdrovicky. The first years of the marriage weren't easy. The couple lived for a time with her parents, before moving to a three-family house.

In the early 1970s, Taccetta moved to Florida, ostensibly to open a restaurant. Authorities claim there was a more nefarious motive. He went to be "schooled" by his mob mentor,

Anthony Accetturo, who had been forced to flee New Jersey to evade a subpoena requiring him to appear before the State Commission of Investigation.

The SCI, as the organization is commonly known, was conducting an investigation of organized crime in New Jersey. It was a legislative body, not a police agency. But it could do things that no police agency could; namely, it could put people in jail for refusing to testify. A number of prominent mob figures found that out and endured extensive jail stays as a result of their reluctance to talk to the state investigators.

Accetturo was by then the king of the Newark streets, and state law-enforcement agencies were making a career out of toppling kings from their thrones. Accetturo knew his turn was coming and decided discretion was the better part of valor. He ran. Taccetta, who had become his protégé in Newark, followed close behind.

Taccetta's stay in Florida was not an auspicious one. He was out of money and out of luck. He ate pasta with tuna sauce, and he tried to survive. His business ventures included an attempt to open a lounge in a Florida hotel, which met with disaster when someone detonated a stink bomb on New Year's Eve, 1973, scattering the customers. A foray into the excavation business proved similarly unsuccessful when a hoped-for contract to dig the foundation for a motel project never materialized.

Shortly after that, Taccetta came back to New Jersey, which proved a much more profitable climate.

In 1983, *The Star-Ledger* of Newark carried a small notice that a Florham Park woman had won the New Jersey State Lottery. She had won $611,979, to be paid out over a twenty-year period. The article identified her as Mrs. Michael Taccetta, the wife of an "oil company consultant."

Mrs. Taccetta was not the only person to experience good fortune.

That same year, Lieutenant Colonel Justin Dintino of the New Jersey State Police, addressing the U.S. Senate Judiciary Committee on the structure of organized crime in New Jersey, identified Michael Taccetta as a rising star within the ranks of the underworld. Taccetta, Dintino reported, "controls a significant portion of the illicit gambling activities in northern

New Jersey and New York City. Taccetta is capable of utilizing violence and is suspected of committing several murders relative to his illicit activities. He is also involved in loan-sharking, race-fixing, smuggling of untaxed cigarettes and a major narcotics network."

When, as a youngster, Michael began working for Anthony Accetturo, he started as a numbers controller, the man who oversaw delivery of the "packages" of gambling slips and proceeds to the "bank," which tabulated the winnings and held the money.

By the time he came back to Jersey from Florida, he was a "boss"—he was Accetturo's number-one man. And the gambling and loan-sharking empire that Accetturo had left behind when he fled the Garden State had now passed into Taccetta's hands for safekeeping. He was Accetturo's duly-appointed delegate, and as far as New Jersey was concerned, the tough kid from the streets was now the top dog.

From gambling and loan-sharking, the operations expanded. He became involved in cigarette smuggling, importing untaxed cigarettes from southern states for sale on the black market in New Jersey. He opened up a separate sports-betting operation and, also, a private social club in Orange. He also stepped into a supervisory post overseeing Accetturo's interests in contracting firms in north Jersey. And through it all, he made sure that "Tumac" received his piece of the pie.

And the "boys" who gathered around Michael were as loyal as they came.

"They should take a poll. . . ." Cataldo declared in another conversation recorded by the FBI. "Talk to everyone, and we'll roll along. I can't think of nobody else in this whole outfit that I'm really not crazy about. Everybody here is good. Of course, ya love certain guys more than others. But still, everybody here, I'm crazy about. . . ."

The camaraderie of the Taccetta organization was explained in part by family relationships. Many were cousins. They served as godparents to each others' children. They had come from a common background, a common neighborhood, and they shared a common goal—making money.

But there was something else beyond just money that

bound them together. Defense attorney Michael Critchley tapped into it when he expressed his own view of the defendants.

"I found instinctively that these were guys that I liked. I'm not making any moral judgments. Because if we could make the pure moral judgments and knew everything about everybody, however you define morality, very few people would measure up. Because everybody has a skeleton in the closet.

"Some people may be involved in gambling, and they're criminals. And some people may be involved in loan-sharking, and they're criminals. And then you have some multinational corporation who's polluting the ocean and making us all turn purple."

There was no doubt in Critchley's mind which was the greater evil.

When the indictment was returned in the Accetturo case, the government was certain the case would never come to trial. They would break, one by one. It had happened before. Take a guy who's willing to do a five-year rap for gambling and elevate it to a racketeering charge that carries a twenty-year sentence, and all of a sudden, he's not such a stand-up guy anymore. The trusted organization member becomes a trusted government informer, desperately trying to save himself at the expense of his buddies.

It is a pattern that is repeated over and over again. The question is not if someone will break, but who the first person to break will be. And the others quickly jump on the bandwagon.

That's what the prosecution believed would happen in the Accetturo case. And they believed it right up until the day they all went to trial together.

The deals were offered by the government, and they were rejected. The prosecutors claimed they were reasonable. The defense claimed they were absurd.

Judge Harold Ackerman sounded the warning bell. "The train," he told the defendants and their lawyers, "is leaving the station. . . ."

But they all stayed on board.

It was only *after* the trial was long over that the truth of the situation began to surface. Accetturo had been all in favor of guilty pleas—for everybody but himself. He had not achieved the prominence he had in the underworld without possessing a shrewd and perceptive mind. It didn't take Accetturo long to realize that although he was the lead defendant in the case, there wasn't a great deal of hard evidence against him. There was plenty of evidence against some of the other people, but it was relatively sparse when it came to his personal involvement.

He realized what the prosecution was up to. It planned to "dirty him up" with the testimony about the others, and hoped the general patina of guilt would wash over him as well. And under the RICO law, the individual charged with being the head of a racketeering enterprise could be found guilty even if there was no direct evidence that he was personally involved in the commission of many of the crimes.

For the past ten years, he had kept himself insulated from the day-to-day operations. Now that insulation threatened to peel away. The only sure way to avoid conviction, as far as Accetturo was concerned, was to make sure he would not go to trial. And one way of avoiding trial would be to have everyone else plead out. The case against him was too weak to take to trial by itself.

Only Accetturo miscalculated. For more than a decade, he had ruled in absentia. He was still the nominal boss of the New Jersey organization, still had a piece of the action. But Michael Taccetta had become more than just his stand-in—he had become his replacement. It was Taccetta's organization, and the loyalties were to Taccetta, not Accetturo. And no one was going to bail out on Taccetta.

It was a reality that Accetturo failed to grasp until many months after the trial . . . and by then it was too late.

But no one rises in the ranks of organized crime by being a nice guy. Taccetta had another side. At least one informant has characterized him as violent, aggressive, and treacherous—a man who does what he has to do to get ahead, and stay there. The New Jersey State Police tagged him by the nickname of "Mad Dog." By some accounts, it was a name well-earned.

It was shortly after 10:20 on the morning of June 12,

1984, when Vincent J. Craparotta, Sr., fifty-six, pulled his Mercedes Benz into his parking garage on the ground floor of a Jersey Shore used-car lot.

Craparotta was one of the most successful building contractors in the area, specializing in the construction of commercial office space and luxury homes. But according to New Jersey State Police, he had another speciality: gambling. Craparotta, authorities said, had for the past twenty years, been a "prominent gambling operative" for the Lucchese crime family, and as such, he worked for Michael Taccetta.

That morning, Craparotta parked his car in a rear garage and headed toward his second-floor office, located above the used-car business. He had built the building himself and maintained office space for his construction firm there. It was centrally located along Route 9 in Dover Township, and it provided him with all the space he needed.

He headed for the stairs. But he never got there.

Three men wearing stocking masks stepped out of the shadows, and before he could cry out or run, they were on him. They had golf clubs in their hands, and they were swinging them at his head. . . .

When police arrived, they found Craparotta facedown in a pool of blood in the bay of the garage. He died several hours later at the Kimball Medical Center in nearby Lakewood.

An autopsy by the Ocean County Medical Examiner's Office attributed his death to lacerations and hemorrhages of the brain.

The attack had been so ferocious, authorities said, that the golf clubs wielded by his killers had left divots on the concrete garage floor. A police officer, versed in graveyard humor, quipped afterward that it took three men to kill him: two to swing the clubs and a third to serve as caddy.

Authorities later would claim that Craparotta, whom they alleged had helped supervise efforts to expand Lucchese family operations in South Jersey, had committed one of the cardinal sins of the underworld: failing to pay the proper "tribute" to his mob superiors, a clear sign of "disrespect."

To teach him the value of that "respect," authorities claim, the Lucchese organization dispatched several of its top operatives to pay Craparotta a visit on the morning of his death.

They took golf clubs with them, authorities said, "because baseball bats break."

Michael Taccetta was one of twelve men called to testify before an Ocean County grand jury convened to investigate the murder. Taccetta appeared, but did little more than give his name and address.

For nearly seven years, the case would remain officially unsolved.

According to an FBI informant, when all else failed, murder and violence were the preferred means of disciplining wayward associates.

One report excluded from the trial claimed that Taccetta personally dealt with a troublesome member who was suspected of talking too freely to police by luring him to an isolated spot under the guise of rendezvousing in preparation for a "score." Instead, Taccetta allegedly blew the man's head off with a .45-caliber handgun and then threw the body from the car. The informant claimed that he met Taccetta at the victim's wake and was told the man had "gone bad and that's why he's dead."

The story of another murder, which FBI reports also link to the Taccetta organization, even found its way into a column by the nationally syndicated muckraker Jack Anderson.

Anderson had written that the victim, a thirty-two-year-old Parsippany–Troy Hills resident named Richard DeMary, was tortured and murdered because he was suspected of informing on a huge "buttleg" operation.

Anderson's column dealt with the extent to which organized-crime figures had become involved in the smuggling of cigarettes from states with low cigarette taxes, such as many of the southern states, to the more heavily taxed northern areas, including New Jersey and New York.

DeMary's brother had been one of seven men arrested during a law-enforcement crackdown on the smuggling operation, which authorities claimed was reaping millions of dollars a year in sales. Since DeMary was not included in the arrest, he was suspected of being an informant. His beaten and bullet-riddled body was discovered in a swamp near the East Hanover Airport in Morris County.

According to an FBI informant, it was not an easy death.

DeMary was reportedly lured to a deserted area near a Morris County reservoir and kept captive for several days before his murder. Although accounts differ as to what actually happened to him, police at the time said DeMary had been tortured.

According to the reports, the suspected informer died slowly over the course of days. After being taken captive, he was first immobilized by gunshots that shattered his knees, elbows, and shins. For two days, he was kept alive. Finally, his assailants told him it was over—they were going to let him live.

Desperate, frightened, and weak from pain and loss of blood, DeMary began to crawl his way through the murky ground that bordered the Passaic River. He didn't get far. One of the men pulled a .38-caliber revolver out of his jacket and fired a single shot into the back of DeMary's head.

According to police accounts, it was not a death that would have been mourned by many. Authorities said DeMary had a long criminal record that included rape. In addition, he had been sought as a suspect in two armed robberies, and police speculated he might have been involved in narcotics as well.

One thing authorities did state definitively, however, was that if DeMary was killed because he was a suspected informant, he was killed for nothing. The "buttleg" arrests had been sparked by information obtained from surveillance and possible wiretaps. DeMary had nothing to do with it.

When Taccetta was eventually brought to trial in the federal racketeering case, the formal charges contained no mention of the murders. Although privately convinced of his involvement, authorities lacked the corroboration to prosecute him for the killings. They tried to introduce some mention of the deaths, but the material was ruled inadmissible.

Although reports of violence and brutality followed Taccetta throughout his rise to power, others who have known him have found him charming, articulate, and reasonable.

A federal prosecutor once remarked that he had the impression that if ever a dispute arose with Taccetta, the mob boss would try, at least initially, to resolve the situation amicably.

Now, in the corridor outside Ackerman's courtroom, he was frequently overheard interspersing his conversations with quotations from Greek philosophy. He expressed admiration for the themes of loyalty to personal principle over government policy, as espoused in the life of Thomas à Becket, the twelfth-century archbishop of Canterbury who was murdered because of his opposition to the policies of Henry II toward the Church.

He has been described as devoted to his family, and was quoted as telling one of his sons that he was not to be regarded as such a "smart guy."

"A smart guy," he reportedly told the boy, "wouldn't be facing sixty years in jail."

There was no doubt, however, that Taccetta was indeed a "smart guy."

A voracious reader, as well as a compulsive eater whose weight changed as frequently as the seasons, Taccetta knew how to play the game. He knew how to deal with his own people; and he knew how to deal with law enforcement, as well. For years they played a game of cat-and-mouse.

It was a game he and his associates were still playing. The question was, would the jury take the bait?

23

Anthony Accetturo shifted in his seat and stared at the painted, carved, and recessed ceiling that added a sense of bygone grandeur to the ceremonial courtroom.

The velvet drapes hung thick and heavy, filtering out the light of the afternoon sun.

The seasons passed, but the world inside this courtroom remained unchanged. The summer sun could be shining brightly or the clouds heavy with a brooding winter storm, it was all the same within the courtroom. The chandeliers cast their dim light over the proceedings.

And as the shadows fell across the craggy face of Anthony Accetturo, the reputed crime lord closed his eyes.

He had come a long way from his days as a "street-corner" hoodlum to occupy the top position in a major racketeering trial. . . .

Anthony Accetturo was born in the suburban Essex County community of Orange on October 18, 1938. He was raised in what was known as the "Valley," a depression in the landscape that was bordered by the West Orange Mountain to the west and the hills of Orange that gave Tremont Avenue (*tre-mont,* three mountains) its name.

They called him "Dirty Pants" then, and he was a scruffy youngster with a perpetually runny nose and clothes that would have been rejected by a Salvation Army fund-raising drive.

Today, sources claim, Accetturo is one of the wealthiest Mafia figures in the nation, with a hidden net worth estimated by some to be about $35 million.

But it wasn't always that way. As a youth, Accetturo lived in one of the poorest sections of the city, in what were later to become tenements. Streets were lined with narrow wooden clapboard homes and rickety apartment buildings. Today those streets are a ghetto, a decaying monument to a city whose dreams have faded and that has slipped into a decline from which it may never recover.

But in the 1940s, it was a workingman's city with a large immigrant population, a city with a small-town atmosphere, where everybody knew everybody and friendly waves and sidewalk conversations were the hallmark of sociability.

The Irish kids banded together, as did the Italians, vying for recognition and their own little piece of the world. They shot baskets in the school playgrounds and attended the local dances. Many, their families strict—or at least prone to give lip service to the orthodoxy of the Roman Catholic Church—sent their children to Our Lady of the Valley Church, the central religious institution in that area of the city.

It was here that Accetturo grew up. His family operated a produce market, and other relatives owned a butcher shop. But these were not the dreams of Anthony Accetturo—his were grander.

By his early teens, Accetturo was already known as something of a troublemaker.

"At the time, he was a punk, running around, breaking into candy stores, and robbing the vending machines," recalled a source who grew up with Accetturo and knew him well.

His career, however, was almost cut short before it began.

The vending machines he was robbing belonged to "Ham" Delasco—the boss of a Newark-based organized-crime group. Delasco wasn't happy and issued his orders: "Bring me the kid."

A car was sent out, and a pair of Delasco's boys found Accetturo on the street. There was a brief tussle, and the older men convinced him to join them for a little ride.

The ride brought Accetturo to an East Orange social club, used by Delasco as his headquarters, where he was ushered inside without ceremony.

In the dim light of the club, filled with tables where members of the organization and associates spent the day over drinks, conversations, and cards, Delasco puffed on a cigar and looked at the youngster appraisingly while his men gripped the boy's shoulders.

"So this is the punk who's been robbing me?"

Accetturo shook off the hands of Delasco's men and just glared back at the older man.

"What of it?"

Delasco's face flushed with anger, and he puffed harder on the cigar, turning the tip a bright red. Then he let out a breath.

"What are we going to do with him?" the men asked.

Delasco stared at the defiant, tough-guy face in front of him and made his decision.

"Kid," he said, pulling the cigar out of his mouth and jabbing it at Accetturo's face, "you think you're pretty good, right?"

Accetturo smiled. "I'm all right. I got your attention, didn't I?"

Delasco laughed at the boy's bravado.

"You know, I've got a choice. I can't have you robbing me like this. It sets a bad example. Others might get the same idea. I could just get rid of you. But that would be a loss."

He pondered the situation for a moment and then proposed his solution. "I think I could use somebody like you. You want to come to work for me?"

The look on Accetturo's face was answer enough.

From the first, Accetturo earned his money.

It was a time of change in Delasco's territory. Newark was in a state of violent flux, and the increasingly large black population in Newark was beginning to become restless. The residents were fed up with white domination and exploitation, and their rage would eventually boil over into the riots that ravaged the city during the 1960s.

And among the criminal elements, there was a sense of unrest as well. Long a stronghold of the old-line Italian crime groups, such as Delasco's, inner-city Newark was now becoming a bastion of black independence. It began slowly, with black numbers operators moving into the formerly white area. At first they worked with the Italians, but then they began to develop on their own, and with the expansion of the black operations, the profits to Delasco and his cohorts began to decline.

Not only that, but more daring black operators began kidnapping white numbers runners and stealing the proceeds. It was not a situation that Delasco could tolerate, so he assigned Accetturo to take care of it.

No one knows for certain how he accomplished it—some say by violence and murder. One source said Accetturo is rumored to have killed some twenty-eight black operators during that time.

But Delasco was satisfied. Accetturo managed to gain "respect" in the black community, and Delasco retained his control over the area.

From Delasco, Accetturo learned his trade: running numbers, "edging" bets, and establishing the "banks" to finance the operation. Accetturo was his driver and his top aide.

These were the days of hanging out in the candy stores, setting up minor "scores," and making the contacts that would later serve to form the core of his own organization. He was rumored to have picked up extra money carrying out "contracts" for the higher-ups in the mob; but if that was true, no one ever charged him with it.

But those who knew him did come to fear him. It was during this time they nicknamed him "Tumac," after a club-wielding caveman played by Victor Mature in a movie that was then popular. It was an apt appellation since Tumac, the movie character, was portrayed as a barbarian, who, when confronted with members of a more "civilized" tribe, tried to grab all the food for himself.

That was Tumac, then and today. Always grubbing; always grabbing; and always out for himself.

Even on his lunch hour during the federal racketeering trial, Accetturo was out supervising business deals, making sure that he was getting his cut and not getting ripped off.

But when Delasco died, Accetturo confided to an associate that he felt he wasn't prepared and that his "schooling" hadn't been completed. Nonetheless, with the ruthless efficiency that was later to become his trademark, Accetturo found little difficulty in stepping into Delasco's shoes. Within months, he was the boss. And the organization was working for him.

The one thing Accetturo never lacked was luck. Although his police record dated back to 1956 and reflected more than a dozen charges, he never served any sentence longer than four months.

There were convictions for larceny, gambling, and extortion—but always, he escaped with little or no jail time. The one sentence he did serve was at a northern Florida facility regarded as a sort of country club of prisons.

When he fled New Jersey in the early 1970s after being called to testify by the New Jersey State Commission of Investigation, Accetturo was only one of a flock of notorious mobsters who migrated out of New Jersey to other parts of the country, where the SCI subpoenas could not be enforced.

The favored area for many was Florida: Simone Rizzo (Sam the Plumber) DeCavalcante, Gerardo Catena, and other ranking, if lesser known, mob figures were among those who flocked there, basking in the warm breezes, enjoying the sunshine, strolling the golf courses, and running their operations from afar.

Accetturo was one of this group.

Anthony Accetturo's decision to leave New Jersey had not been a precipitous one.

Things had been closing in on him; the state was turning up the heat on organized crime and the atmosphere was becoming decidedly uncomfortable. The situation ultimately reached a boiling point one afternoon when an unmarked state police car pulled to a stop on a quiet, tree-lined street in Livingston, New Jersey.

As the urban sprawl had spread westward from Newark, Accetturo and his associates had followed the trend, emigrating toward the increasingly more affluent and fashionable suburbs.

Accetturo's home was a well-groomed brick estate on a dead-end street in Livingston, in a house surrounded by shrubs and trees.

Inside the unmarked police car, a state-police investigator watched the house, sipping coffee.

As the trooper watched, a dark-colored van pulled slowly up the street and backed into Accetturo's driveway.

The trooper drained the last of the coffee from his cup and craned his neck to see into the yard. He wanted to find out what they were loading into the truck—or taking out of it.

The shrubs were too thick, and from where he sat, the truck and its contents were hidden. The trooper started the engine, and moved slowly up the street to get a better view.

There was a movement at one of the windows. The trooper knew he had been spotted.

He had a choice: slink away and give up the surveillance, or just go ahead with it anyway. He chose the latter. They had already seen him, so what the hell, it didn't matter how obvious he was now, the object was to get a look at the truck.

The trooper started the car and pulled closer to the front of the house.

It was too late. Whatever was going on was over, and the truck engine revved into life. The truck pulled out of the driveway and bounced over the curb as it pulled onto the street.

The trooper started up his own car again, determined to get the plate number of the vehicle.

As the unmarked police car raced after the truck, Accetturo, who had been inside, now rushed out of the garage, his teeth gritted in anger, and pulled open the door of his green Lincoln Continental. He slammed the door shut and headed after the police car.

The trooper spotted the Lincoln racing toward him.

Accetturo pulled up behind him, then swerved the wheel sharply and shot into the oncoming lane. He pulled abreast of the police car and raised a clenched fist, mouthing an obscenity through the glass. Then he wrenched the wheel and swerved again. The police car swerved to avoid the impact as Accetturo tried to cut him off.

Now the trooper was pissed.

Accetturo floored the accelerator and shot ahead.

The trooper floored his pedal and pulled out in pursuit.

The truck was in front, and it obscured the view.

As the trooper pulled out to pass, he blinked. There was Accetturo, skidding into a U-turn and heading straight toward him.

The trooper hit the brake and pulled back. As the green Lincoln shot by, he turned his own wheel and hung a U-turn, determined to catch the crime boss.

Accetturo wasn't running.

Several hundred yards up the street, the tires of the Lincoln screeched again as Accetturo swung the big car in another half-circle. He was headed back toward the police car.

This time, the trooper was ready. He pulled his car across the road and forced Accetturo to a halt.

The trooper reached under his seat and activated a tape recorder, hoping to catch Accetturo threatening him. It wasn't much, but it would be enough to arrest him.

Accetturo, his face hot, flung open the door of the Lincoln and jumped out. He swaggered over to the police car.

"What are you doing, you fuck? You want me to come up to your house?" he growled.

The two men glared at each other for a moment, and then there was a flash of recognition in Accetturo's eyes.

"You," he said, "I know you."

The trooper smiled. He had known Accetturo as a boy, grew up in the same neighborhood, and even chased him home on occasion when Accetturo insisted on hanging around with the older gangs.

Accetturo laughed. "I don't believe it. You're with the state police?"

The trooper smiled. "We've come a long way, Anthony."

Suddenly, Accetturo's face lit up with excitement. "Wait here," he said. The crime boss turned and ran to his own car and reached inside. When he returned, he was holding a small bottle of an expensive perfume.

"Here," he said, "for old times' sake."

The trooper just laughed. "You've got to be kidding."

Accetturo registered surprise. "No, no," he protested, "it's not a bribe, nothing like that. It's for old times."

"Forget about it," the trooper said.

As they talked, Accetturo accepted the trooper's invitation to sit in the car. The conversation rambled on, then turned to the old days in Orange and where they had gone from there.

"The state police," Accetturo said. "I still don't believe it."

"Listen, Anthony" the trooper joked. "With a flick of a pen, I can make you a *capo,* and you can eat in all the restaurants in Newark for nothing."

"Or," he said softly, "I can make you a truck driver."

Accetturo slapped the seat and laughed. "I've got a better idea," he said. "Suppose I save you all the trouble. Why don't we work this out. You can call me up in the morning. I'll give you my itinerary. Then you don't have to follow me around. You can submit your reports, and your boss will be happy."

As the conversation progressed, Accetturo expressed curiosity over the surveillance. "What's the state police want with me?" he asked.

The trooper looked into his face. "It's more than that, Anthony. It's the SCI. They've got paper on you. It's all over."

Accetturo just shook his head and gestured his hand in dismissal. "Don't worry about that," he laughed. "I'm getting the hell out of this state . . . you can put it down right now. I'm leaving for Florida. If you want, you can pick me up and bring me to the airport."

Accetturo was true to his word.

Within a week, he was on his way to the Sunshine State.

Florida and Anthony Accetturo went together like a roach in a sugar bowl. He ate it up.

When Accetturo arrived in Florida, it was an "open state." The South American drug cartels had not yet gained a firm foothold. The indigenous crime organizations were weak, and the state's climate had made it the perfect retirement retreat for the aging overlords of organized crime. Just to keep their hands in, they began to explore the market for their type of service.

As time passed, Accetturo began to set up his own operations—gambling, loan-sharking, and whatever else the traffic would bear. He had the expertise, and unlike many of his counterparts from other crime families, who had decided to enjoy their declining years strolling across the golf courses of the state, Accetturo was still young and hungry. And he had a feast.

According to one government document, Accetturo eventually became the dominant organized-crime figure in southern Florida, while maintaining his control over an ever-expanding organization in New Jersey. He treated these organizations like his children, and he raised a fine family of crime.

Justin Dintino, the New Jersey State Police investigator who also served as the organized-crime expert for the State Commission of Investigation, said Accetturo had the potential to become the national leader of the Lucchese crime family if he continued unchecked, taking his place on the honor roll of the high Commission of the Mafia—the nine-member body that has controlled organized-crime operations in America since the days of Al Capone.

Newspaper reports traced his career.

In 1977, the *Miami Herald* reported that Accetturo was charged with extorting twenty-nine thousand dollars from a Miami Beach hotel operator through an elaborate ruse involving a murder hoax and blackmail.

According to the press account, Accetturo was instrumental in attempting to blackmail the hotel operator with tapes of him during a conversation with a woman in which the two discussed their "romantic relationship." The plan was to threaten to play those tapes for the victim's wife and young son if he failed to pay. But when the victim balked at the plan, it was charged, Accetturo and his cohorts arranged to stage a bloody "murder" for his benefit—and then charge him another fifteen thousand dollars to cover up the crime.

As part of the scheme, authorities charged, Accetturo took the victim for a ride in a Cadillac Eldorado, and then pretended to shoot one of the conspirators in the plan, pushing him to the floor of the rear seat and splashing fake blood all around the car.

They then threatened to kill their real victim if he talked, it was alleged, and told him he'd have to ante up fifteen thousand dollars to get rid of the body.

Sources said it was typical of Accetturo to become involved in such a scheme. Although reaping huge profits from his other enterprises, Accetturo, they say, stayed true to the reputation of "Tumac"—he would never miss an opportunity to glom something else.

Even the ubiquitous bingo game was not beneath Accetturo's reach. In 1979, according to a *Miami Herald* report, Accetturo was identified as having a hidden interest in bingo halls in southern Florida, as well as a company that supplied materials for the games.

Despite the public impression of bingo as a game for the elderly or a fund-raising ploy for charities, Accetturo apparently saw it as another jackpot for profits.

In 1989, a ranking FBI official linked Accetturo to a bizarre scheme in which he claimed the Mafia attempted to control high-stakes bingo games on a Florida Indian reservation by infiltrating the tribe. Anthony E. Daniels, a deputy assistant director of the FBI, said Accetturo tried to set up a management firm to tap into the lucrative, but little-known, gambling market on Indian reservations. The scheme was interrupted, Daniels said, when Accetturo was indicted in New Jersey.

Accetturo was sentenced to four months in jail on the hotel-operator extortion case. It was the longest prison term he ever served, and he wanted to make sure it was the last.

In the mid-1970s, Accetturo, along with a number of other mob figures around the country, suddenly discovered that one of the best ways to evade prison was to avoid trial.

A racketeer from New Jersey, John DiGilio, was the master of such strategies. DiGilio, a former prize fighter turned Mafia enforcer, had risen in the ranks of the Genovese crime family to become one of the most feared and respected figures on the New Jersey waterfront. Authorities claimed that DiGilio had his hands in everything from labor-union racketeering to gambling, extortion, and murder. And every law-enforcement official in northern New Jersey was eager to get his hands on DiGilio.

DiGilio was a onetime pugilist, who once staged a punch-out with a codefendant in the halls of the federal courthouse in Newark (he decked his opponent with one punch) and also once offered to "go a few rounds" with a federal prosecutor. His notoriety was further enhanced when he arranged for the theft of his own dossier from FBI headquarters in Newark by enticing a young female clerk to smuggle out the papers hidden in her panties.

The government prosecuted and convicted him. But on appeal, DiGilio invoked a loophole—prosecutors had failed to place a monetary value on the stolen material. As a result, the charge was lowered to a misdemeanor, and his jail exposure cut to only six months.

DiGilio, however, managed to stave off further prosecution for years by invoking variations on a theme: his poor health. His years in the ring, DiGilio claimed, had left him a victim of "organic brain damage," which made him unfit to stand trial.

The ploy worked for years. DiGilio spent more time in prison hospital than in prison. At one point, he urinated in a grand-jury room. On another occasion, he simply told a judge, "Fuck you, Your Honor," and directed U.S. marshals to end the session by taking him out of the room. He had himself declared legally incompetent and had his wife appointed his guardian.

Eventually, DiGilio was convicted, not by the courts, but as one law-enforcement official quipped, "by a jury of his peers." He was found shot to death when his body floated to the surface in a mortician's body bag near a marina in the Hackensack River.

But DiGilio had proved one thing in his career. Mental disorders are hard to diagnose, and they are almost impossible to refute.

Accetturo knew DiGilio well. Representatives of Accetturo's organization had regular meetings with DiGilio, and Accetturo soon found out that what worked in New Jersey for John DiGilio could work just as well in Florida for Anthony Accetturo.

In 1977, Accetturo groaned and moaned in a courthouse corridor while his attorney argued that he had suffered a nervous breakdown.

It was not his only health problem.

In 1980, authorities charged that he was the mastermind behind a race-fixing conspiracy, which involved drugging of horses at tracks in Florida and Pennsylvania by slipping dope into their drinking water.

The problem was bringing him to trial.

In 1981, a federal judge ruled he was incompetent to stand trial. Discounting protests from prosecutors, U.S. district judge Edward B. Davis held that Accetturo's memory was so poor, he could not understand the legal proceedings or help lawyers prepare his defense.

Medical experts called on behalf of Accetturo had claimed that the mob figure was suffering from Alzheimer's disease, the progressive disorder that is often confused with premature senility and that destroys its victim's memory.

Accetturo claimed he had suffered a concussion during a fall in a fish market and that the condition had been worsening every year. To bolster his claim, Accetturo had spent his time in court napping, yawning, rubbing his eyes, and moaning. His behavior was in fact so convincing that Judge Davis held that Accetturo was obviously "befuddled and confused" and "had the look of someone who was lost."

Fourteen months later, however, U.S. prosecutors were back in court arguing that Accetturo was snookering the court. This time, they had videotapes to prove it. And they had testimony.

Authorities portrayed Accetturo dining with the stunning owner of a Memphis supper club. She testified that he had identified himself as a gentleman plumber who, while not the greatest conversationalist in the world, was "extremely nice."

A local marina operator testified that Accetturo became irate over a bill for berthing his boat. And a forklift operator at the marina described Accetturo skipping across Port Everglades in a red speedboat at speeds in excess of fifty miles per hour.

The tapes showed Accetturo going about his daily routine, using telephones and attempting to negotiate the purchase of a condominium.

Concerned over the new disclosures, Judge Davis ordered Accetturo to undergo further mental testing, this time under controlled conditions. The suspect was ordered to the federal prison hospital in Butner, North Carolina.

During his stay, he was observed by a number of physicians. He acted troubled and confused.

Since he was charged with fixing races, one of the doctors asked him what he knew about racing. Accetturo said he had never been to a racetrack and wouldn't know how to cash a winning ticket if he had one.

During the evaluation, one of the physicians asked him the name of the people who ride horses. When Accetturo pleaded ignorance, it was explained that the horse was the one with the "saddle on top" and that a man rode in the saddle during a race.

Accetturo's face suddenly brightened. "Oh," he said. "You mean the little guy? When we were kids, I think we called them jockeys."

One morning, Accetturo was in the prison shower. He was carrying a clean towel but dropped it into a puddle on the floor and asked a nearby attendant for another.

The guard stepped around the corner. By the time he had returned, Accetturo was wobbling on his feet, holding his head in his hands. The guard watched helplessly as Accetturo tried to take a step, then stumbled and fell to the floor.

The guard rushed to his side and called out. When Accetturo didn't respond, the guard triggered an alarm.

As the sound of the alarm bell reverberated through the shower area, Accetturo suddenly opened his eyes.

"Where am I? What happened?" he stammered.

Shortly after, Accetturo asked to see the psychiatrist. "I feel like my memory is returning," he said.

He was a changed man. No longer dull and confused, he was now talkative and emotional.

"Isn't it funny," he told one doctor in seeming amazement, "one bunk and then another bunk, and then my memory comes back. Bunk, bunk."

There was still one difficulty, however: The cure was not complete. Accetturo now claimed he had no memory of anything that happened in the eleven years between the two bunks.

This time, his performance was panned by the court, and Accetturo was ruled fit to stand trial. Fatefully, however, it was another health-related development that once again saved Accetturo from conviction. When he eventually came to trial, the government's star witness experienced his own medical drama: He suffered a heart attack on the witness stand.

Accetturo's own "cure" had made him a free man. But the cure was only temporary. The federal indictment confronted him with an even greater threat to his well-being.

24

In mid-June, the skies were sunny and the days were bright. But for Harold Ackerman, things were looking ever more bleak. The trial was into its seventh month, and it seemed every time he tried to get the trial moving, some new delay would crop up. Indeed, no sooner had the trial begun when the health problems started.

It began with a juror who complained of blinding headaches. The juror was eventually dismissed, but not without causing a recess in the trial.

Shortly afterward, one of the defendants, DiNorscio associate Gerald DeLuca, collapsed in the courtroom. His condition was transitory, but the trial was again halted for several days until the problem could be diagnosed.

On the 1987 Memorial Day weekend, another defendant, Robert Spagnola, the reputed boss of the New Jersey sports-gambling operation, was hospitalized with possible cardiac symptoms. And there was another delay.

Then there was the tragic death of the infant daughter of defendant John Redman, a reputed middleman in the DiNorscio drug operation. The judge adjourned the trial to permit the defendant time to attend services out of the state.

The trial was no sooner set to resume from that setback when a second juror fell ill. After a week of adjournments, the judge finally made a decision to excuse that juror too, and to proceed with the trial.

It was all going smoothly, until the next incident.

At approximately 11:30 P.M. on the night of June 15, an emergency squad ambulance was called to the Livingston home of yet another of the defendants, Jerome Voglino.

Voglino, who authorities claimed supervised loan-sharking operations for the Taccetta organization, had been complaining of severe back pain and muscle spasms. His wife called the emergency medical team, and he was rushed to St. Barnabas Medical Center.

Fourteen days later, Voglino was still out, and the trial was still in recess.

"I have concluded," Ackerman told lawyers in the case, "that this trial can bear absolutely no further delays." He had formulated a policy, he said, that would apply to all future illnesses: no further interruptions. Having said that, Ackerman then made his position clear—Voglino was to return to court, in a bed, if necessary.

Turning to Strike Force prosecutor Barbara Miller, he said, "Miss Miller, I will expect the government to make the necessary arrangements so that counsel can have his client here each morning and can be returned each day."

Ackerman said he had conferred with Voglino's physicians, who had assured him that Voglino was capable of attending the proceedings, as long as an orthopedic bed was provided.

"I am absolutely satisfied," Ackerman declared, "that the man can attend this trial."

So, on June 30, those present in the courtroom witnessed the unlikely spectacle of a key defendant arriving at court carried by an ambulance crew and placed onto a hospital bed in the middle of the courtroom.

Voglino looked like a man in his final hours—he lay on his back, his eyes closed, moaning softly. His wife was at his side, holding a cold compress to his head.

Before the judge could call the trial to order, Voglino's attorney, John Sogliuzzo, was already on his feet. Pointing to the bedridden defendant, he protested, "I would submit it's not a coherent client I have in the courthouse. . . ."

His protest fell on deaf ears. Ackerman had made up his mind. "He is ill," the judge acknowledged, but said, "I have ordered him to court in a bed with the approval of all physicians."

Sogliuzzo, however, addressed the court: Then what should Voglino do if he has to go to the bathroom? The answer, Ackerman said, was simple. Place him in a wheelchair.

"And I will specifically ask you, Mr. Sogliuzzo," the judge said, "if you would be so kind, because I don't want him falling out of a wheelchair, to assist us in that regard. . . ."

Undeterred, Sogliuzzo insisted on a competency hearing. Voglino was on painkillers. He wanted testimony on whether he would be able to participate in the trial.

Ackerman, however, was unyielding. The doctors had said there would be no problem, so there would be no hearing.

"Now," the judge said, "I would like to proceed with the trial. . . ."

But first, DiNorscio had something to say. "I have never really seen nothing like this, Judge. My concern is, if Jerry Voglino or any one of us died in this courtroom, could we have the funeral here too, Judge?"

Ackerman was not amused. "I want to tell you something, Mr. DiNorscio," he said, "I consider that very insulting. I'm no ghoul. . . . And I don't care for it."

But DiNorscio was not the only one to object to moving ahead. The next to lodge a protest was defense attorney Robert Brown. He expressed concern over the effect of medication on Voglino's ability to participate in the proceeding. If Voglino had appeared in court to plead guilty, and it had become apparent that he'd been under the influence of a painkiller, his plea would not be admissible, he said. So how could Voglino *attend* a trial in that condition?

"I know there's a lot of public pressure to move this trial and so forth," he continued, and then noticed Ackerman glowering at him. "You're frowning at me, Judge," he said, cutting his argument short.

Ackerman was agitated. "I don't know what you're talking about—public pressure. I am impervious to pressure. And, Mr. Brown—"

"You're better than most, Judge," Brown interrupted.

"You're better than most. But if you haven't reacted to any pressure whatsoever, then you don't walk on the same earth that I do. . . .

"And what I'm saying to you, Judge, most respectfully, is the fact that there's a lot of pressure in this case or else that man wouldn't be seated over there like a corpse in a bed where he can't even see the witness stand."

Then Brown added, almost as an afterthought, "And it would seem to me, if he's going to be here, could you angle the bed so he can see the witness stand? He's laying there looking up at the ceiling. . . ."

He paused for a moment and then noted, "Mr. Voglino is making choking-type gurgling sounds that I can hear on the other side of the room. . . ."

Brown was joined in his objections by attorney Dennis Mautone, who was scheduled to begin cross-examination of a government witness when the trial resumed.

"I have to concentrate on my questioning of the witness," Mautone protested, adding that he could not afford to be distracted by the "pathetic" sight of a "gurgling, vomiting individual just off to my right. . . .

"It's difficult enough to cross-examine a reluctant witness without doing it with that kind of distraction constantly at my back."

But, distraction or not, Ackerman was not prepared to permit any further delays. He turned to the court clerk, "Would you bring the jury out."

Voglino's wife sat quietly by the hospital bed, rubbing his head and rising occasionally to press ice cubes to his lips. Voglino said nothing—he only moaned.

"It hurts," Voglino said in an agonized voice, his legs shaking. "I can't move . . . I can't take it."

But those moans were not the only noises Ackerman was to hear. At the end of the day, Sogliuzzo was again on his feet. "I think Your Honor has noticed," he said, "that Mr. Voglino has not been, to say the least, an active participant in this lawsuit today. He has been laying here in an incoherent state. . . ."

But Ackerman was not sympathetic. If Voglino elected to sleep through the day, Ackerman said, it was his choice.

"I've seen people in this courtroom out cold in the middle

of the afternoon with their heads back. I could easily see why sometimes you just get bored by the proceedings. You know that's a fact—and I know that's a fact. . . ."

As if to prove the point, attorney Raymond Brown then rose and pointed to the front row of spectator's benches, where a reporter was sitting with his head slumped over to one side.

"Judge," Brown said, "the press is asleep. Could we awake them for the benefit of the Republic?"

25

When the trial resumed again, the next government witness was William Russell Hawley, another career criminal and narcotics associate of Jackie's, whose life in crime started on a quiet Wednesday evening in early 1967. As Hawley told the jury, he was then a nineteen-year-old janitor at Monmouth County College in central New Jersey, when he entered the tiny stationery store owned and operated by Mary and Louis Pascucci in the peaceful Shore community of Long Branch. It was 7:35 P.M.

Wearing a ski mask and holding a gun, Hawley walked into the store, spotted Mary Pascucci behind the counter, and demanded that she turn over the store's receipts.

"Put the money in a paper bag," he ordered. "Hurry up or I'll have to shoot."

Hawley hadn't noticed eighty-year-old Louis Pascucci, who'd been sitting inside the door watching television while his wife tended the counter.

As Mary Pascucci, terrified by the gunman, moved toward the cash register, Hawley heard a sound. It was Louis. Frail and elderly, he was nevertheless trying to protect his wife from the young assailant. He'd grabbed a chair, as if to hit the stickup man.

"I was getting the money from the woman," Hawley recalled, "and this old man came up behind me. I didn't even know he was in the store. I heard a voice and turned around. He was right behind me holding a chair, and he was shot. I shot him.

"I was startled," Hawley said. "Guns don't discharge unless someone pulls the trigger. Yes, I pulled the trigger."

Hawley hesitated for only a moment that night, then turned and fled, racing toward the sound of the ocean in the darkness. Behind him, he left Louis Pascucci, his lifeblood slowly seeping out into a puddle on the floor of the little store.

It took less than twenty-four hours for police to identify Hawley as a suspect. A witness provided police with the lead they needed, and a search of Hawley's room turned up the murder weapon. He was arrested the following morning, pleaded guilty, and was sentenced to life imprisonment.

He was eventually paroled seventeen years later, despite the objections of Monmouth County authorities, who portrayed him as "violent and dangerous."

But for Hawley, the adjustment to freedom would be just as difficult as it had been to life behind bars.

Within two years of his release, he would be in trouble again. Only this time, he would find a way out. He had got to know people—notably, Jackie DiNorscio. The FBI was interested in the people he knew. He would offer to talk, and they would be eager to listen.

After his release from prison, Hawley found work at a Warren County, New Jersey, horse farm operated by the brother of his prison psychologist. Their agreement was that the job was to be only temporary, just to get his feet wet in the outside world. So after six months, Hawley moved on.

His next stop was an upholstery and furniture shop in Nutley, which was run by an ex-convict whom he had known from prison. In addition to his upholstery business, however, the man had opened a second line of work—narcotics—and he made good use of Hawley in both operations.

Initially, Hawley served as a courier, delivering and picking up packages of drugs and money. Then one day his friend in the upholstery business asked him "to come over to the house." He said they needed somebody down in Florida, Hawley recalled, "to baby-sit for Jackie, is the words he used."

The "Jackie" his friend was referring to was, of course, none other than Jackie DiNorscio.

A year later, when Hawley eventually left Florida, things had gone from bad to worse. He was a fugitive from a gun-possession charge there, and found himself back in New Jersey, but with no one to turn to.

Hungry and out of money, he broke into a Passaic County grocery store and began foraging for food. He was in the middle of one of the aisles, gobbling down produce, when the police arrived and found him. They charged him with shoplifting, and placed him in the local jail. A record check had turned up the Florida gun charge and a detainer was placed on him. So, temporarily at least, Hawley remained behind bars.

At the time of that arrest, he was also on parole from the 1967 murder charge, but at that point, possibly due to a bureaucratic mixup (Hawley had legally changed his name while in Florida), his new arrest had not yet come to the attention of New Jersey parole authorities, who had the power to revoke that parole and put him back in jail. But he had made a decision, he said. He was "tired of the bullshit."

"I was tired of the way I was living," he said. "I was tired of the people I was with."

So he asked to be put in contact with the FBI. And a week later he received a visit—from V. Grady O'Malley and Dennis Marchalonis.

The three men talked, and Hawley told them about the people he knew. In particular, he told them about Jackie DiNorscio. He wanted to make a deal. It was another offer that the government could not refuse.

Hawley had been starving and penniless when he was arrested. He didn't stay hungry or penniless for long.

It was disclosed that in return for his testimony, Hawley was given three hundred dollars a week in payments from the government and a promise of a new life under yet another identity when his testimony was over. It was a good deal. It was a lot more than anyone had offered Louis Pascucci twenty years before.

The story Hawley now told of his Florida year was compelling.

When Hawley found him, Jackie was in bad shape. He

had become an inveterate cocaine user, who was showing increasing signs of paranoia and was terrified of being alone. He needed people with him at all times, and that was Hawley's job, just as his upholsterer friend had described it—to be Jackie DiNorscio's live-in baby-sitter.

Hawley had once declared that all he wanted from life was, "To be left alone. Eat a damn hamburger at McDonald's . . . work at a job." He wound up getting a lot more than he ever bargained for.

Hawley flew to Florida around mid-June of 1985. He was picked up at the airport by Jackie's daughter and driven to Jackie's house.

Jackie greeted him warmly. The two had met during one of Jackie's many prison terms. He wanted to show Hawley around, so he took him on a round of collections from customers of his drug business, chauffeuring his new companion in his red Mercedes 500 SL.

Jackie had a number of cars, mostly large new ones. But he also had a beat-up 1983 Oldsmobile, which he let Hawley use. Hawley nicknamed it the "Ratmobile."

Hawley's first job was to answer the door and handle phone calls for Jackie, screen callers, and take messages. Only certain people were allowed to get through to the Fat Man. In essence, Hawley was a "go-fer." In return, Jackie gave him pocket money and a car.

Jackie was, in the words of O'Malley, a "conspicuous consumer," and, according to Hawley, that assessment was entirely fair. It would be nothing, he said, for DiNorscio to spend fifteen hundred dollars for a night on the town. In a week's time, he could easily run through $30,000, $40,000, $50,000.

But Jackie was developing a problem, Hawley said. He was moving past merely snorting cocaine to freebasing—smoking it in large quantities.

Thus, where Amador and Fisher had portrayed DiNorscio as a high-living wheeler-dealer, Hawley's portrait was of a man slowly being driven crazy by his own drug abuse.

"He'd look out the window," Hawley said. "All the trees in the front yard were turning to FBI agents. He would go through the house, ranting and raving and screaming. He'd be running out on the balcony in his underwear, back and forth. . . . Crazy stuff."

Hawley said Jackie had become fearful of "bugs." "Electrical bugs," he explained, "not *bug* bugs."

Hawley said Jackie ordered him to look into light sockets as he ripped them off walls and told Hawley to fix them. Jackie also purchased electrical devices to screen the house for listening devices.

"These little types of antibugging devices," Hawley said, "he used to turn them up too high. I mean, the fluorescent light would set them off. He'd go crazy and freak out when the thing started buzzing. It wasn't buzzing because there was a bug in the house. It was because he had it set too high."

DiNorscio sat with an amused expression on his face throughout much of the testimony.

As Hawley related his narrative in court, he was finally asked to point out DiNorscio. He smiled and gestured toward Jackie, who was seated against the wall. Jackie just grinned.

Asked what connection Gerald Cohen had with the DiNorscio operation, Hawley's answer was almost incomprehensible.

O'Malley paused and looked at the witness. "Would you do me a favor?" he asked Hawley gently. "Would you take the piece of candy out of your mouth?"

Hawley looked surprised. "It's a cough drop," he said, defensively.

O'Malley had an expression of impatience. "Do you really need it?" he insisted. "I think it's a little bit hard for all of us to hear."

Hawley grabbed a tissue from a nearby table and did as instructed. The questioning resumed.

According to Hawley, Jackie was the front man for the operation, while Cohen handled the business end. For his part, Hawley said, he helped package drug shipments for a small army of couriers employed by DiNorscio. Among those he identified was Manny Montiero, the defendant charged with being a runner for Jackie.

It wasn't the most discreet operation in the world. He recalled one associate mailing a half-kilo of cocaine to his father in prison by concealing the drugs in a food package surrounded by cans.

Hawley also said he helped count up profits, and he described how the drug money was divided into four piles of cash. One, he said, was for Jackie; one for Cohen; one was for "Goo" Suppa, who was Accetturo's right-hand man in Florida; and the last was for Accetturo himself.

He described one incident in which he was ordered by Jackie to take his beloved "Ratmobile" out and burn it for the insurance money. Hawley was surprised. The car was a mess—it couldn't have been worth the trouble.

"I tried to talk him into giving it to me," Hawley said, but recalled that Jackie refused, telling him, "I want it burnt."

The instructions from Jackie were to take it out to Alligator Alley, a road that cuts across the Everglades, abandon the car, and torch it.

As recounted later, Hawley and an accomplice drove the car out onto a desolate stretch of the road and got out. They then doused the car with gasoline and ignited it. Only Hawley was standing too close, and he wound up getting blown into a ditch. The car was still burning when the police arrived at the site.

Meanwhile, another patrol car heard the explosion and shortly afterward spotted a car speeding away in the opposite direction, whizzing by at about 85 mph. The patrol car flashed its lights and pulled over the speeding vehicle. Inside were Hawley and his accomplice.

Although he escaped from that scene without anything more than a few scratches, he eventually wound up getting in serious trouble when he accepted a phone call from another one of Jackie's friends.

It was late, after midnight. Jackie was behind closed doors and had given orders not to be disturbed—he was in bed with two of his girlfriends.

The caller wasn't to be dissuaded. "There's a lot of money involved," he said. Hawley banged on the door to Jackie's room and told him to pick up the phone.

When the conversation was over, Jackie instructed Hawley to go out, pick up the caller from a nearby apartment building, and take him wherever he wanted.

They made an odd couple. Hawley was wearing a strap T-shirt, shorts, and sneakers. The man he was sent to meet was wearing several coats and still looked cold and sick. But Hawley did as he was told. He followed the man's instructions and wound up making several wrong turns, including one that took them the wrong way down a one-way street.

Suddenly, they spotted flashing red lights. It was a police car. Hawley started to pull over, almost out of instinct.

The man in the overcoats started mumbling. "We got to hide these," he said. Hawley didn't know what he was talking about. Then the man opened up his coat. He had two guns inside.

Hawley hit the gas. He was trying to lose the cop car. He managed to pull ahead for about fifteen seconds. "Throw them out the window," he called to the man in the overcoats. He wouldn't. Instead, he stuck them under a seat.

The chase didn't last long. The patrol car pulled alongside, and Hawley stopped. The police searched the car and found the guns.

"I didn't do nothing," Hawley told authorities. "I just took a guy for a ride is what I did. My prints were on none of those guns. There was two firearms, and there were two men in the car, yes, but my prints weren't on none of those guns."

When he later returned to New Jersey and was arrested in the supermarket, however, it was the charges surrounding those guns that were to keep him from being released until he eventually made his decision to talk to the FBI.

Hawley's days as a member of Jackie's entourage were numbered. The last one came on Christmas Eve of that same year, 1985.

Jackie was planning a big Christmas party for some Jewish friends and, instead of turkey, he was planning on serving chicken. Hawley's job was to get the chickens.

"I was supposed to go out and pick up all these dozens of these chickens," he said. "And I didn't pick them up."

Instead, he said, "I went to the beach."

As far as Jackie and his friend were concerned, Hawley recalled, "They didn't eat that night. Well, they didn't eat them chickens anyway."

When Hawley got back to Jackie's house, he expected Jackie's wrath to extend past that incident. On the way home from the beach, he had got drunk and wrecked Jackie's car. He had slammed it over a dividing island, and nearly tore out the back end. But when he saw Jackie, Jackie was too drunk to really care. He looked at Hawley and hollered at him briefly about the chickens. Then, as if too weary to continue, Jackie looked at him and said, "Go back to sleep. I'll see you in the morning."

The next day, Hawley was on a plane back to New Jersey.

The courtroom was filled to overflowing when Jackie waddled to the podium to face Hawley. Rumors had been spreading throughout the defense camp—Jackie was in rare form, and the performance was about to begin.

"Good morning Billy," Jackie said cheerfully, then paused. "Billy," he said softly, "I'm not here to ridicule you, but as you know, I'm a *pro se* attorney. And if you insist on lying here today, then I must bring out your real background and show them, the jury, that you're really a liar."

O'Malley was already livid and on his feet with an objection.

Jackie shuffled through his papers briefly, then continued. "Isn't it true, Billy," he asked, "that the real reason you were sent home that day [was] . . . that I refused sexual advances from you to me?"

There was an undercurrent of nervous laughter in the room as people waited for the response.

"Come on, Jackie," Hawley laughed, looking disdainfully at the three-hundred-pound defendant. "Look at yourself. Are you kidding?"

The snickering from the defendants and the audience almost drowned out the exchange.

Then DiNorscio shrugged and walked toward the witness, his hand extended. "I don't want you getting upset," he said. Then the jury saw what was in his hand—a lollipop. Jackie looked at the witness and handed it to him. "You want to suck on this instead for a while?"

With that, the jurors, defendants, lawyers, and spectators began roaring in laughter.

O'Malley was furious. "It's apparent that this was a calculated move by Mr. DiNorscio to embarrass the witness, and it's apparent that that's the tone of this cross-examination. . . ."

Ackerman retained his composure. "You want to take the lollipop back, Mr. DiNorscio," he demanded rather than asked. "We're not playing games, nor is this a candy store. . . ."

DiNorscio looked stricken. "You know it's not a game," he said, "you know he's homosexual."

The exchange was actually not entirely unexpected. Jackie had raised the issue in a conference outside the presence of the jury. Hawley, Jackie had contended, was testifying against him because Jackie had rebuffed his homosexual advances.

"Are you familiar with a blow-job, Judge?" DiNorscio had asked as plainly as possible. "That's what this guy was trying to give me . . . a blow-job, when I woke up. That's why I chased him out of the house on Christmas Eve," Jackie told Ackerman. "It was cold, but I did do that. . . ."

Critchley, not able to resist the line, had interjected a wisecrack muttered by attorney John Vantuno, who he said "made the suggestion he tried to go up his chimney."

The lawyers, and even the judge, laughed.

But Jackie appeared serious. "I'm accused of being a racketeer," Jackie said, "accused of being a muscle, a jerk. I'm not going to be accused of being a fag."

O'Malley had tried to head off the situation by seeking a court directive barring DiNorscio from suggesting any homosexual motivations to Hawley's testimony. But DiNorscio was insistent. He swore on his ailing mother to prove his sincerity.

"Judge," he began, "on my mother, much as I love that woman—and you know I love her—at least have a little consideration." He motioned to O'Malley, and continued his appeal to Ackerman. "He's here telling me not to defend myself, and he's lying his ass off."

Ultimately, Ackerman decided the issue in DiNorscio's favor. "If he wants to try to bring out that the reason he [Hawley] has such animosity toward him is because he attempted to commit an act of fellatio upon Mr. DiNorscio, and that Mr. DiNorscio, in a rage, threw him out of the house," Ackerman said, "then he should be permitted to do this."

Jackie didn't need any further urging.

"Have you ever been called 'Mary' in jail?" he asked the witness. Some jurors held their hands over their mouths to keep from laughing aloud.

"No," Hawley said, with a tone of disgust.

O'Malley started to protest again when DiNorscio turned to face the prosecutor.

"It's hard enough for me to do this testimony, without you interrupting me."

O'Malley ignored him. "I would ask the court to ask Mr. DiNorscio not to address me during the course of my objection."

"Could I make a similar request? . . ." Jackie quipped in response. He apologized to the court for the indiscretion and went on.

"Remember you testified in front of this jury that I was paranoid because I was doing too much coke? And behind every tree was an FBI agent? That's what you said?"

Hawley nodded in agreement. "That's what you said."

DiNorscio, a smile on his face, then swiveled and faced the jury and audience. He held up his hands in a gesture of helplessness. "Was I wrong?"

There was no stopping the laughter: The entire room convulsed.

Ackerman tried to maintain the decorum. "What I want to say to you, Mr. DiNorscio," he admonished, "is I want you to ask questions. This isn't Dial-a-Joke."

But Jackie didn't seem quite so certain of that.

"Have you ever used any drugs in your arms?" he asked, and then demanded that the witness display his arms to the jury.

"There's no marks," Hawley declared heatedly.

"Could we show them?" DiNorscio taunted.

"I don't want to show them nothing," Hawley said, his voice growing harder and angrier.

"Then we're going to assume there are marks there," DiNorscio said.

Hawley called out to O'Malley.

"Mr. O'Malley," Jackie taunted, "help him now."

"If Mr. O'Malley tells me to, I will," Hawley shouted.

"Mr. O'Malley ain't questioning you," Jackie said in a flare of temper. "I'm questioning you, Mr. Hawley. Go to the jury, show them."

Angry and defiant, Hawley stood, pushed up his sleeves, and stepped down from the witness chair. He walked to the side of the jury box, and turned toward DiNorscio. "You stay away from me . . . there ain't no holes in my arms, you knucklehead."

DiNorscio made a prissy face. "Sticks and stones would break my bones—"

Ackerman cut into the exchange, "Nursery rhymes are not needed here in this courtroom."

DiNorscio pouted. "He said 'knucklehead.'"

In a rare display of humor, O'Malley stood and added his own comment. "Judge, I'll concede that Mr. DiNorscio is a knucklehead."

The jury laughed at that too.

"Did I ever treat you bad in my home?" Jackie demanded as he neared the close of his interrogation.

"Yes," Hawley laughed, "you did."

"Didn't I feed you, Billy? You had no money."

"I feed my dogs too," Hawley responded.

"I don't have no dogs," DiNorscio retorted. "I only had you."

Hawley looked at him with contempt. "Yes," he said, "you had a dog. I was your dog."

DiNorscio laughed and glanced at the jury.

"I didn't call you Spot, did I?"

The laughter in the room nearly drowned out Hawley's reply. "Close to it, guy. Close to it—"

26

The prosecution was becoming increasingly frustrated. The evidence, the testimony that had been presented on direct, was devastating. The actual words coming out of the witnesses' mouths were damning, yet the dynamics of what was taking place in the courtroom didn't reflect the strength of that testimony.

Cross-examination was going off on tangents that had little to do with the actual case. Days had been spent recounting the circumstances surrounding Alan Amador's arrest in Ohio. Robert Fisher had been led through days of testimony about his own private misadventures, including a description of a shoe collection that made him sound like the Imelda Marcos of crime. And Hawley had been forced to detail every aspect of his past life.

What was happening was a blurring of the evidence. The witnesses were being placed on minitrials for their own crimes, with Critchley leading their prosecution and Jackie providing a laugh track for the stories.

The government would present testimony in less than a day, and then the cross-examination would go on for weeks. The actual importance of the testimony was being buried under an avalanche of irrelevancies.

Yet in some ways, the very witnesses the government needed were the fatal flaw in the prosecution.

The government had wanted Accetturo, and they knew him to be tied to Taccetta. There was ample evidence linking Taccetta to gambling, loan-sharking, and credit-card fraud, but not to Accetturo. So they needed Jackie to make the connection.

And in order to get Jackie, they needed Alonzo, Fisher, Amador, and Hawley.

But what the government found itself confronted with was a spectacle far different from the one it had hoped to present. The sins, not of the defendants, but of the prosecution witnesses, were being paraded at length before the jury: the specter of Joey Alonzo, in a drug-dazed state, banging down a woman's door with a log and sitting incoherently on her sofa and a blackboard full of drugs consumed by Alonzo over his lifetime; the movie of Amador and his confederates being seized by the DEA in Cincinnati; and Billy Hawley cold-bloodedly murdering an old man in a mom-and-pop grocery store.

The sideshow had developed into the main event. The government witnesses had pedigrees that the defense held out as examples of humanity at its putrid worst. And there was not just one of them, but a steady stream of them, whose careers were dissected over a period of months. And the jury was constantly reminded that it was the government that had sat down with them and made deals.

Accetturo's lawyer, Milton Ferrell, had quipped at the outset of the trial, "When you lay down with dogs, you get up with fleas."

The government case had become infested with vermin. And while the prosecution case had lacked any allegations of violence on the part of the defendants, and while the lurid qualities of a *Godfather* story were missing from the actual charges, the jury had not been disappointed. All the luridness of a Mafia movie was being presented to them—only it involved the government's own witnesses.

27

When it came to dealing with Jackie, there were times during the course of the trial when Critchley found himself performing double duty. In addition to representing his own client and acting as lead attorney for the defense, it was necessary, from time to time, for him to serve as a sort of emissary to Jackie, who along with Gerald Cohen, Gerald DeLuca, and Manny Montiero, was being held in custody as a result of a previous drug conviction.

Although they sat together with the other defendants during the courtroom sessions, they were isolated during the breaks and luncheon recesses and brought back to the holding cell in the U.S. marshals' complex on the fifth floor of the courthouse.

There were any number of reasons why Critchley had to speak with Jackie, from simple hand-holding, to let him know he was still part of the process and part of the team, to briefings about what was coming next in the trial.

There also were times Critchley had to tone Jackie down. He explained to Jackie that his outbursts of temper in the courtroom benefited no one. If it got out of hand, the judge could simply order in more marshals and FBI agents and turn the courtroom into an armed camp. And no one wanted that.

Since he was only able to see him a few minutes in the morning in court, Critchley made a point of periodically going upstairs to talk with him and the other detained defendants. He wanted to make sure they understood what was going on and reassure them they were not being left out there by themselves.

Invariably, everyone would be waiting his turn to talk, interested to discuss the case and what was going on. DeLuca would be quiet, Montiero would be lying down, and Cohen would simply listen. But no matter what the conversation involved, Jackie would interpose himself.

And for Critchley, it was disconcerting.

"He always seems to do the unusual," Critchley recalled. "In the courtroom, he does the unusual. Out on the street, he did the unusual. Now in a jail cell, what can he do that's unusual? Well, it's rather unusual to go up to a jail cell at lunch to talk to people about the trial and see four people, three of whom are fully clothed, and one who is naked except for his jockey shorts."

That was Jackie's routine: He would strip down to his underwear and just dominate the conversations—"You don't know what the fuck you're talking about. Let me ask Mike this question."—while he stood there "naked as a jaybird, except for his jockey shorts."

The marshals, he said, had come to expect the unusual, and essentially came to tolerate it. "They had rules for everybody else—and then they had rules for Jackie."

28

Leon Schenck took his seat at the front of the courtroom. He was dressed neatly and looked relaxed. He glanced around the room at the men on trial. The faces stared back, and Schenck just waited.

Schenck was an FBI agent. He was one of a parade of agents who had participated in searching the homes and automobiles of suspects in the case during the first part of the investigation, several years before the indictment was returned. Now, those agents were being brought back to tell the jury what they had found.

Under questioning by Barbara Miller, Schenck explained that he had been with the Bureau for approximately ten years. He was, he said, currently assigned to investigations of international terrorism. His specialties were hostage negotiating and antiterrorism tactics. He described the searches he had made and the weapons he had found.

Except for some interplay between Miller and DiNorscio, it was all routine.

Then Jackie waddled toward the center of the courtroom, his shirt partially out of his pants. Approaching the podium, he stared intently at Schenck. Schenck stared back, almost militarily erect in his seat. The agent was black—and his race was about to become a major issue.

"What did you say your position was with the FBI?" DiNorscio asked Schenck.

"Special agent."

"A special agent," DiNorscio repeated, casting a glance at the jury. "What do you specialize in?"

"Special agent is a term designated to all agents of the FBI."

DiNorscio moved toward Schenck, holding some papers in his hand. "How many years have you been an FBI agent, sir?"

Schenck answered as if by rote, "I've been an FBI agent for ten years."

Jackie smiled and glanced at the jury. "And in your ten years, every gun you have got was never registered?"

Schenck translated the jumble of words in his mind. "Every gun I ever owned was registered properly."

"Not you," DiNorscio scoffed.

"The procedure I go through to get a weapon is like anybody else. You have to fill out proper paperwork. You have to have the permit to have it."

DiNorscio walked back to the podium and leaned on it for support. "The question before you is: In your ten years as an experienced special agent, have you ever come across a gun that was legal when you went out on them raids?"

"Yes, I have," Schenck replied.

Jackie looked genuinely amazed. Legal weapons? Properly registered? "You did? You did?" he demanded.

"Of course," Schenck said.

There was a moment of hesitation. Jackie seemed confused. He went back to his notes. "Are you aware of the Second Amendment?" he asked.

"You mean the right to bear arms?" Schenck asked.

"Yes," Jackie said.

"I have a general knowledge of it, yes."

Jackie put down his notes. "You have a little knowledge of it? And as far as I gather here today, you're a special agent, and you teach tactics of jungle fighting."

"No," Schenck responded politely, "I didn't say anything about jungle fighting."

"What is it?" Jackie demanded.

"Terrorism," Schenck clarified. That was what he taught, how to combat terrorism.

Jackie was muttering, "We do have a little terrorism in this country," and swept his arm toward the defendants in the courtroom, "but nobody here is involved in terrorism as of yet, is that correct?"

Schenck simply shook his head. "I have no idea about that," he said.

Jackie took a last look at his notes and then shrugged. "I have no further questions," he said, and shambled back to his seat.

The performance had been, even by Jackie's standards, a poor one. His questioning of the witness was not only irrelevant, but more irritating than amusing.

But it did accomplish one thing—it lit a fuse that caused a major courtroom explosion. The jury was barely out of the room when attorney Raymond A. Brown erupted from his seat.

Brown was one of the best-known trial lawyers in New Jersey—and he was black. He had grown up in Hudson County, an area of New Jersey that was virtually an Irish enclave controlled by old-line ward bosses, whose idea of equality was to allow dead men, black or white, to cast votes for their candidates on an equal basis with the living.

Today, his racial sensitivities had been rubbed raw by DiNorscio's treatment of Schenck. His voice rising in volume, he pointed at DiNorscio, his eyes narrowing and his finger jabbing. "And if anybody ever again addresses a black agent as a jungle fighter, he's going to deal with me."

There was a collective gasp in the courtroom, and a host of side conversations were cut short as heads swiveled to hear what was going on.

"I've sat here and taken a lot on behalf of my client," Brown went on, "and it's time somebody calls a shot here."

DiNorscio waved his hands. "Let me explain to you—"

Brown cut him off. "Let me finish. You haven't run into a buzz saw, yet."

Now DiNorscio was growing angry himself. He wasn't used to being spoken to that way.

"Yes, Mr. Brown," he insisted. "I ain't said no fucking jungle fighters. I need your shit like I need a hole in the head. Look, Mr. Brown, who's talking about jungle fighters?"

"You did," Brown shouted.

"What does that mean? 'Nigger'?" DiNorscio demanded.

"That's what it meant to me," Brown shot back.

The courtroom was buzzing. Lawyers and attorneys were looking at each other in amazement.

"Could we have a recess?" Critchley called, trying to take control.

Brown, who was standing in a row in front of him, shouted down the request. "I don't want any recess. I represent somebody here who is having his rights threatened."

Brown was not only angry at DiNorscio, he was concerned over the impact of the remark on black jurors.

"He has no right to say what he just said," DiNorscio blustered, ignoring a court order to be seated.

Ackerman was on his feet, fuming over the use of the word "nigger." He thundered at DiNorscio, "Never utter that word in my courtroom."

Now chaos was breaking loose. Michael Taccetta, who throughout the trial had sat quietly at Critchley's side, sometimes looking more like a professor than a mobster, with reading glasses perched on the edge of his nose, leaped to his feet.

"Judge," Taccetta called out in DiNorscio's defense, "he did not mean that. . . ."

Brown swiveled to glare at Taccetta. "He said it."

Taccetta shook his head, his voice hoarse and bellowing. "He didn't mean it. I know he didn't mean it. Anybody ever disrespected you?"

Brown nodded in agitation. "Many times."

Taccetta was gesticulating wildly. "If he said it, we would all have jumped on him."

"Many times," Brown insisted.

Taccetta jabbed a finger at Brown. "Name one."

Now Assistant U.S. Attorney Braunreuther attempted to intervene. "Judge . . ." Braunreuther began. He didn't get far.

Taccetta waved him down. "Excuse me, Joe," he said. "I didn't get up before. I never said nothing."

Taccetta turned back to confront Brown. "That's not so," he continued, countering the accusation about DiNorscio, and he looked at the court. "What he's saying right now is not so, and it's never been done."

"Good, good," Brown taunted, "say what you want."

Taccetta leaned over the table toward Brown. The room was in near riot. Other defendants were on their feet like a Greek chorus, repeating Taccetta's words.

"If you had something to say, you could have grabbed him, asked him personal. You talk about people getting on shows. . . ."

"Prejudiced," DiNorscio shouted, deriding Brown's accusations, "that's what you are, Mike."

"We're not prejudiced," Taccetta shouted back.

"You ought to read the tapes," Brown charged, referring to racial remarks that had been picked up by FBI "bugs" that recorded some of the defendants' conversations.

Critchley rubbed his hand over his face. "Recess," he called forlornly.

Taccetta turned to the others and pointed to Brown. "What is he doing in this case?"

"Wait," Ackerman shouted, "wait a second."

But the judge was drowned out by the other voices.

"He did not mean that," Taccetta repeated in defense of DiNorscio.

Now almost everyone in the courtroom was on his feet.

"Could we have a recess?" Braunreuther asked.

"I think we should have a recess," Ackerman agreed.

But Brown was not ready to let it go. "I don't think we should have a recess," he shouted.

"We may not need it," Ackerman said, "but we're taking it."

"I want to tell you something," Brown said to the others in the room. "People sit on the jury who are black."

"He didn't mean that," Taccetta insisted, his voice hoarse and loud. "You could have grabbed him alone and said it."

Brown turned to Taccetta again. "I don't have to grab anybody alone. You think the people on the jury think he meant—"

Jerome Voglino, another of the defendants, joined the fray. He addressed Brown. "I don't think anybody thought he meant what you said."

DiNorscio waved his hand to Voglino. "I'd appreciate it if you don't say no more to Mr. Brown."

Ackerman leaned into the microphone. His voice boomed. "We'll adjourn for the day."

29

On August 2, 1987, a news story broke on the front page of *The Star-Ledger* that set off shock waves among government officials, the court, and the employers of some of the jurors.

It was disclosed that federal authorities, who had initially given assurances that the trial would last no more than six months, had written a letter to another judge in which it was reported that the trial was expected to last at least another year, possibly longer.

As it turned out, the estimate was entirely accurate.

The new data on trial length was contained in a letter sent to another federal judge in connection with a possible conflict in the scheduling of another mob-related trial in federal court in Newark. The letter was prepared by an associate of O'Malley's at the U.S. Organized Crime Strike Force, who said he had obtained the information from O'Malley himself. Nevertheless, the public disclosure of the document infuriated members of the prosecution.

The news also alarmed the judge, who—nine months into the trial—was struggling to keep the jury intact. He and the prosecutors shared a common concern. The news could cause the trial to self-destruct.

Employers already were becoming agitated. The trial was, obviously, disrupting work schedules. Jurors were being passed over for promotions and raises. Employers were contacting the court to find out if the trial "really" was in session. Last-minute cancellations would leave jurors with no choice but to report for work late. Irregular scheduling made it almost impossible for offices to know when the jurors might be returning to work—or for how long.

And accompanying comments by some defense counsel only served to spotlight the potential crisis.

"We're clearly breaking new ground," Critchley declared during an interview for the news report. "In the history of this country, this is probably going to be the longest trial ever."

"Obviously," he said, "the jurors never planned for this. A lot of employers may have agreed to bite the bullet to permit them to participate in a six-month or even nine month-trial, but they didn't expect to have to swallow the gun."

Ruhnke was not quite so florid in expressing himself—but he was direct. He was quoted in the newspaper story as saying he expected trouble to arise when jurors began to realize "the trial doesn't seem to be ending." He was right on the money.

The jurors did not know what was coming, and with every witness, some began to hope that the end was in sight. Those hopes were dashed each time the government called a new witness to the stand. And the grumbling began to grow.

"More than anything else," declared Lisa Horton, the courtroom deputy who was in charge of overseeing the jury, "it was an intrusion on their lives. They were disappointed when new evidence was introduced. When they thought they were seeing the light at the end of the tunnel, suddenly it was very black."

Some jurors were becoming depressed; others started coming in late, lingering across the street from the courthouse in a coffee shop until the very last minute.

An exasperated Dennis Marchalonis, the FBI agent who had personally developed the case with O'Malley, shook his head one morning as he washed his hands in a rest room off the jury assembly room in the courthouse. Marchalonis was a meticulous and punctual sort, and he was critical of the tardy jurors.

"When you know people are depending on you," he muttered, "I can't understand how you can keep them waiting."

But despite their frustrations, the jurors showed an almost slavish dedication to their oath.

One man came into court despite the fact that his father had died the night before. It was only when another juror noted that he seemed to be preoccupied and upset that the situation became known. Judge Ackerman immediately directed that the trial be adjourned for the day.

"He made an oath," Lisa Horton said, "and he was going to be here."

The jurors had been directed not to read news accounts of the trial, but even if they strictly obeyed those instructions, the court could not prevent family members or friends from learning that the trial might never end—at least not in the foreseeable future.

"We just don't know what will happen," Ruhnke declared at the time, "when the jurors find out [about the trial length]."

Ruhnke also expressed concern about the impact a two-year-long trial would have on a jury's ability to render a decision in accord with the law.

"We just don't know what happens when we take a diverse group of people and put them together in this kind of setting for that long a period of time. . . ."

"Our American system of justice," he declared, "is simply not designed to handle something this big."

No one ever knew for certain if the jurors, who were under a news "blackout," ever read the articles. But Ruhnke's comments were to prove more perceptive than he ever dreamed.

30

They weren't exactly the best, or for that matter, even the brightest. But they were what the government had to offer.

Not content to allow one witness to regale the jury with the alleged misdeeds of the men on trial, the government was attempting to bolster the testimony of each with the testimony of the other—the theory being that the jury would see the pieces fitting together, as in a puzzle slowly taking shape before their eyes.

What the jury saw, however, was a rogues' gallery of convicted criminals, each admitting to crimes seemingly as bad as or worse than those attributed to the men who were actually on trial.

Jackie, at least as far as the jury knew, had never attempted to kill anyone. Joey Alonzo had. Yet Alonzo was the witness and Jackie was the one on trial.

Billy Hawley had actually committed murder. There were no charges close to the gravity of that pending against the defendants in that courtroom.

The latest member of this club to take his place in the lineup was Raymond Pinto, Jr., a low-level narcotics trafficker.

Pinto settled uncomfortably into the seat behind the makeshift witness box to tell the story of what was to become his last drug deal.

It was the early afternoon of June 5, 1985, and Pinto was preparing to make a sizable delivery of three pounds of top-grade cocaine when he and two associates pulled into a rest area along the Garden State Parkway in Wall Township, New Jersey.

Waiting for him were the DEA and the New Jersey State Police. An undercover DEA agent had set up the meeting with one of Pinto's associates and had arranged for a rendezvous at a commuter parking lot located near Milepost 98.

At approximately 2:15 P.M., a new Chevrolet Blazer drove into the lot. Pinto was in the front passenger seat.

The truck pulled up behind the car in which two DEA agents were waiting. Pinto opened the passenger door of the Blazer and held out a plastic zip-top bag containing white powder, wrapped in silver duct tape.

"Here," he called out to the agents, "get your bag and get in the truck."

At this point, the lead DEA agent gave a signal over a hidden radio transmitter. The agents pretended to reach into the back of their vehicle for money. As Pinto stepped out of the truck, one of the DEA agents got out as well. As he approached Pinto, he lifted his badge. At this point, the other agent was out of the car as well. "Police," they both yelled. "You're under arrest!"

One of Pinto's accomplices dived into the rear of the Blazer. Pinto, who said all he could remember seeing was "this big chrome gun," jumped back into the truck, pointing at one of the agents. He shouted to the driver, "Hit him, get out of here!"

"I was so scared, I didn't know what I said," Pinto later recalled.

The driver engaged the gearshift and accelerated.

One of the agents drew his gun. He saw the vehicle speeding toward his partner. He fired, hitting the right rear tire. The tire exploded, and the Blazer swerved, grazing the second agent, who spun off the front left fender.

The Blazer smashed over a curb onto the grass and sped across the dividing strip onto a local street.

By now, the other surveillance teams were in action.

The Blazer sped toward a construction site, skidded into a turn, and headed back at the pursuers. The agents opened fire, shattering the driver's window and hitting the windshield.

"They were shooting at us," Pinto said. "They shot all the windows out."

As the getaway car picked up speed and raced through the back roads of Wall Township, jumping off the road across fields and back onto the streets, other police cars joined in the chase.

Pinto tossed the package of cocaine out of the window.

For some seven miles, Pinto said, the chase continued, until the vehicle was stopped by a police roadblock.

Pinto was pulled, struggling, from the Blazer, and placed under arrest.

Pinto, it turned out, claimed he had got his drugs from none other than Gerald DeLuca—the man authorities had identified as the New Jersey contact for DiNorscio's Florida drug operation. He said he had met with DeLuca near a Bloomfield bar and then followed him to a "stash house" where he and DeLuca sampled the drugs before he agreed to purchase them.

Pinto said he eventually met DiNorscio during a trip to Florida and then encountered him again during a meeting at a New Jersey motel.

"He was laying in bed, talking to someone on the phone and snorting cocaine," Pinto said.

His story was just what the government wanted to hear, another link in the chain. Pinto was another potential informant. Within a month, he had become a cooperating witness. And within two months, Grady O'Malley was writing letters to the court on his behalf.

While Pinto did what he was supposed to do during the trial, which was to "dovetail" with the accounts of other witnesses and fill in gaps in their testimony, his most memorable performance was not on direct examination, but rather on cross.

It had little to do with the facts of the case, but it was a classic example of how a courtroom question-and-answer session could become a "Who's on First" routine that would have done Abbott and Costello proud.

Pinto, it turned out, had once been shot in the head by a former wife. Critchley, through a series of increasingly frustrating exchanges, was attempting to pin down the facts of the shooting. The task should have been easier than it was.

It began with an innocent-enough inquiry.

"When did this take place?"

Pinto was vague. "I can't remember the precise date."

"I don't want the exact day," Critchley explained. "How about a year."

Pinto thought. "Roughly 1966."

"Was this your first wife or your second wife?" the lawyer asked for clarification.

Ackerman, however, sensing some confusion, interjected an attempt at simplification.

"He's already answered that," the judge said. "He told us it was the second wife, is that correct?"

"Yes," Pinto replied.

So Critchley continued. "When did you remarry?"

Again, Pinto was vague. "I'm not sure of the exact date."

"But it was obviously before 1966?"

"No," Pinto declared. "It was after that."

The jurors were beginning to exhibit some confusion themselves.

Critchley turned to the judge. "That's what confused me, Judge. The dates did not coincide with his second marriage."

Pinto volunteered an explanation. "I lived with her for a long time before I got married. I'd say it was roughly in '84."

Critchley took a step back. "So she shot you when she basically was your girlfriend prior to marriage, is that correct?"

Now Pinto was perplexed. "I don't understand your question."

Ackerman, attempting to help, rephrased the question. "In other words, what he wants to know is, she shot you and subsequently she married you?"

But that wasn't right either.

"No," Pinto protested. "She shot me after I married her."

Critchley was still game. He jumped back into the fray. "That's what I want to find out. When did you get married the second time?"

Pinto thought and then added to the confusion a wholly new date: "I believe it was 1974."

By now, some jurors were rolling their eyes, and the lawyers had placed their faces in their hands.

But Critchley was not deterred. "Okay, then, you got married in 1974 the second time? She shot you after you got married?"

"Yes," Pinto said, seemingly confused by the confusion he was creating.

"So it would have to be sometime after 1974 that you got shot?" Critchley suggested.

"Right," Pinto agreed.

"So when you said 1966, you were off by many years, correct?"

"Correct."

Now it seemed Critchley had a handle on the situation. "Approximately how long after you got married to her did she shoot you?"

"Maybe five years."

Then, Critchley concluded, the witness must have been shot around 1979.

"I guess so," Pinto said.

"Why," Critchley asked, "did you say 1966 before?"

Pinto was straightforward. "I just got confused, that's all."

But he wasn't the only one. Moments later, he volunteered that he was used to having several girlfriends at one time. This intrigued Critchley, who made the mistake of asking when was the last time he had enjoyed such a bountiful social life.

"Nineteen Seventy-four to 1984," Pinto replied.

"I'm sorry?" Critchley asked, suddenly looking pained.

"Nineteen Eighty-four."

"So, while you're married, you have three or four girlfriends simultaneously?"

"I wasn't married in 1984."

"Did you get divorced from your second wife?"

"Yes."

"When were you divorced?"

The answer brought audible groans from some of the jurors. "In '77."

Even the judge began to rub his face in exasperation.

Critchley, however, was nothing if not persistent.

"Now, I'm confused. I thought you were shot by your wife five years after you were married?"

Pinto was becoming testy. "I said roughly. I don't remember the dates, all right?"

Critchley was conciliatory. "Please, I'm not—all I'm trying to do is clarify something. When were you divorced from your second wife?"

"I believe it was in 1978. Or 1977."

"And you were shot around '79 or '80?"

Ackerman was shaking his head.

"Were you still married to your second wife when she shot you?" Critchley asked.

"Yes."

"And after she shot you, you were divorced."

"Yes."

"Did your wife find out about your three or four girlfriends?"

It was the wrong question. Pinto looked confused again.

"I didn't have any girlfriends back then. . . ."

When the cross-examination was over, Joseph Braunreuther made what should be regarded as one of the most brilliant strategic decisions ever made by a federal prosecutor. He said he had no further questions.

31

The jury had left the room, and the judge was preparing to go to lunch, when Jackie DiNorscio lumbered to his feet. It was September, ten months into the trial.

Ackerman, who was adhering to a rigorous diet, was hungry and was anxious to get back to his chamber and his allotted luncheon ration. After all, for a man who liked to eat, something was better than nothing.

He looked at Jackie almost with an expression of martyrdom. Jackie was waving his hand, and the judge could hardly ignore him.

"Looks like I'm not going to get lunch," Ackerman muttered. Then, to Jackie, "What is it you want to say?"

Jackie gestured out to the audience section of the courtroom, where a portly, balding little man sat unobtrusively. Jackie wanted to get to him, but the marshals who were guarding Jackie wouldn't let him. It was not an act of insensitivity, it was a security precaution.

Jackie's father, the former mob *capo,* was in the spectators' gallery that day, and Jackie wanted to visit with him. But visiting was not permitted in the courthouse: There were regular visiting hours at the Metropolitan Correctional Center in Manhattan (MCC), where Jackie was being held during the trial. If someone wanted to see a prisoner, that was where he was supposed to do it, not in the courtroom during the lunch break.

Jackie gestured to Ackerman. His father, he claimed, had brought him some information about a witness. A defense attorney quipped that it was more likely a veal-cutlet sandwich that his father had brought him. Whatever it was, Jackie was desperate.

"I'm detained here," he shouted, "you're not letting me do what I want to do."

"Mr. DiNorscio," Ackerman said formally, "with respect to any problem of security, the marshal—"

Jackie wasn't in any mood to listen. "I'm not going for it anymore, you hear me? I know if you don't let me talk to him, I'll talk to him in front of the jury." He looked at the judge in defiance. "How's that? Before we get a problem . . ."

Ackerman interrupted him. "If you want to embarrass yourself . . ."

Jackie shook his head, his hair falling down over his brow. "I'm not going to be embarrassed when this court's full of shit."

Ackerman stopped in midstride as he was stepping down from the bench. He looked at DiNorscio in incredulity. He could not believe his ears. "What did you say to me?"

DiNorscio didn't blink. He stared right back at the judge. "This court's full of shit." He shouted and pointed at the prosecution table, where the government lawyers looked on in amazement. "You're acting just like them," he said.

Ackerman blustered, his face going red. "Mr.—"

DiNorscio was on a roll. He cut the judge off, "I don't care what you're doing. When the jury is in, I'm going to talk to him."

There was a momentary silence that seemed to go on forever. When Ackerman spoke again, his voice was low and cold. "Mr. DiNorscio," he said, "you listen to me very carefully."

"No," DiNorscio said, flinging himself forward, his hands perched on the table for support, "you listen."

He gestured to the court stenographer and pointed to the judge. "He's hollering again. Put it on the record."

Ackerman nodded his head. "That's right," he whispered, "I'm mad."

DiNorscio bellowed again, "This court is full of shit." He took a deep breath and glared at the judge. "Now you can do what you want."

Ackerman had his hands on his hips and glared back. "I'll do what I want at an appropriate time."

"Do it in front of the jury," DiNorscio taunted. "You going to let me talk to my father?"

"You heard me," Ackerman replied.

"He's got some information about the witness," Jackie insisted. "You're denying me the right?"

"You heard what I told you," the judge repeated.

Jackie was hot. His shirt was unbuttoned, and there was sweat on his face and spreading damp marks under his arms. "You denying me the right to get some information on this guy?"

"Calm down," Ackerman suggested.

"No," Jackie shouted again, louder than before, "you calm down. You going to let me talk to my father or aren't you?"

"You heard me," Ackerman said stubbornly.

"That no?" Jackie demanded. He signaled the stenographer again. "Is it on the record I'm being denied my right for my father to do some investigating work for me because I have no other choice?"

"I told you, speak to the marshal," Ackerman declared.

"I spoke to the marshal," Jackie said. "He said no." He pointed at the judge. "No, it's up to you to tell me that I can talk to him."

"You heard me," Ackerman said again.

"Are you telling me no?" Jackie rasped, out of breath and in a frenzy. "You denying me the right to speak to my father about this business?"

"Your father can visit you at the MCC."

Jackie stuck out his chin. "My father doesn't have the facilities to go to the MCC."

"He got to the courthouse," Ackerman shot back.

"He got driven down here."

"Then let somebody drive him to the MCC."

Jackie's eyes blazed. "Let someone . . ."

This time, Ackerman was on the offensive. He stepped down from the bench and walked toward Jackie, his finger pointing and his arm outstretched.

"Don't you ever address me in the manner which you addressed me just a little while ago. Don't you ever . . . I have treated you with respect."

Jackie sounded like an angry Rodney Dangerfield. "You're treating me with no respect," he told the judge.

"I have treated you with respect," Ackerman repeated, "and understanding."

Jackie laughed sarcastically. "Judge," he said, "then take your understanding and put it in the law book, because I'm tired of it too."

He turned back to the marshals who were flanking him and let them take him by the arm to be let out of the courtroom.

There was an air of expectancy when court resumed after lunch. Everyone had witnessed the blowup. No one had talked to a judge like that since mobster John DiGilio told Ackerman's colleague, U.S. district judge Dickinson Debevoise, "Fuck you, Judge," and stormed out of the courtroom.

But DiGilio had claimed to be brain-damaged. Jackie had never made any such claim for himself.

There were some brief legal issues discussed perfunctorily and then a silence as DiNorscio stood.

"Yes, Mr. DiNorscio?" Ackerman asked politely.

"If Your Honor please, Your Honor," he began. "I spoke to Mr. Critchley during the lunch break, and he really reprimanded my actions today."

He wiped his forehead with a handkerchief. "I want you to understand one thing, Judge, whatever I said today, I meant no disrespect to you, Your Honor. Because I do respect you more than any judge that I ever met, Judge. And I mean no disrespect to the court. I want you to know, Judge, I should be reprimanded for it and held in contempt."

Ackerman nodded solemnly. "Thank you, Mr. DiNorscio. Thank you very much."

"Would you accept my apology, Judge?"

"I accept your apology," Ackerman said. "Thank you."

32

The bloom was off the rose for both sides.

The smoke was beginning to clear, and Critchley realized that despite all the maneuvering, the defense still had serious problems.

One by one, the witnesses had lined up and told their stories. And although they were fed through a meat grinder of cross-examination, their basic accounts remained intact.

The defense had made fun of them, humiliated them, denigrated and excoriated them; but it didn't change what they had to say. Joey Alonzo may have been a drug addict, and he may have tried to kill Jackie, but at one time he was indisputably a member of the "inner circle." Whatever they said about him had to rub off, to some extent, on the defendants themselves.

The same held true for Hawley, Amador, and Fisher. Whatever their own dirty linen, some of the stench had to stick to the defendants.

But Critchley and the defense team were not alone in their concerns—the prosecution had its own worries.

O'Malley was upset over the tone the trial had taken. He wanted to change it and was visibly frustrated when he couldn't. Braunreuther didn't like it either, but he was more inclined to accept the inevitable.

Braunreuther, however, was increasingly concerned over the length of the case. Despite the cross-examination, the efforts by the defense to obscure the real issues in the case, he remained confident that the government could win on the evidence. But what he didn't have confidence in was that the trial would ever reach a verdict. There was simply too much that could go wrong.

The trial had already gone on longer than anyone ever anticipated. The government had been expecting a swift victory, sensing that the defense would fold in the stretch. But that, obviously, wasn't to be the case.

At the same time, the defense realized there might be a better way—cut losses before it was too late. President Nixon had used the phrase "peace with honor" in describing his plan to end the Vietnam War, and the defense team had something similar in mind.

Although the prosecution wasn't willing to negotiate "peace" with the mob, the prosecutors let it be known that they were willing to talk deal. And Critchley was more than willing to talk to them. He knew, despite all the bravado, that the defense was on shaky ground.

There were indications that the government had something it was holding in reserve—a witness, the prosecutors hinted, who would be so formidable that the defense would be devastated as soon as he took the stand. Once he testified, however, his cover would be blown. He could never go home again, and he would be of little use to the government in the future.

"Once we burn a guy like that," Braunreuther said, "his value diminishes."

So word went out, "There's a witness we're going to have to reveal," the prosecutors told the defense. "And once we reveal that witness, there's no coming back."

The subsequent meeting was set up like a mini–summit conference in an anteroom in the courthouse. Critchley and Dave Ruhnke sat on one side; O'Malley, Braunreuther, and Miller sat on the other.

"It was like a peace-treaty conference," Critchley said, "where they sat on one side and we sat on the other side, trying to work out a deal."

Critchley explained his position: "We realize we're in trouble," he told the prosecutors, "but you can't be looking for the numbers you're looking for."

The prosecution stressed its strengths; and the defense hammered at the prosecution's weaknesses.

The defense offered to tie everyone in to the deal, except for Accetturo. Accetturo wouldn't buy any deal. He had vowed privately that he had made one mistake in his life, and that was accepting a prosecution deal years before. He would never do it again. He also realized that without the other defendants in the case, the government had virtually nothing on him. Any hope of convicting Accetturo depended on spillover from the evidence against the others.

Critchley tried to make it sound as attractive as possible. "We're giving you a complete package here, from A to Z, with the exception of Accetturo. That's not an easy thing to do. If you guys think that I can just whip this together and give you twenty people and a guilty plea and think it's simple—it's not."

The talks continued throughout a series of meetings.

The government broke the defendants into tiers—upper, middle, and lower—and set out what it wanted in terms of jail time for each. It was not an easy task. Even the defense lawyers were in disagreement as to who should be lumped in what group.

The top level included Michael Taccetta, Thomas Ricciardi, and Michael Perna, alleged to be managers of the organization. As Critchley recalled it, the government wanted a minimum of twenty years for each. The prosecution, Critchley continued, was willing to settle for less for the lower tiers, twelve years for the middle and five to seven years for the lowest.

The government indicated it was willing to negotiate downward for some of the people. Without actually stating it, the prosecution indicated that it would be willing to accept pleas to fifteen-year jail terms for Taccetta and the others, and that the other terms would be structured downward from there.

The defense called a meeting at the Elks Club in Orange, renting out the meeting hall. It needed the space to accommodate the numbers.

It was a far cry from the first meeting at the Newark restaurant. Money was running short for some of the defendants. Instead of a grand banquet, they were down to coffee and cake for refreshments.

Critchley outlined his proposal. It was not an easy sell. Some of the defendants were willing to go for it. Some defense attorneys refused to participate in the talks. Other defendants actually demanded an apology, contending their rights were being violated—they were not going to plead.

"But then," he said, "everybody, reluctantly, agreed."

For a brief moment in time, Critchley believed he had a package.

He said the plea discussions were in no way an admission of guilt or innocence on the part of the defendants, but were viewed by defense attorneys as a possible "insurance policy" that would set limits on the jail terms facing many of their clients.

"We realized that [for the top people] a guilty verdict meant virtual life imprisonment, and against that very scary possibility, there was a need to discuss an alternative," Critchley said.

Taccetta was willing to go for ten years, and Critchley believed he would have been able to reach a compromise at twelve, with the other levels coming in at eight years and four years each.

But the government said no.

"They thought it was ridiculous," Critchley said.

And by then, things were coming apart at the seams.

Defendants started making new demands for "wraparound pleas" that would immunize them from any further prosecutions anywhere. They wanted to be certain they were not going to plead guilty in New Jersey and then be indicted two months later somewhere else.

"We couldn't take that plea," Braunreuther said. "We were supposed to go to New York, California, Florida—they wanted to wrap up everything in the whole world. Even things they didn't know about."

"We weren't even close," Braunreuther said. "These guys wanted the moon."

Eventually, the talks became acrimonious.

"You're dead," said one of the prosecutors.

Critchley tried to be conciliatory. "Guys," he said, "we're

not here talking because we feel we're in good shape. But we do feel that this is a case that, cosmetically, is not so damaging to us. 'Cause all you've got is a gambling case. You have nothing else. . . . And that jury doesn't look like a bad jury."

Critchley came to see Ackerman.

"Are you close?" the judge asked.

Critchley grimaced. "Judge," he said, "I'm at ten. I can get to twelve. I can't bullshit you. I don't have anything else. That's it."

Ackerman looked almost sad. He knew what the government was willing to do, and what it wasn't.

"That'll never go," he said. "That'll never go. . . ."

33

In the early autumn of 1984, a letter had been written to FBI agent John Thurston by an inmate at New Jersey's Southern State Prison. It was a brief handwritten note, covering one side of a lined sheet of notebook paper.

It was an appeal for help.

In it, the author asked the FBI agent to get in touch. In return, the inmate promised, "I'll write you and explain my problem and try to tell you what I would like you to do for me."

But the FBI is a bureaucracy, and like all bureaucracies, its wheels turn slowly. Thurston had once been assigned to the New Jersey office of the FBI, but he had since been transferred, and the letter took time to catch up to him.

A month later, the inmate was still waiting for an answer. So he tried again.

"Hello . . ." he began. "A friend from Newark, New Jersey, is in trouble and would like to speak to you. He needs your help. . . ."

It was a good thing it wasn't an emergency. That letter too went unanswered. But the inmate was persistent, and on November 21, 1984, he wrote again. This time, the letter contained a little more detail.

He reminded the agent that they had known each other in Newark during the 1970s. Now he wanted to make a new deal. He was willing to do some work for the FBI, but he wanted a promise in return. "If you recall, you'll remember I'm a man of my word, and over the period we did business I never lied to you. If we do work together, my word would become my bond. In return," he wrote, "I would expect the same from you and your agency, being my life would be put on the line."

The inmate was serving a five-year jail sentence, and he wanted out. Because of the nature of his conviction, which involved "profiteering" from drugs, he was afraid the parole board would write him off and he would "max out from behind the fense [sic]."

And then he explained what he would be willing to do: "I would be willing to get directly involved with helping destroy corruption in all the major areas that I know. . . ."

The next line contained the bombshell: "I would be interested in working for a couple of years in order to bury all of Newark and vicinity."

That inmate was to become the government's secret weapon in the Accetturo prosecution, a witness whose testimony would consume four months of trial. His name was Nicholas Peter Mitola, Jr. He was thirty-seven years old, had grown up in West Orange, and had lived a life of crime. Now, he said, he was "just starting to understand what life's all about."

"My so call [sic] friends and business associates of the last twenty-four years have done a good job of destroying my life," he complained.

Nicholas Mitola never did meet Thurston again. Instead, Thurston referred the matter back to someone in Newark who might be better able to make use of the information. That someone was Dennis Marchalonis—and Mitola was just the ammunition he needed.

Three years later, Nick Mitola set out to keep the promise he had made the FBI from prison—his promise to "bury" his old friends.

It was late morning on August 26, 1987, when Mitola walked into the federal courtroom. He was dressed casually, wearing a pullover shirt. His thinning hair was dark, brushed back from a round face. His eyes appeared to narrow nervously as they darted about the courtroom. The faces were all there. Familiar faces. Faces of the people he had talked about—the people he had come to bury. He had known them, worked with them, been friends with some. And now he had turned on them. And they stared back at him with cold and undisguised contempt.

"Mr. Mitola," Judge Ackerman said gently as Mitola was led to his seat at the front of the courtroom, "as you can plainly see, that's a microphone in front of you."

Mitola reached out and grasped the metal pole that anchored the microphone in a floor stand directly beneath the desk in front of him.

"If you can . . . speak right into it at all times keeping your voice up, so we can all hear you, I would appreciate it very much," the judge said. Then he settled back to listen to what Mitola had come to say.

Grady O'Malley stood and walked by the jury, his face grim, his eyes intent.

"Mr. Mitola," he asked in a loud voice, "from your personal experience, is there an organization that engages in criminal activity in the New Jersey area headed by Michael Taccetta?"

His testimony was everything that the defense had feared.

In 1964, Mitola had been a student at West Orange Mountain High School. It was a reasonably good school, a cut above those in the neighboring communities and certainly more prestigious than those in Newark. It had snob appeal in the world of Essex County, where the pecking order ran from Newark westward toward East Orange, Orange, and then West Orange. The people in West Orange had money. They were the people with the big houses on the hill. They looked down on the neighbors in the valley, where Accetturo and Taccetta had been born and raised.

But Mitola and Accetturo had something in common—they liked gambling. The only difference was that Accetturo had seen the potential in taking bets from others: While Mitola didn't mind taking them, he preferred making them.

Mitola started gambling in high school, on football games. He made money by taking his own action. He handed out cards that, for one dollar, gave bettors a chance to pick winners in four to ten football games. The kids in high school were willing customers.

After graduation, Mitola's passion intensified. He attended college in Emporia, Kansas, and there he found a niche. He was the city slicker from the East, and he found a ready-made clientele in the corn-fed environment of the Midwest. He began running weekly card and crap games.

From Emporia, Mitola returned to New Jersey, where he became a "sports bettor," going to the racetrack and hanging out in clubs in Newark and the Oranges, shooting craps, playing poker and gin rummy.

The clubs, he said, were social clubs, a cultural phenomenon common to Italian neighborhoods. There, neighborhood residents would gamble on blackjack, poker, and dice, while the "house" took a cut of the action for its own profit.

He described one club in Orange as ostensibly a political club; although the real activity was the politics of poker, not elected office. When players sat at the table, the "house" would supply the cards and chips. There was an hourly charge for the use of a table, and on top of that, the "house" took 5 percent of the bets.

There was no problem from the police, he said. In fact, one local detective was actually a partner in one of the clubs.

He learned the business from the ground up, starting with writing "numbers" for the mob, calling it "on-the-job experience."

In the course of his testimony, Mitola was asked by O'Malley to describe another social club in East Orange, which shared space with a heating and air-conditioning firm.

"What is it?" O'Malley demanded.

"It's where the Michael Taccetta organized-crime group hangs."

He described the interior of the social club. Inside was one room with couches and a television set. To the right was a half-empty room containing two video machines and a portable crap table. Both of the front rooms opened onto a rear "book room," where there were tables to play poker, gin rummy, or whatever the game of the night might be.

The upstairs was the lounge area, where there was a big bar and TV room, tables, and couches.

"It was a meeting place," Mitola said, "where gamblers and bookmakers met and went over various figures, and played cards, ran crap games."

It was also a place, he said, where he sold counterfeit credit cards and where he discussed cocaine and drug dealing.

"It wasn't a plumbing-supply house, that's for sure," Mitola quipped, as the trial recessed for lunch.

When the afternoon session began, O'Malley went straight to the point. Who was the boss?

"Michael Taccetta," was Mitola's reply.

He had three immediate subordinates, Mitola added: his brother, Martin, Thomas Ricciardi, and Michael Perna.

Martin, Mitola said, was the *consigliere,* the man Michael sent to represent him in resolving disputes within the organization. Ricciardi, he said, operated the firm's interests in the distribution of illegal gambling machines. And Perna, he said, had taken over for Cataldo in managing the operations at the Hole in the Wall. It was, he said, like "one happy family. Each individual had a specialty. . . ."

"Who was the boss above Michael Taccetta?" O'Malley demanded.

The answer was what everyone anticipated.

"Anthony Accetturo," Mitola said. The defendants merely snickered.

The subsequent story Mitola told was one filled with *Godfather*like touches, including payments of "tribute" and ritual kisses of "respect."

Mitola described Taccetta as holding court at the East Orange social club, and said he had witnessed subordinates going to Taccetta's table for huddled discussions to which Taccetta would either nod his assent or disapproval.

His own specialty, he said, was in the distribution of drugs, and he stated that the operations were coordinated through electronic paging devices that were issued to members of the drug ring.

"It was like you had your own office in your pocket," Mitola said. "For thirty-three dollars a month, you would never miss a call. Anytime anybody wanted you, all they had to do was beep you. . . ."

"From your observation," O'Malley inquired, "how many of the individuals who were part of this organization had jobs?"

Mitola shook his head and smiled. "To my knowledge, none of them. I mean, I wasn't working, and I was on the street every day, morning, noon, and night, and ran into all them [during the day]. If I wasn't working, how could they be working if they were running into me?" he asked with impeccable logic.

In addition to multikilogram cocaine deals, he described marijuana transactions, including one in which he recalled transferring a garbage bag stuffed with thirty pounds of the drug from the trunk of one car to another.

In a more bizarre episode, Mitola recounted a meeting with two marijuana dealers at a restaurant in West Orange.

It was winter, and it was cold. He had made arrangements to meet his contacts around 9:00 P.M., but the time was flexible. They planned on having dinner there and told him, "When you get here, you get there."

He arrived as they were ordering their soup, a specialty of the house, mushroom soup. Joining them at the table, he watched them finish the soup, and go on to plow through a Caesar salad and cheeseburgers.

When they were done, one of the individuals stood up and went to the rest room. About five minutes later, he returned. His face was puffy and red. Then the second man stood and went to the bathroom. He came back in the same condition.

Mitola looked across the table at them, sitting there glassy-eyed.

"What, do you got some stuff?" Mitola asked, certain that they had taken a few "hits" on some drug.

The two of them just laughed in response.

"No," they said, "we just went and threw up. . . ."

Mitola laughed as he told the story. "Their idea of being macho at the time was being skinny. Every time they ate, they went down and threw up."

Monday nights, Mitola said, were a night when everybody got together at the "club." That was the night the organization's bookmakers would get together with their records for a weekly rundown. Most bookmakers in the New Jersey area worked on a Monday-to-Sunday week. After the Sunday night games were over, the figures would be entered onto a master sheet. Then the week's final results were tallied up. On Monday nights, those records were turned in to the organization.

The man in charge, Mitola said, was Robert Spagnola. Spagnola, a former cop who had done time in jail, had, authorities said, worked his way up to a key position within the Taccetta organization.

The betting figures were written on "water paper," a parchment-type material that dissolves almost instantly in water. It was insurance; if there was ever a raid, a quick drop in a bucket would dispose of all the incriminating evidence.

Tic Cataldo and Jerry Voglino, identified as the main controllers of the numbers operations, would also report to the "club" that night to tote up their results.

To operate a successful gambling operation in New Jersey, Mitola said, you had to have a "rabbi," someone with enough clout in the underworld to go to bat for you in the event of a problem. Without that kind of support, you were an outlaw, "open game for anyone who had power or authority that could muscle in on you."

In fact, he said, it was common practice among the mob-backed operations to absorb the independents by allowing their own people to bet into them heavily, and then, if there was a problem in meeting the payoffs, just to take them over. The practice, he said, was known as "taxing."

Sometimes, however, the mob made its own problems for the independents. By way of example, Mitola told the story of Angelo, a bookmaker who ran a restaurant in Garfield.

Mitola and several of his friends had been betting heavily that year, and around Thanksgiving, they had lost some ninety-seven thousand dollars to Angelo.

There was some general grumbling and moaning about how they were going to pay it, since they didn't have the money, and then they hit on the simple solution: Rip Angelo off.

"I was told," Mitola said, "that Angelo was going to have a problem."

And what was the problem?" O'Malley asked.

"Well," Mitola explained, "he was going to get paid and robbed at the same time."

It was the first or second Friday after Thanksgiving when Mitola met his friend at the "club." One of them was preparing a bag of money. "He stuffed it with maybe three- or four-hundred dollars in one-dollar bills to make it look like an exorbitant amount of money," Mitola said. Then, the final arrangements were made.

Three of the other guys in on the deal were to take a ride to meet Angelo at his bar. One of the men, known as Randy, entered the bar, met Angelo, and had a drink with him. Then the two men headed for the bathroom, where Randy handed Angelo the money-stuffed bag.

Moments later, the second member of the rip-off team walked in with a gun. He grabbed the bag, slapped Angelo around, and walked out.

When Angelo came out of the bathroom, Randy was waiting.

"Well, I paid you," he told the distraught bookie. "It's not my problem anymore."

Angelo ran out of the restaurant, jumped in a car, and took off after the holdup man. But he lost him on Route 80, somewhere near Parsippany.

O'Malley waited a moment for the impact of the story to settle in on the jurors.

"Was this scheme authorized by anyone?" he asked.

"Yes," Mitola responded.

"Who was it authorized by?"

There was a brief silence, and then Mitola said the name: "Michael Taccetta."

He was also present when Taccetta outlined his philosophy to "Billy," another independent bookie who found himself the subject of some attention from the organization.

Billy had been brought to the club and introduced to Michael for a little talk. As Billy sat across the table, Michael explained the situation: "If you're eating one steak, that's fine. But when you get to have two steaks in your plate, then you should eat only half of the second—and give the second half to us."

Jackie DiNorscio had sat quietly while Mitola told his story; but when details of the testimony produced a heated exchange between O'Malley and a defense attorney, he decided to weigh into the fray.

"Your Honor," he said, waving a hand toward O'Malley, "he's got to stop hollering like that."

DiNorscio looked pained. "He's scaring me."

The courtroom grew silent. Then titters began to break out across the defense camp. Ackerman grimaced. This couldn't be for real.

"He's scaring you?" the judge asked incredulously.

DiNorscio wobbled a finger at O'Malley. "He's doing a lot of hollering in this court, and I want you to make him stop."

Ackerman looked exasperated. "Mr. DiNorscio," he said, "I'm sorry you're scared."

DiNorscio blinked. "Not for me, Judge. He's scaring one of the jurors also. . . ."

It was later that morning when the judge was adjourning court for the luncheon recess that he mentioned to the attorneys that he would be out of his office during the lunch break because he was taking his secretary, Judy Parker, out to lunch. No one made any note of the comment until DiNorscio raised his hand.

"Yes, Mr. DiNorscio?" Ackerman said politely.

DiNorscio stood with a broad grin on his face. "Would you consider taking us to lunch today?" he asked.

Ackerman chuckled and replied, "Did you ever hear the expression 'Two's company and three's a crowd'?"

DiNorscio raised his eyebrows in mock surprise. "Does Mrs. Ackerman know about this?" he inquired.

The judge was not concerned. "Mr. DiNorscio," he said, "next time she is here, you can tell her."

DiNorscio paused for a moment and then offered a word of cautionary advice about the danger of informants. "Just don't let Mr. Mitola know about it. . . ."

34

As time passed, O'Malley grew more grim.

The hurdles he had passed in putting the case together had been only the beginning.

Nobody had wanted to testify against the Taccettas. One man had walked out of the grand jury and muttered, "I'm a dead man. . . ."

His own daughter had been taunted by relatives and friends of defendants. His wife had received mysterious phone calls.

But the obstacles he had overcome in bringing the case to trial seemed minor in comparison to the situation that had unfolded in the courtroom. The case was becoming personal.

He had been cursed and vilified by the defendants on an almost daily basis. But on top of everything else, there was Jackie, the self-anointed court jester, whose antics made O'Malley fume.

"I turned this trial around," DiNorscio once boasted. And in large measure he did. Because when Jackie joked, O'Malley's anger grew.

Jackie charmed the jury.

At one point, he joked about a drug-sniffing government dog named "Sergeant Bandit." "Wasn't he killed trying to sniff the white line in the middle of the road?" Jackie joked.

Another time he kissed a government witness, a woman who had once worked for Aron and Aron in Florida. Still another time he challenged O'Malley to a wrestling match while defendants took odds on who would win and whether Jackie would use a baseball bat to even up the match.

O'Malley, in his own words, was "rip shit." DiNorscio, he felt, was "a fucking guy who's a career criminal," whose antics were turning the trial into something that "took on the flavor of a circus."

For his part, O'Malley remained tight-lipped. "I wouldn't laugh," he said, no matter how outrageous Jackie's antics became, "because I refused to let the jury think that I was on the same wavelength as Jackie DiNorscio. This was serious business."

It may have been serious to O'Malley, but the defendants were doing their best to play it for laughs.

One, Gerald DeLuca, even wrote a poem:

Twenty-one defendants are here today
The scales of justice they're hoping to sway.
Charged with RICO and organized crime,
a law which makes justice truly more blind.

The government says we're a danger to the community
as they grant their informants total immunity.

So with lawyers like these planning our attack,
Why are we counting on a fat man named Jack?

35

The storm that had been brewing between O'Malley and DiNorscio finally erupted in early October.

Ackerman had called a luncheon recess in the trial and was preparing to leave the bench.

Jackie DiNorscio made a motion with his hand and began to speak. "Everybody is going to lunch now," DiNorscio complained, his voice that of a petulant child.

Ackerman looked down at him questioningly.

DiNorscio took the glance as reason to continue. "The prison cut back on their food budget, and we really haven't eaten [anything] in three days," he protested.

There were muted chuckles from various areas of the room. Ackerman raised an eyebrow and surveyed Jackie's portly form. He was less than sympathetic in his response.

"You look good to me," he remarked offhandedly.

DiNorscio smiled and stood. "Only because I drink a lot of water." He paused. "Is there any reason why we can't have a little more lunch?"

Ackerman shrugged. "Ask the marshals."

DiNorscio shrugged back. "I asked the marshals. They said no."

Ackerman rose from his seat. Jackie looked at him plaintively. "In that case, would you bring me back a little French fries?" DiNorscio asked.

Ackerman shook his head in regret. "I'm not permitted to bring you French fries."

He turned and left the room before Jackie could respond.

But as the defendants filed out of the room, O'Malley allegedly passed a comment about the incident that was overheard by some of the other defendants. They, in turn, lost no time in relating the remark to DiNorscio.

The alleged comment did not sit well on DiNorscio's empty stomach.

When the trial resumed after the lunch break, DiNorscio was on his feet.

The judge nodded permission for him to speak.

"Your Honor," he began benignly, "I made a promise to this court, Your Honor, especially to you, that I won't start no more trouble."

Then, with a movement that seemed almost impossibly swift for a man of his bulk, Jackie swiveled, extended a meaty arm, and jabbed a pointed finger toward O'Malley. He was no longer benign.

"Next time he calls me a fat motherfucker," DiNorscio snarled, "I'm going to kick his fuckin' ass."

He looked up at the judge to explain. "Mr. O'Malley called me a fat scumbag motherfucker."

He again pointed with a pudgy digit to the prosecutor, his voice now growing hoarse and his face florid. "Did you say it, you yellow motherfucker? He called me a fat scumbag motherfucker, Judge."

DiNorscio then took a deep breath and sat down.

"I apologize to the court, Your Honor," he said mildly.

O'Malley appeared stunned.

The defendants were snickering, and the judge glared in amazement.

O'Malley rose to his feet. "Judge," he protested, "I don't ever recall having a conversation—"

At that point, John Redman, the defendant who was seated to O'Malley's rear, jumped to his feet, shouting at the top of his lungs and gesticulating wildly. Heads whirled to see what was going on.

"You said it walking out of the courtroom," Redman blustered. "I heard it. You said, 'The fat scumbag motherfucker has got thirty years, [and] he's worried about lunch?'"

The courtroom was taking on the atmosphere of a barroom brawl.

O'Malley tried to remain composed.

"Judge, if I said what they claim I said, it was said to other individuals."

There were hoots and catcalls. Redman was still livid. He pointed at Marchalonis. "And your fuckin' puppy behind you agreed with you. That little jerk on the side of you."

There were scattered applause and shouts.

Ackerman was attempting to restore order. He addressed Redman's lawyer, John Vantuno. "Mr. Vantuno," Ackerman called out, "would you try to control your client? Just try." He gestured for O'Malley to resume.

"Judge," the prosecutor said, "if I made any comments to my colleagues and it was overheard, I have no other comment to make. . . ."

The situation, O'Malley protested, was no different than when he had heard his own name "disparaged" in the hallways. There were snickers from the defendants.

Ackerman paused and then admonished O'Malley.

"Two wrongs don't make a right. . . ."

"To say the least," the judge declared, "it isn't professional. I realize, you know, someone said this is war at the beginning of the trial. But if I may say that my job isn't made any easier in trying to administer a trial by these unnecessary intrusions. In plain English, will you keep a zipper on your sipper?"

The attorneys laughed, and O'Malley, red-faced, sank back into his seat.

The judge's chastisement of the prosecutor seemed to appease DiNorscio.

"I apologize to the court, Your Honor," Jackie said, smiling.

36

Late in 1982, a team of FBI agents performed what is known in the trade as a "black bag" job. Under the cover of darkness, they broke into the Hole in the Wall luncheonette in Down Neck Newark and planted a series of hidden microphones, each capable of picking up conversations and transmitting them to remote tape recorders set up a short distance away. They planted one near the freezer in the back room, and they tapped the telephones.

For months, FBI agents equipped with earphones listened as the habitués of the Hole in the Wall talked—and they recorded it all.

These recordings, some three hundred of them, were to be the backbone of the prosecution case. They would lend credence to the stories the informants had to tell. They would illustrate how the gambling and loan-sharking operations worked. Jurors would hear firsthand how the mob installed video-gaming machines in bars.

As conceived, the plan was a sound one, as many of the conversations were clearly about gambling and other illicit activities.

But rather than providing shocking glimpses of life in the

underworld, the dialogue sounded curiously benign. There was no one plotting murders. There was no whispered plan for any "big score." It was pretty much the routine workings of a blue-collar betting crowd, no worse than what you might hear in any bar where the friendly bartender was taking bets. As the jurors listened, they appeared to grow alternately bored and amused.

And the situation wasn't helped by the fact that Nick Mitola, who had helped the prosecution identify the speakers on the tapes, had changed his mind several times about whom the voices belonged to before the transcripts were prepared for the trial.

In the end, what the tapes were finally most notable for was the curious insights they presented about life in the mob. Indeed, unlike the television portraits of gangland figures as silksuited dons, chauffeured about in black limousines while dining at fine eateries, the FBI tapes revealed that these same men were just as apt to bicker about nickles and dimes as they were to wage "war" over "beefs" about big money.

In fact, the tapes portrayed much of the daily activity of the Lucchese organization as centering on how to avoid being cheated by its own operatives and how to keep a lid on expenses, as well as cut down on the cost of Christmas presents to customers and employees.

The jurors were even treated to a debate between Michael and Martin Taccetta over whether to allow their wives to attend a Tupperware-type lingerie party being thrown in their neighborhood.

In addition, the tapes included references to a roster of characters, all talked about in code names that could have come straight out of a Batman comic book. There were "the Riddler," "the Penguin," "the Cow," "the Panda," and "the Bad-News Bear." And there were "Tomahawk," "Cochise," and "Ironsides."

Then there were the numerous faceless voices and names who were discussed in less than laudatory tones by the members of the "Hole in the Wall" gang.

There was "Sallie," who owed money but "slipped on the ice or something" and died before he could pay.

"That dirty motherfucker! I have to call him that even though he's dead. . . . I met him on the street about a month ago, and I said, 'What you gonna do about that tab you owe us?' I knew in my heart he was doing something."

And there was Al, a bookie for the organization who wanted two dollars more to cover an increase in his telephone costs. "I call from Cranford, sometimes Westfield. . . . A dollar-fifty with overtime," he said.

But the mob had no sympathy. "Two dollars a day is fourteen dollars a week! We're only giving you two dollars extra!"

"You believe this fucking guy?"

There were also the problems with the deadbeats.

"Let me tell ya something. They're a lot of stiffs in this fuckin' book, and they think we are suckers all the time. . . .

"Ya got to keep on top of these guys, ya have to. I'll tell ya what I'm gonna do. When they come in, I'm gonna slap them in the fuckin' mouth. I'm gonna slap every one of them in the fuckin' mouth. . . .

"They won't pay. They are just degenerate cocksuckers. They don't know what it is to be nice. . . .

"We're taking [off] the Santa Claus suit. There are a lot of guys who are going to start getting hurt."

And there were a smattering of other tidbits, like a reputed organized-crime figure offering some "big brother" advice to a younger sibling.

"Do yourself a favor, go get a job. . . . You're not going to survive out there. I know how stupid you are. . . ."

There was also some resentment over the inroads that legalized state lotteries are making in the numbers business.

"Ya know, they told Swifty when he went for sentencing . . . the prosecutor told him, he said, 'Listen, the state of New Jersey now, ah, has gambling operations. We don't want ya having anything to do with it. . . ."

The mobsters appeared to recognize that, like the dinosaurs, their era might be growing to a close. Referring to the legitimate lottery officials, one said, "This is their game, you understand? They're the 'wiseguys' here."

37

As the days passed, like a soap opera, Mitola's story continued:

It was a Saturday afternoon in the winter of 1982 when Marty Taccetta walked into the "club" with a proposal for Nick Mitola.

Smiling, Marty clapped Nick on the shoulder and asked, "Would you like to go to work in Haiti?"

It was an offer, Mitola told the jury, that took him by surprise. It was also an offer that he eventually decided to refuse.

According to government reports, leaders of the Lucchese organization had hoped to expand their operations into the Caribbean and had sent Marty Taccetta down as a sort of goodwill emissary to check out the possibilities of establishing a gambling resort on the island of Haiti.

In order to carry out their plan, authorities said, they hoped to enlist the support of the since-deposed dictator of that island nation, Jean-Claude (Baby Doc) Duvalier.

The reports suggested that the "boys from Jersey" were already skimming money out of one Haitian gambling casino, and hoped to establish another gambling base on the island.

A "bagman" for the New Jersey organization was already making routine trips to the island, and picking up proceeds and funneling them back to New Jersey.

The long-range plan, according to the government, called for the organization to skim the proceeds from the first casino until they drove it into bankruptcy, and then form a new corporation to purchase another resort on the island.

A telephone call intercepted by the FBI portrayed Taccetta in conversation with a contact on the island, apparently setting up the groundwork for the deal.

"Hello, how are ya?" Taccetta greeted his associate.

"All right," he acknowledged, but added, "the Frenchman still hasn't showed."

As the two discussed the situation on the island, they referred to the feasibility of setting up their own corporation, and discussed the accessibility of certain locations on the island.

"There's a nice place on the beach maybe fifteen or twenty minutes from there," the man in Haiti told Taccetta. "But I don't know whether this airfield will handle even smaller jets."

"All right," Taccetta responded moments later. "You let me know what you need."

The conversation continued as the Haitian contact told Taccetta it would be necessary for the New Jersey mob boss to establish his own corporation and "use local lawyers [to] meet with your lawyers" to work out the details. It would also be necessary to receive permission from the Haitian minister of the interior.

"All right," Taccetta replied again. "But then we got to set up, ah, an appointment with their minister then, right?"

"But that's no problem," the contact assures, "once you start to form your own little company and make your petition. . . ."

Mitola said he became aware of the plan after meeting Marty Taccetta shortly after the mob leader returned from a trip to the island. Mitola said he was asked by an associate to obtain plane tickets for a number of the other "boys" for a subsequent visit to the Caribbean nation.

They were welcomed in style. Government documents reveal that members of the Lucchese family were invited to dine on a meal of roast pork with then-dictator Baby Doc Duvalier at his home, during which time his personal bodyguards armed with .45-caliber guns watched over the guests.

The plan, however, was never brought to fruition. Not long afterward, Duvalier was ousted in a bloodless coup and was last reported living in exile on the outskirts of Paris.

When the story of the Caribbean connection was disclosed during the trial, Critchley made light of it. He charged that the allegations had transformed the basic case from a gambling conspiracy that centered on the activities at a Newark sandwich shop to a case of international intrigue involving the apparent takeover of a Caribbean gambling empire, complete with "meetings with dictators on Caribbean islands."

"Are we going to be in a position to subpoena 'Baby Doc'?" Critchley protested at Ackerman's decision to allow the evidence into the case.

"The next thing you know," Critchley said, "we'll be charged with overthrowing governments. . . ."

38

In many ways, Marty and Michael Taccetta were opposite sides of the same coin.

Michael looked like what he was—a guy from the streets. Marty looked like a Hollywood image of a young on-the-rise mobster—and he fit the role perfectly. One newsman covering the trial suggested that he had not seen Marty wear the same outfit twice. His dress, his hairstyle, and his soft-spoken bearing showed a sophistication that had carried him well beyond the streets of Newark.

A close associate had once described the brothers' relationship as almost symbiotic. While Michael appeared sedate, almost philosophical in demeanor, Marty was the spark plug for the organization. He was the one who was venturing into new areas, expanding the scope of operations from New Jersey to California, and even to the Caribbean.

The trial years, however, were not the best years for Marty Taccetta. The trial had made him restless. The FBI was monitoring his movements. He was on a tight leash held by the court, at least as far as his travel went. Whenever he wanted to leave the state to, as he claimed, attend to his "business interests" in California, he had to get permission from the judge. He wasn't in jail; but at the same time, he wasn't free.

But Marty had always skated on the edge of danger. And there were times when it seemed as though the thin ice would finally give way.

Around 2:00 A.M. on February 5, 1976, a twenty-four-year-old West Orange resident was stabbed to death as he was exiting a local basement discotheque known as Dimple's.

The victim was David W. Dowd, Jr., the son of a former New Jersey State senator and former Livingston mayor. The younger Dowd had worked as a leather craftsman and owned a shop in the Shore community of Point Pleasant. He had moved to West Orange just a year before his death.

As outlined by authorities at the time, a dispute had broken out in the bar when a customer spotted a woman he knew and tried to strike up a conversation. The woman, however, was somebody else's date, and her escort and several other men objected to the attention. The dispute, marked by heated pushing and shoving, spilled out into the lobby. There, the first man was punched and knocked to the ground.

Authorities said Dowd tried to stop the fight and was stabbed once in the back. He was rushed to St. Barnabas Hospital in Livingston, where he died on the operating table.

Martin Taccetta, then twenty-four, and a companion, Michael Ryan, then twenty-five, surrendered to authorities shortly after the incident. They were both charged with murder.

Ten months later, however, both were cleared of the charges. Although the state's key witness had testified that he had seen a metallic object in Ryan's hand, possibly a knife or ice pick, he could not identify Ryan as the man who stabbed Dowd. A jury acquitted Ryan of the murder charge, while a superior-court judge directed that the charge against Taccetta be dropped for failure by the prosecution to produce sufficient evidence.

Marty didn't stay out of trouble long, however. Three months after the acquittal in the Dowd case, he and Ryan and several others were indicted again, this time for the brutal beating of an alleged extortion victim in the men's room of a

Union County night spot. Taccetta, it was claimed, had been trying to enforce the payment of a ten-thousand-dollar debt allegedly owed to Anthony Accetturo.

Although Marty had stayed out of the headlines after that incident—he still appeared to be a magnet for trouble. In fact, new problems started for Marty not a year later, just before the start of the Accetturo trial. As some of the "boys" put it, Marty was in "deep shit."

The incident that started the latest round of difficulties occurred while the court was gearing up for jury selection.

It was two in the morning on September 1, 1986. Marty and some friends had been socializing at a neighborhood watering hole in Florham Park. Sitting near them at the bar were a bunch of "good old boys" from the Deep South, who were apparently itinerant dog-show operators in the process of promoting a canine beauty show in New Jersey at the time.

What they found in that bar was not "southern hospitality."

One of these "boys" thought he had found a friend. For approximately forty-five minutes, he chatted with Marty about pedigree dogs. According to some accounts, he punctuated his remarks with a couple of "good old" punches to Marty's arm. Then he got up and went to the bathroom.

When he returned, Marty was still seated at the bar. Marty muttered a brief greeting as the dog-show man sat down. The stranger returned the greeting, only, this time, he reached over and gave Marty a friendly "chuck" on the cheek.

Whatever the strictures of southern etiquette, they apparently don't mesh well with northern mob protocol. One thing people in New Jersey learn early on: You don't touch someone you meet in a bar, and you particularly don't get overly familiar with the *consigliere* of a Mafia family. This "good old boy" apparently didn't know that.

It was late, they had been drinking, and there wasn't time for a long, complex discussion of manners. So the Jersey boy decided to teach the southern friend the meaning of "respect." Marty didn't say anything. He merely picked up a beer bottle off the bar and smashed it over the head of the dog-show operator.

The police arrived shortly afterward.

"He blindsided me," the dog-show man complained. "I never saw it coming." He was lucky he could say anything. He was treated at a local hospital and received seventy-five stitches.

Two days later, Marty was arrested at his home on a charge of aggravated assault.

As a result of the incident, Marty was placed under a curfew by the court that remained in place throughout the trial. He was specifically ordered to be in the house by nine at night and to stay out of any establishments where alcohol was served, unless in the company of his wife. He was also instructed to "not directly or indirectly threaten or intimidate anyone."

A little over a year later, Marty appeared to have violated every one of those directives. At approximately two o'clock on the morning of Nov. 18, 1987, he was arrested for drunk driving. And he allegedly threatened and attempted to assault the arresting officer.

When it was over, Taccetta was issued five separate summonses. The police called his wife, who in turn called his brother, Michael. Marty was then led into the police-station lobby to wait for a ride home.

As he waited, he continued to taunt the arresting officer, who sat behind a window at the front desk of the police station. At one point, he walked to the window, looked at the officer, and spat at him through the opening. Then he went back to his seat.

Michael arrived shortly afterward and quietly led Marty out to his car.

"He's not to drive," the officer called out. It was, at best, an unnecessary reminder.

The upshot of the incident was an order by Judge Ackerman further clamping down on Taccetta's movements. Prosecutors had urged the judge to revoke Taccetta's bail. Ackerman, however, was more lenient—he merely confined Taccetta to a form of house arrest.

39

Critchley and several other lawyers noticed the commotion shortly before Mitola was set to resume his testimony after a lunch break.

DiNorscio was conferring with his legal adviser, Al Gellene, and his voice was becoming increasingly loud and agitated. The other lawyers tried to ignore it, but the volume grew until the words became clearly audible. "You stupid son of a bitch; you stupid son of a bitch," DiNorscio shouted at the young lawyer. "I told you that wasn't it; I told you that wasn't it."

Now the others were staring. Obviously, Gellene had done something to really set Jackie off. A moment later, the reason became obvious, "I told you," Jackie shouted. "I told you I wanted *creamy*, not crunchy, peanut butter."

When Nick Mitola returned to the stand, his testimony turned to what happened the morning he picked up his buddy Ron to meet two more friends at a Livingston sporting-goods store.

"C'mon," Ron told Nick as they entered the store, "we got a new scam. You're going to enjoy this one."

They were pursuing the Great American Pastime of shopping. Only unlike most consumers, they had no intention of paying for the goods.

It was, as described by Mitola, like a high-stakes game of "Supermarket Sweeps," the old television paean to greed in which shoppers raced the clock to grab as much merchandise as they could carry.

The key to success in this version of the game, Mitola said, was a ready supply of counterfeit credit cards.

It was late September 1982. Mitola and his companions entered the small sporting-goods store, chewed the fat with the owners for a few moments, and then proceeded to pick out a supply of sneakers and clothing, including jogging suits, shorts, and even some hats.

They didn't skimp. The total of their purchases came to around $600–$700 each.

Ron, Nick said, pulled out a handful of credit cards and handed them to the store owner.

One at a time, the owner called in the number for a charge authorization and then rang up the sale. If the credit card was rejected—if the purchase exceeded the account's limits—the card was handed back, and they tried another.

The store owner was happy to cooperate, Nick recalled, because rather than discount prices for the items, the charges were processed at full retail value. That way, Mitola explained, the owner shared in the profits.

It was, he said, a "nice thing."

The cards came from a makeshift embossing shop located in a garage in New York City, somewhere around Forty-third Street, while the cards' numbers themselves had been obtained from a variety of sources. They were generally good until the real owners of the cards noticed the bogus charges on their bills and reported them to the credit-card companies.

For the mob, it was a "victimless crime," or almost. The credit-card owners didn't have to pay the charges—they simply had to alert the credit-card company that they hadn't purchased those items. The stores got paid, regardless of whether the cards were counterfeit or not. It was the banks that footed the bill. And as far as the "boys" were concerned, the banks could afford it. After all, some mused privately, credit cards, with their 18 and 20 percent interest rates, were nothing more than legal loan-sharking. The banks, they contended, deserved what they got.

When Mitola and his friend brought the first load of cards back to the "club," which they'd purchased, Mitola said, for $100 to $150 a shot, they were an immediate hit. Michael Taccetta had given his approval for them to sell the cards to his "boys" for a fifty-dollar profit. They moved like hotcakes at a firemen's breakfast.

In addition to peddling them at the "club," Mitola and his friend Ron also brought them to the Hole in the Wall and sold another batch there.

It was like instant money.

Next they spawned a series of mob shopping sprees that allowed the "boys" to roam the shopping malls of the Garden State, running up huge charges on phantom accounts and stocking their homes with carloads of high-tech electronics gear, jewelry, appliances, and clothing.

Mitola related how mob figures systematically utilized the cards to purchase big-ticket items such as a giant-screen television, a one-thousand-dollar pair of shoes, and tens of thousands of dollars in clothing and other merchandise.

The mob bosses, he said, didn't actually make the purchases themselves—they had their own home-shopping network. They merely drew up a "shopping list," which they gave to their subordinates and let them go out and buy the merchandise and arrange for it to be delivered to their posh suburban homes. In some cases, he said, the "boys" would be sent out with shopping lists provided by Michael Taccetta or his brother, Martin.

Mitola claimed that on one occasion, he and a friend purchased four 19-inch portable RCA television sets, which he personally delivered to Michael Taccetta's home in Florham Park. The house was still under construction at the time, Mitola said, and a carpenter let them in through a garage door.

That same day, he said, they delivered additional merchandise—a 45-inch TV and two 19-inch portable RCAs—to Marty's home.

Mitola said he was also present when they delivered a refrigerator and a gas range to Michael Perna's home in Belleville.

The shopping sprees began in the early 1980s, Mitola said, and ran for years, with his mob friends using more than fifteen hundred different bogus cards, many of which they charged right up to the credit limit.

"It was a common practice," Mitola said, "that everyone would go out every day trying to create a new opening [contact a new store] for us to go into." The boys would then gleefully swap information on stores where they found it easy to use the cards, so they could obtain different types of merchandise.

In one instance, he described broaching the subject of the cards with a salesman at a Parsippany appliance store, who in turn brought Nick to meet the store owner, who was having coffee at a nearby luncheonette. They sat down together and outlined the scheme, Mitola said, and the owner was all for it.

That same day, they went in and charged $7,000–$8,000 worth of merchandise.

Within minutes of meeting the store owner, Mitola's pal Ron called some other "boys" on their portable beepers. An hour later, they joined in the shopping expedition.

But simply charging the items on bogus cards wasn't enough. While some of the shoppers kept the owner and salespeople busy, Mitola and another associate kept themselves busy—they simply stole the merchandise they wanted.

"At that time," Mitola said, "we were stealing—VCRs were stacked near the door—and [we were] throwing them out in the trunk."

As he described the scene in court, some of the defendants began to laugh openly.

O'Malley looked grim. "I don't see anything funny about that, Judge," he declared.

Others, however, did. Some of the jurors were laughing along with the defendants.

According to Mitola, the shopping sprees were so successful, they were running out of things to buy.

In the case of the Livingston sporting-goods store, he said, "after we had used the store twenty or thirty times, we were all loaded up with racquetball equipment, ski equipment. So one of the owners came out with some catalogues. . . ."

That was all they needed. They simply ordered more merchandise, even though the store didn't carry it.

Some of the "boys" ordered motorized minicars for their kids. A more dapper sort ordered a one-thousand-dollar pair of shoes from a Texas wholesaler. And some even picked out European-style ski jackets—only the sizes turned out to be all wrong.

"Basically," Mitola said, "the ski jackets were made for thin guys, and we were heavy guys trying to get into thin jackets."

While many of the cards were used with the cooperation of merchants or salesclerks who were willing to go along with the scam in exchange for commissions or inflated sales profits, it was possible, Mitola testified, to hit stores that were unaware of the deception. In those cases, he said, they would just "take a shot" that the cards would pass.

At one location, an electronics store in Bloomfield, Mitola said, a clerk who was helping them with the scheme was becoming nervous. There had been inquiries about bad charges from the banks. But one of Mitola's friends wanted a large-screen TV for his house—and he told the salesman he wasn't leaving without it. He got it.

There were other purchases. Items like ten-thousand dollars' worth of gold jewelry picked up one afternoon from a booth at a shopping mall in Morris County, and even an above-ground swimming pool. They rented limousines and bought fur coats for wives and girlfriends. Mitola said he personally purchased tires, gasoline, and oil for his car and would even charge tune-ups.

"I went to liquor stores, I went to furniture stores, I went to appliance stores, restaurants, jewelry stores, flower shops. . . .

"Sometimes," Mitola said, "we went into stores with so many credit cards the owners didn't want to be bothered, so they would let us go in the back room, use the phones, and call in the name, number, and get authorization numbers for each individual card that we were using at the particular time."

Most of the cards, he said, had credit limits of between $1,500 and $3,000 each; but, he added, there was little danger of exposure if the credit limits were reached. "The worst that would happen," Mitola said, "is that the card would be reported overcharged and that you couldn't use it. But you would never get to the point where you'd have to run out of the store because it was reported stolen."

As a safety precaution, Mitola said, they would periodically make their own authorization checks on the cards—using stores' numbers they knew—to ensure that the accounts had not been closed down. As added protection, he said, the "boys" were able to obtain copies of the weekly booklets issued by the credit-card companies to make sure the cards they were using had not yet been listed as stolen.

As Mitola concluded his story of the shopping sprees, he added one ironic note: "I've used the card at my uncle's store to send fruit baskets and turkeys to certain gentlemen in this audience at Christmastime and at Thanksgiving," he said, with a wry smile on his face.

O'Malley asked the names of the beneficiaries of Mitola's generosity. At the top of his list were the bosses of the organization.

"Martin Taccetta, Michael Taccetta . . ."

"Why did you send them to Michael Taccetta?" O'Malley inquired.

Mitola smiled again. "That was my way of paying tribute," he said.

After a subsequent break, DiNorscio added his observations to the situation.

Defense attorneys were seeking permission to rent—at the court's expense—an expensive "stop-action" video recorder needed for their clients to view videotapes of their activities which had been recorded on special time-lapse equipment by the FBI.

Ackerman considered the request for a moment and suggested that one of the lawyers look into the rental costs.

Jackie, however, had his own solution.

Standing, he raised a hand. "Just put it on my credit card," he offered.

40

Mitola had told a great story. He had described the Taccetta-Accetturo organization in intimate detail. He had identified its members; he had described their operations from the perspective of a true insider; and he had explained the significance of hundreds of their tape-recorded conversations. In sum, he had done everything expected of him by the government—and more.

It was that "more" that caused the problems for the government.

In May of 1986, some two-and-a-half years after Mitola had first approached the FBI with the offer to "bury" his former associates, the then-head of the U.S. Drug Enforcement Administration (DEA) office in New Jersey was also looking at Mitola.

The DEA, it seemed, had learned something that the FBI didn't know, which was that although the FBI was coddling Mitola as a favored informant, he was at the same time playing Marchalonis and the Bureau for fools: He was out on the street dealing drugs. The FBI had arranged his early release from prison to work undercover in the Lucchese probe; but

Mitola wasn't satisfied with that arrangement. He decided to commit his own crimes, and he jumped back into the narcotics trade right under the noses of his FBI controllers.

The situation was made even more embarrassing because, although Mitola was able to dupe the FBI, he blundered right into a DEA investigation. The problem was, the DEA never knew he was working for the FBI.

So that May, DEA special-agent-in-charge Glennon L. Cooper filed a memorandum with the chief of narcotics investigations for the U.S. Attorney's Office in Newark requesting funding for a full-scale task-force probe involving both federal and state law-enforcement agencies. The target of the probe was to be none other than Nicholas Mitola.

The memo said Mitola had supplied a DEA informant with one ounce of heroin for $5,200 and that Mitola claimed he could obtain multikilogram quantities of the drug on one-day notice for a cost of $190,000 per kilo. Mitola claimed the drugs were to be obtained from Turkey or Pakistan.

And that was not all.

The memo also disclosed that Mitola and an associate met with an undercover DEA operative in connection with a scheme to obtain large quantities of machine guns, which were to be used in a potentially violent, armed drug "rip-off" in an unidentified Latin American country.

The memo disclosed that Mitola's associate told the DEA operative that he wanted to acquire a hundred Israeli-made Uzi machine guns to be used in a "one-shot deal" in which a very large amount of drugs would be "ripped off," possibly in South America.

As a result of this information, the DEA designated Mitola a suspected heroin "kingpin" and sought authorization for further undercover investigation, as well as electronic surveillance of the probe target.

Records showed that the task force was formed in June 1986 and a federal grand-jury investigation was initiated. Government documents indicated that some twenty agents from various federal and local agencies were assigned to coordinate the probe.

In the memo, Cooper said he anticipated that a case could be developed that would result in the "immobilization" of a major smuggling organization "sanctioned and/or operated by New Jersey–based organized crime families."

It never came to pass.

The FBI pulled Mitola off the street and inducted him into the Federal Witness Protection Program before the DEA probe could be completed.

The story garnered front-page headlines in the local press: STAR WITNESS IN MOB TRIAL DUPED FBI AS DRUG DEALER LEADING "DOUBLE LIFE."

It was not the government's most memorable moment.

It also added new fuel to the defense fire.

"We know who protects us from the criminals," Critchley said, "but who protects us from the informants?"

It was indeed a question worth pondering.

A chronology prepared by the defense showed that Mitola had been released on parole from a drug sentence in August 1985. He was released on a Tuesday, and he committed his first crime the following Monday. He began earning tens of thousands of dollars dealing drugs; he participated in an armed robbery in Maryland; and he sold heroin to an undercover DEA operative.

It was not until early 1987—while jury selection in the trial was well under way—that FBI agent Marchalonis learned that his star informant was out working behind his back.

It was, as defense attorney David Ruhnke phrased it, a "probably unwelcome St. Patrick's Day gift" for O'Malley when Mitola sat down with Marchalonis on March 17 of that year and confessed what he had done.

41

Michael Critchley picked up his notes and walked to the podium. He nodded toward the prosecution table, which was adjacent to where he was standing. Barbara Miller sat near the end.

"Could I ask Miss Miller to move?" Critchley asked the court. "I know it's very tight," he said, indicating the cramped courtroom space, but added, "she's very close to me."

Miller seemed amused.

"I'll be happy to, Judge . . . I'll be happy to move. . . ."

Mitola was brought into the courtroom and took his seat. Everyone stood as the jury was then led in and the jurors took their seats.

"Good morning, Mr. Mitola," Critchley began mildly.

Mitola did not smile. "Good morning, Mr. Critchley."

The defense attorney shuffled his papers.

"Now, you indicated that you worked in Pueblo, Colorado, is that correct?"

"Yes, sir," Mitola said.

"And at Arby's Roast Beef?"

"Yes, sir."

"And why didn't you stay at Arby's Roast Beef?" Critchley asked, a wry smile on his lips.

Mitola grimaced. "Because I couldn't be bonded."

Critchley feigned amazement. "You could not be bonded, you're telling us, to sell roast-beef sandwiches? . . ."

Some jurors began to snicker.

"No," Mitola corrected hoarsely, "I couldn't be bonded as a manager handling the funds of the corporation."

"Because of your prior record?" Critchley asked.

"Yes, sir."

Critchley put down his papers and leaned over the podium. "You could not be trusted to deal with the proceeds of Arby's Roast Beef because you couldn't be bonded?"

"Objection!" O'Malley shouted.

Critchley rephrased the question, but the impact was still the same. "You could not be bonded to deal with the money of Arby's Roast Beef?"

"Yes, sir," Mitola admitted.

Then Critchley raised his voice. "But the government asked you to be bonded to sell testimony here. Isn't that a fact?

"And it's fair to say," Critchley continued, "that for the past twenty years, you have been a walking crime wave, is that not a fact?"

Mitola lowered his head. "I've been a career criminal, yes."

"You have committed," Critchley shouted, "and I don't use this term loosely, you have committed literally thousands of crimes?"

"I never counted them," Mitola said, "but there were quite a few, yes."

Critchley walked closer to the witness. "In effect," he began, "Mr. O'Malley gave you immunity for anything that you were going to talk about."

"Yes, he did. Except murder," Mitola responded.

"Well you didn't go in there and say, 'I want to tell the truth.' Before you went in there, you bargained, did you not?"

"I asked for certain things, yes," he admitted.

"When you asked for certain things, you were selling

something, and they were looking to buy something. . . . You were looking to sell something, and my adversaries were looking to buy something, isn't that a fact?"

Critchley kept up the pressure. And Mitola buckled.

"Yes," Mitola acknowledged.

"And you were looking to sell testimony, and they were looking to buy testimony, isn't that a fact?"

Mitola's voice was low. "I don't know if it was so much testimony. I was looking to give them information that I knew about criminal activities . . . and I was looking to help myself."

Mitola admitted that three months after he was sentenced to prison on drug charges, he attempted to contact the FBI with his proposal.

"And what you said to them, in effect, was get me out," Critchley suggested. "And lo and behold, after three-and-a-half months in jail . . . who shows up?"

"The FBI," Mitola answered.

"In the form of who?" Critchley inquired.

Mitola pointed toward the prosecution table. "Mr. Marchalonis and another agent."

Critchley swept his hand over the prosecution team. "And as a result of Mr. Marchalonis showing up, you go before a grand jury, is that correct?"

"Yes, sir," Mitola admitted.

"You get a pass for all your criminal activity. And now you're out of jail because of the intercession of Mr. Marchalonis. Correct?"

"Yes," Mitola said abruptly.

Then Critchley zeroed in on his main point. "And how many days was it before you committed your next crime?"

"Monday after the Tuesday . . ."

"So it took you six days?" Critchley said, shaking his head in a gesture of amazement.

"Yes, sir," was all Mitola could say.

Bit by bit, Critchley hammered away at the deal Mitola had been given by the government. O'Malley, he disclosed, had written a letter to the parole board, saying that he was not aware of any prior convictions against Mitola. Critchley, however, pointed out that Mitola had, in fact, been convicted of grand larceny in Kansas.

He also noted that Mitola had told the court he had not committed any crimes of violence.

"What would you consider an armed robbery to be?" Critchley demanded.

"I participated in an armed robbery, but I wasn't carrying any guns," Mitola said. "I don't even know if the guns were loaded or not."

According to Mitola, Critchley said, armed robbery did not constitute a crime of violence. "That's a very liberal interpretation, is it not?"

"That's my interpretation, Mr. Critchley," Mitola responded.

Critchley focused on Mitola's early life, a good school, a good home, parents who sent him to college, in short, "all the advantages." But instead of making the most of them, the lawyer suggested, he turned to crime. And shortly after that, he turned informant. The one time he was arrested, he cooperated and was let go. Now, he admitted, he was prepared to testify against his brother if necessary.

"You'll do anything to save yourself, including testifying against your brother," Critchley sneered.

"Yes," Mitola acknowledged.

"But at all costs, you want to make certain you get the best deal . . . and on the back of your brother you may hope to get zero."

Critchley looked at Mitola with undisguised contempt. "Do you know what it is to be a man and face up to any responsibilities of life? I mean . . . everything for you, Mr. Mitola, is immediate self-gratification, is it not? Haven't you run your life based on that principle?"

The charge drew a sharp response—Critchley had hit a nerve. "That's not true," Mitola declared. "I am no different than any other criminal on the street, trying to survive."

Later in his cross-examination, Critchley began to poke fun of Mitola.

"I'm not a greedy person," Mitola had said in response to a question. "I gave away more than I kept, that's for sure."

Critchley looked at him with a sarcastic smile on his lips. "Are you the Mr. Rogers of crime?"

The defense attorney started to sing the theme song from the children's show *Mr. Rogers' Neighborhood.*

"You say you're a loan shark," Critchley said. "People beat you left and right, and what you do is just get them more loans and forget about it. You're like a friendly loan shark?"

"Yes," Mitola muttered, "that's how I was. That's why I wasn't successful at all."

Critchley started to sing the children's-show theme again: "Won't you be my loan shark? . . ."

He made a similar jibe about Mitola's career as a bookmaker.

"Won't you be my bookmaker? . . ." he taunted.

Some members of the jury were laughing, as were the defendants, and even the judge appeared amused. But not O'Malley.

"Judge," he said, rising to his feet, "I'm going to object to at least the singing. At least he can ask the questions without the singing."

Critchley raised his arms in a shrug. "My brother Joe always criticized my singing, Judge. . . . I'm a frustrated Irish tenor."

Ackerman grimaced. "Can you make the questions devoid of melodiousness?"

The most devastating element of the cross-examination, however, dealt not with Mitola's actual testimony, but with his relationship with the FBI and Agent Marchalonis in particular. Critchley essentially cast himself in the role of prosecutor, and the defendant was the prosecution team itself.

Referring to DEA reports showing that Mitola was continuing to deal drugs even while working as a DEA informant, Critchley described Mitola as a "renegade informant" who was "leading two lives."

"So we have two informants out there," he said, "two federal agencies basically running into one another."

Ironically, Critchley pointed out, not only was an undercover FBI informant dealing with an undercover DEA informant without either agency realizing that the other was an informant, but the DEA informant was cheating the DEA. In the spirit of true American entrepreneurs, the DEA informant claimed to be buying drugs from Mitola at a higher price than Mitola was actually selling them and, apparently, pocketing the difference.

As a result of the DEA probe, however, Critchley noted that Mitola had been designated a "kingpin" by the federal agency and, as a result, could have faced life imprisonment if he were convicted.

"You wouldn't be sending letters after three months to the FBI, you'd be in there without parole," Critchley told the witness.

The key question Critchley was raising, however, was what happened to the DEA investigation. Mitola had told how he kept in touch with his drug partners via an electronic beeper that was like having "an office in your pocket."

Critchley noted, however, that the DEA had obtained a court order to essentially "bug" his beeper calls with a duplicate beeper that would monitor whoever was calling him. But within weeks of the DEA obtaining the court order, Mitola turned in his beeper.

According to documents submitted by Critchley, he did it one day after records showed that Marchalonis made an "emergency" call to Mitola on his beeper.

"On October twenty-second," Critchley asked Mitola, "did Marchalonis, when he beeped you, let you know that the phones you were using, the beepers you were using, were being monitored by the DEA? Or is it just coincidence that the very next day after Marchalonis calls you, you turn them in?"

The question drew a stir from the defense camp but was adamantly denied by Mitola. He claimed an associate had learned he was under surveillance from a friend with a radio scanner that picked up DEA transmissions.

Critchley didn't stop there, however. Not only did the records show that Marchalonis had tried to reach Mitola on the twenty-second, but they also showed that Mitola had received a telephone call that came from another familiar number—the U.S. Justice Department Strike Force.

"And it's the next day," Critchley demanded, "you turn in those beepers."

"Yes, sir," Mitola muttered in response.

"And that's just coincidence that those calls from the government appeared on your digital-display beeper the day before you turned them in? Is that just coincidence?"

"Yes, sir, it is," Mitola insisted.

"And you know who the strike force is, right?" Critchley asked, turning to the jury.

"Yes," Mitola replied.

"Who's the strike force?"

Mitola's voice was barely audible. "That's—that number is Mr. O'Malley's number. . . ."

Critchley continued his grilling.

If it wasn't to warn him about the DEA investigation, why were O'Malley and Marchalonis trying so desperately to reach him? Mitola didn't remember. "But," he insisted, "it had nothing to do with them telling me to turn in my beepers."

"October twenty-second, when they're trying to reach you, the day before you turned in the beeper—didn't you say the only time Marchalonis would try to reach you would be in terms of emergency?"

"Yes, sir."

"You don't recall what that emergency was on October twenty-second?"

"No."

Critchley walked closer to the witness. His voice was harsh and accusatory. "Emergency was, you're being tailed by the DEA. You're going to make him look bad because their star witness is going to get busted as a heroin kingpin. Then how does he look? Didn't he tell you that?"

Mitola shot back, "That's not true."

O'Malley was on his feet. "I would object to the question."

Ackerman waved him down.

"Objection overruled."

Critchley continued, "Isn't it a fact, he told you, 'Hey, our case is going down the drain, you jerk. You just dealt with a DEA agent'?"

"That's not true," Mitola shouted back.

"That they'd take ten minutes to convict. You're being investigated as a kingpin and you're facing life in jail?"

"No, sir," Mitola insisted again.

"Just coincidence . . ." Critchley mocked. Was it just a coincidence that agent Marchalonis tried to reach you twice on October twenty-second, the day before you turned in the beepers that were being monitored, not by the FBI but by the DEA?"

"Yes," Mitola reiterated.

"That's just coincidence?"

"Yes, sir, it is."

Critchley turned to face the jury again. "And you can't tell us what he reached you for?"

Critchley smiled knowingly at the jurors, as he allowed Mitola to finish his answer. "I don't recall," Mitola insisted. "I had numerous conversations with Mr. Marchalonis, but none of them was to inform me of what you're alleging."

"No," Critchley said softly as he walked back toward the podium, "of course not."

Several days later, Critchley ended his interrogation of the witness. He began, "You're a thief?"

"Yes."

"Armed robber?"

"Yes."

"Shylock, a gambler, a con artist, a liar, and a deceiver?"

O'Malley appeared irritated.

"Is that one question, Judge?"

Critchley nodded. "That's one question."

"I would object, Judge," O'Malley called.

Critchley rolled his eyes. "Have I left anything out?"

Some of the jurors smirked at the exchange. Then Critchley turned back to Mitola.

"If you were over here," he asked, pointing toward the jury box, "would *you* believe you, knowing everything about you? Honestly, would you believe you?"

For the first time, Mitola seemed uncertain of what to say. "I couldn't answer that question," he said.

Almost two weeks went by before Jackie got his turn at bat. And although his performance didn't produce the grand slam he had predicted, he did manage to score with at least some of the jurors.

DiNorscio was waiting at the podium for Ackerman to give him the nod to proceed. It was November, and Jackie looked less like a perspiring porpoise—he was becoming an old hand at this.

"Morning Mr. Mitola," he called to the witness in a cheery voice.

"Good morning, Mr. DiNorscio," Mitola muttered warily.

"Beautiful weekend, wasn't it?" DiNorscio inquired.

The jurors shifted in their seats as DiNorscio continued to wade through his notes. Despite the passing of summer, DiNorscio was beginning to sweat again.

"Judge," he asked, "could we have the window open in here? It's a little hot."

DiNorscio raised his voice. "Mr. Mitola, if I was to say to you in front of this jury—I'd like you to watch the jury—and I said to you, 'Mr. Mitola, I put the gun to your head, and if you don't tell that jury that you're lying, I'll blow your brains out,' you'd tell them you're lying, wouldn't you?"

Mitola looked at him appraisingly. "You'd have to pull the trigger, Jackie."

DiNorscio swiveled his bulk and pointed to O'Malley and the others. "Is there any difference between this table's gun and the one I would use? Only theirs shoots time and threats . . ."

As Mitola quietly denied the accusations, DiNorscio gathered up his papers and stuffed them back into a manila folder. He started to walk away and then paused.

"Mr. Mitola," he said with venom, "get off the stand. You disgust me."

As he walked back toward his seat, Ackerman looked up. "What's that?"

"No further questions at this point," DiNorscio muttered.

Ackerman was livid. "Don't tell the witness to get off the stand. This court will tell the witness when he may leave the stand. Are you finished?"

DiNorscio ignored the tirade and turned back to Ackerman, a broad smile on his face.

"Being you stated that, Your Honor—they'd let him get away for even killing you, Judge." He pointed at the prosecution team. "They would do that."

Then DiNorscio pulled himself up to his full height and stated firmly, "But with every strength I have, Judge, I'd stop them. Because I love you."

As some of the jurors began to laugh aloud, DiNorscio flushed and waved his hand. "I don't mean *that* way, Judge." He tapped his heart in a gesture of platonic sincerity. "This way . . ."

* * *

As the weeks progressed, other defense attorneys took their own shots at Mitola. At one point, Ackerman had to admonish spectators who began whistling whenever points were scored.

"This is not a ball game," Ackerman cautioned. "This is a trial."

One attorney, Miles Feinstein, played another sort of game with the witness. He challenged Mitola's accounts of what the witness claimed were tape recordings of a loan-sharking transaction.

An FBI tape had recorded one of the defendants, Joseph (Scoops) Licata, discussing the sale of a Jeep that cost $10,900 and had ten thousand miles on it.

Mitola claimed that "Jeep" was a code word for a loan and that the tape conversation was actually about a $10,000 loan with a $10,900 payback.

Feinstein had suggested, however, that another tape recording of Mitola speaking with his former associates might cast doubt on some of Mitola's claims. The attorney then reached into his pocket and brandished a cassette tape before the witness.

Mitola backtracked. Confronted with the cassette, he acknowledged that such a conversation had, in fact, occurred.

Feinstein looked more than satisfied—he had wrung an important admission from the witness. As he returned to his seat, the attorney suddenly stopped and turned back to face the witness, displaying the tape in his hand.

"You know what it was?" Feinstein asked, "'La Bamba.'"

As the court erupted in laughter, Ackerman quietly asked Feinstein, "What's 'La Bamba'?"

"'La Bamba,'" Feinstein replied, "the Richie Valens song. . . . I'll play it, Judge. It's a great song."

Ackerman declined the offer. "I never heard the song, and I didn't see the movie," the judge remarked.

"Would it be a bribe if I gave you the tape?" Feinstein asked.

Ackerman smiled, then addressed the attorney. "Yes," he said, "it would."

Moments later, Feinstein approached the witness once again. He suggested that Mitola had turned informer in an attempt to "buy" his way out of prison.

He then handed the witness a small card and asked if the FBI had provided him with a similar one. Feinstein turned to the jury and displayed the card. It was from a Monopoly game, and it read, *This card may be kept until needed or sold. Get out of jail free.*

42

On November 30, 1987, Nicholas Peter Mitola, Jr., had a final comment for the jury. "I'm all talked out," Mitola said.

For four months, he had sat in the witness seat testifying about what he claimed were the innermost secrets of one of the most powerful mob empires in the nation.

He had answered hundreds of questions, in fact; for nine weeks, he had been interrogated by federal prosecutors and by a seemingly never-ending array of defense lawyers, all seeking to portray him as the worst sort of criminal—a "rat" willing to sell his testimony for a promise of freedom.

"I'm telling a story," Mitola had told the court. "You can call it a rat. The code of silence in the Mafia. You know—when I'm not talking and I'm going in front of a judge and I'm keeping quiet and lying for them, then it's great. But when I'm a rat, does the public see me as a rat? I don't know. But the defendants do because they know I'm telling the truth. . . ."

Day after day, Mitola, who was under tight government guard, was ushered into the federal courtroom in Newark and led to a special desk where he sat staring into the faces of the very persons he agreed to help convict.

At night, he was taken back to a windowless room in an undisclosed location where he waited for the next day of interrogation to begin.

"I've been here since August," Mitola said, "you know, getting tired. And it's very difficult for me, and I'm going to make mistakes and say stupid things that you guys laugh at. That's a fact of life. I'm doing the best I can."

His testimony had been startling.

He claimed to have been a trusted associate of mob bosses in both New Jersey and Las Vegas, and told how he personally delivered $100,000 in casino "skim" money to the late "godfather" of the Nevada gaming resort, Anthony Spilotro.

On the witness stand, Mitola gave an account of his involvement with not only the New Jersey branch of the Lucchese crime family, but also with the New Jersey mob organization once controlled by Richie the Boot Boiardo.

The defense had attacked his story mercilessly. Much of it, they said, was too melodramatic to be believed. They suggested that some of it had been lifted intact from crime sagas such as *The Godfather* and the television series *Crime Story.*

Mitola detailed his own criminal career, which spanned his college days—where his academic records showed that the only course he excelled at was bowling—to his life as a professional bookmaker, gambler, and drug dealer.

He told how he had once gambled $100,000 in a single bet on a Super Bowl Game, and how he kept $420,000 in cash stashed under his socks in his dresser drawer: "Money," he explained at the time, "is only a tool to gamble with. It means nothing to a gambler."

But his testimony had also made him the subject of denigration and ridicule.

Attorney Peter Ryan goaded him, "You're just a rat testifying, aren't you?"

Ryan went on to call him worse: "A degenerate criminal . . . a degenerate who cares about nothing."

But in the end, Mitola seemed almost resigned. His ordeal—possibly the longest ever endured by a government witness—was finally over.

"I've given a truthful account of my criminal activities," he declared.

"You [the defense]," he began, jabbing his finger at the

defense lawyers, "accused me of committing six thousand crimes. Who did I commit them with?" He gestured about the room.

"Then" he said, "it was the code of silence in the Mafia for me. Now, when I'm telling a story that you don't want to hear, you're calling me a liar. . . ."

43

Michael Critchley, wearing a gray suit and lugging his ever-present briefcase, stepped briskly up the front entrance ramp of the federal courthouse.

A year had passed since the trial began—the seasons had changed from winter to spring to the heat of summer and back to autumn. To some participants, it seemed as if this was something they had always done. It was becoming as regular and routine as any nine-to-five office job. For many defendants used to hanging out at pool halls or social clubs, it was probably the closest they had ever come in their adult lives to holding a real job. Only instead of a paycheck, they were working for something a lot more critical—their freedom.

Government officials had originally predicted the case would last no longer than six to eight months. Now there was open speculation that the trial, which had begun in November 1986 and already lasted until November 1987, would continue on through the summer of 1988—and possibly beyond.

"I am numbed by the experience," Critchley declared at the time. "It has taken a drastic toll on everyone involved."

As he entered the courthouse on the one-year anniversary, Critchley grinned broadly for a television crew on hand to mark the occasion. "Happy anniversary," he called out cheerfully. His client, Michael Taccetta, wearing a blue windbreaker and open-neck sport shirt, remained impassive.

Several other defendants, Tommy Ricciardi, James Gammero, and Michael Perna, followed behind in a group.

"Bring us a cake?" one of them quipped to the television reporters, while another muttered that he hoped they wouldn't be there to celebrate the trial's second anniversary.

Another defendant, Danny (Bobo) Ricciardi, dressed casually in a red windbreaker with a gold chain around his neck, paused to ham it up for the cameras. Pointing to a budding potbelly, he beamed, "See how much weight I've gained in a year? Look at last year's picture."

Moments later, the two lead prosecutors, Grady O'Malley and Joe Braunreuther, crossed the street from the Federal Office Building that housed the headquarters of the U.S. Attorney's Office and the U.S. Justice Department Strike Force. O'Malley pulled a wire cart laden with documents up the entrance ramp, while Braunreuther followed closely behind, sipping a last-minute cup of coffee.

O'Malley paused in the doorway and flashed a rare smile for the cameras. "Of course there's an end in sight," he declared in response to a question. "It's not discouraging at all. That's what we're getting paid to do. . . ."

On the morning of February 16, 1988, Anthony Accetturo pushed the buzzer outside the chambers of Judge Harold Ackerman, as the judge's secretary watched his image on a closed-circuit television monitor mounted over the outside door. The secretary, Judy Parker, pressed the lock release, and Accetturo entered the chambers. He was alone, and he wanted to see the judge.

Accetturo smiled and said "good morning" to the young blond woman behind the desk. She smiled back and explained that the judge was busy but that she would tell him Accetturo was waiting. Accetturo lowered himself into a green high-back chair and sat quietly, occasionally exchanging small talk with the secretary.

Accetturo seemed unusually subdued and anxious. He was dressed casually, the way he always was for court, looking more like the local grocer than a mob boss.

But this morning, there was something on his mind; something that he alone knew; something that could change the course of the entire trial—or bring it to an end.

A few moments later, the door to the judge's inner chamber opened, and Ackerman was at the door. He nodded courteously. "Mr. Accetturo," he said formally, "I understand you would like to see me."

The news Accetturo had come to deliver was devastating. Milton Ferrell, Sr., the lawyer who had represented him from the start of the trial, was dying.

Ferrell had become ill during a brief break in the trial. He had begun experiencing severe back pain and had flown home to Florida. He was admitted, for tests, to a hospital, where the diagnosis was grim: a cancerous lump and degeneration of the spine—he had only weeks to live.

He was never to return to New Jersey.

For Ackerman, the news was doubly shocking. Not only was he faced with the imminent death of a man he had come to know, but the situation created problems for the court that were even more immediate—what to do about Accetturo?

Here was the key defendant in the case, the government's prime target, the man whose refusal to plea-bargain had without question undermined any effort to resolve the case without trial—and now he was without a lawyer.

Later, when Ackerman convened court, there was a hush as the multitude waited to hear what would be done next. The judge cleared his throat and pulled the microphone closer. He spoke slowly and softly.

"At this moment," Ackerman said, as he stared out at the sea of faces before him, "I do not have a solution to this problem."

Ackerman could only instruct his clerk to call the jurors and alert them that the case had been put on "hold"—indefinitely.

Henry Asbill, who had shared a rental home in New Jersey with the elderly Ferrell, was shocked when he learned of the situation. He immediately made arrangements to fly down to Florida.

Ferrell was staying in his son's house. Bedridden, he spent his days propped up with pillows, nodding off periodically from the medication he had been given. But he was alert and brought his children and loved ones together to say his last good-byes.

Asbill stayed with him for a few days. There was a bond that had developed between the two men, and he had become a part of the old man's life—and the old man a part of his. As Asbill prepared to walk out of the room for the last time, he gripped Ferrell's arm and stared into the old man's eyes, his own wet with emotion.

"I enjoyed knowing you," the young lawyer said, and then added, "we're going to win this one for you."

For Matthew Boylan, the death of Milton Ferrell, Sr., was to signal a watershed event in his own legal career, a career that had already spanned four decades, and that had propelled him to the peak of professional recognition within the legal community in New Jersey.

Boylan was at a meeting at the headquarters of Ciba-Geigy, the giant international pharmaceutical conglomerate, in Ardsley, New York, when he received an urgent telephone call from his secretary.

"Yes?" he asked as he took the phone.

It was late in the afternoon, and there was a note of concern in her voice.

"Judge Ackerman has been trying to reach you," she said. "He says you should call his office immediately."

The judge had left his personal number, which Boylan took down on a pad and ripped off. He was already on his way out, and his driver was waiting. He decided to call from the car.

The vehicle was at the door when Boylan emerged from the building. Boylan's transportation was like Lieutenant Colombo's raincoat—old and rumpled. Although he was regarded as one of the most preeminent attorneys in New Jersey, Boylan's transportation of choice was a brown 1977 Chevrolet station wagon with over two hundred thousand miles on the odometer. It looked like something on its way to a scrap-metal-recycling center.

But he did allow himself the luxury of his own driver, a man who had previously served for nine years as the personal driver for a general in the Turkish Army. The driver held the door open and ushered Boylan into the rear seat. As always, Boylan took his place directly behind the driver, a position the chauffeur insisted upon because he believed it to be the only place a person of stature should sit—farthest from the people who might be on the street attempting to do "God knows what" to the occupant.

On this day, as the car turned onto the highway, Boylan picked up the car phone and dialed Ackerman's number. It rang twice before it was picked up. Ackerman answered himself, and there were few preliminaries.

"You've been reading about it in the paper, you must know what's going on."

Boylan was at a loss—he had no idea what Ackerman was referring to.

"What are you talking about?" he said.

There was a brief pause and static. The reception was bad.

"C'mon," the judge said. "The case, Accetturo . . ."

In a few short sentences, Ackerman reviewed the situation. Accetturo's trial attorney was dying and would not be able to resume. Boylan had handled some of the pretrial motions in the case, and the judge wanted Boylan to pick up the ball.

"I want you in court tomorrow," Ackerman declared.

Boylan hesitated. He had other obligations, and as far as he was concerned, the trial had gone on without him. He had nothing to do with it.

"I have to be someplace else. . . ." he told the judge.

Ackerman slowly repeated himself. "I want you to be in court tomorrow," he declared.

Boylan was silent for a moment, as he considered the situation. This was a federal judge issuing him a direct order, and one couldn't really ignore a federal judge.

"Well," he said in resignation, "if you want me to be in court, I'll be there."

When Boylan saw Accetturo in the courthouse corridor, nearly two years had passed since the last time he had seen him, and time had taken its toll. Accetturo's hair, which had been salt-and-pepper, had gone entirely white. He had gained at least forty pounds, and he had the shambling gait of a much older man.

The two men barely acknowledged each other that day. Accetturo wanted no part of Boylan, and Boylan wanted no part of the trial.

In the courtroom, Ackerman looked weary. He had a crisis on his hands. On one hand, the prosecution was enraged.

What had become the longest criminal trial in New Jersey history was now on indefinite hold, and government lawyers feared that if Accetturo was severed from the case, he might never again be brought to trial. The costs of the prosecution had already become enormous, and it was unlikely that a separate prosecution—of equal length and expense—would be authorized.

O'Malley made his position as clear as possible. "We want the trial to continue and will oppose any motions for mistrial or severance. The concern that we have is to keep the trial going and to keep Mr. Accetturo in the case."

At least one government attorney grumbled privately about Accetturo "planning it all"—deliberately hiring a man with a terminal illness in order to provoke just such a crisis and ensure his own freedom.

The government's formal-motion papers filed with the court, however, were only slightly less accusatory. Accetturo, they charged, was engaging in a "blatant manipulation" of the situation.

The government attorneys were right about one thing: However tragic Ferrell's illness might be, it could prove a stroke of fortune for Accetturo. And Accetturo knew it well. He wanted out. Out of the court, out of the state, and out of the government's grasp.

The other lawyers in the case, however, were attempting to place the court in a "catch-22" situation. Ackerman wanted to delay the trial by a month. That was what was needed, he said, for another attorney—presumably Boylan—to bring himself up to speed on the developments in the case. But that delay, the other defense lawyers argued, would jeopardize the rights of the other defendants, and so they planned their own legal protest.

Meanwhile, many participants began to voice concerns over the prolonged delay and its potential impact on the jury. Federal prosecutors, at least publicly, maintained that they were confident the trial would be brought to completion. Others were not so sure. But Ackerman was determined not to let it unravel.

When court convened, the judge was already irritated. At least one of the attorneys had been late to court, another was absent, and a third was in the bathroom. He waited for the court to settle down and spoke in carefully modulated tones as he addressed the defendant by name.

"Mr. Accetturo," he said, "may I address you, sir?"

Accetturo stood and nodded his head. "Yes."

Ackerman asked him, "Have you been able to secure an attorney to argue whatever motion you want to argue this morning?"

Accetturo shook his head and shrugged helplessly.

"I'm trying to get people that know the law. I don't know the law," he protested. "I don't know the first thing about it. I've only been accused of breaking it."

The next day, February 25, would be one that Matt Boylan would never forget.

Ackerman issued his ruling. The trial, he said, would be placed on a one-month "temporary suspension," and Boylan would be appointed to pick up the pieces.

Ackerman's logic was simple: Under the local rules of court, once an attorney entered an appearance in a trial, he was considered under an obligation to remain with that trial until formally relieved of the responsibility. Boylan had unquestionably been in the case during the pretrial period. The attorney had tried to cover himself by presenting letters stating that he had only become involved for purposes of limited pretrial hearings. But according to Ackerman, those letters didn't hold water. Boylan could not unilaterally decide to limit his involvement in a case. That was a power reserved to the judiciary—and it was a power that Ackerman was now invoking.

The outcome was less than surprising. Boylan knew what to expect. The judge was backed into a corner: He could sever Accetturo—thereby virtually ensuring that the man authorities portrayed as one of the most powerful mob figures in the nation would go free—or he could attempt to invoke his powers to compel Boylan to take on the case.

The problem was solved for the court when Boylan, as he described it, was "dragooned" into service. Boylan, like it or not, was back in the case.

And on the morning of March 18, the trial, on hiatus for more than a month, was back in session.

But Accetturo wasn't one who gave up easily. In the corridor, he greeted Boylan like a long-lost brother. Then he pulled him aside. "I'm going to have to say some things when we get into court," Accetturo confided. "Don't take them personally."

It wasn't long before Accetturo, wearing a ratty white sweater over a white pullover shirt, was on his feet in the courtroom, and Boylan found out what Accetturo had been referring to.

"Judge," Accetturo said, nodding toward the tall lawyer at his side, "in all due respect to Mr. Boylan, he's doing what you told him to do. But I didn't hire him, *you* hired him."

Ackerman grimaced. He had thought this was over—apparently Accetturo didn't. Carefully, the judge outlined the legal reasons why he had ruled that Boylan was obligated to stay in the case. "You selected Mr. Boylan to represent you. . . . I just state it as simply as possible, sir, without in any way meaning to antagonize you or get you excited."

Accetturo waved away the apology.

"Judge, nobody is antagonizing me, and I ain't antagonizing you. I only state a point. I hired him for one purpose . . . he was supposed to come here for pretrial, that's it. That's all he was hired for. Now you chose to bring him back here. I think I deserve for you to tell this jury that you brought him here. I don't need this jury to think that I went and hired the biggest law firm in New Jersey to come here because Milton Ferrell, Sr., is dying. I don't think it's fair to me."

Accetturo was clearly upset. Throughout the trial, Ferrell had been almost silent. That was part of the strategy. There was very little direct evidence against Accetturo. Most was circumstantial, or hearsay, what somebody told somebody else. What Accetturo didn't want was a visible role in the proceedings—he wanted to remain in the background. Even his style of dress was designed to suggest a store owner rather than a multimillionaire mob boss. And no simple store owner would have hired Matthew Boylan.

"I refuse to tell the jury that I hired Mr. Boylan," Ackerman said firmly.

Accetturo was belligerent. "Who hired him?" he demanded, "just for the record, who hired this man?"

Ackerman was beginning to smolder with anger. "You," he shouted.

"I did not," Accetturo insisted.

Ackerman composed himself. "Well, I'm sorry, sir, we have a—"

Accetturo shrugged and cut him off. "There's going to be a disagreement, because I didn't hire him."

Ackerman merely glared in anger. Accetturo sat down. The judge called in the jury. Despite the defendant's protests, Ackerman did what he said he would: He introduced Boylan to the jury as Accetturo's new lawyer.

45

It was April 4, 1988, when the jury filed back into the courtroom.

It had been six weeks since they last met, but it might have been yesterday. It was warmer, and the sense of spring had crept into the air. But inside the courtroom, it was as if time had been standing still.

The defendants and lawyers stood as the jurors were ushered to their seats. There was a slight buzz in the room as the jurors swept their eyes over the defendants. They were just as they had left them—except maybe a little fatter.

Moments later, Ackerman greeted the jury, "Good morning, ladies and gentlemen . . . Let me just say on behalf of all of us, welcome all of you back. . . ."

Matt Boylan stayed with the trial just long enough to accomplish something the defense had been trying to do from the start, which was, effectively, to get Accetturo out of the case. When the episode was over, Accetturo would still be sitting there in the courtroom, but he would be virtually immune from conviction.

For the earliest pretrial stages, the government had adamantly opposed severing Accetturo from the trial. The whole concept of the prosecution was to prove that he was the "boss" of a RICO enterprise. But it had become apparent that without the evidence they had compiled against the alleged members of his organization, there was little chance of proving him the boss of anything, much less a major crime organization.

The actual hard evidence against Accetturo was almost nonexistent. There was testimony by Alonzo, identifying him as the man in charge, and corroborating testimony by some of his sycophants from Florida. But these were words, and the words of men the defense had incessantly reminded the jury were liars and thieves. Never mind that that was what the government claimed the defendants were: The defendants weren't testifying, the witnesses were—and a more unsavory crew would have been hard to round up.

One of the few items of solid evidence to support Alonzo's contentions was a receipt from a Florida diet center that showed that Accetturo and DiNorscio had attended sessions there together and that DiNorscio had picked up the tab. But as yet, no one had made it a crime to be fat.

The government's best hope was to show association. If it could prove that Accetturo had regular dealings with the other defendants, this could be used to support the argument that those dealings were not entirely social.

There was another item: a receipt from a Newark flower shop for a basket of flowers. The flowers had been sent to another organized-crime figure, and according to the receipt, the message on the card had read, *From Tumac and the Boys.*

The other potentially solid link between Accetturo and the "boys" in Newark were three telephone calls. The calls, the government contended, were placed by Accetturo to the Hole in the Wall and monitored and recorded by the FBI. FBI agent Dennis Marchalonis testified in court that he was certain he had recognized Accetturo's voice on the tapes—and that the voice on all three tapes was the same.

The calls were innocuous in and of themselves. "How's the weather?" "The weather is nice." Not exactly the stuff of which convictions are made. But they were at least something on which the government could build its argument of association. Even in exile in Florida, Tumac was keeping in contact.

But on May 6, even that slender thread of evidence began to unravel.

Boylan submitted to the court a sworn declaration written by Mark Jackovich, the inmate-systems manager at the Federal Correctional Institution at Butner, North Carolina. The declaration confirmed that "Anthony Accetturo was confined at the Federal Correctional Institution, Butner, North Carolina, from February 18, 1983, to April 29, 1983."

This was the time when Accetturo was undergoing court-ordered observation for Alzheimer's disease. It also was the time period during which the phone calls to the Hole in the Wall were made.

"Mr. Accetturo was housed in the Mental Health Seclusion Unit on March 2, 1983," the declaration read. "A review of the telephone log book maintained on secluded inmates does not indicate that a phone call was made by Mr. Accetturo. Normally, phone calls placed by an inmate are logged by a Correctional Counselor."

Further, the report went on to say, "No records exist which would indicate that Mr. Accetturo placed phone calls on March 22 and March 23, 1983."

On March 6, Ackerman gave the government the bad news. After reviewing the submissions from Boylan, he had no choice but to bar the government from attempting to introduce the phone calls as evidence against Accetturo.

Federal prosecutors, Ackerman said, had failed to produce "clear and convincing" evidence that Accetturo was, in fact, the speaker on the tape-recorded phone conversations. The judge noted that despite Marchalonis's sworn claims to have recognized the voice, he felt that "whatever [his] suspicions [were], whatever reasoning" was used by the agent to reach his conclusion, "to me, when you add it all up, the government has missed the mark."

As a result, Ackerman directed that Accetturo's name be stricken from the wiretap transcripts and the jury instructed that the name be deleted.

Stephen Skoller, an associate of Boylan, smiled broadly as he left the courtroom. "Out of hundreds of tapes made by the government," Skoller mused, the government had been able to select only three to use against Accetturo. "Now," he said, "there are none."

It was the beginning of what was to become a slow but inexorable downhill slide for the prosecution. The government had mountains of evidence yet to introduce—but they were mountains the jurors were growing too weary to climb.

As the days wore on, the momentum of the case seemed to slow as the weather warmed.

The case had been stretching on interminably. The government was introducing its paper proofs, along with its corroboration witnesses. These were primarily documents designed to support the live testimony. There were no startling revelations or allegations being aired. Even the press had curtailed its daily coverage. The jury was becoming visibly restless. One young woman juror was gouging out a hole in the back of the wooden jury box with her high heels as she rocked in her seat.

And a good third of the trial still lay ahead.

Braunreuther was still optimistic—he believed in the case. He believed that whatever defense tactics were being used to divert attention from the facts of the prosecution, the jury would ultimately see through them. After all, they were the good guys.

But the defense was intent on blurring that distinction.

When FBI agent Jerry Sullivan took the witness stand in late April 1988, the testimony was clearly designed to be dramatic. He had attended a birthday party for Anthony Accetturo at a Florida restaurant. It had all the trappings: music, wine, and kisses of tribute and respect.

At the hands of defense attorneys, however, the account that emerged sounded less like a scene from *The Godfather*, and more like an episode of *The Three Stooges Meet the Mafia*.

On direct testimony, Sullivan had told how he drank and mingled with the bar crowd and then ate dinner while Accetturo and a gathering of some sixty persons dined at a nearby banquet table. Most of those present, he said, appeared to be "Italian males."

He claimed he was later introduced to Accetturo himself by one of those "Italian males" and said he kissed the hand of the crime boss in a show of respect.

When Critchley confronted him, however, the defense lawyer turned the testimony into a joke. How, Critchley demanded, could Sullivan pick out "Italian males" at a glance?

The answer in at least one case was simple: "He looked Italian to me. With his hand gestures and everything else," Sullivan explained.

As the audience of defendants and attorneys snickered, Critchley played the scene broadly. He asked Sullivan to describe how he had kissed Accetturo's hand. Then he went one step further—he asked for a demonstration.

Sullivan stood in the witness stand and extended his own hand. As muted laughter filled the courtroom, Sullivan's pose resembled that of a royal princess waiting to be acknowledged.

As Sullivan was holding his hand out, Critchley reflected and then asked the agent, "How do you get your lips on his hand?"

It was easy. "I just brought it up," he replied.

46

The line for the bathroom had thinned. The defendants were on their way back to the courtroom, some lighting up for a quick smoke before the case resumed.

Critchley was standing at a urinal, concentrating on his aim. Braunreuther stepped to the next urinal.

It was a cramped bathroom. There were only two urinals, and two stalls. It was poorly lit, and the tiles had a grimy look that no amount of scouring by the maintenance crews could remove.

"We kicked your ass today, Joe," Critchley quipped.

Braunreuther snorted. "You think so? We crucified you."

It was the usual banter that had been engaged in since the trial began—only today there was something else.

There was a whole phase of the case that had yet to be dealt with—allegations involving Taccetta's involvement in Carmata Fuel, a heating-oil supply company located in the Morris County community of Whippany.

When the original indictment was announced, Carmata had been described as a key part of the charges outlined by U.S. Attorney Greelish. The company, he said, had become a "captive" of mob interests and had been operated "for the benefit" of the Taccetta organization.

The government claimed that the firm engaged in fraudulent billings, while Taccetta used the company as a sort of personal bank, dipping into its assets as he needed for loans and cash.

The problem was, to prove those charges could extend the trial well into the next year.

"C'mon, Joe," Critchley told the prosecutor, "what do you say we do something about this Carmata stuff. The jury's going to throw something at us if we keep going."

"It's not me," Braunreuther said, referring to his colleagues, who were handling that portion of the case. "It's not my decision to make."

"Look, Joe," Critchley said, "I've got checks to prove those transactions were loans. I've got the checks going back into the company."

Braunreuther was a practical man. He knew that if the government had not proved its case by then—with testimony of drug deals, mob sit-downs, and tape recordings of gambling operations—going off on a dry, document-laden tangent was not going to do it for them either.

"If you can convince them," Braunreuther said, staring at the wall, "I think maybe we could do something."

"Let's go over and talk," Critchley said.

The two men zipped up their flies, washed their hands, and headed back to the courtroom.

That afternoon, the deal was struck. The prosecution agreed to drop those charges against Taccetta, as well as a codefendant accused of participating in the scheme.

And on April 28, Grady O'Malley made an announcement that the Carmata Fuel Company phase of the case was being dropped as part of a "tactical decision" that he said would cut three to four weeks off the trial.

He predicted that the case would be over by early June—he was wrong.

In June of 1988, in the twentieth month of trial, the U.S. Court Clerks' Office in Newark confirmed that it had received notice from the Administrative Office of the Courts: The *U.S.* v. *Anthony Accetturo et al.* had become the longest criminal case on record in the federal courts of the nation.

47

There was an abiding concern in the back of Joe Braunreuther's mind—Dennis Marchalonis was about to take the witness stand.

For years, the FBI agent had tracked the activities of the Lucchese crime family. He had sat outside clubs at three-thirty in the morning, copied down license-plate numbers, took note of who came and who went, and, when he could do so without drawing attention, he took photographs. He saw, he watched, and he waited.

And in the spring of 1988, six years after his initial surveillance operations began, Marchalonis was finally being given the opportunity to tell what he knew, which was exactly what Braunreuther was afraid of.

Braunreuther himself had been frustrated. The rules governing the admissibility of evidence had been cumbersome, to say the least. There were materials that the government had thought were clearly permissible that were excluded. There were others that were admitted only after long and exhaustive arguments.

Braunreuther had had his own trial by fire early on in the case, when he presented Alonzo's testimony. Alonzo knew a lot more than he was allowed to tell in court. Braunreuther had had difficulty presenting Alonzo's story in any coherent pattern. He was forced to present "previews" of the testimony to the court the day before, just to make sure there wouldn't be any surprises that would violate the rules of evidence. Even Alonzo was cowed. There were times when he didn't know what he was allowed to say and what he wasn't. It gave a halting quality to his testimony that was exploited by the defense. It made him seem unsure of what he was saying. He wasn't—he was just unsure as to whether he could say it.

Now Marchalonis was about to testify, and he knew as much about the "boys" as they did themselves. What Braunreuther was afraid of was that he would decide to tell it.

The prosecutor had sat beside the FBI agent throughout the trial, and he had seen him growing increasingly impatient and angry. The defense was making a mockery out of the case—the strictures placed on the prosecution were absurd.

Doubly frustrating was the fact that many of the defense "revelations" about the government witnesses were actually based on material that under court rules was provided to the defense by the prosecution team itself.

"I was afraid," Braunreuther recalled, "that Dennis might say what he really thought."

Taking the witness stand, Marchalonis was polite but cocky. He knew the case better than anyone, as he had worked on it longer and harder. He knew the informants, and, most of all, he knew the defendants.

There were photos he identified: of Tic Cataldo outside the Hole in the Wall, shaking his finger and berating an associate, of Martin Taccetta, driving up to the Hole in the Wall in a cream-colored Mercedes Benz convertible; and of Michael Perna loading clothing into the trunk of a Chrysler Fifth Avenue. He saw Danny Ricciardi, his brother Tommy Ricciardi, Jerry Voglino, the man with the bad back. He saw Cadillacs, other alleged members of the organization, he saw Lincolns, all converging on the dingy storefront luncheonette. And on some occasions, he even saw Michael Taccetta.

For over a month, Marchalonis sat in the witness seat. Braunreuther questioned him, showing him stacks of photographs for identification, which were then distributed to the jury.

The jury, however, appeared to be listless. The jurors looked as if they were becoming bored. As Marchalonis answered the questions put to him by the prosecutor, some of the defendants just put their heads back and slept.

In the silence, there was a steady undercurrent of *crunch-crunch* and cellophane paper being torn and crumbled. It sounded like rats in the walls, but it was really only Jackie and his friends, munching on their caches of candy.

After the stacks of still photos were introduced, the government began to screen videotapes of the FBI surveillance operation. The Bureau had made more than 380 hours of videotapes of people coming and going, walking into the Hole in the Wall, walking out of the Hole in the Wall, locking the door. The most interesting of the movies had the "boys" playing a game of touch football on a warm afternoon. And although the FBI had edited down the tapes into a one-hour compilation of excerpts, the screening still seemed to take forever.

Marchalonis correlated the dates and times of the surveillance films with the voice recordings introduced into evidence earlier in the trial.

Some of the jurors were yawning openly.

It was only after days of numbing testimony that Marchalonis finally turned to what was to become a focal point of his testimony: his meeting with Michael Taccetta in June of 1985.

Three years later the jury heard the story, and Marchalonis described the incident in detail: how he had encountered Taccetta during a search of an associate's home, how the two men sat down at a kitchen table and talked for three hours.

The jury was listening intently. They had seen Michael Taccetta, and they had heard about Michael Taccetta's alleged leadership of the organization. Now, the FBI case agent, the man who spent years almost single-handedly putting together the case against Taccetta, was describing his face-to-face confrontation with his arch nemesis.

It was a polite, friendly conversation as Marchalonis related it. It ranged from a practical discussion about "stool pigeons" and the money to be made in illegal gambling to more esoteric contemplations of morality and ethics. They talked of the "code of the streets," Marchalonis said, and the danger of mistakes.

The jury was mesmerized. Here was a startling personal portrait of Taccetta, a man of violence who was also a man of letters—it was an incongruous duality.

The discussion, Marchalonis said, turned to "the teachings, if you will, or discussion of Socrates."

And there was a discussion of political philosophy, Marchalonis said, that centered on the theories of Machiavelli, as presented in his tract *The Prince*.

It was then that he told the jury that Taccetta had related Machiavelli to his own profession and stated that the "overall theme of Machiavelli is the idea that power corrupts, and absolute power corrupts absolutely."

It was a fascinating account. The problem was, it did little to bolster the prosecution's case. If anything, it probably only served to do what the defense had been trying to do all along—humanize the defendants.

These were not evil men, the defense had repeatedly suggested, these were just a bunch of good-natured juvenile delinquents who never grew up. And here was the FBI agent who was trying to convict them dealing with the leader of the pack as though he were an equal—they were discussing their mutual philosophies of life. And rather than looking like cinematic caricatures devised by Francis Ford Coppola, the defendants were beginning to look like real people.

For nearly two years, the jurors had sat in the same room with them. They had laughed and, at times, they had even cried. There was clearly a bond that had grown. In a way, they were all captives—the defendants, their lawyers, and the jurors. And the prosecution was responsible.

The witness stand is often referred to as the "hot seat." People who testify in court frequently find themselves being grilled until they are well done. But it was unlikely that any FBI agent had ever been grilled the way Marchalonis was grilled when the defense began its cross-examination. He seemed to be almost smoking.

It was the culmination of nearly two years of pent-up antagonism. The defense had portrayed Marchalonis and O'Malley as a team. DiNorscio had derided the agent as "Hopalong Cassidy," the man who was ready to hop on any plane to anywhere to rope in a new witness.

Marchalonis was a precise and meticulous man, and he

had grown increasingly intolerant of the defense's game-playing, which was turning the trial on its ear. And now those same defense lawyers were trying to do the same to him.

Critchley was working like a professional fighter: He was bobbing, he was weaving, and he was throwing his questions like punches. Marchalonis warded off a lot of them, but a lot of them appeared to strike home.

It had been the heart of the defense team's overall strategy to put the government on trial, not the defendants, and to call the prosecution's motives and actions into question. The prosecution team was supposed to be the good guys, but if the jury saw them as crossing the line, the defense would be on its way to winning the game.

As he continued to pummel Marchalonis, what Critchley did was to turn the agent's own work against him. Marchalonis had been involved in virtually every aspect of the case—interviewing witnesses, attending hearings where plea bargains were agreed upon, driving Alonzo to his methadone program, and supervising Mitola, who was apparently dealing drugs right under the FBI agent's nose.

And Alonzo, Critchley reminded the jury, had "hoodwinked" the agent by using FBI money to buy drugs even while he was under daily supervision by Marchalonis.

"You couldn't determine, while you were with him almost on a daily basis, a law-enforcement officer for seven years, that he was under the influence of drugs?" Critchley demanded.

Critchley suggested that Marchalonis had, in fact, "closed his eyes" to Alonzo's drug abuse.

"Now I guess we can understand why he wanted the protection of the government," Critchley declared. "We're giving him money to buy drugs, we're giving him a car, we're keeping him in hotels and giving him room service at approximately sixty-five dollars a day. That's not bad."

Then there was Mitola, the government's second star witness. He had got out of jail early because of his deal with the FBI.

The government, in a letter from O'Malley, had told the parole board that Mitola had no prior convictions that they were aware of.

"The parole board was lied to in that letter, weren't they?" Critchley demanded.

The defense lawyer continued to jab at the witness. Marchalonis acknowledged that Mitola had admitted to participating in an armed drug robbery in Baltimore, but no charges had ever been brought against him.

The FBI, Critchley charged, was "giving this guy a pass."

And when the DEA began targeting a task-force probe of Mitola's own drug dealing, Critchley reminded the jury, there were suddenly two phone calls from Marchalonis—and no reports to explain what they were for.

"October twenty-second, you contacted him twice," Critchley said. "And on October twenty-third, the next day, he turned in his beeper, didn't he?"

And as a result, Critchley noted, the DEA could no longer monitor Mitola's beeper calls.

"You told him about this investigation, didn't you?" Critchley demanded.

Marchalonis was adamant in his denial, but Critchley plowed ahead anyway. They had already bludgeoned Mitola with the same issue, but he was just an informant. Marchalonis was supposed to be the one wearing the white hat. Critchley was trying his best to splash a little dirt on that hat.

"You turned him on to that investigation, did you not, because you did not want to see your star agent being arrested by a DEA operation?"

Marchalonis said no, he would never do such a thing.

So Critchley then demanded an explanation. What, in that case, was so important that he had called Mitola twice?

Marchalonis said he could not remember.

"You told him," Critchley shouted, "about the DEA investigation, didn't you? . . ."

The answer was a denial. But Critchley wasn't interested in the answer—he just wanted to be sure the jury heard the question.

Even Braunreuther knew that Critchley had scored a home run, even though he himself was convinced that Marchalonis had played by the book, that he had never done anything wrong. But he was enough of a realist to recognize that the circumstances could be construed as suspicious and that Critchley had succeeded in doing what he set out to do: dirty up the white suits of the good guys.

When Critchley turned to the meeting with Michael Taccetta, his strategy was simple: He suggested it had never happened.

Critchley pointed out that before he became an FBI agent, Marchalonis had taught history. And the subject he taught was political science, which included Machiavelli. The question Critchley raised was, was this a true account of a real conversation, or was it an embellishment of the truth by an FBI agent who was attempting to bolster his own case?

"Do you know what it means to 'gild the lily'?" Critchley asked.

The attorney expressed marked skepticism over the story. Within fifteen to twenty minutes of meeting Taccetta for the first time in his life, Critchley asked, almost incredulous, Taccetta was discussing his "profession" with an FBI agent?

"All I can say is what he told me, what I told him, sir," Marchalonis replied.

Critchley noted that despite the fact that other government agents were in the house, the only person who was a party to the discussion was Marchalonis himself. Also, there was no tape recording of the exchange.

Critchley was trying to plant a question in the jury's mind. Did Taccetta really have that discussion with Marchalonis? He began gently, asking Marchalonis about his own interpretation of the Florentine statesman, letting him demonstrate his own command of the subject, leading him into a discussion of the historical perspective of Machiavelli's writings.

Machiavelli, Marchalonis said, was essentially a "nationalist," which to Marchalonis was a man who believed "my country right or wrong."

"Basically," Critchley suggested to the agent, "he espoused the theory of totalitarianism, did he not?"

Marchalonis was talking about Machiavelli. Critchley, however, was talking about something else, and Marchalonis played right into his hands.

"His basic theory," the agent responded, "to my understanding, was, you do what you have to, to accomplish what you want to accomplish. If it means you step on your friends, you step on your friends. If it means you need your friends for something, you utilize your friends."

Critchley nodded, as if trying to grasp what Marchalonis had said.

The agent went on to say that Machiavelli was regarded as "immoral at the time, unethical at the time."

Critchley, almost striking a classic "Lieutenant Colombo" pose, scratched his head and attempted to recapitulate what the agent had said. Machiavelli's political philosophy, Critchley asked hesitantly, didn't it amount to "the end justifies the means"?

"I don't know if I'd go as far as that," Marchalonis agreed, "but you're on the right track."

Critchley nodded toward the agent. "You're fairly knowledgeable about Machiavelli, aren't you?"

He was almost done with the questioning when he tossed in his final point, "Power corrupts, and absolute power corrupts absolutely. That was Machiavelli who said that, wasn't it?" he asked.

"That would be my understanding," Marchalonis said, biting at the bait. "The idea you want the power, you'll do anything to get the power. When you do get the power, the greed and the other factors play into it, and, finally, it destroys itself."

Critchley paused as though in thought. That was the same thing Marchalonis had said Taccetta had talked about during his discussion with the agent.

Critchley nodded as if considering the answer. Then he walked back to his desk and picked up a thick volume. It was a copy of *Bartlett's Familiar Quotations*. He walked back to the podium and leaned over it, looking at Marchalonis. "Do you know who Lord Acton is?" Critchley asked.

Marchalonis looked confused.

"Lord Acton?"

"A-C-T-O-N," Critchley spelled the name.

"No, sir," Marchalonis said warily.

"Well," Critchley said, holding the book up for the jury to see. He noted that Acton was English and lived between 1834 and 1902, three hundred years after Machiavelli. "He's the author of that particular quote . . . not Machiavelli."

There were a few audible snickers from the defense camp as Critchley placed the book back on his desk.

Moments later, as the attorney walked out of the courtroom, he joked with reporters, "I think I cleared Machiavelli's name—he's not part of the Lucchese crime family."

He had done more than that. He had suggested that Marchalonis was a "student" of Machiavelli. And Machiavelli, he had reminded the jury, was willing to do whatever was necessary to achieve his goals, which was exactly what he was implying the government had done in putting the case together.

The prosecution never bothered to suggest that Critchley may have been doing the same thing.

48

At 3:51 P.M. on June 3, 1988, a tired and haggard-looking Joseph Braunreuther stood and formally announced to the court, "On behalf of my colleagues, I am pleased and proud to announce that the government rests its case."

There was only the briefest of pauses before the defense responded with a spontaneous outburst of applause.

There was nothing Ackerman could do but wait for the demonstration to subside. "I am gratified," he declared, "that we appear to be seeing the light at the end of the tunnel."

Critchley wiped his brow in relief over the government announcement. "I never thought we'd see the day," he declared. "I never thought I'd be that happy to hear those words."

Ruhnke was less exuberant. "It's nice to know it's ending," he declared, "but there's an awful lot more to go. . . ."

The prosecutions's announcement had been a long time in the coming. The case, once heralded as the most significant organized-crime prosecution ever to be undertaken in New Jersey, was at an end. It had set records: It had lasted nearly twenty months. More than 35,000 pages of transcript had been compiled, comprising 240 volumes; some 850 exhibits had been introduced; and more than seventy-five persons had taken the witness stand. Plus there was the fact that hundreds of thousands of dollars had been spent on providing protection for government witnesses, while more than $150,000 a month was spent providing court-appointed attorneys for defendants who were unable to afford their own lawyers.

Braunreuther was clearly exhausted but for him, it was not over yet.

"We have a lot to do in terms of getting the summations ready," he declared. Given what was to come, his assessment was a monumental understatement.

49

Joe Braunreuther sat alone at the kitchen table. The night was hot and thick with humidity—and anxiety.

It was all coming to a climax. Nearly two years of trial, including sleepless nights, decisions, and worries, was soon to be over.

It had been difficult. Joe's wife had given birth to their first child just before the trial began. They had been living in an apartment in Weehawken then. In some ways, life had been a lot simpler.

Midway through the trial, they had decided to move to a home in the suburban Essex County community of Maplewood, where tree-lined streets and a good school system had created a sort of utopia for yuppies.

The house they purchased was old and in need of work. Joe tried to find time to tackle some of these projects while pouring himself into the trial, but there just wasn't enough time to go around.

As the trial had progressed, Braunreuther had slowly emerged as the dominant personality on the prosecution team. It had been O'Malley's case from the start: He had worked with the FBI during the investigation; he had drafted the indictment; and he had presented the opening arguments. But Braunreuther had gradually come to play a larger and more significant role in the case. In many areas, he began to call the shots. In some ways, it was a deliberate strategy, since the defense had set about targeting O'Malley and Marchalonis as the villains of the story—making deals that offered freedom to the lowest forms of criminals in a desperate attempt to score a victory. To some degree, Braunreuther was insulated from those attacks. He had not come into the case until it was already complete; he had not dealt with the informants; he had not made the deals.

At the same time, his personality was not such as to allow him to take a backseat. He was in the case, and was therefore determined to be a major part of it.

The kitchen table in his home was littered with documents, pages of transcript, and notes. The night was still, and the sweat welled out of his pores as his eyes swam over the materials. It had become an all-consuming effort.

The Braunreuthers had had their second child while the trial was still in progress. As he worked, the baby would cry, and their older child would wake.

There was no air-conditioning in the old house, and the heat mingled with his thoughts and the cries of the baby. There was so much to put together.

O'Malley and Miller had done their part. So had Marchalonis. The summations were to be broken into three sections: an introduction and outline to be presented by O'Malley, an analysis of the credit-card-fraud charges to be presented by Barbara Miller, and a detailed overview of the entire case to be presented by Joseph Braunreuther. It was a massive undertaking.

The prosecution team had summer interns prepare page references from the transcripts. Joe had a computer readout indexing all the key evidence by witness and subject.

In organizing his thoughts, he wanted to put himself in the place of jurors. They couldn't question that crimes had been committed. What he wanted to do was compile the evidence against each individual. If he could do that, he was certain, the jury would have to convict.

50

The walk to the courtroom was a long one. Joe, Grady, and Barbara rode down the elevators in the Federal Building and crossed the street to the old courthouse. Inside, the thick walls insulated the building from the glare of summer heat. It was July 9, 1988.

Outside the courtroom, the crowds had begun to gather—defendants, lawyers, and their families. Other prosecutors had come too. The final act in what had become an epic drama was about to be played out.

There was an air of almost breezy nonchalance as the defendants filed into their seats. No one spoke to the prosecutors.

Ackerman entered the courtroom, his black robes swirling behind him as he ascended the bench.

For a moment, there was silence.

Grady O'Malley looked grim. The jury looked weary as they entered the room in single file. The defendants looked resigned. The evidence had all been presented. The tapes had been played, and the witnesses had testified. It was all over except for the summations.

The jurors shifted in their seats as O'Malley rose to his

feet. There was an undercurrent of voices. O'Malley waited for the silence to resume.

His voice was loud, his expression determined. There appeared to be an edge of anger in his delivery, as he began to address the jury for the final time.

"Fact or frame-up, ladies and gentlemen?" He turned his body and swept his hand over the defense camp. "Reality of criminal enterprise, or is it a monstrous government conspiracy that has gone on for years, a vendetta against these gentlemen here in the courtroom? Two diametrically opposed theories are presented to you for your consideration."

"The government suggests—in fact has charged in its indictment—that these defendants, with many others, have engaged in a criminal enterprise for at least a period of nine years, starting in 1976."

He paused.

"The defense has claimed that the evidence you've heard in the case, the physical evidence that has been presented to you, is a fabrication—has been created out of whole cloth."

He turned to the jury and softened his tone.

"I don't even know how to say this, really. It's difficult to put into words how we feel about the sacrifices that you people have made. . . . To say thank you is probably a very, very weak attempt. It was an arduous task. I'm sure there were many personal sacrifices that you people made.

"There were trying times during this trial, and there were some humorous times during the trial, and I'm sure the personalities came to the front from everybody's perspective. Individual jurors viewed specific individuals in certain ways."

The prosecutor appeared strangely uncomfortable. He sounded almost apologetic as he talked about personalities. He was, by nature, an aggressor, but for the moment, he seemed almost contrite.

"And I ask you, and I'm sure the court will suggest to you in its charge, that personalities should not play any part here; that you should put those from your mind and focus specifically on the evidence that has been presented."

O'Malley took a breath and then went on to the facts of the case itself.

His presentation lasted for two days.

He described "sit-downs" in luxury automobiles, "business" meetings at fruit stands, and cryptic telephone conversations replete with references to characters such as "Tomahawk" and "Cochise."

Drawing on the tape recordings and photographs amassed during the trial, O'Malley outlined to the jury what he portrayed as "compelling, devastating evidence" that revealed the anatomy of a powerful organized-crime family.

From discussions of deals in bootleg cigarettes to examples of what he termed the "courtesy and etiquette" of organized crime, O'Malley described a tightly regimented "chain of command," which he said was used to control the operations of the crime organization.

From hangers-on at an Irvington pool hall, O'Malley said, the members of the group evolved and matured into a professional criminal enterprise that controlled an empire of gambling, loan-sharking, and narcotics operations in both New Jersey and Florida.

As he spoke, the air conditioners whirred in the background. The outside temperature was nearly 100 degrees, and the humidity was thick enough to drink.

"We have overwhelming evidence," O'Malley told the jury, "that shows this organization functioned, had a structure and hierarchy.

"This enterprise," he went on, "like a business, like a corporation, delegates duties, delegates specific authorities to do specific acts."

Referring to conversations regarding moneylending, which had been picked up by FBI taps at the Hole in the Wall, O'Malley raised his hands in an appeal to common sense.

"Let's be frank here, ladies and gentlemen. Nobody lends money out of a diner in Down Neck Newark just to be friendly. That's not what it's all about. . . ."

And collecting on those loans was part of the plan.

"The Taccetta organization's reputation in the community was such," O'Malley declared, "they didn't have to threaten people—they knew . . . They knew if you don't pay it back, they're not taking you to court. They knew that if you didn't pay it back, you're going to have a problem. . . ."

The presentation was alternately shrill and bombastic, soft and staccato. The jurors sat impassive.

As he neared the end of his speech, O'Malley became demonstrably more emotional. He defended the government; he defended the use of informants; and he defended Marchalonis.

The government didn't cheat, he said. The FBI didn't embellish or "gild the lily." The evidence was as it was presented. He drew himself up to his full height. His muscles seemed to bulge beneath his jacket.

"So, ladies and gentlemen," he concluded, his voice filled with fire, "for the government to have constructed this monstrous conspiracy to get these defendants, dozens of people would have had to have been included—judges, law-enforcement [officials] from all over the country, local law enforcement, civilian witnesses, we would have had to have planted evidence. . . ."

"And I suggest to you, ladies and gentlemen, that in fact, there is no conspiracy on behalf of the government. What you've heard here is a realistic view of what went on."

When he stopped talking, there was only silence.

And then court was adjourned.

It was the last time O'Malley spoke to the jury—until the day of the verdict.

Outside the courtroom, the defendants and their attorneys milled about. Their voices were loud and raucous, and the noise drew the attention of at least one of the other judges in the courthouse, who filed a protest to Ackerman. Moments later, Ackerman convened the gathering and requested that they try to keep the noise level under control.

Ruhnke, however, protested that it would be virtually impossible to reduce the noise, simply by virtue of the number of people involved—some forty lawyers and defendants and an almost equal number of spectators.

"I think if there were eighty federal judges standing outside in the hallway, there would be a clamor even if everyone tried to speak quietly," Ruhnke declared.

Ackerman seemed in no mood to argue. "Well," he said, "pretend that you're in a Trappist monastary. . . ."

O'Malley's speech was, in the context of the Accetturo trial, the towering prosecutor's last hurrah. Miller was next to present her summation, and she was low-key and confined almost exclusively to the credit-card aspect of the case. The main summation was yet to come, and that would be delivered by Joseph Braunreuther.

Braunreuther's summation was as epic in scope as the trial itself—it lasted seven days.

And when the defense finally ended its own marathon series of closing speeches, he came back for an encore rebuttal that lasted yet another three days.

Indeed there was so much to say and so little time. For Braunreuther, even a week or ten days was too little. The case had taken nearly two years to present, and now he was going to try to condense it—it was an impossible task.

He wanted to read transcripts, he wanted to play tapes, but he knew he could not.

"I cannot do it," he told the jurors. "I won't put you through it."

As he spoke, Braunreuther painted a verbal portrait of an organization ruled from afar by all-powerful bosses, who give their orders with nods of approval while maintaining iron-fisted control over one of the most lucrative racketeering empires in the nation.

There was, he said, a "common thread" of connection that led through the maze of criminal dealings that had been presented to the jury during the course of the trial.

He described the lavish life-styles led by some defendants, and he reviewed a "classic confrontation between organized-crime families" that arose during an attempt to take over the mail-order gem operation in Florida. The clash, he said, was sparked when one of the defendants told another ranking mob figure, "Go pump gas in New Jersey."

Accetturo, he said, never came into direct contact with the criminal acts but served as a sort of absentee director.

"We don't maintain that Anthony Accetturo ever touches gambling records. He doesn't touch cocaine. But he is the ultimate leader of the organization."

Taccetta, Braunreuther said, served as Accetturo's "surrogate" in New Jersey, and the prosecutor described his role in a similar fashion.

"He doesn't touch the gambling records. He doesn't have his fingerprints on the cocaine. He is, in the hierarchy of the organization, one who gives approval, one who benefits, and one who takes responsibility for his actions like anybody else in terms of his leadership role."

Regardless of their roles, however, Braunreuther charged that each defendant, boss or soldier, was "equally culpable" for the staggering array of crimes committed by the organization.

For the next week, Braunreuther plodded on. He played tapes, he displayed exhibits—some jurors paid attention, some seemed to drift. But Braunreuther knew the facts of the case, and he was determined to present them as forcefully and cogently as he could. It was up to the jurors to decide what to make of those facts.

His final words settled on a simple thing. An item found during an FBI search at the Hole in the Wall luncheonette. A receipt from a flower shop. The flowers, he said, had been sent with a message—from "Tumac and the boys."

"Whoever sent it knew there was Tumac and the boys," Braunreuther declared. "And whoever received it knew there was such a thing as Tumac and the boys."

"That's what this case is about," Braunreuther said softly, leaning toward the jury box, "Tumac and the boys."

He ran through the defendants, one by one, reflecting on their individual roles in the organization, leading up to Michael Taccetta and, finally, to Anthony Accetturo himself.

"These are the guys who hung together for years," he declared. "Make no doubt about it, ladies and gentlemen, we say it's Tumac and the boys."

Taccetta, he said, was the "chosen one."

"Michael, who can sit back and pontificate and philosophize about his role in organized crime and brag about it and walk around with the Taccetta name on the street, which is respected." He paused. "Or is it feared?"

Pointing to the defendants, Braunreuther pushed his hair back from his face.

"Tumac and the boys," he declared, "the legacy of Anthony Accetturo. That's what we're dealing with here, ladies and gentlemen. The outfit, the edge . . ."

Braunreuther was right about one thing. There was a legacy to be left by Anthony Accetturo—and for the government, it would be a devastating one.

51

There was almost an air of celebration in the court when it came time for the defense team to start summations. They had sat, and they had listened, as Braunreuther attempted to marshal the evidence to convict.

Now it was their turn.

One by one, the galley of lawyers took turns presenting their arguments, most of which were brief. They all had points to make—critical bits of testimony with which they had to deal. Some were simple and direct.

Tic Cataldo, who along with DiNorscio had been representing himself, made an appeal that was at once poignant and eloquent.

The government had charged that the defendants were no different than the informants the defense had excoriated. That made Cataldo angry. Alonzo, he said, was a dope dealer and attempted murderer, a man who had terrorized an innocent woman and child.

"And you heard the government get up and say, well, they're part of them, they're just like them."

He tightened his lips. "Ladies and gentlemen," he said with all the dignity he could muster, "I'm not like him."

He then turned to the other informants, Mitola and Hawley.

"I've done some things that I'm not proud of," he said, referring to his previous convictions for gambling. "But I paid the price. I'm not like them."

He pointed to the prosecutors. "They've been living and dealing with the Mitolas and Alonzos of this world too long. . . . They make you ashamed of the word 'respect.' Friendship is a dirty word. . . ."

With him in that courtroom, he said, were both friends and relatives.

"I grew up with them. I've been with them all my life. I played ball with them. I went to catechism with them. I did a million things with them. I slept over at their house, they slept over at mine.

"Ladies and gentlemen," he said, his voice now filled with emotion, "some guys in this room, and some relatives of mine, I loved them when I was a little boy. I loved them when I made my opening, and I love them today. And nobody is going to make me take a backward step from them—no one is going to take my manhood away and make me back down from that. I love my friends and relatives. And I respect people, and I hope they respect me."

Some of the summations were workmanlike, some were inspired, and some were, in keeping with the trial itself, bizarre.

Stephen Skoller, a young lawyer from Matt Boylan's firm who had gradually assumed the dominant role in the representation of alleged crime-boss Anthony Accetturo, used a projector to display a cartoon of the wolf from *Little Red Riding Hood.* Pointing to the drawing, he likened the government informants in the case to the wolf in the fairy tale.

There was another summation that stood apart from the others as well—the one delivered by Miles Feinstein, which began with him singing a refrain from "La Bamba," making an obscene gesture to the other attorneys, and making several ethnic remarks about Jews and Italians.

The jury, which had become virtually insensate by now, suddenly looked alert—and amazed.

Feinstein recited poetry. He referred to *Laugh-In* and told the jury that Henry Gibson was his idol. He paraphrased the news alert from radio station WINS—"Give me an hour of your time . . . and I'll give you reasonable doubt." He sang a Frank Sinatra song; he jumped in the air; he shouted; he played a harmonica; and he did an impression of Howard Cosell. He ran back and forth in front of the jury box, likening the case to football plays. He ripped open his shirt and showed a T-shirt emblazoned with LA BAMBA.

Finally, he hyperventilated and had to ask for a break.

After watching him, Ackerman commented, "I want to tell you something—I got the first headache I've had in almost a year and a half."

While the judge was not amused, fortunately for Feinstein, the jurors were. As he reentered the courthouse after the luncheon recess, several of the jurors were gathered outside the front entrance. They smiled, they laughed, and they cheered him on.

52

Mike Critchley had his hands full.

As the defense team was summing up, the lawyers were facing a nightmarish task of coordinating logistics, of weeding through evidence that had been compiled over the length of the trial, of sifting through the facts, and of attempting to marshal them in such a way as to support the defense theory of the case.

It would be Critchley's job to carry the main burden. Everyone else was to play a part as well; but they couldn't have lawyers stepping all over each other, repeating points, making the same arguments over and over again. It involved diplomacy at its best, and everyone involved was capable. But there could only be one quarterback.

Beyond all the other concerns, there was one other: Jackie DiNorscio. He was a wild card. All along, things he had said during his own forays into cross-examination could have blown up in the faces of the other defendants. The same was so now.

Dennis Mautone recalled an incident in which he had cautioned Jackie during the trial to be careful how he questioned the witness. There were areas that could prove damaging to his client, Manny Montiero. In fact, Mautone, who sat near DiNorscio, had asked him to reconsider questioning the witness at all.

But Jackie was intractable. "My people, they expect me," Jackie told him, waving toward the jury. "My jury, they want me—I got to go."

Mautone shook his head despairingly. "Just don't talk about those areas," he pleaded.

As might have been expected, Jackie did what Jackie did. He talked about the very subjects Mautone had wanted him to stay away from.

When DiNorscio returned to his seat, he was beaming. "So, how'd I do?" he asked, obviously anticipating an accolade.

Mautone only glared at him. "You're an asshole," he muttered.

The reaction took only a moment. Jackie was out of his chair faster than anyone had ever seen him move. He was headed for Mautone.

Montiero saw what was coming and tried to hold Jackie back.

"What the fuck did you say?" DiNorscio hissed to the lawyer.

Ackerman could not see everything that was happening. He only heard the commotion.

"What's the trouble?" he asked innocently.

Mautone put on a smile and waved his hand in dismissal. "Nothing, Judge."

DiNorscio was fuming in his seat.

"Nothing?" he muttered in a voice audible only to those close to him. "I'm going to throw him out the fucking window."

Fortunately for Mautone, the fit of temper passed.

Now Critchley had his own worries. He wanted to be absolutely certain that Jackie could be contained during his summation—that he would not do anything that would be totally disruptive to the overall defense strategy. But with Jackie being Jackie, he knew he could not be certain of anything.

Critchley made arrangements to visit Jackie at the Metropolitan Correctional Center in Manhattan, where Jackie had been held throughout the trial. He knew Jackie was preparing his own summation, and he wanted to try to impose some restraints, to let him know what he could do and, even more important, what he could not do.

Critchley was ushered into the visiting area to meet with DiNorscio. It was a large, open room with tables bordered by a private conference area.

One thing inmates were never shy about asking for was free legal advice. When they spotted a lawyer, they peppered him with questions. That even applied to the so-called "big guys."

And Critchley had become a familiar face. As he was waiting, he became embroiled in conversation with a number of the organized-crime luminaries who had already been convicted—including the boss of the Genovese crime family, "Fat Tony" Salerno and his top aide, Matthew (Matty the Horse) Ianniello, both of whom were facing lifetime sentences for racketeering.

Moments into the conversation, Jackie walked in carrying his legal folder. He was an impressive sight—huge, sweaty, and shambling across the floor in slippers. When Jackie walked into the visiting area, people recognized that someone different was walking in.

He looked indignant. Critchley had come to see *him*, not the top crime bosses of the metropolitan area.

"Fuck those guys," he said, cutting into the conversation. "They're doing a hundred years each. I got to get ready for *my* summation."

Salerno and the others could only stare and laugh at the audacity. Jackie was used to getting his way.

When indeed it came time for Fat Jack's final bow, it was a performance that began with raucous laughter, irreverent disputes with the prosecutors and the judge, and even a silent message personally delivered to one former juror, who was widely perceived—rightly or wrongly—to have been unamused by DiNorscio's Falstaffian antics.

As the juror glared at DiNorscio, another attorney watched in horror as DiNorscio mouthed a silent, but fully visible, "Fuck you" to his perceived nemesis. Fortunately for the defense, that juror was dismissed before the case reached deliberations.

Now, as DiNorscio lumbered to the microphone, he tapped it and counted. "One, two, three, four—" He looked at the jurors. "That's not the counts I'm involved in, I'm just loosening up."

He hesitated, and rushed through a few quick one-liners relating to his girth.

"Most people," he said, "don't really like fat people."

"See my feet?" he asked. "Well, I can't."

The jurors laughed.

He referred to the off-color quips with which he had begun the trial and admitted that he had deliberately chosen the role of "court jester and jokester" to try to win the goodwill of the jury.

"I didn't want you to be mad at me at the end of this trial," he said.

The laughter and outrageous behavior was over. What remained was a poignant plea for leniency for the men he called his friends.

Noting that he had only a sixth-grade education—"I know it's hard to tell," he joked—DiNorscio told the jury, "I was afraid, ladies and gentlemen, but never of the truth, just of the lies."

He pointed to the other defendants in the courtroom. "Most of the men in this courtroom I've known all my life." He paused. "And it's not sinister to have friends. Remember me telling you at the beginning of this case loud and clear that I was gonna deal with this case from the heart? And that's what I've done, and that's what I'm doing here today. I want you to believe that sincerely."

Referring to his lengthy prison record, DiNorscio declared, "I done my time, ladies and gentlemen. I ain't never said I did right or I did wrong. I've paid for it. I danced, and I paid the fiddler."

Had it not been for his relationship with Joey Alonzo, he said, the other defendants would never have been brought to trial.

"Believe it or not," he said, "I don't even hate the guy. Between me and him, there's been a love-hate thing since we were kids. . . .

"Well, ladies and gentlemen, I was shot on February 10,

1985. I went to sleep in my home, and I was shot while I was sleeping." He lowered his voice: "Now if I had died there, there wouldn't have been no trial here."

Braunreuther rose to his feet with an objection, but DiNorscio continued on.

"Well," he said, "I lived, and I didn't tell on him. If he didn't tell on me, there wouldn't have been no trial. And that's the truth."

At that point, DiNorscio said, Alonzo "went over a line that would make him, like, less than anyone in this courtroom."

DiNorscio picked up a sheaf of papers that he had rested on the podium, a thick pile of yellow legal sheets. He waved them in front of the jury.

In a dramatic flourish, he ripped the pages in half and tossed them into a wastebasket. "Believe me," he said, pointing to the torn speech, "this is a waste of time."

He steadied himself at the podium.

"See these men?" he said, looking slowly around the courtroom. His voice was choking with emotion. "They all got something to go home to . . . I know every one of their families; I know every one of their kids."

His voice dropped to a hoarse whisper as he referred to his own family. "I lost mine because I did it to myself."

It was late in the afternoon, and despite the summer day, the shadows were deepening in the courtroom, the light filtering through the heavy velvet drapes.

DiNorscio took a deep breath and held himself erect. He looked at the prosecution table and then back to the jurors.

He told the jurors that if they felt they had to convict someone, they should convict *him* in his place.

"If you feel they got to you," he said, gesturing at the prosecutors, "would you let these people go home and you find me guilty? Because without me, there wouldn't have been no trial." He lowered his head. "I told you I'm not guilty, but I'm used to this."

He looked at the jury for a final time.

"I don't have nothing further to say, ladies and gentlemen. Thank you very much."

53

Michael Critchley was like a racehorse vying for the Triple Crown. He was both figuratively and literally breaking into a sweat. They couldn't keep him penned up for long.

Critchley had planned to go last, but the plans had changed. He and the other defense lawyers realized that after a seven-day government summation, the jury would be comatose by the time his turn came. To wait for nineteen other defense summations to conclude was too much to ask. If he waited until then, it would be all over—no one would be awake in the courtroom to listen.

And so on July 26, he was turned loose.

There was a tumult of conversation in the courtroom as the crowds of lawyers, defendants, and spectators waited for the session to begin.

Ackerman had ordered the jury brought out, when suddenly, to his right, he noticed Jackie DiNorscio frantically waving his hand.

"Could we have it quiet, please?" he called out. As the clamor subsided, he nodded to DiNorscio to speak.

"Judge," DiNorscio complained, pointing to an easel set

up in the middle of the courtroom, "I'm blocked by this." He pointed over at the far end of the courtroom. "Do you think I could sit over there?"

Ackerman shrugged.

"I have no problem. . . . Where do you want to sit?"

DiNorscio again pointed over past the prosecution table. "Just so I can see."

"You have to show me," Ackerman replied.

DiNorscio stood. "Not with the prosecutors," he clarified, to a few chuckles, "in the far corner, right there."

"You mean where Mr. Sogliuzzo is?" Ackerman asked in clarification.

"Yes."

Ackerman assented. "I have no problem."

Attorney John Sogliuzzo rolled his eyes—there was barely room for the people already there. "What, does he want to sit on my lap, Judge?" he muttered.

Ackerman watched as the three-hundred-pound DiNorscio lumbered toward the corner of the room.

"Better yours than mine," he said.

When Michael Critchley rose to speak, there was silence in the room. This was the moment everyone had been waiting for, the moment that could make or break the case for the government. Critchley's cross-examinations had been brilliant. He had used humor like a scalpel, slicing away at the facades of the government witnesses. They could have been telling the truth—it wouldn't have mattered. Under his questioning, even the most reasonable of people could appear absurd.

But that was behind him. O'Malley had been right—the case was not to be judged on personalities, on who had the most winning smile or who told the best jokes. Braunreuther had spent seven days spotlighting the facts of the case. He had fit them together into a giant puzzle that supported the government theory of guilt for each of the defendants. Now it was Critchley's turn to take that puzzle apart. He was going to draw his own picture—the defense version.

He was not a classical orator. His voice didn't resonate like Raymond Burr delivering a speech in a Perry Mason movie. His voice was of the street; in fact, he could have been one of the defendants, since he spoke like one of them.

He started with a confession. He didn't know quite how to begin.

"I don't know," he said. "I thought about it, I agonized over it. I tried to work as hard as I can to do exactly what a summation is supposed to do, summarize it cogently, reasonably. But after I tried and tried, I said to myself, Mike don't you wish you were back in school?"

He paused, pacing back and forth as though to gather his thoughts. He raised his head.

"When I grew up, approximately ten years, seventeen to twenty-seven, I was a roofer. The good thing about roofing is that when you're done at four o'clock, the job is done. You just had to worry that it doesn't leak."

There was a smattering of chuckles.

"But for all practical purposes, you were done. You went on to something else. The problem that I have now with my profession that I agonize over is that I'm never done. No matter what happens with you, the case, you live with it." He touched his chest. "Somehow, it gets inside of you. It gets into your bones and into your marrow. Because you do know that you've been given a God-given responsibility."

He looked hard at the jury. "You have an awesome responsibility," he told the panel, "because, ladies and gentlemen, I have in my hands the fate of Michael Taccetta."

He strode around the well of the court looking alternately at his client and the jury.

"I can't do any better than I can do. If I were like my brother Joey, I can break out into 'Danny Boy' periodically, and we might be a little lightened up. Or like my brother Jimmy, do a little tap dance." He clicked his shoes on the courtroom floor. "He's a good dancer."

Braunreuther, he said, had cautioned the jury not to be misled by histrionics. Well, he said, sometimes it is necessary to be dramatic.

"But yet," he said, "sometimes you do have to yell. I was the youngest of six boys growing up not too far from here, three miles from here, yes, in a cold-water flat. If you don't yell sometimes in those circumstances, you don't eat. Not that my brothers were denying me, but, you know, you give and take and you learn to scrap and scramble."

He paused again and gritted his teeth. "My mother told

me something—if she were alive, she'd be sitting right here." He gestured at the front row of spectator benches. "When you're the youngest of six boys in my neighborhood, she said, 'Mike, don't worry about how big or small you are; somebody comes at you, you stand up to them; if they're a bully, you stand up to them.'"

Suddenly, Critchley turned and pointed at the prosecution table, at O'Malley, Marchalonis, and Braunreuther. "And, Helen," he vowed, "as best I can, I'm standing up to these bullies." His voice grew louder and more defiant. "They're not going to scare me, they're not going to frighten me, they're not going to cause us to turn away. Because like all bullies, you bark back. And when you bark back, sometimes their bark is not that loud."

He quieted and turned back to the jury. He shook his head in a gesture of amazement. "Whoever dreamed, my God, that I'd be talking to you this late July of 1988 when we started to convene a jury on November 19, 1986 . . . but you know, a long journey is difficult. And it becomes more difficult in the final steps. For we're almost at the end of that journey, but we're at the final steps, and those final steps sometimes are more difficult than any of the other steps." He took a deep breath and puffed out his chest. "You have to suck it up," he said, pounding his chest, "you have to suck it up and go the distance."

He glanced at O'Malley with a sly smile. "If I can make a sports analogy: In a basketball game, you can watch that game, but then you can turn on that last two minutes. That's when it's going to be won or lost." He looked at the government prosecutor, the former pro-basketball player. O'Malley was impassive, his expression a deadpan scowl. "That's when champions are made," Critchley went on, "or champions are destroyed, the last two minutes of a game. Because that's when you have to suck it up. And in a football game, they call it the two-minute offense and the two-minute defense. They don't talk about the other minutes that precede it. Because that's when champions are made and that's when champions are destroyed."

He nodded to the jury. "We're at the last two minutes, ladies and gentlemen." He paused. "But this is not a game—this is life.

"But before my job is done, we've got a lot of traveling to do. Whether you like it or not, ladies and gentlemen, you're coming with me. And when I'm finished, with all sincerity, I'm going to say, 'Let my people free!'" He looked out over the crowded courtroom at the silent faces with their eyes turned to him. "Because justice is going to tell you to set them free."

Critchley took a step back. The jury was rapt. Rarely do courtroom speeches equal those of television or motion-picture dramas, but this one did.

He began to name informants. O'Malley, he said, claimed those witnesses came into the case in "various ways." He laughed to himself. "Although they may have come in various ways, there is one constant—they all came in handcuffs."

The jurors laughed along with him.

"Then," he continued, "Mr. O'Malley said, you know: 'We're not asking you to embrace these people, we're not asking you to take them home with you.'"

He looked at the prosecutor, his voice shrill. "But they're asking you something more. They're asking you something far more. They're asking for you to take them with you to all eternity. Because this is not something where you say, 'Okay, I think I made a mistake, I want to change my vote.'" He was shouting. "The decision you make is final." He lowered his voice. "The decision you make in this particular case lives with you for the rest of your life."

It was a sobering thought. "At that last moment in life," he quipped, "the last person we want to be thinking about is Joseph Alonzo."

The speech was a warm-up—a prelude to the main act. Critchley gradually shifted gears. He began to pick apart the prosecution witnesses, comparing them to the Joe Isuzu character on the television commercial—the character who lies with a smile and says, "Trust me."

The key government informants, he charged, had lost the ability to tell the difference between lies and truth; their ability to make a moral distinction between right and wrong had disintegrated.

"So they're able to get up there and lie with a straight face, because it's built into their characters. It's in their soul and in their being. And they became very good at it. Because it had almost become to them a way of life. They have survived on the ability to manipulate other people's choices, to cause people to do things . . . and it gives them a lot of power."

He looked at the jury intently. "I'm asking you to take that power away."

"You know," he said, gesturing toward the government table, "my adversaries sometimes seem to operate under the assumption that they know what's best for all of us. They know what's best. They will tell us. They're the repository of all good. But we know that's not always the case. Not only this case, but history has told us that they're not always right.

"In this case, what they have done, they have given us Mitola, Alonzo, Hawley, and their ilk. And automatically changed them from what they were for the past thirty years—individuals who have figuratively raped, pillaged, and plundered society for thirty years. And now, with a flick of a switch, they are the guardians of goodness. They are the ones who are going to protect us. They're going to bring the light."

He stopped and waited. "It just doesn't happen," he said softly. "I mean, Mother Goose is not real. The Tooth Fairy is not real. And their witnesses aren't. It's a fairy tale."

It was like a lecture on the nature of morality and truth. Critchley quoted from Saint Augustine. He accused the informants of bartering testimony for freedom.

He slowed for a moment. "I'm sitting here, there's something, God darn"—he slapped himself in the forehead in a gesture of a dawning truth—"I know what this case is about. It dawned on me what they're doing. This is a case of Marshal Marchalonis and his posse of misfits out to get the Hole in the Wall Gang."

The jury chuckled at the concept.

He created a mock dialogue between a cooperating witness and a prospective informant, one incredulous and one with the slick assurance of an old-time snake-oil salesman:

"We found a better way."

"What's that?"

"We cooperated."

"You cooperated? You don't go to jail anymore?"

"No, we cooperated."

"When you get arrested?"

"You cooperate."

"What about parole?"

"Silly. You cooperate."

"What about when you need money?"

"You cooperate."

"What happens when you run out of money?"

"You commit more crimes."

"What happens when you get caught?"

"You cooperate. . . ."

The only requirement is, he said, you have to be prepared to testify. Against anyone. Even your brother or your mother.

"Perjury," he said, "forget about it."

Testimony. He held up government wiretap transcripts and evidence files. "You get all kinds of transcripts, you get these things. See these books? All these books? You study them."

The jury was laughing out loud.

"You study them. It's called transcripts—the script . . . You know the question before the answers. Like in school . . . And you go over it again. Day and night."

Critchley took a breath and pointed at the prosecutors. "And then they have the gall, they have the gall to say, 'You know, everything he said was corroborated.' My God! He had three months to get it together!"

It was nearing the noon hour. Critchley looked at the clock. It was almost time for a break.

The government, he said, had promised to take the jury on a journey, and evidence was to have been the fuel for the trip.

"Only something happened along the way," he said. "They ran out of evidence. The fuel stopped."

"But," he said, "my adversaries' case is like a runaway train. Powerful. Very powerful. And out of control." His voice was compelling and convincing as he spoke directly to the jurors. "But we have to make certain we put that runaway train under control. Because if we don't do that, ladies and gentlemen, we are going to wreak a lot of havoc and cause injury to a lot of innocent people.

"What I'm about to do, ladies and gentlemen," Critchley said calmly, "I'm about to put that train under control."

For five days, Critchley kept the jury spellbound. Using charts and blowups of evidence, he spoke extemporaneously, reeling off a staggering array of facts. He assembled the government case and then took it apart, piece by piece.

"They tried to make a case," he charged. "They tried to find a case, and when they failed," he declared, "they said, 'The hell with it, we'll go out and buy a case.'"

He was alternately serious and humorous, boisterous and quiet. It was the performance of a lifetime.

As he neared his conclusion on the fifth day, the tension in the courtroom became visible when Braunreuther attempted to interpose an objection.

"I'll be done in ten minutes, please," Critchley snapped. "You've kept us here for two years. Give me the courtesy of another ten minutes."

As he drew near the end, Critchley pulled away from the case and turned to the law. There was something more important than this case at stake in this courtroom, he said, and that was the law itself.

"We are a nation of laws and not men," he asserted. "And the reason we are a nation of laws and not men is because men come and go. . . . You cannot let the foibles of men, the prejudice of men, the weaknesses of men, decide or dictate at any given time what is right, what is wrong. It is not the man's choice. It's the law. The law governs. Because the law is constant. . . .

"It's our birthright as citizens. It is the thing for which blood has been shed on beaches all the way from the Revolution, all the way to the Battle of Verdun, to the Normandy beaches, to Korea, to Vietnam. . . .

"It is a fundamental principle that every American—regardless of race, color, or creed, regardless of your ethnic background—when you are in this courtroom, those sacred Constitutional principles will protect you, no matter who you are and no matter who your accuser is, no matter how powerful they may be—you are within the protection of the Constitution of the United States of America. . . .

"When I look at this jury," he said, his voice now only a whisper, "it's not people with blond hair, it's not people with red hair, it's not people with black hair. It's not just Italian people or Irish people or black people. It is the combination of what makes this country great. You are the blood of America. You are the conscience of America."

Everyone, he said, is bound by the same law. "Rich, poor, powerful, weak, law-enforcement officer, private citizen."

And, he said, "If we blind our eyes or we condone the defiance of law by those in authority, regardless of who they are, regardless of who they work for, if we condone that violation of law, then we forfeit our credibility as citizens to preach law and order to the rest of society. . . .

"We are a feisty nation," he continued, one that believes that the sovereign is not always right, "that the sovereign can do wrong no matter how powerful or mighty."

It was that concept, he charged, that the government was attempting to distort in this case, claiming that because "we are the sovereign, it must be right.

"But that concept is distasteful and odious," he said, "and violates fundamental principles of justice that were in existence when this Republic was new."

Looking into the eyes of the jurors, he put the responsibility on them, to act as protectors of the Constitution, and not as partisans for the government.

"Because, ladies and gentlemen, it's important. It's not only important for Michael Taccetta." He pointed out into the audience at Taccetta's wife. "It's not only important for Carol Taccetta. It's important for me. It's important for you. It's important for your children. It's important for your loved ones. Because it is the fabric that causes this country to keep going and going. It is something that we will pass on to our children and our children will pass on to their children. And it must never, ever, break down. Never."

Critchley strode back and forth across the courtroom, his head down, deep in thought. He stopped and looked up at the jury.

"Soon, soon," he said, "my participation in this odyssey that began several years ago will come to an end. I'd like to look at my client and his wife and say, Carol and Michael, I've given you all I've got. I have no more. I got no more. I can do no more. I hope I did enough. . . ."

He turned to face Carol Taccetta, who sat quietly, her eyes glistening with tears. "No matter what it is, Carol, when you talk to the kids, I hope you can say Michael Critchley gave it all he had."

He grimaced for a moment. "People ask me: How do you

feel? How do you feel after giving two years?" He shrugged. "Mixed emotions. Mixed, mixed emotions. I'm happy . . . and sad. Happy, ladies and gentlemen, that the evidence has indicated that we fought a good fight. We stayed, we stayed."

He looked out at the defendants and the sea of attorneys. "I will never forget them," he said. "We have been here together. . . ." He looked at the jurors' faces. "They're going to object to this," he said, pointing at the prosecutors. "I love all of you. Because you have taken that task, that responsibility as citizens, and seeing to it day after day, that it's going to be done. To see that justice is going to be done."

He pointed again to the prosecutors. "Please," he appealed for a final time, "pay attention to the evidence. Don't let them wow you because of who they are. They're nobody special. . . . They're just like us. They just have more power than us. Consider the evidence and end this injustice and say [to the government], never again, never again, should you attempt to do what you've done here."

With that, Critchley paused for a final breath and then whispered his closing like a half-spoken prayer. "I thank all of you. And I'm passing my client's fate to your hands."

There was silence in the courtroom as Michael Critchley returned to his seat.

For all practical purposes, the trial was over.

54

Joseph Braunreuther looked both tired and relieved. He had done all he could, and all that was left was the waiting. It had begun as O'Malley's case, but now he had become a part of it—it was just as much his. He had not created it, but he had done the very best he could with what was there.

The government prosecutor planned to take off the following day, Friday, to drive his wife and children out to a campsite in Long Island, where they were to meet up with friends and family for a long-awaited week of vacation. He was going to return the next day and wait out the verdict. He hoped to have time to return to his family once the verdict was in.

He popped his head inside the pressroom, a narrow, cramped cubicle where news reporters had gathered to await the verdict and exchange small talk.

It was a room strewn with yellowing newspapers, overflowing wastebaskets, and walls papered with headlines and cartoons carefully culled from various publications. There was one framed plaque on the wall, displaying a quote from Sherman Reilly Duffy: "Socially the reporter stands somewhere between the whore and the bartender, but spiritually he stands besides Galileo. He knows the world is round."

Everyone knew that the Accetturo trial could bring some surprises.

"I'll be away tomorrow," Braunreuther said. "I'll be back on Saturday."

One of the reporters looked at him. "This verdict is either going to be long or short," he said. "It's either going to be two weeks—or it's going to be two days. I wouldn't stay away too long."

Braunreuther shrugged. The trial had taken forever. He did not expect a verdict to come quickly.

Ackerman had presented the jury with the legal "charge," the technical instructions on how to apply the law, and deliberations began on Thursday, August 25, 1988.

For nearly two years, they had filed into the cavernous federal courtroom in Newark and sat silently as they were confronted with what appeared at times to be an endless stream of testimony and cross-examination.

They had donned earphones to listen to hundreds of tape recordings, and they had stared at television monitors displaying days of video surveillance tapes. They had also waited patiently in a tiny anteroom behind the court, as prosecution and defense attorneys argued about the law.

Now, as the trial was preparing to enter its final phase, the strain was finally beginning to show. The six-man, six-woman panel retired to a cramped jury room located in a corridor behind the courtroom to begin their review of the evidence. They took their places around a large conference table, as a deputy U.S. marshal closed the door behind them.

As the jury assembled on Friday morning for its second day of deliberations, Braunreuther was packing up the family. He left home in Maplewood that morning to drive out to his wife's family's home in Lyndenhurst, Long Island, about an hour and a half's ride from New Jersey.

He loaded his wife, Theresa, and their two children in the family's red Dodge Caravan and set out on the expedition. They were headed for Montauk Point for a camping trip that had become an annual event for his family and close friends. He had gone to the same spot for almost twenty-five years, to a campsite right on the ocean. There were playgrounds for the kids, and the adults played volleyball on the beach, drank beer, and had barbecues at night. It was a perfect getaway, and the vacation had been planned since January. The three previous years, he had had to cut the trip short because of the case. Two days away from the deliberations was not too much to ask to get his family out to the site.

The plan this year was for him to stay with his in-laws Friday night, drive his wife and children out to the campground Saturday morning and get them settled, and then drive back to Newark.

On Friday afternoon, Braunreuther and his family arrived in Lyndenhurst. He left his wife and children at his in-laws' house and headed by himself to pick up a trailer-camper in Hempstead, Long Island.

The ride to the trailer-rental garage took about half an hour. He had to have a hitch installed on the Caravan to handle the trailer, so he left the vehicle at the garage to let them take care of the hookup. He had more than an hour to kill, so he strolled to a nearby shopping mall to wander through the stores while he was waiting.

In Newark, the second day of deliberations had begun.

As the jury met behind closed doors, attorneys and defendants milled about almost aimlessly in the courthouse corridors. In the court assembly room, some trickled in to watch news accounts of the trial on a television. The news accounts were interspersed among soap operas and reruns of prime-time police shows.

The day outside was sunny and hot. A television camera crew had stationed itself outside the courthouse. Some lawyers started up an impromptu game of softball on the courthouse green. Defendants leaned lazily against railings outside the front of the courthouse, dressed casually in short sleeves. They laughed and joked.

The jurors sent out a message. They wanted a lie-detector machine that had been seized from DiNorscio's home. And they wanted to open it. No one could even speculate as to what they wanted with it.

The problem was, it was locked. In an off-the-cuff comment, DiNorscio offered to open it up. The offer was not accepted.

At lunchtime, defendants seated themselves around long

tables in the assembly room. Someone delivered a carton of cheesesteak sandwiches ordered from a legendary neighborhood restaurant, and they dug in. When midday newscasts on the television mounted at the end of the room showed interviews with the defense attorneys, they broke into applause. When the cameras focused on the prosecutors, the defendants jeered.

O'Malley had given a brief interview. "The evidence," he had said, "was overwhelming." There were catcalls in the assembly room when he appeared on the screen.

Even Ackerman wandered into the room. And everyone waited.

It was shortly before 3:00 P.M. when word broke.

The jury had sent out another note. A marshal entered the room and handed Ackerman a slip of paper. This was the moment they had been awaiting for two years—the jury had reached a verdict.

The laughter ceased. The lawyers put on their jackets, and the defendants gathered outside the courtroom for the final time. This was the moment of truth. They harbored no illusions. If they were convicted, many of them would receive prison terms that could put them behind bars for the rest of their lives. There was no doubt about what Ackerman would do. He had given them a fair trial, but if the jury went against them, he would be Draconian in imposing the price for their crimes.

Some turned over car keys to friends and relatives. Others took off rings and jewelry. One clutched a bag of clean underwear he had brought with him to take to jail in the event he was convicted. They were prepared for the worst.

One of the defendants rushed to the bathroom. He wasn't certain if he was going to be sick.

"If they offered me a deal right now," he muttered, "I'd take it in a minute."

Taccetta and Accetturo only shrugged. They knew the rules. And they were prepared to play by them. If the jury went against them, well, as one defendant had quipped, "It's been a great ten years."

Critchley was somber. He walked into an empty room just to gather his thoughts. He was happy and he was afraid. It was a moment that had seemed as if it were never going to occur. It had seemed like a journey without an end—only now the end was in sight.

O'Malley and Marchalonis filed into the courtroom and took their seats. This was to be their moment. Marchalonis had already received a promotion to supervisor, which was, at least in part, a result of his work on this case. O'Malley had never lost a case. If he won this one, his record would be unbroken—and he would be credited with winning the largest mob prosecution ever brought in New Jersey.

As the remaining participants slipped into their seats, several approached DiNorscio. Those who knew him from childhood gathered around him. This could be the last time they would see him. If they were convicted, they would all be taken away to jail. But even if some were acquitted, Jackie was still facing a thirty-year jail term from his previous conviction on drug charges. They might go home, but he never would. Taccetta embraced him; others shook his hand. Marty, whom DiNorscio had once carried on his shoulders as a child, gripped his arm in a final farewell. Whatever happened, they had stuck together. They had not broken.

As the judge entered the room and ascended to the bench, the murmurs quieted. Lisa Horton, the petite blond courtroom deputy who had supervised the proceedings for the bulk of the trial, signaled to a deputy U.S. marshal to bring in the jury.

It seemed to take forever for the jury to arrive.

There was a dead silence as the panel filed in. The jurors looked solemn. The defendants looked anxious. Family members had tears in their eyes as they squirmed in their seats. Michael Critchley reached over to Michael Taccetta, put his arm around his neck, and gave him a brotherly squeeze. Then he looked at the ceiling. He might have been saying a prayer.

"Madam forewoman," Lisa Horton called out, "have you reached a verdict?"

Carrin Nexon, the dark-haired young forewoman, rose to her feet. The sunlight was filtering through the heavy curtains behind her, and the rays of sun cast swathes through the dusty air of the dark, dimly lit courtroom.

One of the defendants glanced at the engraving on the front of the judge's bench—LET JUSTICE BE DONE.

"Yes," Nexon said, "we have."

"Is your verdict as to all defendants, as to all counts, or is it a partial verdict?"

Nexon did not hesitate. "As to all defendants and all counts."

Then, the clerk asked the question that had been years in the coming: "What is your verdict?"

Nexon raised her head and looked out over the assemblage. There was no sign of nervousness or hesitation. She almost shouted it, loudly and clearly. "Not Guilty."

There seemed to have been a collective intake of breath that sucked the oxygen out of the air. It was as still as the interior of a bell jar, a moment frozen in time, a miniature tableau preserved for eternity—mouths open, eyes wide, and hands clenched.

Lisa then read down the jury verdict sheet, which listed the name of each defendant and the specific crime with which he had been charged. Nexon called out the same response: "Not Guilty." The phrase was repeated over and over again, more than seventy-five times, until it began to sound like an echo reverberating in the room.

Critchley had been ticking off the counts on a verdict sheet. Midway through, he stopped and put down his pen.

Taccetta turned to his lawyer. "What are you doing?" he whispered.

Critchley stared dead ahead. "It's over," he said.

Suddenly, as the last "Not Guilty" faded into the shadows, defendants and attorneys rose to their feet as one, clapping, cheering, and waving their arms in wild jubilation.

Ackerman waved the courtroom to silence.

"Was the verdict as rendered by the forelady a unanimous verdict?" he asked.

"Yes," Nexon replied.

Ackerman turned to O'Malley, who appeared as though he had gazed upon the forbidden face of the Gorgon—his face was ashen and set in stone. "Do the parties desire to have the jury polled?" the judge asked.

O'Malley barely spoke the words, "No, Judge."

It was a decision that would haunt him for the rest of his career. For within days, one of the jurors would come forward and admit that she and others had disagreed with the verdict and would have said so if she had only been polled. It would have meant a mistrial, and the government would have had the option of trying to convict the defendants yet again. Now it was over. There was nothing left to do.

O'Malley had been defeated. And at that moment, the case that he had spent much of his career developing had crumbled into dust like some ancient and withered corpse. He sat as if dazed, his long legs stretched out before him, just staring into space.

The courtroom, which had been simmering since the initial outburst, erupted again. The verdict was in. It was final. It was official. It all was at an end.

"God bless you! God bless you!" defendants shouted over and over again to the panel as they broke into tears and kissed and embraced, while pandemonium erupted in the courtroom.

Critchley turned to David Ruhnke, who had been his chief lieutenant throughout the proceeding. He stood just feet away and gave a thumbs-up sign. They had been victorious.

Taccetta turned to Critchley and hugged him in a great bearlike embrace.

"It couldn't have been done without you," Taccetta muttered.

The jurors had remained calm as the decision was delivered, but their demeanors turned jubilant as they were led out of the courtroom for the final time by U.S. marshals.

As they exited, a female voice could be heard echoing down the marble corridor, "We're proud of our verdict."

Taccetta and the other defendants appeared almost disoriented. A moment before, they had been facing fifteen, twenty, even forty years' imprisonment. Now they were free.

Except for Jackie. He stood at his seat, smiling broadly. He was flanked by marshals. He was not free—he was still in custody from his earlier conviction. He faced a minimum of seventeen years in jail before he could even be considered for parole. Michael Taccetta approached him and embraced him. The two men kissed. Critchley stood beside Taccetta, and he too hugged Jackie.

Jackie stood rigid, his lips tight, his eyes moist.

"It's you and me, Mike," he stammered. "I told you—I told you. I told you we could do it."

But as the defendants left the room, hugging wives and children, Jackie stood alone. The others were going home. He was going back to jail.

O'Malley seemed almost to shrink visibly, slumping into his chair, as his companion, Dennis Marchalonis, the FBI agent who had spent the better part of his own career putting together the case against these men, shook his head and muttered to no one in particular, "What a disgrace."

As the crowd thinned, Dan Wakin, a reporter from the Associated Press, pushed his way through the double doors at the entrance to the courtroom and walked toward the front of the room, where O'Malley sat silently.

O'Malley had waved away other reporters who sought his comments. Now, as the din subsided and the courtroom began to empty, he finally turned to Wakin and asked, "What is there to say?"

O'Malley was angry. He would be angry forever. He had lost the biggest case that he would probably ever try.

He had put in his time and years of effort. He had been plagued with telephone calls to his home. His teenage daughter had been harassed by relatives of the defendants at school. And he had watched as the defense had turned what was to have been a landmark prosecution into something that took on the flavor of a circus.

During the course of the trial, he had been forced to take medication to avoid an ulcer. But he had consoled himself with the thought that when the trial was over, he would be the one to have the last laugh. Now the only laughter he heard was from the defendants, as it echoed down the corridor.

He had set his own standard: You win, you're a hero. You lose, you're a bum.

And he had lost.

Joseph Braunreuther was in Long Island, dressed in jeans, T-shirt, and sneakers, wandering through a department store, waiting for his trailer hitch to be installed. He was fairly relaxed. He was confident. With the weight of the evidence presented, he thought, the jury had only one choice—to convict. It was going to be a great vacation. He had done the best job he could, and soon it would be all over. He felt a little guilty about not being there, but expected that the amount of evidence would take days, if not weeks, to analyze.

Something compelled him to make a phone call back to his office, just to check on what was happening. He dialed the number of the strike force. Barbara Miller answered. She was clearly distraught.

"Joe B.," she said. "They let them all go. They let everybody go. How could they do this? I can't believe it. They didn't look at anything, Joe B. . . ."

He was standing near the appliance section of the store, and he suddenly realized what he was watching. There were scenes of the Newark courthouse and the people standing outside.

As he put the phone down, he wandered closer. Now he could see the pictures clearly, and he could hear the voices.

He could see Accetturo; he could see Taccetta.

"Never again," one attorney was saying, "never again."

Braunreuther could only stare at the screens.

The verdict was a stunning defeat that was reflected in the headlines of every major metropolitan paper.

MOB TRIAL DOWN THE DRAIN blared the banner front page of *New York Newsday*. TWENTY LUCCHESE HOODS GET OFF SCOTT FREE trumpeted the *New York Post*. *The New York Times* was more sedate but just as definite: ALL 20 ACQUITTED IN JERSEY MOB CASE.

From Boston to Richmond, Virginia, from Philadelphia to Denver to St. Louis, Florida, and Chicago, the stories were all the same. One of the most heralded antimob prosecutions ever mounted had gone up in smoke.

It had taken two years for O'Malley and the prosecution team to present their case, but it had taken the jury less than two days to render its verdict.

As news of the verdict spread, even in prisons, celebrations and cheers echoed through the bars.

And as Jackie was taken back to the Metropolitan Correctional Center in Manhattan, he was greeted with makeshift banners and applause from the inmates.

As far away as Fort Leavenworth, Kansas, where another New Jersey mob figure, Tino Fiumara, who had, like DiNorscio, been a target of Project Alpha, remained behind bars, spontaneous applause erupted when the news was announced.

Outside the federal courthouse, the twenty defendants gathered at the rear entrance, determined to wait until the jurors were brought out of the building by the U.S. marshals who had served as their escorts during the trial and the subsequent deliberations.

"They waited two years for us," one of the defendants remarked as they stood on the sidewalk surrounded by reporters and cameramen. "We can wait an hour for them."

As the jurors finally emerged from the courthouse, some with tears streaming down their cheeks, they waved and smiled to the defendants as they were led by marshals to a waiting government van to be taken back to the hotel where they had been sequestered since deliberations began.

The defendants broke into spontaneous applause and raised clenched fists in signs of victory and salute. The defendants were kept apart from the jurors, as much as possible, by deputy marshals. But there were exceptions. Marty Taccetta reached out his hand and shook the arms of one beaming juror. The lead defendant in the case, Anthony Accetturo, a broad smile of victory on his craggy face, stepped forward and kissed one of the female jurors on her cheek; while another juror, a hospital maintenance worker, threw up his arms in a victory salute.

Tic Cataldo was crying openly. He hoisted his youngest child onto his shoulders and waved at the jurors.

"God bless them for having the courage," he cried. "That's what saved us. We love them."

As the jurors were led away, the defendants and attorneys moved en masse down the block behind the courthouse, camera crews and press photographers trailing behind as the celebration shifted to a tavern located in the basement of a building near the rear of the courthouse. It was the first stage in an all-night bout of revelry that had attorneys and defendants dancing on the sidewalks, while a crowd of family, friends, and well-wishers flowed five deep into the downstairs bar.

As drinks flowed and rock-and-roll music blared, defendants and their supporters toasted their victory with champagne and beer, while passing automobiles saluted the celebration with a cacophony of honking horns.

Attorney Maria Noto, who was the only female defense attorney in the case, flashed a broad smile and a thumbs-up sign for the camera.

"They were sending a message to the prosecution team," she declared. "Don't ever try to do this again."

Critchley flashed a *V* for victory, while others chanted "Never again, never again."

Critchley held up a toast to one camera. "I'm very happy," he said, laughing, "ecstatic—and drunk."

Robert Spagnola, who had been one of the key defendants, remarked with obvious relief, "I feel like I've gotten a reprieve from purgatory."

There were more hugs and kisses and dancing. Defendants took over the bar, pouring their own drinks. And when the barroom celebration ebbed, the crowd moved on to an Italian restaurant on the border of Newark's North Ward.

There, a television crew filmed the festivities, broadcasting live. Television news personality Pablo Guzman sat at a table at the restaurant, surrounded by attorneys and defendants as they raised their glasses in celebration.

Harold Ackerman, meanwhile, had left the bench almost immediately after the verdict had been returned and had walked slowly back to his chambers.

It was very clear what had happened: The jury had simply rejected the government case outright.

As the judge walked into his inner sanctum, the door outside the chamber buzzed. The defendants were milling about. His secretary told him what they wanted, which was to come in and say thank you. It was an awkward moment for the judge, who would later become what some termed the "designated scapegoat" for the government's loss. Ackerman was profoundly embarrassed.

The explanations for what had occurred were as multitudinous as the defendants. An Associated Press report quoted O'Malley as speculating that the jury "just resented the length" of the trial. A *New York Times* editorial posed the question, "How could the government spend twenty-one months trying a case against the Mafia—and then fall flat on its face?"

The editorial suggested a combination of factors: the extreme length, the government's "absurd" decision to try so many defendants, virtually assuring an unwieldy trial, and the pace of the trial itself.

"It became," the paper declared, "a gross imposition on the lives of the jurors. For that, the prosecution and the judge are to blame."

The explanation was only partially correct.

There had been errors by the court. A slip of the tongue by the judge in presenting the final jury instructions might have confused some. But that was not the answer either.

One juror later reported that most of her colleagues on the panel had made up their minds to vote for acquittals long before deliberations even began.

One elderly juror had complained during summations that the government was merely "wasting my time." Another said after the case that the government's heavy reliance on informants had "left a lot to be desired."

An annual report by the U.S. Attorney's Office had no answers. It only summarized what had already been reported in the media about the length of the case.

What had caused it? The length, certainly. The rejection of the informants? Very possibly. But there were other factors, factors that were probably unique to that case alone.

In his summation, O'Malley had pleaded with the jury not to be swayed by "personalities." But in many ways, the trial was one of personalities. It had been a trial of O'Malley's own personality, as well as that of Braunreuther, Miller, and Marchalonis. And of a faceless government bureaucracy that had brought everyone together in that courtroom.

And there was another factor. Critchley had virtually fused his own personality with that of the defendants. To convict Michael Taccetta, the jurors would, in many ways, have had to convict Michael Critchley. And that, they clearly were not prepared to do.

The trial had taken on a life of its own. Whatever heinous crimes these men may have committed, they had not been presented in court. Jackie had succeeded in making even drug dealing seem funny. There were no murders, and the case was strangely lacking in violence. One Associated Press reporter had quipped years before, after scanning the indictment for some reference to *Godfather*-type violence, "What did they do, order pizza pies sent to the homes of their victims?"

All of the truly heinous crimes presented to the jury had been committed not by the defendants, but by the informants: Alonzo, Hawley, Amador, and the others. And they were aligned with the government, so that in the end, it was really the government itself that was on trial.

As Harold Ackerman drove home alone the night of the verdict, he tried to sort through what had happened. Years later, he would offer his personal explanation: "Too much was charged against too many, which took too long and resulted in jury nullification."

It was as good an explanation as any.

It was echoed by G. Robert Blakey, now a Notre Dame University Law School professor. Years before, he had served as chief counsel to the U.S. Senate Committee on Criminal Laws and had been the man who drafted the RICO law under which the Accetturo case had been tried.

"What happened in Accetturo?" he mused. "Who knows? How do you explain unique events?" In the end, he said, it was "a fluke."

On the evening of the verdict, U.S. Attorney Samuel A. Alito, Jr.—who had inherited the case when he took over the office months after Thomas Greelish had left—sat alone in the library on the fifth floor of the Federal Building, surrounded by camera crews and a handful of reporters.

O'Malley and Marchalonis were not present. Braunreuther had spoken with Alito on the phone and had offered to come back. But it was over—there was nothing that could be done.

Alito faced the camera by himself.

"I certainly don't feel embarrassed," he said, "and I don't think we should feel embarrassed. I think we should feel proud for what we tried to do. . . . I do not have a dollar figure for what this prosecution cost, but I'll tell you this: Every penny was well spent. How much money do the people of New Jersey think it's worth to eliminate organized crime?

"We have nothing to apologize for," Alito said. "We have nothing to be embarrassed about."

A day later, Alito would acknowledge that the government had learned a lesson from the trial.

"We plan to try to avoid any future trials like this," he declared. "I think you'll see faster, simpler trials."

As the evening wore on, the defense celebration was pared down to a hard core of lawyers, relatives, and close friends, and the party moved to the palatial suburban Florham Park home of Michael Taccetta, the man reputed to be the underboss of the Lucchese organized-crime family in New Jersey.

There, amid throngs of friends, children, grandchildren, mothers, and grandmothers, as well as trays of Italian food, an outpouring of congratulations was beginning to swell for Michael Taccetta, the soft-spoken, charismatic man with the barrel-chested wrestler's build, whose acquittal would eventually propel him to a new pinnacle of prominence and stature within the underworld power structure. Within months, his success in court would be regarded by the mob hierarchy as a personal triumph that would make him the pivotal figure in an underworld drama that has yet to play its final scene.

Joe Braunreuther returned to his family at his in-laws' home on Long Island that night. He talked with his wife. He watched the news again on television. He had a beer and went outside. It was a warm night, the stars were visible in the sky, and the shadows were just beginning to thicken. He began to jog, slowly building up speed. Soon he was running. He ran into the night until he found himself in a park near a schoolyard. And when he was done, he walked slowly around the park.

Michael Critchley left the celebration at Taccetta's house early. He had been drunk, intoxicated from both liquor and the exuberance of victory. But now he felt tired—very, very tired. It was as though something had burst, and everything inside that had carried him for two years, had rushed out of him. He had been living with the case since its inception, when the first search warrants were executed. And now it was over.

The next morning was as beautiful as the day before. It was summer and sunny and bright. He sat up in his bed with the sun streaming in through the curtains.

"Son of a bitch," he said softly to himself. "We did it. . . ."

POSTSCRIPT

The jubilation that buoyed the leadership ranks of the Lucchese family upon the verdict was to be short-lived.

According to the New Jersey State Commission of Investigation, dissension within the ranks had already begun to grow during the latter months of the trial, and the once close relationship between Taccetta and Accetturo deteriorated rapidly into a power struggle for control of the crime organization. Within weeks of the verdict, sources reported, a murder contract was issued for Accetturo, and the once-powerful crime leader, now ostracized by his own "family," dropped quietly out of sight.

Eventually, it was revealed, he was traced to a stronghold in the mountains of North Carolina. On September 19, 1989, Accetturo was taken into custody by New Jersey authorities and ordered jailed for contempt of court for refusing to testify before a state grand jury conducting an ongoing probe of Lucchese operations in New Jersey. Loyal to the oath of *Omertà* or "silence," that every crime family member must take, Accetturo was relegated to a basement prison cell in a state facility for an indeterminate sentence. While in custody, he pleaded guilty to a federal income-tax charge filed against him in Florida. He would eventually spend twenty months behind bars before finally winning his freedom. Even then, his release was to be conditional, with a judge agreeing to set him free only after a bail of one million dollars was posted. And that freedom was to be tenuous. A state investigation was under way that would subsequently confront Accetturo and his former associates with what could be the most serious threat they have ever faced.

Although Michael Taccetta appeared to have won the struggle for dominance of the Lucchese organization, his victory was less than complete. On January 4, 1989, Taccetta, facing prosecution on firearm-possession and income-tax charges, shocked authorities when he walked into the federal courthouse in Newark and agreed to plead guilty. Sources said Taccetta was concerned that he could have been convicted under a "special dangerous offender" law which would have substantially increased his possible prison time and decided to "cut his losses" by entering a plea bargain. He subsequently was sentenced to five years, and is serving the term at a federal prison in Minnesota. He is scheduled to be released no later than July 1992.

His troubles, however, were not over. On September 14, 1990, Taccetta was indicted by a state grand jury on charges of extorting more than $100,000 from the owner of a Roseland, New Jersey, construction company in order to ensure labor peace.

Meanwhile, the SCI reported that during Michael's imprisonment, his brother Martin Taccetta had been entrusted to take over the day-to-day operations of the Lucchese organization in New Jersey. But Martin was not immune to trouble of his own. A New Jersey grand jury subsequently indicted him on charges of conspiring to defraud more than $400,000 in auto insurance claims.

Then, on April 18, 1991, the New Jersey Attorney General's Office called a press conference to announce even more serious and far-reaching charges against the leadership of the Lucchese family.

Anthony Accetturo, Michael Taccetta, Martin Taccetta, Thomas Ricciardi, and another of the original trial defendants, Michael Ryan, were indicted on racketeering charges linking the five to a plot to take over an array of businesses located along the boardwalk in Point Pleasant, one of the premier amusement and vacation resorts along the Jersey Shore.

In addition, the five were charged with conspiracy in the "savage" murder of Vincent J. Craparotta, the South Jersey contractor who had been found beaten to death on June 12, 1984. The indictment specifically charged that Martin Taccetta, Ricciardi, and Ryan beat Craparotta with golf clubs after he failed to pay the proper "respect" and "tribute" to the mob hierarchy.

Nor was Jackie DiNorscio to be immune from his own share of continuing troubles. On March 31, 1989, he and his fellow Accetturo trial defendant Gerald Cohen were among a group of men named as defendants in a seventy-nine-count racketeering conspiracy indictment filed in federal court in Florida. The charges accused DiNorscio and Cohen of fraud in relation to their activities in the mail-order gem-investment business.

DiNorscio and Cohen both pleaded guilty to a conspiracy charge and were sentenced in May 1991 to ten years' imprisonment, to be served concurrently with the sentences they were already serving on the prior New Jersey drug conviction.

On New Year's Day, 1990, U.S. Attorney General Dick Thornburgh abolished U.S. Organized Crime Strike Force offices throughout the nation, and merged their operations with those of U.S. Attorney's Offices in the respective states. Thornburgh was quoted as explaining that his new plan would end "turf battles" between the two offices and would offer "substantial managerial benefits" that would strengthen the Justice Department in its fight against the mob.

Grady O'Malley remained with the strike force and joined the staff of the U.S. Attorney's Office in Newark when the two agencies were merged. Although his defeat in the Accetturo case remains a raw nerve, he has continued to successfully investigate and prosecute organized-crime-related cases and is regarded as one of the most formidable prosecutors in government service.

Joseph Braunreuther remained with the U.S. Attorney's

Office in Newark and successfully prosecuted a series of securities-fraud cases before returning to private practice with a prominent New York law firm in February 1991.

Barbara Miller, upon the breakup of the strike force, transferred to a U.S. Attorney's Office in another state.

FBI agent Dennis Marchalonis was named a supervisor of organized-crime investigations in the Newark office of the FBI.

Thomas W. Greelish, who as U.S. Attorney had authorized the Accetturo prosecution, returned to private practice and died at age fifty-one, after suffering a heart attack while attending a picnic in Morristown, New Jersey, on Sunday, June 23, 1991.

Joseph Alonzo, the government's star witness, died of natural causes on September 24, 1990, while living under an assumed name under the protection of the U.S. Justice Department.

U.S. District Judge Harold A. Ackerman continues to preside on the federal bench in Newark.

Defense attorney Michael Critchley and his colleagues on the defense team continue to practice law in New Jersey.

"We have organized crime on the run in this state."

—Colonel Justin Dintino of the New Jersey State Police
April 18, 1991

"This is, however, no time for kudos and relaxed vigilance. There are plenty of young, hungry, and vicious hoods who will try to lay claim to the pieces of this broken empire."

—Robert J. Del Tufo, New Jersey Attorney General
April 18, 1991

INDEX